The new networked learning society

1. Your neural network
Your unique brain, mind and body 'talent' and how to develop it.

2. Your personal learning network
Home, school and community in a linked interactive learning environment.

3. Interactive information network
How you can interact with the new world of instant communications.

4. Your creative network
How to think for new ideas and innovate in partnership with others.

5. Your talent network
Worldwide sharing of skills, abilities and professional knowhow.

6. New organisational networks
New 'social movements' linked to cooperative open partnerships.

7. Global learning networks
Education based on shared information, talents, cultures and 'digital tools'.

Quick recap of The Learning Revolution

English language simplified

- ❏ Has a total of 615,000 words
- ❏ But 2,000 make up 90% of all speech
- ❏ 400 words make up 65% of most writing
- ❏ 43 words make up 50% of daily English

- ❏ 10 linking words make up 25% of most English
- ❏ All words made from only 26 letters
- ❏ English uses only 44 sounds
- ❏ And all sounds spelled in only 70 ways

To learn anything better, faster and more easily:
- ❏ **Simplify it,** so the key points are easy to grasp (as above).
- ❏ **Then to learn it, do it:** speak it, count it, type it, write it.
- ❏ **Then play games:** board games, phonic games and sound games for language: card games and dice to learn math.
- ❏ **Then label it:** so you can categorise what you've learned.

The 20 easy steps to faster, better learning: from Page 185.

Three ways to learn anything

First this   Then this   Then this

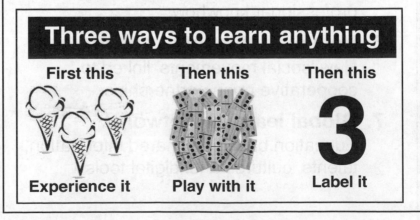

Experience it   Play with it   Label it

Now: how revolution works in practice

Nine-year-olds used to colour-in scrapbooks.

Now they make colour computer-animations in three dimensions.

Page 454

Seven-year-olds used to play in parents' clothes.

Now they digitally play any role in fantasy or as any historical character.

Page 28

Once only written exams showed "what you know".

Now students can keep digital portfolios on line to prove their talents.

Page 444

Russian and US students came up with a new idea.

Now their Google website can scan 8 billion pages in half a second.

Page 15

How to skim-read this book in 30 min.

Six main pathways into the brain

 What we
SEE

What we
TOUCH

What we
HEAR

What we
SMELL

What we
TASTE

 What we
DO

1 Every second page in this book is a 'poster page': either a summary like the page above or a photo or graphic, sometimes a contrast between old and new methods.

2 'Poster pages' at the start of each chapter summarise its theme, and generally list some key points covered in that chapter.

3 To get a complete big-picture overview of the book, we suggest you read both the Contents pages and the summary pages at the start of each chapter.

4 This book is also a multi-level brain-friendly book, so that you can absorb its contents in two distinct ways:

a. First skim the left-hand 'poster pages' (it's best to do this fast, one chapter at a time, so you skim the whole chapter like a slideshow).

b. Then read the complete text of the book on the right-hand pages. In this way you embed the message through different pathways in the brain, for better recall.

How to remember all the main points

If you're a teacher or trainer

Duplicate any 'poster page' in this book on a photocopier. Then enlarge that page and print on bright coloured poster paper. Display the posters on walls as permanent reminders of main points. To make your posters more attractive, print each one in a different solid background colour with the type and illustrations "reversed" so the black printing and pictures appear as white against the solid backgrounds of different colours.

If you're a student of any subject

Make a Mind Map® of any chapter you're studying. A good Mind Map* starts like the illustration above, computer-generated by Dilip Mukerjea, of Singapore, and reprinted from his book *Superbrain*. Mind Maps record information as the brain does, like branches on a tree, and make it very easy to recall key points. See pages 203-207 for simple tips.

* Mind Map is a registered trade mark of Tony Buzan.

5

Also by Gordon Dryden and Jeannette Vos

Book, video, audiotape and CD-rom series:

The Learning Revolution

Also by Gordon Dryden

Books:

Out Of The Red

The Reading Revolution (with Denise Ford)

Parenting programme:

FUNdamentals (with Colin Rose)

Television series:

New Zealand: Where To Now?

The Vicious Cycle
Right From The Start
The Vital Years
Back To Real 'Basics'
The Chance To Be Equal
The Future: Does It Work?

16-part United States series:

The Learning Revolution

Also by Jeannette Vos

Doctoral dissertation:

An Accelerated/Integrative Learning Model Programme

The New Learning Revolution

How Britain can lead the world in
learning, education and schooling

**Gordon Dryden and
Dr. Jeannette Vos**

with a foreword by Sir Christopher Ball

the
learning
web

The New Learning Revolution

How Britain can lead the world in learning, education and schooling

Published by:

Network Educational Press Ltd.
P.O. Box 635
Stafford
ST16 1BF
United Kingdom
www.networkpress.co.uk

in association with

The Learning Web Ltd.
P.O. Box 87209
Meadowbank
Auckland 1130
New Zealand
www.thelearningweb.net

ISBN: The New Learning Revolution Dryden/Vos 978 1 85539 183 3

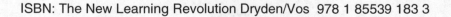

Contents

Contents

Contents

A reader's guide to style

Currency and measurement

Most currencies have been converted into United States dollars at the mid-2005 exchange rates. International metric measurements throughout, occasionally translating into "imperial "measures" where appropriate.

Billions and trillions

We have used American terminology: thus 1 billion equals 10,000 million and 1 trillion equals a billion billion.

Repetition

Because the book is designed to be read both as a complete work and for those seeking information from individual chapters, occasionally we recap information from previous chapters for easier, single-chapter reading.

▬▬▬▬▬▬▬▬▬▬▬▬▬▬▬▬▬▬▬▬▬▬▬▬▬

First: the dream—now the new learning revolution in action

This is not the book we set out to write.

Fourteen years ago the co-authors first met by chance, seated next to each other at an international conference on new methods of learning.

One: a Dutch-born, Canadian-reared American educator who had just obtained her doctorate in education after a seven-year research project into those new methods.

The other: a New Zealand-born television presenter and producer who was completing six one-hour TV documentaries on the same subject.

When we compared notes, we found our findings dovetailed neatly: the academic research and the graphic television images of new ways to learn, teach, think, create and communicate. So two years later we wrote the first edition of *The Learning Revolution*.

Since then we've updated that work three times and it has gone on to become the world's biggest-selling nonfiction book. And, with ten million copies sold in China: a dramatic example of how the learning revolution is impacting on a land where the average city family spends 35 percent of its total income on the education of their one child.

Last year we started on the fifth edition. By the end of the year we'd virtually completed it.

And then it hit us: in fourteen years the entire world has almost completely reinvented itself.

❏ When we first met, early in 1991, the World Wide Web had just been launched but few people had heard of it. We didn't even mention it in our first edition at the end of 1993.

Today almost a billion people have instant access to the Web. Within five years that number will double.

❑ In 1994, when we updated a second edition for American and British readers, the world had never heard of Netscape or Internet Explorer. Now almost a billion people use their Web-browsers.

❑ In 1997, when we prepared a third edition, the world had never heard of Google, although Russian-born student Sergey Brin and American student Larry Page were working on it. Now Google scans 8 billion Web pages in half a second to provide answers to almost any question.

❑ In 2000, when we rewrote a fourth edition, the results of the Human Genome Project had not been announced. Now genetic scientists have unlocked many of the secrets of life itself. These breakthroughs, and others in neuroscience, are completely challenging many of the myths and dogmas on which education, schooling and testing have been based.

❑ Fourteen years ago I was able to show my new co-author a primitive black-and-white static PET scan of my brain: taken for the television series. Now scientists and medical experts can view the brain in action, in living colour as it actually learns to learn.

Every one of these breakthroughs has transformed the world.

But amazingly this new revolution has left much of "education" largely unchanged. In a world of instant, electronic and interactive communication and technology, hundreds of millions of students, sitting in rows, still face their teachers in classrooms designed for a different age.

Yet in the same fourteen-year timespan, the learning revolution we predicted has already started. But so far only in pockets around the globe. Yet it has the power to completely change learning, education, teaching and schooling more than anything else in history.

More importantly, it is now possible to instantly share those breakthroughs with the rest of the world's 59 million school teachers and 1.5 billion students.

So we've completely rewritten much of our earlier work, to produce what we hope is a completely new synthesis. A few middle chapters have simply been updated from the earlier edition. But the total book now represents a complete "operating system" for *The New Learning Revolution*. And not only for "education", but hopefully for a more creative, cooperative, sharing world society.

Gordon Dryden, co-author and editor

Foreword by Sir Christopher Ball ▬▬▬▬▬▬▬▬

A 21st-century catalyst to change the way we think, learn and teach

When the first United Kingdom edition of this remarkable book appeared eleven years ago, I read it quickly—and then reread it more carefully.

I realised that this was the book that I had always wanted to write, but didn't know how.

Since then I have kept two copies close at hand, one for reference, the other to lend to friends. It is a masterpiece.

The appearance of a new, completely revised and updated edition is a cause for celebration and gratitude. Study it, and see for yourself.

It tells the story of not one but three revolutions. Each started some years ago; all three are now are in full flood. They cannot be stopped.

The first is the breakdown of traditional schooling. The second: the emergence of a new understanding of how people learn best—and how best to help them. And the third: the explosion in new methods of sharing information, knowledge and ideas.

The first is negative, painful, slow, and frightening for those who see no alternative to school education.

The second is positive, hopeful, imminent, and welcome to adults and children alike.

The third is shaking traditional thinking to its very roots.

This book explains what is going on in the gradual collapse of the old model of education and the advent of the revolutionary new models of learning. And it is written in a style that makes it a joy to read.

Gordon Dryden and Jeannette Vos demonstrate that "the old school model is as dead as the industrial revolution that spawned it". The flight of both pupils and teachers from traditional schooling will soon become an embarrassment for governments in developed countries. Neither the curriculum (what is taught) nor the pedagogy (how it is taught) is any longer sustainable.

Well-meaning reforms have not made a significant difference. Education is in crisis.

What is to be done about it? The authors set out what is needed to transform the new understanding of how humans learn into a global movement to change the way the world learns.

I particularly welcome their insistence on the importance of the early years, their optimism about human talent, and their emphasis on the challenge to develop global citizens.

But what lies at the heart of this book is a shift of focus from teaching to learning, and a recognition that a new philosophy of learning must lead the curriculum. The reverse does not work.

If you get the "how" of learning right, the question of "what" people should learn will solve itself. The truth is: people are brilliant natural learners, as every infant demonstrates. Sadly, traditional education often does more to frustrate that ability than to foster it.

Does it matter? Of course it does! Our health, wealth and happiness depend on successful learning—our own and that of everyone else.

This has indeed always been the case. But the accelerating rate of change in the modern world means that now more than ever before the rewards of the good life will go to those who are most adaptable—who learn best.

It will also go to those who learn to use and share the new world of interactive technology, instant communication, collaborative innovation and multimedia creativity. And to those who can add the new sciences of learning to the art and inspiration of great teaching.

This book will help you learn how to do that, and how to help others. Whether you are a student, parent, teacher or politician, I advise you to read it—and reflect.

Christopher Ball
Foundation Chair
Britain's Campaign for Learning
Oxford, United Kingdom

Eight-year-olds used to go to the movies

Now they can produce their own movies as they use the real world as their classroom

In photo: Children can now use Apple iMovie or Microsoft MovieMaker software to edit video they have shot, and then create and add music, commentary and titles. At Sherwood Primary School in Auckland, New Zealand, six-year-olds learn to shoot video from their first week in school.

History's newest revolution: to change the way the world learns

Education is about to change more than it has in almost 300 years—since the Prussian Government invented compulsory schooling in 1717.

We've called this change *The New Learning Revolution*.

But it is much more than a single revolution. Dynamic, expanding networks are converging to provide the synthesis for a new creative age.

They challenge each one of us to completely rethink what we mean by learning, teaching, schooling and education itself.

And Britain has a unique opportunity to lead that change.

Not only in one country. But to play the major part in spreading that change to the world's one billion people who live on under $1 a day and the other billion who live on less than $2 a day. The tools to bridge that digital divide are finally here. And we know how to use and share them.

The forcing catalysts for that change are blindingly obvious:

❑ *The new world of instant information:* the combined knowledge of humankind at out fingertips.

❑ *The new world of interactive technology:* and the individual power for each person to use it—from early childhood till late in life.

❑ *The explosion of "mass innovation":* where hundreds of millions of people co-create their own future. Millions already are doing that.

❑ *The "computer in your pocket" revolution:* as the students of the world interact personally with online music, video, digital photography —in their own creative, multimedia learning workshops.

❑ *The community revolution:* and the chance to turn schools into

19

**Google already scans 8 billion
pages in half a second. But soon . . .**

Everyone everywhere will be able to carry around access to all the world's knowledge in their pockets.

GOOGLE'S GOAL*

*Quoted in *The World Is Flat,* by Thomas Friedman,
published by Allen Lane (Penguin), London.

Regular updates: www.thelearningweb.net

new community learning centres—soon to be lifelong learning centres in the villages of the world's poorer countries.

❏ *The sharing revolution:* where the world's finest teachers combine with the world's best multimedia producers to create new ways of learning . And then share them with the rest of the world's 59 million school teachers and 1.5 billion students.

❏ *The upside-down revolution:* where we finally realise that health, education—and dare we say it: Government—are concepts we do for ourselves. Not something someone else "delivers" to us.

❏ *The genetic, neuroscience revolution:* already starting to shatter the myths and dogmas on which much "education" is based.

❏ *Above all, the new Open Revolution:* at long last the possibility of finding a genuine Third Way to reinvent society—the new open-source world of cooperative, collaborative co-creativity.

Overall, what BBC Director-General Mark Thompson calls "the new on-demand, pan-media universe we are hurtling towards".[1]

❏ For the first time in history, we now know how to digitally store all the world's most important information.

❏ And to make it available, almost instantly, in almost any form, to almost anyone on earth—on demand, and *much of it virtually free.*

❏ We also now know much more about how to unleash the almost untapped learning potential of the human brain, mind, body and spirit.

❏ And to personalise that knowledge in ways that enable each of us to create and manage a much more creative future.

But only a fool worships his tools. These provide only the catalyst.

Says Canadian researcher and author Don Tapscott in *The Digital Economy:* "We are at the dawn of an Age of Networked Intelligence— an age that is giving birth to a new economy, a new politics and a new society."

Says British scientist and author Matt Ridley in his book, *Genome: The autobiography of a species:* "I genuinely believe we are living through the greatest intellectual moment in history. Bar none."

And the models to inspire this moment are already working:

❏ At Swedish refugee centres infants from more than 100 countries have learned to speak three languages fluently—even before starting school. And in Montessori preschools around the world, three- and four-

For three centuries teachers have taught with blackboards

Now Britain leads with electronic 'interactive whiteboards': like electronic flipcharts

In photo: One of the digital interactive whiteboards that have played a big part in improving education in the United Kingdom, specially in secondary school. This Promethean ActivBoard comes complete with lessons in subjects such as mathematics and geography. And Promethean 'collaborative classrooms' enable teachers around the world to share their best practices.

year-olds have for years been learning to read, write, spell and count: not in dull classrooms but naturally by using all their senses.

The New Learning Revolution model: The best time to develop your children's learning ability is before they start school—because most of the brain's major pathways are laid down in those vital early years.

❏ In New Zealand's Tahatai Coast Primary School, all students graduate, at twelve or thirteen years of age, fully competent to use multimedia, digital tools to solve any problem they may encounter—at a level generally found only among college-grade computer-studies students. Yet these children are from families with below-average incomes: 30 percent of them from minority ethnic groups.

The New Learning Revolution model: Create the right environment and even children from poor families explode into self-directed learning.

❏ In New Zealand, eleven-year-olds up to three years behind in their reading are catching up in eight to ten weeks through a "tape-assisted reading programme". A typical gain in that time is 3.3 years.

The New Learning Revolution model: Even if you're well behind at school, it's not too late to catch up, using simple learning methods.

❏ Near Newcastle-Upon-Tyne in England, Cramlington Community High School has won rave reviews from Ofsted, the United Kingdom's Office for Standards in Education, for the way it has married interactive technology—specially interactive digital whiteboards instead of blackboards—with accelerated-learning teaching methods.

The New Learning Revolution model: Great methods can be used to dramatically improve learning inside a traditional secondary-school national curriculum.

❏ In Singapore, the Overseas Family School is among the first to introduce the full International Baccalaureate "focused inquiry" curriculum for children as young as three years right through to senior high school. Almost 2,500 students, from sixtyfive nationalities, attend this international school. They are learning to be rounded, open-minded global citizens through a six-faceted universal curriculum.

The New Learning Revolution model: An interconnected world requires a new-style curriculum to develop globally-minded citizens.

❏ "Educators" around the world continue to debate the importance of the *process* of education versus *content, rigorous academic standards, "accountability"* and *"standardised tests"*. But the IB curriculum

New model for global school curriculum

1. Universal culture
Celebrating achievements of all

2. Universal explorers
Skilled in the process of scientific inqury

3. Universal knowledge
To understand all 'the building blocks'

4. Universal network
To link teachers, students, families

5. Universal citizens
Competent to solve global problems

6. Universal qualifications
And digital portfolios to prove talents

INTERNATIONAL BACCALAUREATE*

* IB curriculum as developed by Overseas Family School, Singapore.
(See www.ofs.edu.sg for *The School of The Future)*

already provides a better alternative that combines most of these elements—and more—for 1,595 schools in 128 different countries.

The New Learning Revolution model: Great schools can now end the mindless argument about process, content, accountability and qualifications. As at Singapore's Overseas Family School, they create:

*A **universal culture**: celebrating the great breakthroughs of all cultures, and an understanding of the world, to produce*

***Universal explorers**: skilled in the process of open, scientific inquiry to discover, by themselves and in groups,*

***Universal knowledge**: on a wide variety of projects, linked with one's own culture and personal strengths and talents. Ideally*

*A **universal information-technology network** that instantly links students, teachers, parents and schools with vital information, including all personal study programmes. All to produce*

***Universal citizens**: confident and competent to analyse all important problems and create positive solutions, and with*

***Universal qualifications**: including diplomas and certificates accepted and valued by universities and employers, plus personal digital portfolios to show each student's accomplishments.*

❏ In St. Louis, Missouri, the teachers at New City School have collectively written two books, on how they're teaching every subject at every grade, by catering to many different types of intelligence.

The New Learning Revolution model: There is more than one type of smartness—and we each have a learning style as individual as our fingerprints. Good schools recognise that and cater to it. But teachers can also multiply their own talents into books and online learning tools.

❏ Millions of youngsters have now learned the basics of geography from a CD-rom game devised by two young Iowa trivia-quiz fans: *Where in the World is Carmen Sandiego?*

The New Learning Revolution model: Computer games can transform many aspects of learning. And children themselves can invent them.

❏ In Singapore, Nanyang Polytechnic has been built as a "teaching and learning city" on a campus the size of sixty football fields. To graduate, its students have to produce hi-tech and high-skill projects, often under contract to giant international companies: from robots to animation.

The New Learning Revolution model: Remove the barriers between

How to reinvent universities to end boring lectures

Carnegie Mellon University's Digital U

Digital campus network: First in America. Now connects more than 15,000 students and faculty, with wireless access links to worldwide research sources.

Virtual worlds: with virtual reality on tap, integrating disciplines, through headsets.

Business game: with three years of activity compressed into four months.

Virtual tutors: with software acting as interactive tutors on a variety of subjects.

Team CMU: so students can collaborate online to share projects and documents.

Virtual labs: where chemistry students can "mix" solutions and check results online.

Digital library: with links to latest scientific and business research around the world.

BUSINESS WEEK e-biz*

* 'The Wired Campus', by Steve Hamm, December 11, 2000.

school and work and you reintroduce the proven principle of "learning by doing", but on twentyfirst-century not nineteenth-century tasks.

❏ In Pennsylvania, Carnegie Mellon University has spent $50 million building America's best online campus. But its aim is not to put boring lectures online. "Among CMU's digerati," says *Business Week,* "public enemy No. 1 is the old-fashioned lecture, where a scholar stands before hundreds of snoozing students and drones on for an hour or two. For them the chief role of technology is to help end boredom." [3]

The New Learning Revolution model: Tomorrow's best universities will creatively use IT to transform study, not merely replace black-and-white overhead transparencies with brighter Powerpoint slides.

❏ In California, ex-school teacher Jan Davidson and husband Bob, who borrowed $6,000 from their son's college savings to start an educational multimedia company, later sold it for almost $1 billion. They now concentrate on their non-profit foundation to develop young talent.

The New Learning Revolution model: Great teachers can now teach millions of people, through the marvels of interactive communications: and sometimes create fortunes doing the things they love to do.

❏ In California, the scientist who dissected Albert Einstein's brain, Professor Marian Diamond, has for years reared laboratory rats in different environments. Not surprisingly, she's found that rats reared in dull, boring, impoverished environments, with no stimulation, grow up to be dull, boring adult rats. But those reared with good diets and rich, stimulating activities, grow up to be healthy intelligent rats.

The New Learning Revolution model: Brain research shows intelligence soars in the right environments. And it works for humans too.

❏ There's also a soaring revolution in other "neurosciences". For much of the past century, schooling has been dominated by a string of competing theories in "educational psychology": often presented as dogma. Now the latest genetic and brain research shows that each of these put only one brick in the wall of learning, not the complete wall. [4]

The New Learning Revolution model: New breakthroughs in genetic, brain and mind research are combining to add a new "science of learning" to the art and inspiration of great teachers.

❏ In New Zealand more than 1,100 of that country's 2,700 schools have so far been part of "interactive-technology clusters". Each cluster of up to eight schools is led by one that has shown how to use information and communications technology as the catalyst to reinvent schooling.

Seven-year-olds used to dress up in parents' clothes

The
Spaghetti Fish Fairy
www.BubbleDome.co.nz

Now they can also act out any role in history or create their own digital fantasy characters

In photo: As taught at Southland Innovator seminars, in Invercargill, New Zealand, as part of a five-day Learning Web project to retrain school teachers in how to use interactive technology and instant communications as the catalysts to rethink schooling. Almost half New Zealand's 2,700 schools have now been part of 'interactive technology clusters'. In each cluster, one 'lead school' trains teachers from up to eight other schools.

Regular updates: www.thelearningweb.net

The New Learning Revolution model: It is now easy to use the most advanced schools to help bring others into the twentyfirst century.

❏ Using some of those methods, six-year-olds in New Zealand's "digital classrooms" learn to work together in teams to shoot video and edit it from their first days in class. Then, as they progress, they learn computer animation, to compose digital music, make digital games— and how to use the whole world as their classroom.

The New Learning Revolution model: Twentyfirst-century multimedia literacy is not the same as old-style reading-and-writing literacy. Today's youngsters grow up in a society whose basic communication "tools" are not the same as their parents' or teachers'. And schooling, to be effective, has to build on those differences.

❏ In Alaska, students at Mt. Edgecumbe High School at one stage ran four pilot companies, and earned $600,000 selling smoked salmon to Japan as they studied marketing, business, economics and Japanese.[5]

The New Learning Revolution model: Use the real world as your classroom. And again: to learn it, do it.

❏ In a suburb of England's Bristol city, Brislington High School has built a digital learning centre in its grounds. Outside school hours it becomes a multimedia community learning centre.

The New Learning Revolution model: It's incredibly wasteful to use the big investment in school buildings for only 20 per cent of the time.

❏ Atomic Learning, a company formed by school teachers, now provides more than 12,500 video tutorials online continuously to teach anyone how to use hundreds of computer applications. School subscriptions for the service average around $2 a student for a year.

The New Learning Revolution model: Stand by for an explosion in collaborative online "learning answers" to educational challenges.

❏ Early in 2005 Nicholas Negroponte, co-founder of the Massachusetts Institute of Technology MediaLab, announced its plans to produce, by 2006, a laptop computer to sell at around $100. China already is producing $300 laptops, sold without operating systems, which buyers then download free from the Internet. And the Novatium group in India is also developing a new $100 network PC.

The New Learning Revolution model: It is finally possible to eliminate the "digital divide" that has restricted the world's newest learning technology to rich countries. Link cheap computers with free

Once we were taught there was only one right way to think

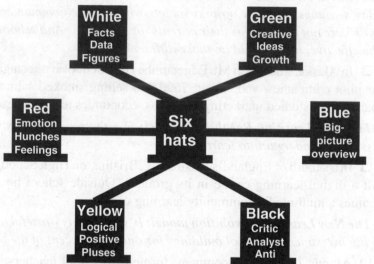

White
Facts
Data
Figures

Green
Creative
Ideas
Growth

Red
Emotion
Hunches
Feelings

Six
hats

Blue
Big-
picture
overview

Yellow
Logical
Positive
Pluses

Black
Critic
Analyst
Anti

Now children don different-coloured hats to think in many different ways

Graphic depicts a Mind Map showing Edward de Bono's concept of Six Thinking Hats: each in a different colour. Even very young children like wearing a white hat to assemble facts; a green one to think creatively; yellow to think positively; black as the critical analyst; red for following your hunches; and blue for taking a 'big picture' overview.

networks and new-type village learning and health centres, and the United Nations Millennium Project can actually achieve its goal to halve world poverty and provide primary education to all by 2015.

Those examples may look like isolated facts. Yet they typify one of the most important revolutions in human history.

The old school model is as dead as the industrial revolution that spawned it. It may have been fine sixty years ago to "educate" 25 percent of the population to be professional workers, 20 percent for trades and clerical jobs, and to leave the rest to be poorly uneducated farm and manual labourers. But that world of mostly labourers no longer exists, and a whole new range of creative and teamwork skills are now needed.

Edward de Bono, creator of *lateral thinking* methods, is appalled that learning how to think is not taught in most schools. And, where it is taught, generally only one form of thinking is involved: logic. His methods, including *Six Thinking Hats,* are now being used successfully in many schools to teach students to think in different ways.

Most important: nearly everyone has the talent to be successful at something. Yet much of the world's education systems are locked in an archaic ritual of rote learning and "standardised testing" for a narrow range of abilities. Even worse, much of this testing actually blocks people with "non-academic" talents from continuing education.

Robert J. Sternberg, IBM Professor of Psychology and Education at Yale University, says America, in particular, is obsessed with tests that reflect only a small segment of a student's ability to succeed.

Most of these assessment systems, such as Scholastic Aptitude Tests and their resulting SAT scores, are based on IQ or "intelligence quotient" tests developed around a century ago.

"But the skills measured by IQ tests," says Sternberg, "are not the only skills that, in combination, constitute intelligence."[6]

He says there are at least three different types of "intelligence":

Analytical intelligence (which tests measure).

Creative intelligence (which tests don't measure). And

Practical intelligence (which the tests also do not measure).

He is convinced that highly creative and practically talented people are being blocked from "educational success", and wrongly labelled as failures, on the basis of faulty, simplistic "standardised test scores".

Howard Gardner, Professor of Educational Psychology at Harvard

Nine-year-olds used to colour-in scrapbooks and later learn to write 'essays'

Now they do computer animations in three dimensions: and learn by doing

In graphic: animation, as published at www.bubbledome.com—part of competitions to involve young children in interactive technology. Bubbledome trainers in New Zealand also help run four-day Learning Web courses in which teachers can learn the basics for teaching eight separate digital technologies, including 3D animations, video editing and desktop publishing.

University, has identified eight and possibly nine different forms of intelligence—defined by some others as different talents.

Professor Raj Reddy, the former longtime dean of Carnegie Mellon University's School of Computer Science, forecasts a revolution emerging in the way universities teach. *"In the future learning will come from doing. You abolish lectures, and you don't just read about history, you participate in a simulation of it."*[7] CMU is already doing that.

Other great schools also reflect this thinking. Unfortunately the big majority don't. But the world's most successful corporations do.

Firstly, they select staff in a way that is completely at odds with the testing methods used in most school systems.

Schools test for unified standards, as if it's important for all students to be the same. Successful organisations hire for high-quality individual talent.

They recognise that widely-different talents are required for different jobs. So they select for *specific talent*. They then ensure that those individual talents fit together in collaborative, results-oriented teams.

Successful organisations build-in ongoing training programmes so their vari-talented people can develop their skills and knowledge as they work. They focus on strengths, not weaknesses. They don't try to train a great surgeon to be a nurse; or a concert pianist to be an opera singer.

General Electric, FedEx, Cisco, Microsoft, Oracle, Dell, Accenture and many other corporate giants also now run their own model universities. Corporate universities are surging ahead in China and South Korea.

For education, this does not mean supporting the overall current business model of winner-take-all in dominant technologies. "Control the standard and you control the industry" is a great model for super-profit, not necessarily the way to organise public schooling.

Here other new and better organisational models are emerging as the world struggles to heal the great divisions that threaten to tear us apart: new free-flowing, more *organic* alternatives.

Some of those new models have already given birth to the Internet, the World Wide Web, revolutionary free browsers and search engines like *Explorer, Netscape* and *Google,* and the open-source software movement inspired by the cooperative-enterprise model of Linux.

Says Eric Raymond, one of the trail-blazers, in *The Cathedral and the Bazaar:* "Linux was the first project to make a conscious and successful

The new law of networks

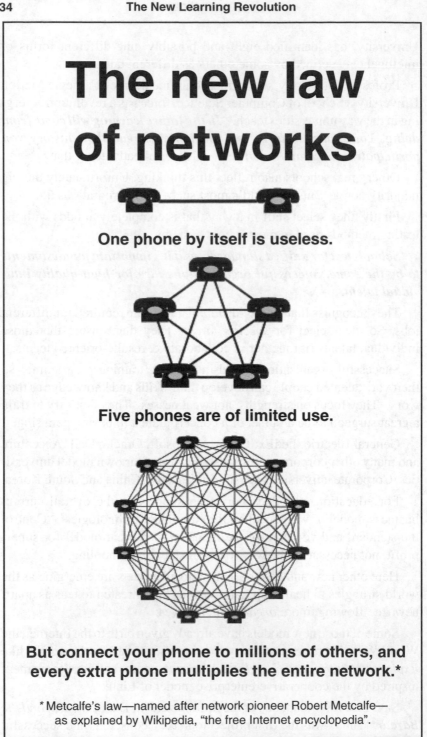

One phone by itself is useless.

Five phones are of limited use.

But connect your phone to millions of others, and every extra phone multiplies the entire network.*

* Metcalfe's law—named after network pioneer Robert Metcalfe—
as explained by Wikipedia, "the free Internet encyclopedia".

effort to *use the entire world as its talent pool."* Linux systems have been collectively designed by thousands of computer scientists in universities and homes around the world, working cooperatively online.

We also live in an era where two "new laws" are converging:

Moore's Law: Intel co-founder Gordon Moore's proven concept that computer power will keep doubling every eighteen months with no increase in price. Add one transistor on a silicon-chip to only one other, and it's no big deal. But double a billion transistors to two billion and you're talking about a revolution in power and miniaturisation.

Metcalfe's Law: 3Com founder Robert Metcalfe's theory on the explosive power of networks. Connect one phone to another and only two people can speak at a time. But connect more cellphones to millions of others, and every extra one multiplies the entire network.

For the first time in history, we also live in an age where children and students generally know more about the dominant communications technologies than most adults. Provide them with the world's best multi-media tools, and they will invent their own future. Combine all these trends, and the challenges become clear:

❏ *Start building new online global learning webs, to revolutionise schooling and learning, in the same way that the World Wide Web has revolutionised the exchange of information.*

❏ *Form the core of those new learning webs from the world's fiftynine million teachers. If business trends are followed, 2 percent of those teachers (1,180,000) are already trendsetting innovators, and 13 percent (7,670,000) of them are early adoptors of new methods. That is an enormous base for sharing interactive learning and teaching models.*

❏ *Then tap into the talents of the world's 1.5 billion students. The innovators are already showing us how to use interactive technology to create an entirely new future.*

❏ *Build simple learning templates: as Apple iMovie and Microsoft MovieMaker software already make it easy for any novice to produce and edit semiprofessional video "movies".*

❏ *Provide most of that information free on the Internet—just as the computer scientists of the world already share their talents. That is the basis of the scientific method: openly share, test and improve.*

❏ *Provide easy-to-use professional-development programmes for those teachers who are not normally innovators or early adoptors.*

Towards a new world-wide learning web

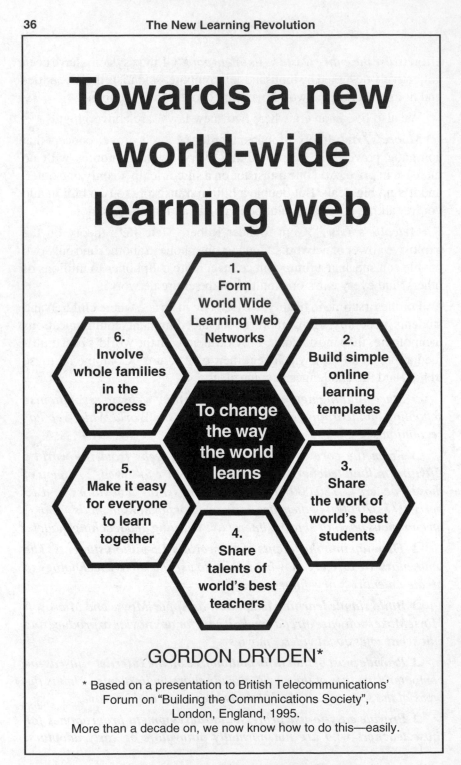

GORDON DRYDEN*

* Based on a presentation to British Telecommunications'
Forum on "Building the Communications Society",
London, England, 1995.
More than a decade on, we now know how to do this—easily.

Regular updates: www.thelearningweb.net

Silicon Valley calls this "crossing the chasm". Others might call it crossing "the fear barrier" to the world of the future.

❏ *Involve entire families, whole communities, in the process,* by *transforming schools into fulltime, lifelong community learning centres, with digital networks linking them to students and families at home.*

❏ *Slash the cost of computers and software—specially to emerging countries—by developing cheap open-source PC operating systems, as Japan, China, India and South Korea are pioneering; and by downloading cheap or free open-source software, as needed, from the Internet.*

❏ *Then transform international aid programmes,* to concentrate *not on handouts but on how to learn a living.*

❏ *And open up a widespread public and political debate to break the traditional ineffective ritual of classroom lectures.* Instead, encourage learners to learn in new interactive, talent-developing ways.

In previous societies, land, natural resources, labour and then industrial capital provided the basis for growth. Today's new "drivers": innovation, leadership, talent, brainpower, information, knowledge and wisdom. Now these can be freely or cheaply shared.

As Gary Hamel summarises it in *Leading The Revolution:* "We are now standing on the threshold of a new age—an age of revolution. Change has changed. No longer is it additive. No longer does it move in a straight line. In the twentyfirst century, change is discontinuous, abrupt, seditious. In a single generation, the cost of decoding the human gene has dropped from millions to less than a hundred bucks. The cost of storing a megabyte of date has dropped from hundreds of dollars to essentially nothing. The Web is rapidly becoming a dense global matrix of connections between people, their ideas and their resources."

In this new world, says Hamel, the future is not something that happens to you, but something you create.

True education in this new society thus enables you:

❏ To identify and develop your own unique talents.

❏ To create your own future, in any field you choose.

❏ To co-create a new global web of shared relationships.

❏ And to create an entirely new approach to lifelong learning, schooling and education—in a new world of creative, networked intelligence, abilities and skills.

Fifteen key trends to shape your future

1 The age of instant communications.

2 Not only instant, but free.

3 A world without economic borders.

4 Five leaps to a one-world economy.

5 Internet commerce and learning.

6 The new service society.

7 The marriage of big and small.

8 The new age of leisure.

9 The changing shape of work.

10 Women in leadership.

11 Cultural nationalism.

12 Removing the poverty trap.

13 The new demographics.

14 Do-it-yourself learning and health.

15 Cooperative, networked enterprise.

Converging revolutions and the birth of the Next Society

History has a way of repeating itself. Even centuries later.

"What happened in the western half of Europe just before 1500 was one of the most remarkable convergences of influential events in the known history of the world to that time," says historian Professor Geoffrey Blainey, in his new-century book, *A Short History of the World*.

"It was like a crossroads where, almost by chance, extraordinary meetings took place between navigators and painters, priests and teachers and scientists.

"There emerged a new way of painting and sculpting and a fresh perspective in architecture which, seen as a whole, was called the Renaissance or rebirth. A religious awakening, the Reformation, swept across northern Europe.

"The technique of printing, a wonderful way of disseminating new and old knowledge, leaped from town to town. An entirely new world emerged with the discovery in quick succession of the American continent and the all-sea route from Europe to eastern Asia."

But now—as then—the biggest transformations emerge from a change in view, a new perspective: by looking at challenges through new lenses. But also by rethinking the social consequences of new technologies.

For centuries millions of people saw apples fall from trees. But only Isaac Newton worked out why. The answer transformed society.

"Between his twentyfirst and twentyseventh year he laid the foundation for the scientific theories that subsequently revolutionised the world."

Education is about to change more than it has since the modern school was created by the printed book over 300 years ago.

PETER DRUCKER
The New Realities*

* Published by Harper & Row, New York.

But we now know that even a genius like Newton discovered only part of much greater truths.*

For thousands of years nearly everyone believed the earth was flat—and the centre of the universe. Then Nicholas Copernicus and Galileo Galilei proved we all live on a planet orbiting the sun at eighteen miles a second. Since then the scientific world view has never been the same.

"For a hundred thousand years," says Blainey, "a human being could see only eight to nine thousand stars on a moonless night. These stars seemed to be affixed permanently—with the exception of the Sun, Moon and five visible planets—on the inside of a great sphere that rotated around our fixed homes, wherever they might be, on earth."

We now know our sun is one of about 200 billion stars in our galaxy; and there are billions of galaxies in outer space. In 1996 the Hubble orbiting space-probe found evidence that the universe has at least 50 billion galaxies. And early in 2004 American astrophysicists detected a galaxy 13 billion light years away from earth.

Until 1451-53 few of our ancestors had access to the printed word. Then the young German goldsmith Johannes Gutenberg invented a form of movable type and a press for mass-producing books. This technology breakthrough was to transform the basis for learning and schooling.

"The printed book in the West triggered a surge in the love of learning such as the world had never seen before, and has never seen since," says Peter Drucker. "It made it possible for people in all walks of life to learn at their own speed, in the privacy of their own home, or in the congenial company of like-minded readers." [1]

But for almost two centuries, says Drucker, that message was largely lost on schooling. "The printed book, fiercely resisted by schoolteachers in the fifteenth and sixteenth centuries, did not triumph until the Jesuits and Comenius created schools based on it in the seventeenth century. "The printed book forced schools to change drastically how they were teaching. Before then, the only way to learn was either by laboriously copying manuscripts, or by listening to lectures or recitations. Suddenly people could learn by reading." And Drucker says we are now in the early

---

* *Like George Washington cutting down the cherry tree, the story of Newton discovering gravity by being hit on the head by a falling apple is a myth—reportedly spread by his housekeeper. What Newton did was realise that the force of gravity follows the same mathematical rules as light. He did this by observing how quickly the moon circles the earth.*

The vice-president of a small Seattle bank reinvented money

Dee Hock developed Visa International as a 'chaordic' organisation: from a marriage of chaos and order. He sees the same principles in the Internet and the World Wide Web.

Now he says the same principles should revolutionise education and almost everything

stages of a similar technological revolution, perhaps even a bigger one."

When Drucker wrote that, in 1988, only 560,000 homes, offices or universities were connected to the Internet. By 2004: 740 million. By the end of 2005: more than 1 billion.   And by 2007: 1.46 billion.

By 1988 the World Wide Web had not yet emerged from the fertile mind of Tim Berners-Lee. Yet within fifteen years one computer company, Dell, was achieving sales of more than $50 million a day on the Web.

"In 2010 there will be over two billion Internet users," [2] says one forecast. Around 30 percent of all households in the world will have personal computers. And over 2.5 billion web appliances will be in use. And the rapid spread of cellphones and cheap networked computers will almost certainly make these forecasts conservative.

If you think that won't write a new agenda for education, think again. We're moving rapidly from the World Wide Web to a potential world wide learning society: a web of interactive, sharing self-learners.

Says Visa-card creator Dee Hock, the man who reinvented money: "The collective memory of the species will soon be no more than a few keystrokes away." He argues that this will affect more than just the way we learn. "Within a few decades, we will look on our present methods of manufacturing, transportation, finance and organisation as quaint relics of an archaic Industrial Age." [3] We'd put education top of the list.

Even as early as 1980 another great American futurist, Buckminster Fuller, was spelling out the core of the challenges and opportunities: "Think of it. We are blessed with technology that would be indescribable to our forefathers. We have the wherewithal, the know-it-all to feed everybody, clothe everybody, and give every human on earth a chance. We now know what could never have been known before—that we now have the option for all humanity to 'make it' successfully on this planet in this lifetime. Whether it is to be Utopia or Oblivion will be a touch-and-go relay race right up to the final moment."

For centuries, too, people were told that students learn best when lectured by others. Then Maria Montessori proved the opposite: *create the right environment and even very young children will become self-motivated, self-acting self-learners.* A century later most school systems still resist transforming themselves around this simple truth.

A little over a century ago, only a small percentage of youngsters went to high school, even though the "elite" in several countries went to

The revolutions converge

The biomolecular revolution

will give us a complete genetic description of all living things, giving us the possibility of becoming the choreographers of life on earth . . . the knowledge to cure disease and feed an expanding population.

The computer revolution

will give us computer power that is virtually free and unlimited, eventually placing artificial intelligence within reach . . . to link all people with a powerful global telecommunications and economic network.

The quantum revolution

will give us new materials, new energy sources, and perhaps the ability to create new forms of matter . . . and the power to build a planetary society.

MICHIO KAKU
Visions*
How science will revolutionise the 21st century

* Published by Anchor Books, New York.

university. Then secondary school started to "take off". And in the United States the Carnegie Foundation set up a commission to recommend what high schools should teach and how they should teach it.

Their recommendation: that high schools should teach what became known as "standard Carnegie units": the specific "units of knowledge"— or "school subjects"—taught then for an academic university education.

This has become the norm for a century—at a time when most other industries have been transformed every few years.

While the Carnegie commission was inventing high school, Frederick Winslow Taylor, with his time-and-motion study, was reinventing factory productivity. Two Europeans were inventing IQ tests to separate "intelligent" people from supposedly unthinking drones. Henry Ford was combining these concepts into the first efficient car-production line. And that model was to become the standard, too, for education and schooling for almost a century.

The converging revolutions

The Ford model was to dominate industry for much of that century. But today we live in an entirely new, emerging era.

Michio Kaku, Professor of Theoretical Physics at the City College of New York, in his far-sighted book *Visions* (subtitled: *How science will revolutionise the twentyfirst century*), says we are now living through the convergence of three revolutions:

❏ *The biomolecular revolution;*

❏ *The computer revolution: and*

❏ *The quantum revolution.*

Says Kaku: "In the past, scientific revolutions, such as the introduction of gunpowder, machines, steam power, electricity and the atomic bomb, all changed civilisation beyond recognition. How will the biomolecular, computer and quantum revolutions similarly reshape the twentyfirst century?

*"**The biomolecular revolution** will give us a complete genetic description of all living things, giving us the possibility of becoming the choreographers of life on earth.*

*"**The computer revolution** will give us computer power that is virtually free and unlimited, eventually placing artificial intelligence within reach.*

You can expect to have on your wrist tomorrow what you have on your desk today, what filled a room yesterday.

NICHOLAS NEGROPONTE
Being Digital*

* Published by Vintage Books, New York.

"And the quantum revolution will give us new materials, new energy sources, and perhaps the ability to create new forms of matter."

Scientist Kaku looks forward to a global society that is not "haunted by brutal sectarian, fundamentalist, nationalist and racial hatred of the past millennia". He envisages a new era in which:

The computer revolution will link all peoples with a powerful global telecommunications and economic network;

The biomolecular revolution will give them the knowledge to cure disease and feed their expanding population; and

The quantum revolution will give them the power to build a planetary society.

All require new ways of looking at everything.

The systems revolution

Peter Senge, Margaret Wheatley and Dee Hock are among many challenging the dominant old-style systems-model of the Industrial Age. All stress the new world model provided by the quantum revolution. They say the old command-and-control model is completely outdated.

Wheatley says the quantum worldview stresses that "there are no independent entities anywhere at the quantum level; it's all relationships". She says most systems should now be seen as "webs of relationships".[4]

Hock stresses the new word "chaordic"—as a combination of chaos and order—to show how institutions should look at reorganising themselves along the lines of nature: as self-organising organic entities.

The Internet itself is a "chaordic" organisation: like nature, an ordered web of networked information, but with seemingly no one in charge.

To build a "new networked learning society" means building it on the firm basis of the other most important trends shaping tomorrow's world. Of those, at least fifteen main ones demand a new kind of vision:

1. Instant communications

The world has developed an amazing ability to store information and make it available instantly in different forms to almost anyone. That ability is revolutionising business, education, home life, employment, management and virtually everything else we take for granted.

Our homes will re-emerge as vital centres of learning, work and

Now more information can be sent over a single cable in a second than filled the Internet in a month in 1997.

GEORGE GILDER
Telecosm*

* Published by The Free Press, New York.

entertainment. The impact of that sentence alone will transform our schools, our businesses, our shopping centres, our offices, our cities— in many ways our entire concept of work.

Our ability to communicate is one of our key human traits. Many historians agree that speaking, thinking and writing are probably the three main abilities separating the human species from others.

Yet our ancestors did not invent any form of writing until 6,000 years ago: first by drawing symbols instead of words.

It took another 2,000 years before they created the first alphabet. That unique concept eventually enabled all knowledge to be recorded by rearranging only twentysix symbols. But not until the eleventh century AD did the Chinese start printing books. And it was not until 1451-53 that German inventor Johannes Gutenburg printed the first European book. This transformed our ability to store and communicate knowledge by making books available to millions. Before Gutenberg, there were only about thirty thousand books on the entire continent of Europe. By 1500, there were more than nine million.

Not until the mid-1800s did we begin to speed up the process, starting with Samuel Morse's telegraph in 1835. The first typewriter appeared in 1872, the first telephone message in 1876, the first typesetting machine in 1884, silent movies in 1894, the first radio signals in 1895, talking movies in 1922, infant television in 1926 and the computer microprocessor and pocket calculator in 1971. Since then the communications revolution has exploded.

By the early 1970s, Californian and Texas engineers were starting to cram 1,000 transistors on a "chip" of silicon. By 2000: 10 million. And by 2010: 1 billion. The computer in your cellular phone today has more power than all the computers during World War II—combined.

The world is becoming one gigantic information exchange. By 1988 a single fibre optic "cable" could carry three thousand electronic messages at once. By 1996: 1.5 million. By 2000: ten million. But now, says George Gilder, more information can be sent over a single cable in a second than was sent over the entire Internet in 1997 in a month.

Gilder predicts that, over the next decade, "new technologies of sand, glass and air will form a web with a total carrying power, from household to global crossing, at least a million times larger than the networks of today".[5]

In a typical year the world now produces over 800,000 different book-

Models for the new information age

Your child's video game

has 10,000 times the capacity of the world's first 1947 ENIAC computer.

Today's greeting card

that sings "Happy Birthday" contains more computer power than existed on earth before 1950.

Most home video cameras

contain a more powerful chip than the huge IBM system 360 computer: the giant that filled hundreds of sq. ft. of air-conditioned space in the 1960s.

Genesis offers a game

with a computer more powerful than a multimillion-dollar 1976 Cray supercomputer.

Sony has a videogame

with a 200 MIPs (millions of instructions per second) processor that not so long ago would have cost about $3 million in mainframe form.

Internet 2

will soon connect more than 100 universities at 600 million bits per second—enough to transmit a 30-volume encyclopedia in less than 1 second.

DON TAPSCOTT*

* Condensed from *The Digital Economy*, and the book edited by him, *Blueprint To The Digital Economy*, both published by McGraw-Hill, 11 West 19th Street, New York, NY 1001, USA.

titles. If you read one a day, it would take you well over two thousand years to complete them all. But what if you could automatically select only the information you want, when you want it, and have it fed to you through this instant-communications network? And what if you could reproduce that information at home in any form: on computer, videotape, compact disc, your home printer or phone-based "computer in your pocket"? The technology is already working. And more and more you won't even need the fibre optics. Google is working with publishers and universities to make collected libraries of books available instantly on line—and free.

Wired magazine's co-founder Kevin Kelly calls the new economy a tectonic upheaval. "The irony of our times is that the era of computers is over. All the major consequences of stand-alone computers have already taken place. All the most promising technologies making their debut now are chiefly due to communication between computers—that is, connections rather than computations." [6]

Kelly says the network economy is "fed by the resonance of two stellar bangs: the collapsing microcosm of chips and the exploding telecosm of connections. These sudden shifts are tearing the old laws of wealth apart and preparing territory for the emerging economy.

"As the size of silicon chips shrinks to the microscopic, their costs shrink to the microscopic as well. They become cheap and tiny enough to slip into every—and the key word here is *every*—object we make."

While the total world population of personal computers is expected to reach 1.5 billion by 2007, "the number of noncomputer chips now pulsating in the world is six billion". And Kelly forecasts there'll be ten billion by the end of 2005 and a trillion not long after. "As we implant a billion specks of our thought into everything we make," he says, "we are also connecting them up." It is the explosion of low-cost—sometimes free—connections that is fuelling the new economy.

"When you go to Office Depot to buy a fax machine," says Kelly, "you are not just buying a box. You are purchasing the entire network of all other fax machines and the connections between them—a value far greater than the cost of all the separate machines." And instead of "fax machines" add the more important networks of PCs and cellphones.

Peter Drucker says the "enormous" psychological impact of the Information Revolution is just about to arrive. "It has perhaps been greatest on the way in which young children learn. Beginning at age four

In poor countries students can't afford expensive computers

Finnish student Linus Torvalds, founder of the Linux movement, which has given birth to the open-software movement.

So the open-source movement creates a new era of cooperative enterprise and free sharing

(and often earlier), children now rapidly develop computer skills, soon surpassing their elders; computers are their toys and their learning tools. Fifty years hence we may well conclude that there was no 'crisis in American education' in the closing years of the twentieth century—there was only a growing incongruence between the way twentieth-century schools taught and the way late-twentieth-century children learned." [7]

2. Not only instant, but free

Even better, it is now possible to get free access—or very cheap access—to this instant supply of information. And even to get free computer software and PC operating systems. The five new building blocks for a world wide learning web are already in place:

1. The World Wide Web itself: conceived by Tim Berners-Lee in 1989 and operating by 1991. Berners-Lee invented Hyper-Text Markup Language (HTML). This enabled millions of Internet-users to create automatic click-through links to thousands of other websites.

2. Linux open-source operating systems. In 1991, too, Finnish computer-science student Linus Torvalds couldn't afford to buy a Microsoft *Windows* operating system for his personal computer. So he designed the kernel of a new system, and "posted" its "source-code" on the Internet, seeking suggestions and improvements. They started to roll in, and soon gave birth to the Linux open-source movement (named after its founder who in turn was named after Nobel Laureate Linus Pauling).

3. Open-source software, too. Now more than 100,000 collaborative groups (http://sourceforge.net) are working round the world to produce open-source software, and share the source-code freely with all others. The result: a burst of collective innovation that will send the cost of much computer software down to zero or near zero.

4. Free browsers: the innovation, started by Mark Andreessen and his *Mosaic* team—and later Netscape *Navigator*—to add graphics to the World Wide Web through free browsers.

5. Free search engines: starting off with *Yahoo* but then booming with the development of *Google*, and its ability to deliver, in under half a second, the answers to almost any query.

"Open source" does not mean stealing inventors' patent rights. It firstly means sharing the "source code" for computer operating systems. That's very much like everyone sharing the "source code" for writing: the various alphabets and grammar. But "open source" also means a philoso-

Bill Gates' fortune is based on Windows and Microsoft Office

Now's he's got a competitor for both, and they're free

*OpenOffice, the free competitor to Microsoft Office,
is now available in eighty languages. Linux open-source
computer operating systems can also be downloaded
free from the World Wide Web.*

phy of cooperative collaboration: a new type of mass innovation.

If these new developments affected the Internet alone, they would be highly important. But "open source isn't just about better software," writes Thomas Goetz. "It's about better everything." He says it is doing for *mass innovation* what the assembly line did for mass production.

"We are at a convergent moment when a philosophy, a strategy and a technology have aligned to unleash great innovation." [8]

"Open source" means those signing a licensing agreement can download software free of charge, including its source-code. But they guarantee to pass on, free to others in the movement, any improvements to that source-code. Developers can still brand and sell their own products.

This has major ramifications for the future of a new world society. Traditionally universities existed to share knowledge without restriction. The Internet itself grew out of the same desire. And the open-source movement works on the principle that *all of us are more intelligent than one of us, so let's share the keys to that collective intelligence.*

More importantly, this "free pass-on principle" has the power to enable the world's poor countries to benefit, free of charge or at much lower prices, from the collective contributions of thousands of researchers, teachers and other students.

Some are already doing that. And they are doing it fast. In the third quarter of 2003, sales of laptop computers in China increased by 56 percent. Their price dropped by up to 90 percent as China officially adopted open-source computer systems. Students can thus buy laptops without operating systems, and download those free from the Web.

OpenOffice (a free competitor to Microsoft *Office,* the world's biggest-selling software suite) is available in eighty languages, including many non-alphabet ones, such as Japanese and Chinese. It includes *Write* (for word processing), *Calc* (for spreadsheets), and *Impress* (for slide and multimedia presentations similar to Microsoft *Powerpoint* and Apple's *Keynote). OpenOffice* also includes software that lets users transfer their finished work into pdf (portable document formats) for open sharing on the Web. By mid-2005, Microsoft *Office* was available through Amazon for $299. And a student version was available for $150. But *OpenOffice* can be downloaded off the Web—free (www.openoffice.org).

OpenOffice has been developed as a partnership between Sun Microsystems and thousands of volunteers working through the International Open Source Network (www.iosn.net). Many of the developers, par-

How developing countries catch up to the rich

❏ Open-source software has particular appeal in developing countries. Because it can be freely modified, it is easier to translate, or localise, for use in a particular language.

❏ Localising software is a tedious job, but some people are passionate enough about it to resort to unusual measures.

❏ The Hungarian translation of *OpenOffice* [the free competitor to Microsoft *Office]* was going too slowly for Janos Noll, founder of the Hungarian Foundation for Free Software.

❏ So he threw a pizza party in the computer room at the Technical University of Budapest. Over a dozen people worked locally, with about 100 Hungarians submitting work remotely over the Web.

❏ Most of the work—translating over 21,000 text strings—was completed in three days.

THE ECONOMIST*

Open source's local heroes, December 4, 2003.

ticularly in education, are also members of the Creative Commons network (http://creativecommons.org).

When the Hungarian translation of *OpenOffice* was moving slowly, more than a hundred volunteers completed it in three days. That's the kind of new creative learning revolution we're talking about. And the entire Creative Commons movement has the power to transform education, with the free sharing of lesson plans and interactive digital "learning tools".

3. A world without economic borders

We are also moving inevitably to a world where most commerce will be virtually as unrestricted as the Internet. Ignore the short-term moves to protect some countries' farming incomes. The genie is out of the bottle: the instant transfer of money around the globe—at least $1.3-trillion a day—has altered the very nature of trade and world commerce.

John Naisbitt, author of *Megatrends* books, lists a global economy as one of his main predictions. "That's the undoubted direction the world is going—towards a single-market world economy. Sure, we have the counter-trends of protectionism along the way, but the main over-arching trend is to move to a world with free trade among all countries." [9]

4. Five different routes to the Next Society

While international finance has spurred the growth of the one-world economy, there are at least five national ways to a better future:

1. The continued leadership of America in the vital field of electronic innovation and in productivity based on hi-tech investment.

2. The rebirth of Europe as a single economic entity, as a working example of how many countries can form integrated communities.

3. The rise of dynamic "Tiger economies"—particularly in Asia—as models for small countries and examples for the world's giants.

4. The resurgence of China, the world's most populous country, as the planet's fastest-growing manufacturing dynamo.

5. The rise of India, to start joining America as a new poor-country model on how to become an information technology powerhouse.

The first stepping stone: the American flair for quickly turning hi-tech research into breakthrough products, services and experiences. In spite of short-term fluctuations, the resilience and productivity of the

What's needed to match Silicon Valley?

1. Major research institution
Like Stanford, Cambridge, M.I.T.

2. One mega-success story
Like Microsoft, Nokia, Lotus, Acer

3. High-tech talent
And the ability to attract it

4. Venture capital
Israel, Taiwan now showing the way

5. Infrastructure
Singapore the Government model

6. The right attitude
Risk-taking confidence

STEVEN LEVY*

Newsweek cover story, *The Hot New Tech Cities*
(November 9, 1998).

American economy remains a strong base for growth through innovation.

Despite some setbacks, California's Silicon Valley is still the model for the future. Even fifty years ago the area south of San Francisco Bay was a county of orange groves and vineyards. Now it has given birth to 240 publicly-listed technology companies with a market worth of $500 billion, annual sales of $170 billion and 377,000 employees—plus at least 4,000 small non-public companies.

But its lesson for the future is probably even more important: a unique series of university-business partnerships. Today half of Silicon Valley's revenues come from companies seeded by Stanford University. And this kind of education-business partnership will provide some of the twentyfirst century's greatest growth models.

America's emerging new catalyst is the way several of its ground-breaking industries are now converging: computers, television, enter-tainment and instant communications. That convergence, too, has tre-mendous implications for education: and the potential to bypass the school system if that system stays locked into an outdated model.

The second stepping stone into a one-world economy is modelled by the European Union. With ten new members added in May, 2004, it now links twentyfive countries and 450 million people. Long in the shadow of the United States, Europe is once again re-emerging as the second global anchor for prosperity and stability. Europe's new single currency, the Euro, links most of its members. And, in spite of high unemployment in some traditional manufacturing industries, Europe's software and telecom companies have been pumping out jobs. Finland's Nokia, Sweden's Ericsson and Britain's Vodafone have shown how the new technologies can revitalise the new century's economies when backed by equally dynamic educational policies.

The third stepping stone is the new model of the internationally-minded small country or state: Taiwan, Ireland, South Korea, Finland, Singapore and Dubai, with pockets elsewhere such as Bangalore, Hyderabad and Madras in India, Tel Aviv in Israel, and Kyoto in Japan.

When co-author Dryden first visited Taipei in 1964, the capital of Taiwan had only one set of traffic lights: turned on only when a visiting dignitary entered town. Now Taiwan, with 21 million people, boasts 14,000 electronic companies with total sales of $75 billion, mostly exported, including 120 high-tech public companies, with a market worth of $100 billion, sales of $27 billion and 72,000 employees. It also

Forty years ago: a sleepy backwater of the third world

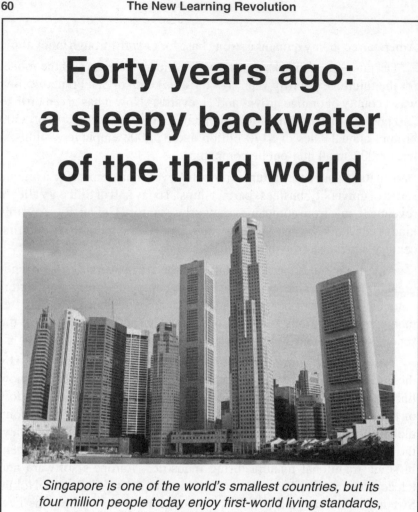

Singapore is one of the world's smallest countries, but its four million people today enjoy first-world living standards, with an technical-education system geared to attract international giants.

Today Singapore is home to 3,200 world hi-tech companies with technical education to match

graduates 10,000 engineers and scientists a year and has an active policy to attract back thousands from Silicon Valley.

Singapore provides equally important lessons. Forty years ago it was a poverty-stricken island. Twenty years ago the Government began a campaign to attract hi-tech multinationals—with tax incentives, an educated workforce, and an amazing infrastructure programme. Fired by an enormous Government-investment policy from compulsory superannuation savings, the island state's biggest infrastructure project, *Singapore One*—worth hundreds of millions of dollars—is designed to connect every household, school and office to the Internet.

Ireland, with under four million people, tells a similar story. Twentyfive years ago it was a poor farming country. But by 2001 it had surpassed the United States as the world's biggest software exporter. It has attracted 1,100 international companies to the republic, and these now have 107,000 employees. The country's annual exports: $25 billion, with a trade surplus each year of at least $11 billion. Ireland's tax incentives to attract hi-tech companies are matched by extensive policies to develop the skilled people to staff them.

Finland has even a more amazing story to tell—and in many ways it is the story of one company: Nokia. Back in the 1980s, Finland's major industry was paper and pulp. Helsinki-based Nokia, the country's largest company, was known more for its rubber boots than tiny phones. But when the economy took a nosedive in the early 1990s, Finland turned to hi-tech for salvation. The Government decided to put 2.9 percent of the gross domestic product into technology research and development. Companies turned to international partners to start electronic ventures, and Nokia discovered a seemingly endless market for cellphones. Soon Nokia was pulling in $32 billion a year from this new phenomenon. As the company grew, it also invested in science parks at universities around the country, which were funded by government-venture capital groups. Today Finland has 400 hi-tech firms. And also a great education system, with one of the world's best teacher-training programmes.

South Korea leads the world in fast, broadband Internet use: more than 75 percent of its homes are connected. And South Korea also aims to dominate the rapidly-increasing market for digital home theatres.

And Dubai, in the United Arab Emirates, has also proven how a small city-state can provide the dynamic leadership model for its larger neighbours. Like Singapore, it has used its own modern airline, Emirates, and

china.net

By 2006: China is expected to have more people on the Net, more broadband subscribers and more mobile-phone customers than any nation on earth.

By 2003: China had twice as many mobile phones as America.

By end of 2004: China had 100 million Web users—second to United States.

By end of 2005: China will have 44 million with broadband access: more than America.

By 2006: China will have 153 million Web users—surpassing United States as world No. 1.

BUSINESSWEEK*

* Cover story, *China.Net,* March 15, 2004.

one of the world's most modern airports to turn itself into a tourist and business hub. Its Internet City houses regional offices of such companies as Microsoft, Dell, Siemens, HP, Oracle and IBM. Its Media City is home to the regional bureaus of several TV networks. And it is now planning a new Knowledge Village, as a Middle Eastern educational centre. And now nearby Qatar is replanning its entire education system with the aim of becoming a world leader.

But the biggest sleeping giant of all is China. After the stagnating years of Mao's Cultural Revolution, since 1979 it has released more people from poverty than any other society in history. In the past twentyfive years it has increased its economy more than 400 percent. In many of the coastal "special economic areas" the economy has been growing even faster. Sure: the country still has big problems, but it is now racing to apply the lessons of Singapore, Hong Kong and Taiwan.

In the past five years its soaring production has made it the world's new manufacturing powerhouse. And an educational one, too. More than 2.8 million students graduated from institutions of higher learning in China in 2004, more than double 2002. In 2005: 3.2 million.

China, too, has an extra "secret weapon": the 51 million Chinese who live outside its borders. Collectively they own liquid assets worth two trillion dollars. Their over-riding ethic is educational achievement. Most of their historic family links are with major areas of growth along China's eastern seaboard. With their investment in those areas, and the country's own internal growth policies, the Chinese economy is set to become the world's largest no later than the 2030s, maybe much earlier.

Already by the end of 2004 China had between 35 million and 40 million households with the equivalent purchasing power of a U.S. household earning $25,000 to $30,000 a year. Around 100 million Chinese are therefore living the middle-class life. Economists forecast that number to double or triple over the next ten years.

Already China's leading personal-computer company, Legend, has acquired IBM's PC division and renamed itself Lenova to pave the way for international expansion. In a reverse drive, Amazon.com has bought Joyo.com—China's biggest online retailer of books and music—to add to the American giant's millions of existing online customers in China.

What China has started to achieve in manufacturing, India is doing with information technology.

By the end of 2003, there were more IT engineers in the Indian city

India's challenges

- ❏ Only 53% of villages have primary schools.
- ❏ 40% of students drop out by age ten.
- ❏ 40% of adults are illiterate.
- ❏ Elitist education system filters top students so that only 2000 a year are selected for the seven big Institutes of Technology.
- ❏ 200 miss out for every one selected.
- ❏ And then this giant poor country exports most of its IT graduates to subsidise Silicon Valley in the the world's richest country.
- ❏ Now some of India's IT pioneers are working to build $100 network computer.
- ❏ And experimenting with setting up computer-assisted learning centres and IT multi-purpose kiosks in villages.
- ❏ Microsoft, Oracle, Intel and other giants are helping with other IT and teacher training.
- ❏ But India is unlikely to achieve UN goals for primary schooling for all by 2015.[1]

EDUCATIONAL TECHNOLOGY IN INDIA*

* Report by Osama Manzar and Dr. B. Phalachandra,
for Quest Alliance/USAid, 2005.

1. This report was written before the 2005 commitment by many major nations to fund the United Nations Millennium Project.

of Bangalore (150,000) than in Silicon Valley (120,000). And Indian schools are pumping out another 260,000 engineers every year.

McKinsey, the giant consulting company, estimates that by 2008 IT services and IT outsourcing work in India will swell fivefold, to a $57 billion annual export industry employing four million people.

India's second richest man, 57-year-old Azim H. Premji—with a net worth of $5.3 billion as the main shareholder in IT giant Wipro Ltd.—has transferred company shares worth $45 million to a new foundation focused on achieving universal elementary education for India. But the Premji Foundation doesn't donate money direct to schools. Instead, it works in with UNESCO to develop models for better teaching methods.

Significantly, in the 2004 election, India's Congress Party swept to power on a policy to double the country's educational spending, and to concentrate this on primary education. To date, India's rapid rise to IT power has rested almost entirely on its preoccupation with higher education. But as *Business Week* reported on the election result: "The real problem is with primary education. When they were at the same stage of development as India is now, South Korea, Taiwan and China focused on elementary and secondary schools. As a result, they achieved nearly universal literacy among youth—the educated workforce that fueled economic takeoffs."

5. Internet commerce and learning

Link these first trends to all aspects of commerce and education and you get an even more astonishing view of tomorrow's world. Not only can people communicate instantly around the globe, but they can *trade* instantly and *learn* instantly.

Peter Drucker picks the "revolutionary" impact of e-commerce as being a dominant change-driver in the early part of this century: "the explosive emergence of the Internet as a major, perhaps eventually *the* major worldwide distribution channel for goods, for services, and, surprisingly, for managerial and professional jobs". He says e-commerce is to the Information Revolution what the railroad was to the Industrial Revolution: "a totally unprecedented, unexpected development".[10]

By mid-1997, Dell was selling computers through the Internet at a rate of $1 million a day. By 2003: $50 million a day. And nearly all of those computers are being "configured" by the users themselves on the Internet, selecting from individual components. The completed orders are

We still buy most of our goods from stores and supermarkets

Meg Whitman, CEO of eBay, with some of the merchandise traded online.

But now 147 million people trade $30 billion a year through world's biggest Web auctions on eBay.

then emailed to FedEx depots, quickly assembled and delivered overnight or within two days to more isolated areas.

*The Dell model for education is obvious: soon everyone will be able
to type individual learning goals on to the Web, and select components
of interactive courses to make those goals possible.*

Similar moves are revolutionising commerce in other fields. By 2003
at least thirty million people a year were buying and selling more than $20
billion in merchandise through e-Bay online auctions: more than the
gross domestic product of all but seventy of the world's countries. By the
end of 2004 the number of registered users had soared to 125 million, with
goods worth $30 billion sold. And by 2005 eBay could boast 147 million
users worldwide, even before buying Skype with its 50 million users.

Still think the Internet revolution won't change education?

By early this century, the giant Cisco Systems corporation was the
world's largest integrator of routers and switches—vital links that connect computers around the world. Its sales have risen from $1.5 million
in 1987 to $25 billion in 2005. Its Internet-generated sales have been as
high as $40 million a day.

And because its network automatically links all its customers—who
share answers to hi-tech queries—this saves Cisco from employing ten
thousand customer-answering engineers. Instead, hospital staff using
Cisco systems in one country can share knowledge and find answers to
similar problems from hospitals around the world.

Similarly, it is now possible and desirable for all the world's best
teachers to share the world's best lesson plans on line. Already, in a world
where corporations are desperately short of skilled information technology specialists, giant IT companies like Oracle, Microsoftt and Cisco are
running their own training programmes in many countries.

Cisco Systems has Network Academies in 152 countries. The academies offer a four-semester course that trains students to design, build and
maintain networks. The total programme links hands-on, practical
training with Internet back-up, and guarantees high-paid jobs. Many of
the 458,000 taking these courses are high-school students; others are at
university colleges.

And one of the Academy Network's big achievements: the large
percentage of young women taking their courses in countries where
females have often been under-represented in education. In the small
Middle Eastern country of Jordan, for example, ten Cisco Academies

Cisco only started its Networking Academy Programme in 1997

A two-fold revolution in Islamic Indonesia: an emancipated woman instructor at the Cisco Networking Academy in Jakarta.

Now it has 458,000 students in 10,000 world academies in 152 countries

have been opened. More than 600 students have entered their IT courses, 65 percent of them women.

6. The new service society

Peter Drucker, John Naisbitt, Kenichi Ohmae, Robert Reich and many other forecasters all agree the next new trend: the move from an industrial to a service society.

Two hundred years ago 90 percent of the people in North America were farmers; one hundred years ago, 50 percent. Now: between 2 and 3 percent.

Both Naisbitt and Drucker predict that within a few years only 10 percent of the workforce in affluent developed countries like America will be working in direct manufacturing.

So if all a developed country's manufacturing can be done with 10 percent of its workers, and all its farm products produced by another 2 percent, what will the other 88 percent of us do?

Some are calling this future "the new service economy". But the very terms "manufacturing" and "service" are now largely obsolete.

More and more, manufacturing is now combined with service: customised for individuals—in the same way that computer hardware now represents a very small part of the total service supplied by a computer company. By far the biggest part is in specialist consulting: customised software systems and training.

The same applies to education. Given the interactive technology and instant-communications tools that now abound, one of the next major industries will be taking the brilliance of the world's best teachers, and selling those services to the world.

But we're not talking only about information-technology companies. Cemex, for example, has quickly transformed itself from a small regional Mexican company to the world's fastest-growing and most profitable cement corporation. It did it in large part by using a new computer network to reinvent the just-in-time supply of cement to building sites.

As Gary Hamel puts it in *Leading The Revolution:* Cemex has a passion for growth, innovation and new forms of service. "This passion has spawned dozens of growth initiatives across the company—from GPS-guided delivery trucks to cheaper fuels to new methods for building houses in the developing world." And he adds: "Cemex never set out to

The most successful corporation of the future will be something called a learning organisation.

FORTUNE INTERNATIONAL*

*Quoted by Peter M. Senge, in *The Fifth Discipline,* published by
Random House, New York.

build a computer network, *per se;* rather, it set out to build a learning and innovation network." That has made it an international leader.

7. The marriage of big and small

In the traditional industrial economy, bigness ruled. GM, Chrysler and Ford dominated world car production for almost half a century; IBM towered over computers; and so on in dozens of different industries.

Even thirty years ago only big companies could afford the giant computers that were then the peak of electronic achievement. That technology helped spur the ride to centralised bureaucracy, takeovers, acquisitions and mergers. Today many of those giant computers are obsolete. The world of the mini has arrived. Sure, many big companies are still there. Many of them, such as GE, are booming. Giant mergers are reported almost every day as different industries converge. And new giants such as Microsoft, Acer, Sun and Oracle have emerged. But the earlier vast air-conditioned computer rooms lie empty or transformed.

And organisational structures are changing fast. Where the giant companies are still prospering, they have generally been split into dozens of small project teams, each self-acting and self-managing, cutting through the old specialisation, the old business pyramid-style hierarchies, the old army-style management.

The biggest growing network by far is the Internet, with its thousands of individual networks, and the opportunity for anyone to sell his or her niche products to customers around the planet.

Here again, eBay, the world's biggest online auction site, shows the shape of things to come. Says a special *Business Week* report: "On eBay more than 150,000 entrepreneurs earn a fulltime living by selling everything from diet pills and Kate Spade handbags to $30,000 BMWs and hulking industrial lathes." eBay holds constant classes, dubbed eBay University, to teach people how to use the site. In many ways the company is revolutionising retailing. Its Chinese centre is now China's biggest e-commerce site.

And in other fields—notably retailing—franchising and computerisation make it possible for small distribution outlets to link with major international systems-suppliers, from McDonald's to computer and software manufacturers.

Some analysts say that by early this century 50 percent of all retailing will be through franchises (mostly self-operating small units linked to

In 1930 on average we lived to 60, and leisure time was limited

New leisure pursuits such as white water rafting and adventure travel are turning tourism into the world's fastest-growing industry, with 'educational tourism' a key part of lifelong learning.
Online photo from: www.costaricajungletours.com

Now we live to 75, with 388,000 hours for leisure, hobbies and learning

giant systems) and direct-marketing networks (mainly individuals linked to world suppliers). Again the examples are startling:

❏ Franchising in America involves $250 billion in annual sales.

❏ The fastest-growing franchise is Subway Sandwiches, with 17,000 outlets in seventythree countries.

❏ Many of McDonald's 29,000 franchises around the world are run by husband-and-wife teams, but all are linked to the one central system.

❏ More than twenty million Americans are now making money from home-based industries. Over 60 percent of them are women.

❏ One of the biggest is Amway, started by Richard DeVos and Jay Van Andel, in the basement of a Michigan home in 1959. Now the company had three million people selling 5,000 Amway products in eighty countries, with global sales of $5 billion..

❏ Japan is the world's biggest direct-selling market, involving 1.2 million women distributors and a turnover above $20 billion a year.

Our prediction: a big rise in franchised educational partnerships. Both universities and corporations such as Cisco will provide some of the online courses and back-up. Other specialists in interactive technology, and specially "games simulation", will add expertise. So will students, creating teaching software as part of their studies. And local franchise-holders, including schools and businesses, will provide the hands-on experience: sometimes in classrooms but also in the "real world".

8. The new age of leisure

British educator, broadcaster and business consultant Charles Handy puts the figures neatly in *The Age of Unreason*. When he first started work in the 1940s it was standard for each person to spend 100,000 hours in his or her lifetime in paid work, although we never thought of it in those terms. But we generally worked around fortyseven hours a week, for fortyseven weeks of the year for fortyseven years—generally from age sixteen, seventeen or eighteen. And that worked out at just over 100,000 hours. Handy predicts that very soon—at least in developed countries— we will each need to spend only around 50,000 hours of a lifetime in paid work. And he thinks we will each split that into different and convenient "chunks".

The average male in rich countries now lives to around seventyfive years—a total of over 655,000 hours. And if we sleep for 200,000 hours

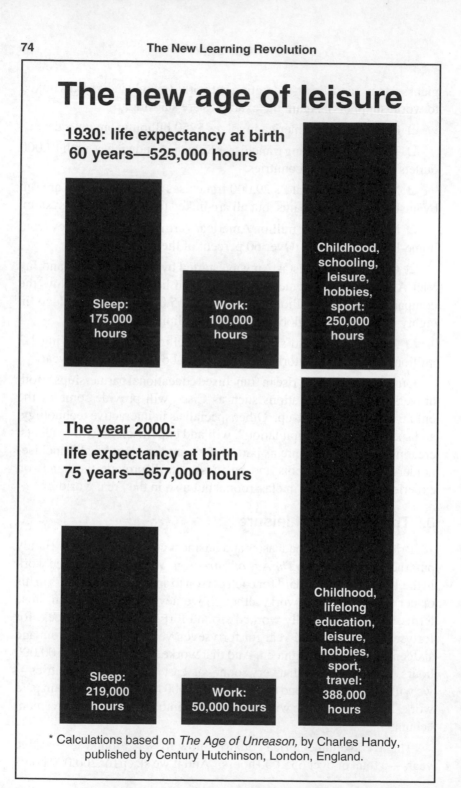

The new age of leisure

<u>1930</u>: life expectancy at birth
60 years—525,000 hours

Sleep:
175,000
hours

Work:
100,000
hours

Childhood,
schooling,
leisure,
hobbies,
sport:
250,000
hours

The year 2000:

life expectancy at birth
75 years—657,000 hours

Sleep:
219,000
hours

Work:
50,000 hours

Childhood,
lifelong
education,
leisure,
hobbies,
sport,
travel:
388,000
hours

* Calculations based on *The Age of Unreason,* by Charles Handy,
published by Century Hutchinson, London, England.

Regular updates: www.thelearningweb.net

and spend only 50,000 hours in paid employment, we will have over 400,000 hours to spend on leisure, education, travel, hobbies and everything else.

Leisure, tourism and lifelong education will be among the major growth industries. Already some of the trends are obvious. Half a billion tourists travelled each year in the 90s. By 2001, the billion mark was in sight. And tourism for many countries is already the fastest-growing source of employment, with all that entails in foreign-language, social and presentation skills.

9. The changing shape of work

Handy forecasts that soon a minority of working-age adults will be employed in fulltime permanent employment by traditional-style companies. Those will generally be highly-trained people, probably not starting work until their mid-twenties—with graduate and postgraduate qualifications. They are likely to provide the essential core management services. The rest, predicts Handy, will work in three separate clusters:

Cluster one will involve project groups: people coming together for specific projects, often for short periods. This is the prevailing method of organisation in the movie, television and multimedia production industries. It typifies, we suggest, one of the main themes of this book: that the most successful organisations of the future will be those, in all fields, that learn from these industries how to select people on the basis of their specific talent, and how to blend and organise that talent to produce outstanding results.

New Zealand is one country where that lesson shows up in the movie industry, based around Peter Jackson's headquarters near Wellington international airport. Multi-talented teams reassemble and combine as production moves from *Lord of The Rings,* to *King Kong* and beyond.

The second cluster will be part-time and seasonal workers: those who work part-time in supermarkets or the tourist industry. These will be among the few outlets for the unskilled or semiskilled.

The third cluster will be those who work individually or as a family group—often doing things they love to do. Effectively, the new worldwide information Web enables competent people in any country to sell goods and services to anyone else—and to use databases to identify those customers and services. Families will be able to use such services to swap everything from holiday-houses to ideas.

The first country where women won the right to vote

New Zealand Prime Minister Helen Clark:
the second woman in a row to head a country where women
have had the right fo vote from 1893.

Now it has had women as Head of State, Prime Minister, Chief Justice, top corporate CEO and main TV 'anchor'

And we will have the choice of the world's best educators in nearly every home.

10. Women in leadership

Of the 22 million new jobs created in America in the eighties, two thirds were taken by women. By the 90s John Naisbitt was forecasting that the increase of women in leadership positions in America was now reaching critical mass.

"Forty percent of all managers are now women. Thirty-five percent of computer scientists are women. Half the accountants are women. In medical schools or business schools, half of the freshman class are women. And women are creating new companies at twice the rate of men." [11]

In some countries women have already risen to dominant positions of political leadership. New Zealand, for example, can fairly lay claim to being the world's first fully democratic country: the first where all women joined men in 1893 in gaining the right to vote in national elections. In recent years New Zealand has had a woman Head of State (Governor General), two women Prime Ministers, and women as Chief Justice, CEO of its biggest corporation, Attorney General, main television news-anchor and TV current-affairs interviewer. In the past 15 years its five main cities have each had a woman mayor.

There is also no doubt that in many cases women provide a different perspective. Vicki Buck, the former mayor of New Zealand's Christchurch city, has since played a major part in setting up Discovery 1 and Unlimited, primary and high "schools" that work from small but strikingly-designed multimedia centres and where students then use the entire city as their classroom. Both are fully funded as part of the flexible public system of chartered schooling

Also from New Zealand, Wendy Pye is a guiding light in educational publishing. She has become her country's wealthiest business woman as the founder of Sunshine Books. Its philosophy: teaching children to read. Its theoretical base: New Zealand's rich record in children's literacy and literature. International sales to date: well over 100 million copies, backed by a global TV series, *The Magic Box*. Sunshine is also a leader in learning on the Internet, involving seven-year-olds, and younger, in designing their own books online.

Anita Roddick is another outstanding example. In 1976 Roddick

Never doubt that a small group of thoughtful, committed citizens can change the world. Indeed it is the only thing that ever has.

MARGARET MEAD*

* Quoted by Anita Roddick, founder of The Body Shop,
explaining her own philosophy in
Business as Unusual, published by Thorsons, London.

opened her first retail venture, The Body Shop, in Brighton, England. It now trades in around 1,900 shops in fifty countries, across twelve time zones and in twentyfive languages. Many of them are franchised or run as joint ventures by like-minded people, most of them women.

In her books, *Body and Soul* and *Business as Unusual,* Roddick's perspective comes through on almost every page. "The great advantage I had when I started The Body Shop was that I had never been to business school . . . If I had to name a driving force in my life, I'd plump for passion every time. The twin ideas of love and care touch everything we do." [12]

But the emancipation of women is not happening only in developed countries, if not always as fast as we would like.

In Islamic Iran, for example, the most populous country in the Middle East, 53 percent of new students admitted to university are now women. And in India's 2004 general elections, an Italian-born woman, Sonia Gandhi, led the Congress Party to victory.

11. Cultural nationalism

The more we become a one-world economy, the more we develop a global lifestyle, the more we will see an equal counter movement for what Naisbitt calls cultural nationalism.

"The more we globalise and become economically interdependent," he says, "the more we do the human thing; the more we assert our distinctiveness, the more we want to hang on to our language, the more we want to hold on to our roots and our culture. Even as Europe comes together economically, I think the Germans will become more German and the French more French."

The downside of this is obvious: the "ethnic cleansing" and horror of the civil war in the former Balkan country of Yugoslavia; the Middle East wars, often with religious overtones; rebellion in parts of the former Soviet Union; the racial bigotry in many countries.

But the positive challenges for education are equally obvious. The more technology thrives, the more the striving to capture our cultural heritage, in music, dance, language, art and history.

Where individual communities are inspiring new directions in education, particularly among so-called minority groups, we're seeing a flowering of cultural initiatives—and a tremendous rise in self-esteem.

The other alternative: a rising underclass

The telephone gap

Half the world's population has never placed a phonecall.

The computer gap

Only 20 percent of the world's population uses computers, and even in the rich United States millions cannot afford them.

The unemployment gap

Even in affluent Western Europe, 19 million people cannot find jobs—5 million in Germany alone.

The poverty gap

37 million Americans now live in poverty.[a]

The education gap

More than half of America's young people leave school without the foundation needed to hold a good job.

The violence trap

270,000 American students carry guns to school.

The wealth gap

1 percent of Americans own more household wealth than the bottom 90 percent combined.[b]

The knowledge gap

The have-nots become the know-nots and do-nots.

a. 2005 Census Bureau annual report on U.S. incomes, for 2004.
b. *Business Week* summary, September 26, 2005.

12. Removing the poverty trap

You don't have to move too far from the centre of the city in places like New York, Chicago, Philadelphia and Los Angeles to see the grim signs of a soaring underclass. In developed countries it is mainly associated with colour and educational failure, and is overwhelmingly among unemployed, uneducated youth.

And in the developing world, the gap between the wealthy sections of main cities and faraway villages is incredible. Visit the modern small states of Dubai or Qatar on the Arabian-Persian Gulf and you see the new prosperous potential of the Middle East—and educational models for the rest of that troubled area. But drive even half an hour in any direction from Tehran, the Iranian capital of the most-populous Middle Eastern country, and it's like moving several hundred years back in history.

"Eight million people die each year because they are too poor to survive," [13] says Jeffrey D. Sachs, author of the United Nations' most far-reaching programme to end poverty.

Overall, in a world of plenty, half the six billion population are poor. But "there are three degrees of poverty: extreme (or absolute) poverty, moderate poverty and relative poverty," says Sachs. "Extreme poverty, defined by the World Bank as getting by on an income of less than $1 a day, means that households cannot meet basic needs for survival. They are chronically hungry, unable to get health care, lack safe drinking water and sanitation, cannot afford education for their children and perhaps lack rudimentary shelter—a room to keep rain out of the hut—and basic articles of clothing, like shoes." Sachs says this is the poverty that kills.

"Moderate poverty, defined as living on $1 to $2 a day, refers to conditions in which basic needs are met, but just barely. Being in relative poverty, defined by a household income level below a given proportion of the national average, means lacking things that the middle class now takes for granted."

The World Bank estimates that 1.1 billion people now live in extreme poverty, down from 1.5 billion in 1981, but still a disaster.

Sachs, an American professor of economics, is head of the United Nations Millennium Project, which has the goal to cut the world's extreme poverty in half by 2015.

In his new 2005 book, *The End of Poverty,* he spells out specific ways to achieve that—by boosting agriculture, improving basic health, provid-

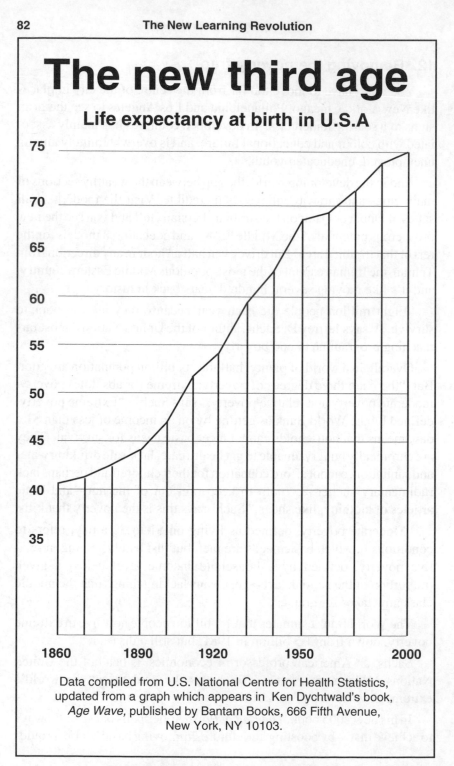

The new third age

Life expectancy at birth in U.S.A

Data compiled from U.S. National Centre for Health Statistics,
updated from a graph which appears in Ken Dychtwald's book,
Age Wave, published by Bantam Books, 666 Fifth Avenue,
New York, NY 10103.

Regular updates: www.thelearningweb.net

ing clean water and sanitation, bringing electric power to villages and investing in education.

Most of the programmes he suggests are simple ones, and could be funded internationally if all countries carried out their existing pledges to donate 0.7 percent of their annual gross national product to sensible international aid, development and educational programmes.

For education, he says: "Meals for all children at primary schools could improve the health of kids, the quality of education and attendance at school. Expanded vocational training for the students could teach them the skills of modern farming, computer literacy, basic infrastructure maintenance and carpentry. The village is ready and eager to be empowered by increased information and technical knowledge."

Some of that empowerment is already starting to flower in India with Internet pioneer Rajesh Jain as one catalyst. Jain set up his IndiaWorld Yahoo-type Web portal in 1995, and sold it four years later for $115 million. Now he's using that as a financial base for a series of educational initiatives. These include building a $100 network computer, and linking millions of these with India's thousands of villages and online lessons.

13. The new demographics

Demographic changes are also a big driving force in this new century. And the most striking trend in many countries is two-sided: the active aging of the population and the decline in the percentage of young people.

A hundred years ago only 2.4 million Americans were over sixtyfive, under four in every hundred. Today there are over thirty million— around one in eight. By 2050: over sixtyseven million—almost 22 percent of the population. Since 1920 in America, average life expectancy has increased from fiftyfour years to seventyfive. In most developed countries, the average male reaching sixty can also expect to live to at least seventyfive, and the average woman over eighty. At current rates of growth, by the year 2025, the world's over-sixties population will have increased to one billion.

Life expectancy—and with it the number of older people—has been going up steadily for 300 years. But the decline in the number of young people is something new.

Already both extremes are reshaping much of our future. In China, for instance, with its official one-child-per-family policy, in its coastal cities middle-class families now spend more on the education of their one child

Now the 21st-century provides the revolution with a difference

Well over 50 percent of United Kingdom students aged from seven to sixteen now have a mobile phone, and students in eastern Chinese cities are fast catching up.—BBC online photo.

The first revolution where children know more about the dominant technology than parents

than similar families once spent on their four or five children. And in China's major cities it is quite common for families to spend up to 35 per cent of their total income on the education of the single child in most families.

In America, with fewer children and later pregnancies, *second career* and *second half of one's life* have already become buzzwords.

Says Drucker again: "In future there will almost certainly be two distinct workforces, broadly made up of the under-fifties and the over-fifties respectively. The split into two workforces is likely to start with female knowledge technologists. A nurse, a computer technologist or a paralegal can take fifteen years out to look after her children and then return to fulltime work. Women, who now outnumber men in American higher education, increasingly look for work in the new knowledge technologies. Such jobs are the first in human history to be well adapted to the special needs of women as child-bearers, and to their increasing longevity." [14]

Drucker says demographics will be one of the most important factors in what he calls the Next Society. And one of the most interesting trends has already emerged in Asia.

In China, people joke about the new generation of "six pocket children", with two parents and four grandparents devoted to each child's education. In other Asian countries, most families have live-in grandparents. And in Singapore, with an early childhood centre in each big state-provided apartment complex, grandparents play a big part in preschool education.

Conversely, Finland is one country that at one stage selected 5,000 bright computer-minded children to train their teachers in how to use intreractive technology.

Already some people are calling the new generation—those who have grown up with the "new technology"—"digital natives". And the pre-computer generation "digital immigrants".

So hopefully the agenda is set to blend the wisdom of age with the technical know-how of the young.

Don Tapscott summarises one of the resulting challenges in *Growing Up Digital:* "I have become convinced that the most revolutionary force for change is the students themselves. Give children the tools they need and they will be the single most important source of guidance on how to make the schools relevant and effective."

14. Do-it-yourself learning and health

The industrial age also gave birth to another phenomenon: the confusion of structures with reality. Just as giant corporations arose to provide standardised mass-produced products to millions of people, so giant organisations arose to "deliver" health and education.

And so we came to confuse education with schooling; health with sickness-treatment and hospitals; law with lawyers. We came to regard education as something someone else provided for you. We believed that health was something you purchased from doctors, specialists and hospitals.

Today that concept is changing rapidly. The new do-it-yourself revolution involves more than painting your home and doing your gardening. It involves taking control of your own life.

Personal computers can now provide the basis for much of what we pay experts to do: prepare wills, handle accounts, buy stocks and bonds, and figure taxes. Every sensible person now accepts that health also comes from what you do: what you eat and drink, and how you exercise. So stand by for "the Wellness Revolution".

And we see this same principle at the very core of education: with learners writing and reframing their own curriculum throughout life. And selecting from the world's best teachers and resources as they personally control their own education, leisure and health.

15. Cooperative, networked enterprise

The 1990s started with the collapse of Soviet-style communism, and we hope that the Enron and other collapses in 2002 herald the decline of gambling-casino corruption in the corporate world. Already new forms of cooperative enterprise are emerging:

❏ **The American model of Atomic Learning:** set up by school teachers and now providing students more than 15,000 online, on-demand video tutorials on how to use interactive digital technology.

❏ **The British model of Richard Branson:** where the Virgin group operates as a venture-capital centre for its employees' ideas. Branson views Virgin's core business as a giant "ideas incubator". Its corporate function is to find new business opportunities that fit the Virgin brand. Nearly all of those have so far come from staff members. The company then lines up management teams and provides guidance and support.

When students can download 15,000 tunes from the Web on to their iPod . . .

can lessons on demand and 'school in a pocket' be far behind?

❏ **The Brazilian Semco model** of Richard Semler: where the company's employees select all new workers and their own bosses.

❏ **The new Google model,** where all staff are required to spend at least one day a week dreaming up new ideas unrelated to their work.

❏ **And the Silicon Valley model**, based on the initial example of Bill Hewlett and Dave Packard: entrepreneurship plus shared ownership.

Peter Drucker, in his view of *the Next Society,* says the new-century knowledge workers will have two main needs: education that enables them to enter specific knowledge work, and then continuing education throughout their working lives to keep their knowledge up to date.

"Continuing education of already highly educated adults will therefore become a big growth area in the Next Society," says Drucker. "But most of it will be delivered in untraditional ways, ranging from weekend seminars to online training programmes, and in any number of places, from a traditional university to the student's home." [15]

That forecast is already being proven in practice:

❏ Apple's new *iPod* and *iTunes* software combine to show one model of the future. Together they let millions around the world download, for less than $1 each, all their favourite music tracks. And to store up to 15,000 of them in a digital box not much bigger than a pack of playing cards. And now Apple has linked it all with a mobile phone too: your personal radio station, school, computer and phone in your pocket.

❏ Pepperdine University in California runs "educational technology" programmes at undergraduate, masters and doctoral levels. But students spend only fifteen days a year on campus: five at the start, five in the middle and five at the end. All the rest is online.

❏ And China's recently-retired Vice-Premier in charge of education, Li Lanqing, sees satellite, television and digital networks playing a major part in re-educating the world's most populous nation. In his new book, *Education for 1.3 Billion,* he spells out how satellite and wireless networks, in particular, will be needed to retrain China's 10 million school teachers, and to provide quality education for all its 120 million primary school and 82 million high school students.

Overall, we see an even more embracing series of new networking concepts will reinvent learning, teaching, schooling and education. No longer will education be synonymous with schooling. In their place: an entirely new networking way to learn, teach, share and create.

The seven networks in new learning society

1. Your neural network
Your unique brain, mind and body 'talent' and how to develop it.

2. Your personal learning network
Home, school and community in a linked interactive learning environment.

3. Interactive information network
How you can interact with the new world of instant communications.

4. Your creative network
How to think for new ideas and innovate in partnership with others.

5. Your talent network
Worldwide sharing of skills, abilities and professional knowhow.

6. New organisational networks
New 'social movements' linked to cooperative open partnerships.

7. Global learning networks
Education based on shared information, talents, cultures and 'digital tools'.

New framework for education
in the new networked world

Visit schools around the globe for more than fifteen years, as we authors have, and the stunning facts emerge:

❑ *Most schools are teaching students for a world that no longer exists.*

Prominent American educator Professor Seymour Papert says the world is currently entering "the most momentous megachange that has ever come to the practice of learning and education".[1] But overwhelmingly, he says, most educational systems are failing to lead the change.

Papert is a co-founder of the Massachusetts Institute of Technology's world-famous MediaLab.

He says the typical school-classroom system is still very much like the production line in the original 1907 Henry Ford Model T factory: "The car moved along and at each station an additional change was made, a piece added, something was checked, an exam was given." He concedes that this model for education might have been appropriate for an earlier age"—when we didn't know any other way to do it. But now we do. And much better ways are working brilliantly in pockets of excellence in many countries, many states or districts.

❑ *Most schools are still teaching in ways similar to the blackboard-and-chalk, desks-in-rows classroom model invented 300 years ago.*

Graham Nuthall, a New Zealand Emeritus Professor of Education, has spent forty years researching classroom practice around the world. And almost everywhere he's found what he calls the same "cultural ritual" of traditional classroom teaching. It's a ritual that has remained largely unchanged for decades—in many cases for three centuries.

Compulsory schooling began in Prussia in 1717 with teacher, chalk and blackboard

300 years later, many schools around world still use the same outdated 'cultural ritual'

His conclusion: "We're locked into a system that inevitably produces failures and inequalities."[2] Nearly all adults have gone through this ten-year classroom ritual—and many thus automatically equate classroom schooling with real learning.

❏ *It's almost as if the biggest communications revolution in history has bypassed most education systems.*

Almost every school system in the world is investing big money in "information and communications technology". But nearly all are doing it ineffectively. Locked into the old classroom model, they're slapping twentyfirst-century technology on to an eighteenth-century design. But elsewhere, a new teaching vanguard is linking the same technology with the latest neuroscience research as catalysts to rethink the entire system.

Even where governments have invested hundreds of millions or billions of dollars in ICT, we still see classes of forty or more children sitting in rows, facing a teacher at a blackboard or static whiteboard while expensive computers lie unused at the back of the room or in nearby "computer laboratories".

William D. Pflaum confirms our experiences. As a designer of educational software, he took almost a full year off to visit schools across America. And the story he tells in his 2004 book, *The Technology Fix,*[3] is sobering: "The average student spends only about an hour a week with a computer at school. Many spend far less." And that's not the worst aspect. Just as many confuse traditional classrooms with real learning, many schools confuse computers with interactive digital technology in all its aspects: the tools that elsewhere are reshaping the Next Society.

❏ *But we're not talking only about a different world. We're talking about a different people. "Our students have changed radically. To-day's students are no longer the people our educational system was designed to teach,"*[4] *says digital-games producer Marc Prensky.*

He says children's brains are now actually "wired" differently. And noted neuroscientist Dr. Richard Restak confirms this in his latest book, *The New Brain: How the modern age is rewiring your mind.*

Prensky dubs today's youngsters *digital natives.* Just as natives of any country speak their own language naturally and in the local dialect, today's young people have grown up in a world that thinks and communicates differently to their parents. Prensky calls those parents *digital immigrants.* Like new migrants to any country, they generally find it difficult to become fluent in the new language of interactive multimedia.

When five-year-olds can create this kind of art on their own computers

Why do you think they find blackboard and chalk divorced from today's 'real life'?

Above: Examples of children's artwork are from Narrabeen North Primary School in New South Wales, Australia: done using KidPix software, to illustrate a cooperative classroom project on Australia's Great Barrier Reef. Outside classrooms, you'll find them studying botany in the school's eco-garden.

Those new digital natives, he says, are being socialised in a way that is vastly different from their parents. "The numbers are overwhelming: over 10,000 hours playing video games; over 200,000 emails and instant messages sent and received; over 10,000 hours talking on digital cell phones; over 20,000 hours watching TV; over 500,000 commercials seen—all before the kids leave college. And, maybe, *at the very most,* 5,000 hours of book reading." [5]

Prensky's inventions include brilliantly-created, complex interactive games for learning. But that's only the start. He wants to see all the world's 1.5 billion students and 59 million teachers, working in networks, together inventing "the new tools" for twentyfirst-century education and schooling. A concept of learning-by-doing, and learning by co-creating. Says Prensky: "The idea is that the educational software we use (all of it—games, non-games and anything else, at all levels, preschool to adult) should be created by the 'world mind', should not belong to any of us, and should be available, for free, to anybody, anywhere, who wants to use it." [6]

❏ *A working model already exists to achieve this: the 100,000-plus collaborative groups working online to produce open-source software, in exactly the same way that the Linux movement has created cheap, and often free, computer operating systems.*

That's how *Wikipedia*, the Internet's free encyclopedia, is compiled.

It's the way students at some of the best schools on the planet are already learning: using the world as their classroom, and using the world's best interactive tools to explore it.

It's just one of several ways that education, learning and schooling need to change.

Above all, it provides the blueprint to solve the problem of the two to three billion people left on the wrong side of "the digital divide". And we are not talking about how interactive technology, and new methods of networking, impact only on education. We're talking about the trends that are creating an entirely new type of society, and how "education" should be a key catalyst for that transformation.

Some lessons from history

But anyone searching for a new theory of human behaviour and learning should recall the words of George Santayana: "Those who cannot remember the past are doomed to repeat it." [7] Most people have

The world our kids are going to live in is changing four times faster than our schools.

DR. WILLARD DAGGETT
Director of International Centre for
Leadership and Education*

*Address to Colorado school administrators, 1992.

a natural tendency to to remain locked in existing mental models.

And the mental model of school began over four hundred years ago. It started with Jon Amos Comenius and the Gutenberg printing revolution. For the first time ever, mass printing made it possible for tens of thousands to actually study *The Bible*—if they could read.

So Comenius, a Moravian-born Czech bishop, invented the modern textbook, complete with pictures—and a schoolroom system to teach reading. Comenius also created a new educational philosophy, called *pansophism,* or universal knowledge, designed to bring about worldwide understanding and peace. He advised teachers to help children learn through all their senses, as well as the printed word. Unfortunately, others distorted his wider vision. But the classroom stayed.

In 1717 Prussia became the first state to make primary schooling compulsory. This started with a schoolroom, blackboard and chalk, and students sitting at desks in rows—facing a teacher. This became the model for much of the world. And, as Professor Nuthall concludes, ever since education has been enmeshed in a "web of supporting myths".

Between 1850 and the 1930s a whole raft of new educational and behavioural theories surfaced. These ranged from two extremes:

❏ **Francis Galton**, with his belief "that all genius and intelligence is inherited"—forerunner of the IQ or intelligence quotient tests. And

❏ **John Broadus Watson**, who resurrected the Thomas Aquinas and John Locke *tabula rasa* theory that everyone is born with a blank-slate mind, waiting to be filled with information and knowledge.

And in between, the full spectrum of competing concepts, often enshrined in dogmatic practice:

❏ **Charles Darwin:** with his theory of the evolution by natural selection: what some others dubbed "survival of the fittest".

❏ **William James:** the champion of instinct as a dominant characteristic of all behaviour, including human.

❏ **Hugo De Vriess,** who rediscovered Gregor Mendel's laws of heredity, including dominant and recessive genes.

❏ **Ivan Pavlov:** with his conditioned reflexes and salivating dogs.

❏ **Sigmund Freud** and **Emil Kraepelin,** with their theories of psychiatry based on personal histories.

❏ **Emile Durkheim:** the pioneer of sociology, and the overriding importance of social trends.

Human Genome Project proves it:

We are all a combination of Nature via Nurture.

MATT RIDLEY
*Nature Via Nurture**

* Subtitled *Genes, Experience and What Makes Us Human*,
published by Harper Perennial, London,

❏ **Franz Boas:** with his insistence that culture shapes nature, not the other way around.

❏ **Konrad Lorenz:** with his view on how the human brain is vitally influenced by "imprinting" from early experiences.

❏ **Maria Montessori,** and later **Jean Piaget**, presenting evidence that children develop through a period of critical stages—although still disagreeing, years later, on the timing and nature of those stages.

In his new book, *Nature Via Nurture,* British scientist Matt Ridley outlines the theories of these key shapers of twentieth-century behavioural and educational psychology. And he reaches a surprising conclusion: "They were right. Not right all the time, not even wholly right, and I do not mean morally right . . . But they were right in the sense that they all contributed an original idea with a germ of truth in it; they all placed a brick in the wall."

Ridley says the Human Genome Project has proven that we are all a *combination* of both nature and nurture. Human behaviour is, in fact, a combination of our genes, our instincts, our environment and our experiences—including our education.

We are also very much creatures of our culture. And the cultural gap between humans and other species is a gulf. Humans have "nuclear weapons and money, gods and poetry, philosophy and fire. They got all these things through culture, through their ability to accumulate ideas and inventions generation by generation, transmit them to others and thereby pool the cognitive resources of many individuals alive and dead.

"An ordinary modern businessman, for instance, could not do without the help of Assyrian phonetic script, Chinese printing, Arabic algebra, Indian numerals, Italian double-entry bookkeeping, Dutch merchant law, Californian integrated circuits, and a host of other inventions spread over continents and centuries." And of course the incredible methods we have invented over the past two decades to change technology, change culture—and the way we transmit it.

One would think this common sense would make us all more than a little nervous about dogmatic theories of education and learning.

Yet entire education systems have been built on rival claims to be infallible dogma. Each of Ridley's "wise men" of behavioural science may have placed a brick in the wall of knowledge, but their followers turned each brick into the whole wall. Many teaching methods are still

100 years ago Henry Ford's production lines transformed industry

Similar theories created standardised lessons and standardised exams to standardise school

based on those rival part-truths—all claiming to be "evidence-based".

And probably the two most conflicting theories are those of the *behaviourists*—led by Watson and his disciple, Burrhus Frederick (B.F.) Skinner—and the rival school of John Dewey.

Watson summarised the behaviourist theory, in part, in 1924: "Give me a dozen healthy infants, well-formed, and my own specified world to bring them up in, and I'll guarantee to take any one at random and train him to become any type of specialist I might select—doctor, lawyer, artist, merchant-chief, and, yes, even beggarman and thief, regardless of his talents, penchants, tendencies, abilities, vocations, and race of his ancestors." [8] He was only slightly exaggerating his beliefs.

This is the theory that drives many school systems today, specially in the United States. At its simplest: if each brain is an empty vessel to be filled in the same way, then "learning" can be measured in a similar way—by the same "standardised test". As Pflaum found on his recent one-year tour of American campuses: "The reality of schools today is that they are all about measurement." But critics would say they're measuring the "wrong thing".[9] As educator John Holt asked many years ago in *How Children Fail:* "How much of the sum of human knowledge can anyone know at the end of schooling? Perhaps a millionth. Are we then to believe that one of those millionths is so much more important than another?" [10]

But visit any major American "educational" conference today and you'll be amazed at the similarity of the commercial displays. The overwhelming majority sell textbooks, instructions to "teach to the test" and "guaranteed ways" to measure and achieve "standardised test results". And all based on a student's ability to memorise and regurgitate a limited selection of the world's knowledge-base. "Standardised test scores" have become the dogmatic mantra that's mesmerised a nation.

Significantly, the Watson-Skinner theories were based very strongly on that early standardised production-line industrial model that Ford introduced so successfully around the same time.

It's unfortunate that Professor Dewey's counter-theories have been placed under one of those academic labels, *constructivism,* that is generally not part of everyday lay language. *Standardised testing* is easier to understand, even in a land like America where *non-standardised* innovation has been the overwhelming wealth-creator.

In real education, said Dewey, we should all:

❑ Learn by doing.

John Dewey's philosophy holds up better:

- ❏ **Learn by doing.**
- ❏ **Learn by experience.**
- ❏ **Learn by linking mind and brain together.**
- ❏ **Learn by constructing your own storehouse.**
- ❏ **Learn from activities that are 'real life'.**
- ❏ **Learn by collaborating.**

JOHN DEWEY*

* A summary of some his major theories from
John Dewey on Education, Selected Writings,
selected by Reginald D. Archambault, Modern Library, New York.

❏ Learn by experience.

❏ Learn by linking the mind, brain and body together.

❏ Learn by actually *constructing* your own mental storehouse of knowledge and creative ability.

❏ Learn by engaging in activities that "mean something to you".

❏ And learn by collaborating with other learners.

Now schools that have built on the Dewey methods for more than half a century are leading the world in using interactive technology and instant communications to successfully reinvent schooling. That's because the new tools enable the creative ability of children to flower. And to do it in much more exciting ways than Dewey could envisage.

This is not to deny that truly educated citizens should be familiar with a core body of knowledge, and be able to read, write, spell, count and understand the basics of history, geography and science.

But we live in an era where around 10,000 new scientific research papers or articles are published every day. And many more from other fields. So it's much more important to learn how to find the new information needed to understand any issue, and to turn that combination into new knowledge, ideas and actions.

Fortunately new research provides us with associated new insights to transform learning, teaching, education and schooling. And to make it easier for students to prove what they know and can do.

❏ *Some of these breakthroughs come from genetic research, unlocking many of the secrets of life itself.*

Says Ridley, in his other book, *Genome: The autobiography of a species:* "I genuinely believe that we are living through the greatest intellectual moment in history. Bar none."

New genetic research, for example, confirms the worst doubts about the "blockbuster magic-bullet" drugs that have been the mainstay of the multi-billion-dollar pharmaceutical industry. And it's highlighting better paths to more personalised health:[11] wellness instead of sickness.

❏ *Some breakthroughs come from outstanding advances in neuroscience: revealing new secrets of the human brain and the mind-body network.*

As American scientist Michio Kaku puts it: "The three and a half pounds sitting on our shoulders is perhaps the most complex object in the solar system, perhaps even in this sector of the galaxy." [12] And now

New research:

Everyone has the potential talent to be good at something.

GALLUP POLLING ORGANISATION
from surveys of 1 million people*

* Summarised by Marcus Buckingham and Curt Coffman
in *First, Break All The Rules,* published by
Simon & Schuster Business Books, London.

scientists are able to view individual brains in action as they learn, think, memorise and interact with mind and body.

❏ *Some breakthroughs have come from organisational and management research.*

Some of the most important come from extensive surveys by the Gallup polling group, into what makes organisations effective.

Among their main conclusions:

❏ Everyone has a potential talent to be good at something, but not good at everything—a complete contradiction of Watson and Skinner.

❏ The trick is "to find that something", and then to develop the skills and abilities so that talent can flourish.

❏ But talent is not merely a specific vocational skill. Rather it is a mixture of each person's personality, behavioural traits and passions.

❏ Great managers select for talent, and then train for skills. But that's also a great lesson for parents, teachers and students: learn how to identify talent, and then develop the skills and abilities to let it flower.

❏ *Some breakthroughs come from the continuing power of "Moore's Law": the doubling of computer power every eighteen months.*

That doubling is expected to continue until at least 2020. So a simple calculation provides the arithmetic: if Intel could fit only 1,000 transistors onto a tiny silicon chip in 1970 and knows it will be able to fit 1 billion in the same space by 2010, then by 2019 they'll be able to fit more than 4 trillion interacting transistors onto a chip the size of your fingernail. That's 4 billion billion—on one chip—by the time today's five-year-old turns nineteen. And those chips will be everywhere, in almost everything—and connected in interactive ways not yet in our dreams.

❏ *Some breakthroughs continue to blossom from "Metcalfe's Law" of exploding networks.*

And not just of individual networks, but the convergence of so many different types: television, radio, movie-making, PCs, laptops, cellphones and those new "computers in your pocket".

As Mark Thompson, Director-General of the British Broadcasting Corporation, says: "We are all hurtling towards an on-demand, pan-media universe".[13] And he adds: the cost of versioning content—video, music, movies, and digital learning—for different kinds of devices "is collapsing and will tend to zero". Already the BBC is well on the way to

People of all ages can learn virtually anything if allowed to do it through their own unique styles, their own personal strengths.

BARBARA PRASHNIG
*The Power of Diversity**

* Published by Network Educational Press, United Kingdom

converting all its excellent television, radio, music and digital libraries into on-demand multimedia services, including interactive learning.

❑ *Other breakthroughs are rewriting the total manual for business as corporations discover the power of the "frictionless web": the ability to weave together new seamless digital networks that completely short-circuit outdated sales and distribution methods.*

The banking, insurance, computer sales, airline travel, publishing, book selling and entertainment industries are all being blown to bits and put together in new ways.

That's happening by the way in which industries are slashing *transaction costs,* largely by selling online. After recording music, for example, it now costs about 50 cents to mass-produce each CD. Sell it in through traditional chains and each *transaction* adds a cost. But make the same music available on the Web, and the transaction costs drop to zero—so you can buy the latest hit for 99c—and not several dollars.

Papert, among others, calls for a similar rethink to all aspects of education. That will probably also include new dynamic ways for "education" to interact with other disciplines—as physics, electronics, generics, biotechnology and computer science are also converging.

The new framework for learning

That interaction will provide a new framework for learning. The broad outlines of that framework, we believe, are already creating the scaffolding to create a new learning society:

1. The diversity of talent:

Everyone does have a talent to succeed at something. And a one-size-fits-all learning-model stops that.

2. The new science of learning:

Neuroscience is exploding: the combined research on how the brain, mind and body work together to make learning easier, faster and more effective—to learn how to learn, learn how to think, learn how to create.

3. The changing role of teaching:

Teachers as coaches and stimulators—not instructors and information-purveyors. Each a guide on the side, not a sage on the stage.

4. The new core of knowledge:

Not as isolated facts to be remembered, recalled for exams and then

New framework for learning:

- ❏ **Identify your talent.**
- ❏ **Science of learning.**
- ❏ **Teachers' new role.**
- ❏ **The real basics.**
- ❏ **To learn it, do it.**
- ❏ **Learn creativity.**
- ❏ **Master skills.**
- ❏ **Balance lifeskills.**
- ❏ **Show you know.**

often forgotten—but as the scaffolding and building blocks for an interconnected, integrated world.

5. The common sense of *doing:*

As Dewey said: to learn it, do it. And to absorb new knowledge faster, embed it with all your senses and in other effective ways.

6. The new art of creativity:

In a new creative age: the ability to combine mind-power and new interactive tools to create new solutions, products, ideas, services and experiences.

7. The mastery of skills and abilities:

"Select for talent, train for skills and abilities" is sensible "shorthand". But as all great sporting achievers demonstrate: great coaches develop *mastery*—both for individual strengths and to produce champion teams.

8. The balance of lifeskills:

The full mix of abilities that make us truly human, including better communications and relationship skills.

9. The proof of performance:

To move away from the narrow concept of "standardised recall tests"; instead to demonstrate living proof —to "show you know".

The seven interlinked learning networks

That new scaffolding will change many things. But it will cause the biggest cultural earthquake in the current *structure* of education, where so many people have a stake in the status quo.

While Amazon, Dell and other industry leaders are slashing their "transaction costs", university fees are soaring. And the traditional way of setting fees, on an annual basis per student, does not encourage more efficient ways of learning.

Papert urges us all to think of the sudden collapse of the former Soviet Union. "It is a system, I think, that was becoming increasingly incompatible with the modern world for reasons not very different from those that operate in the education system.

"It tried to run a country as a production line, as a top-down command economy where what people made would be determined by a committee somewhere. We try in our school systems to decide what people will

Every child has, at birth, a greater potential intelligence than Leonardo Da Vinci ever used.

GLENN DOMAN
author of *Teach Your Baby To Read**

*Author interview at The Institutes for the Achievement of
Human Potential, 8801 Stenton Avenue, Philadelphia,
PA 19118.

learn in this top-down centralised way and, for the same reason, it is not compatible with the modern world ." [14]

We authors believe this modern world demands a new learning theory that links *the uniqueness of individual potential* with the developing world of *interlinked networks* and new models of efficient collaboration.

But we stress that many of these conclusions are tentative. Read any history of science and philosophy over the centuries, and some conclusion are obvious: Plato, Aristotle, Galen, Ptolemy, Newton, Copernicus and Galileo were all geniuses. We can still stand in awe at the breathtaking scope of their theories and the way they changed our world. But in every case major aspects of their theories were later proven to be wrong.

So, as Karl Popper puts it so well in his theory of knowledge: "We make progress not by adding new certainties to a body of existing ones but by perpetually replacing existing theories with better theories." [15]

This chapter summarises our overall "rethink." These conclusions are then expanded throughout the book. They will undoubtedly be improved as new and better models emerge.

1. Your Internal genetic and neural network

and the brain-mind-body talent that makes you unique

That network-model starts with you—and how you, and not schools or systems, are the most important component for lifelong learning.

The human species is unique. But so is every other species, although all are created from the same genetic building blocks or code. Says Ridley: "Trunks are unique to elephants. Spitting is unique to cobras. Forty years of field primatology have confirmed that we [humans] are a unique species, quite unlike any other." But, he says, there is nothing exceptional in being unique. "Every species is unique." [16]

So are you as an individual. That uniqueness stems largely from your DNA, genes, your brain-mind-body network and your experiences. For centuries, scientists could only speculate on some of the most intricate workings of this neural network. Now technologies like positron emission tomography (PET), magnetic resonance imaging (MRI), and *functional* MRI allow scientists to actually see the brain at work as it learns.

So they're providing new evidence of how each of us develops from the continual interaction of "nature and nurture". We are each born with inherited characteristics, and not just the colour of our hair and eyes and

Perhaps schools won't look like schools. Perhaps we will be using the total community as a learning environment.

ANNE TAYLOR
*Creating The Future**

*Edited by Dee Dickinson and published by Accelerated Learning Systems, Aston Clinton, Bucks, England.

the basic build of our bodies. We are all either born with or soon develop our own distinct personality and behavioural patterns. But these then interact with our experiences, our environments and our cultures.

"Armed with these and other tools, we have taken giant leaps in learning," say Marcus Buckingham and Curt Coffman in *First, Break All The Rules,* the summary of major Gallup surveys of effective business. New scientific research reveals similar findings: how we can use that ability to learn much more effectively.

2. Your personal learning network

Linking home, school and the real world together

Traditionally, we've called learning organisations "schools'"—and kindergartens, colleges and universities.

Comenius is rightly regarded as the "father of modern schooling". Building on Europe's mass-printing innovation, he was the first to use pictures in textbooks: in *The Visible World in Pictures,* published in 1658. By the time he died in 1670, he had published 154 books, mostly dealing with educational philosophy. And his concepts of schooling were being taken up in various parts of Europe, though not all. But he was years ahead of his time. Unlike many religious leaders of his day, he contributed greatly to *The Enlightenment.* He was a strong advocate of what today would be called holistic education. He taught that education began in the earliest days of childhood and continued throughout life. He encouraged learning by seeing, hearing, tasting, smelling, touching and doing.

He advocated formal education for women and girls an idea very revolutionary at that time.

His philosophy of *pansophism* attempted to incorporate theology, philosophy (effectively, the prescientific name for *science)* and education in one. He believed that learning, spiritual and emotional growth were all woven together.

This wasn't the model, however, adopted by the Prussian state in its first compulsory public schools. They set the pattern for the regimented, classroom that has continued, basically in the same form. Comenius's schools were established to teach religion along with reading, writing and arithmetic. But to this the Prussian Government added as a main component: to build disciplined "duty to the Prussian nation state".

Some governments—and textbooks—continue that emphasis today, with many history textbook notoriously biassed. But already talented

Baby rats reared in dull, boring cages become dull bored adult rats

But in interesting and stimulating environments they become bright, intelligent rats: a lesson for humans?*

* From author interviews with Professor Marian Diamond, University of California at Berkeley.

Regular updates: www.thelearningweb.net

school teachers are transforming even complex subjects into more interactive learning journeys. And many others are creating environments and networks from which everyone can emerge as a better learner.

And here two combined research-results are vitally important:

❏ *First: create the right environment, and even very young children "explode" into learning.*

Maria Montessori was proving this a century ago in the slums of Rome. By creating multisensory environments, even children thought "mentally retarded" were reading, writing and counting before starting school. But more important, they were also becoming confident, self-acting, enthusiastic learners. And doing that while enjoying themselves.

❏ *Second: we also have different ways to take in information, process it, store it and use it.*

We each have a learning style, thinking style, creative style and working style as unique as our fingerprints. So learning environments need to cater to that diversity, and build on it.

Some of the strongest examples of great learning environments come, surprisingly, from rats. For years, neuroscientists at the University of California at Berkeley have shown what happens to rats reared in both dull and interesting environments.

Place baby rats in dull, boring cages—with bland, uninteresting food—and you produce dull, bored, unintelligent adult rats.

But place young rats in bright, interesting, colourful environments— with plenty of games, colour, movement and multisensory stimulation, plus a good diet—and they grow to be bright, interesting, intelligent rats.

Common sense should tell us that the same simple truths can turn all environments into more stimulating, interesting "learning places".

The family learning network

Our first environment, of course, is inside our own family. Home is our first school, and our family our first teachers.

We also know that each one of us goes through distinct "ideal teachable moments" and "ideal learning moments".

And for parents, those vital moments include five main periods: during pregnancy, from childbirth, from a child's first days at an early-learning centre, when starting school and later when starting at high school. Later chapters will deal with each period.

Schools are becoming technological hubs, for adult computer classes, Internet access and video conferencing.

LEARN & LIVE
*George Lucas Educational Foundation**

* Published by the foundation, and can be downloaded
from its website: www.edutopia.org

Regular updates: www.thelearningweb.net

All children also grow through very specific developmental stages, in sequence. Both Montessori and the Swiss psychologist Jean Piaget have identified such stages. And parents who study developmental-phases, during pregnancy and early childhood, probably learn more from that direct experience than they'll ever learn at school.

And you don't have to spend big money to develop an emotionally-safe and stimulating learning environment in your own home. Several in-home training programmes are now available to help parents develop as their children's first teachers.

New school networks

Schools themselves will continue—but hopefully with a much more expanded role. Amazingly the big majority of primary and high schools around the world are used for only around 20 percent of total time. Any corporate leader underusing the main business capital resource to this extent would be fired. And the models already exist to turn schools into much more effective lifelong-learning centres for all the community.

❏ Brislington High School's new Digital Learning Centre in Bristol, England, is used during school hours by its own students for learning interactive technology. Outside school hours, the centre is used by other schools, parents, grandparents and community groups.

❏ At Brislington and many other United Kingdom classrooms, interactive, digital whiteboards have already replaced blackboards. In this way, lesson plans can be shared through the Internet to classrooms, for use on digital whiteboards—and on students' home computers.

❏ A major report on the importance of early-childhood education, prepared for the provincial government of Ontario in Canada, has recommended that good early-childhood learning centres be built in the grounds of all primary schools.

❏ Many schools in China have created their own natural history museums—with all the exhibits either collected outside school or made by the students.

❏ Singapore's Overseas Family school, with 2,500 students from sixtyfive nationalities, runs its own digital online network to link teachers, administrators, students and families. In 2003, when the Singapore Government closed all schools, because of the SARS virus epidemic, OFS had all class lessons available from its website within one working day.

We learn

- ❏ **10% of what we read.**

- ❏ **20% of what we hear.**

- ❏ **30% of what we see.**

- ❏ **50% of what we see and hear.**

- ❏ **70% of what we say.**

- ❏ **90% of what we say and do.**

VERNON A. MAGNESEN*

*Quoted in *Quantum Teaching,* by Bobbi DePorter,
Mark Reardon and Sarah Singer-Nourie, published by
Allyn and Bacon, 160 Gould Street, Needham Heights, MA 02194.
Note: these figures are broad approximations. We each
learn in our own individual way.

Regular updates: www.thelearningweb.net

❏ Discovery 1, in Christchurch, New Zealand, is a public primary school that uses all of that city as its classroom. Students spend part of their time at its exciting central campus, adjoining the city's main public transport terminal. But they do most of their research and discovery out in the community. They study botany in the city's botanical gardens; bread-baking in a bakery; law and justice in the court system.

And schools themselves work more effectively if the total curriculum is based on how the human brain processes and stores new information, like branches on a tree.

Here the International Baccalaureate Organisation provides a brilliant operating model—for students from age three to senior high school:

❏ All IB elementary-school study is based around global projects, so students can build each theme as a separate branch of that tree of knowledge, and explore its expanding patterns in interactive ways.

❏ In the IB primary years, one "global inquiry project" normally covers six or seven weeks. During that time students will study themes such as the planets of the universe, the minerals of the world, inventions that have changed society, endangered species and the human body. All other "basic subjects", such as reading, writing, mathematics and literature, are integrated into those projects. And because parents know in advance what broad themes their children will be studying, families become involved in using their community and the world as a classroom. So in studying the solar system, the whole family can go to the local planetarium; in studying transport—a transport museum. Or they can watch supporting videos and get library books on the same topic.

❏ No more desks in rows, of course. They've disappeared from good schools years ago. In those schools, students in the main already learn in groups that blend their own talents in with others.

❏ "Change the frame—or viewpoint—and you change the picture" is a good truism. And instead of the "cultural ritual" and narrow perspectives of the traditional classroom, students will develop as multimedia journalists and creators. They'll use the tools of inquiry and discovery. And above all they'll learn by doing and actually creating. But instead of creating only nineteenth-century "essays", they'll be producing their own videos, DVDs, music, movies, animations, artwork and twentyfirst-century, multimedia literacy.

❏ And examinations? Of course academic qualifications will continue to be valued. But, more importantly, all students will keep their own

Since everyone has the talent to be good at something

one way to prove you know 'that something' is to show it in digital portfolios.

personal digital portfolios to actually show their talents in action. Tiger Woods shows his golf talent in every tournament by actually playing— not by filling in a multiple-choice written test on golfing. Peter Jackson shows his film-making ability by producing three giant movie episodes of *Lord of The Rings* and *King Kong*—not by getting a ten-minute written "teacher evaluation" or passing a written test. His team's best *non-standardised* test: eleven Academy Awards in one night.

Good musicians prove they can play in an orchestra by actually playing, and then demonstrating that with their own DVDs, CDs, CD-roms or video cassettes.

❏ Already many schools provide the facilities for students to keep those "digital portfolios" online. Singapore's Overseas Family School keeps them on its school-family network. And in both New Zealand and Australia, many students from as young as five keep their artwork, learning-style summaries and videos of animations and other achieve- ments, on individual websites actually created by each student.

❏ And "standards"? Of course they're important. And of course most educational standards are far too low. But the aim must be to educate for twentyfirst-century standards and needs—not the assembly-line standards of the early twentieth century or the multiple-guess written "standardised test scores" of more recent years.

Community learning networks

Almost everyone will soon have in-home or community access to a wide variety of educational services. The trend is already there:

❏ The New Zealand Government provides grants for every adult to learn computer skills at centres throughout the country.

❏ Community libraries are becoming alternative learning centres, extending their normal book-lending role to provide digital training.

❏ Thousands of Microsoft, Cisco and Oracle specialists now achieve high-earning qualifications largely online, but generally combined with hands-on courses at community schools or colleges.

❏ Many homes will soon have self-contained entertainment, learning and often work centres.

❏ More and more schools are building community-learning and development programmes into their regular curriculum: like students doing project work in association with local industry and commerce.

❏ School adventure camps now operate in many countries—so

Regular updates: www.thelearningweb.net

students can develop confidence-building skills while they explore and video nature. Then, at school, they add music and sound to their videos— and use them to teach interactive technology skills to their teachers.

Significantly, children at New Zealand's leading primary schools learn from year one to use digital cameras and video cameras to explore the real world. Many schools actually bar the use of *Powerpoint* computer slides in early-year grades, as being "non-creative" and "non-interactive". The new world of interactive technology is not the mindless viewing of a TV screen or a computer screen. Instead, even young students become multimedia journalists, creators and presenters.

Teacher networks

Probably nothing is more important than professional-development programmes if teachers are to break out of the "cultural ritual" of traditional classroom practice. Trendsetting schools are now following the example of leading corporations—and building *daily* professional-development programmes into their working life.

At Singapore's Overseas Family School, for example, all elementary students have a daily one-hour foreign-language lesson. They can choose from six international languages. Each is generally taught by a fluent native-speaker from outside the school's permanent staff. And permanent teachers can spend that hour on professional-development, preparing lesson plans or working in with their school's curriculum coordinator.

Online networks

For post-secondary education, online learning is growing:

❑ California's Pepperdine University offers undergraduate, masters and doctoral courses in educational technology—with only fifteen days a year on campus, in three separate weeks: the rest on line.

❑ In China thousands of students are studying for an online MBA degree from the Beijing Academy of Sciences.

❑ China's richest man, Li Ka-Shing, has donated $600 million to education, including $80 million for teacher-training satellites.

❑ India is setting up networks of village-based Internet kiosks, and designing cheap hand-held network computers for rural use. Some ex-Silicon Valley Indian entrepreneurs are now working on plans to develop combined village learning centres that will also engage young students in creating hands-on learning programmes for other developing countries.

Ten years ago you had to find a local partner for bridge

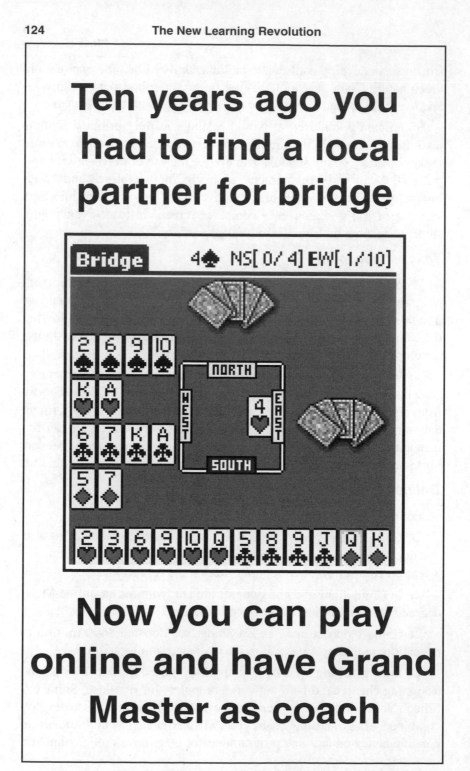

Now you can play online and have Grand Master as coach

❑ Other skills are also easily learned online or from interactive CD-roms—designed by some of the world's best "subject masters". Anyone wanting to learn the bridge card game, for example, can buy a range of software or linkup online to actually "play against the computer". Then she can replay a hand or a series of moves with help from the master himself, simply by clicking the "hint" button on the screen. Significantly, most brilliant bridge players are skilled in the use of mathematical symbols. So they often don't make great teachers as most new players are more likely to learn by seeing and doing, not by mathematical symbols on a board. And because computer bridge games actually show the cards in colour, players can learn to be proficient much more quickly.

❑ But bridge experts don't have to be software specialists to create games. They merely need to find software-design talents to match their own game-playing skills. Great teachers can do the same with any subject. Often they can enlist multi-talented students to make the interactive software—so all learn and create together. And what better way to "show you know" than designing an interactive game that enables other students to learn in a simpler, better, faster way? That's a real exam.

❑ Digital chess games provide even better examples. All players can select their level of competence: from beginner to world master. And then sequentially increase one's skill levels. In a world of cross-cultural study, this is most important. A ten-year-old Chinese student might be at the level of other fourteen-year-olds at mathematics, but at a five-year-old level in English. So new methods of learning will enable anyone to take just-in-time lessons on any subject, at any level, and at any age.

In *The Lexus and the Olive Tree,* New York journalist Thomas Friedman relates the story of his seventynine-year-old mother phoning him one day from Minneapolis. She was perturbed, and when he asked why, she replied: "Well, I've been playing bridge on the Internet with three Frenchmen, and they keep speaking French with each other." When Friedman chuckled, she took a little umbrage. "Don't laugh," she said, "I was playing bridge with someone in Siberia the other day."

Friedman adds: "To all those who say that this era of globalisation is no different from the previous one, I would simply ask: Was your great-grandmother playing bridge with Frenchmen on the Internet in 1900? I don't think so."

Friedman's book was written in 1999. Now his mother can have her bridge-bids translated instantly into French or Russian on

What should be taught?
A brief history*

 Essentialism: The 'essential core' needed for a sound education. Plato started it, and Britain carried on for its elite, with different systems for trades and labourers.

 Encyclopedism: Much broader base and available to all. Comenius started it with the first textbooks, and most European states still follow the same principles.

 The sensory-based early-start model: Aristotle first proposed that knowledge comes first through the senses. Itard, Seguin, Rousseau, Pestallozi, Froebel and Montessori have developed variations.

 The pragmatic child-centred movement: The original American breakaway, with Dewey the pioneer. Now two main strands: one around the individual child, and other to 'reconstruct society'.

5 **The global-curriculum:** As society becomes more globalised, the need arises for a common-sense international curriculum that blends together the best *process* for learning anything and a structured *content* syllabus that helps all students develop as open-minded, lifelong-learning global citizens. And to do that, in part, by collaborating on the World Wide Web.

* Plus the Confucian academic examination model, still popular in Chinese societies, E.D. Hirsch's *Cultural Literacy*, and Jean Piaget's theories of phased intellectual development.

www.babelfish.altavista.com—and sign up with *www.yahoo.com* to find new opponents anywhere on earth—and around her level of competence.

3. New interactive information networks
How to interact with the new pool of instant information

And if grandmother Friedman wants to set up a local bridge club, she can buy programmes where world champions have joined with software designers to make that easy. The experts provide hundreds of sample hands, a system to grade results and computer printouts to show all players how they scored and how they could have done much better.

It also bears repeating: for the first time in history, we now know how to store virtually all humanity's most important information and to make it available, almost instantly, in almost any form, to almost anyone on earth. We also know how to do that in great new ways so that people can interact with it, and learn from it.

It is almost impossible to underestimate the importance of that paragraph: specially when it involves the convergence of all forms of digital communication, including the wireless revolution.

Since the fifteenth century in Europe, until the early 1990s, mass information for education was dominated by the mass-produced book.

Gutenberg's invention not only revolutionised printing: it caused more important revolutions in religion and education—as the Protestant Reformation spurred the importance of reading: and with it, the birth of the modern primary school. By the early eighteenth century, the first British encyclopedias had been born. And then, from 1772, came the first books of the thirtyfive-volume French *Encyclopedia:* up to then the biggest publishing venture in any language.

Most of France's outstanding writers and thinkers contributed to it. "But what made it intellectually and historically important was that it embodied the new attitude to knowledge that Voltaire had imported into France from England—a scientific approach that looked to Francis Bacon and Isaac Newton as its great forebears, married to a philosophical approach that looked, above all, to John Locke [the philosophical 'father' of democracy and equal opportunity]. Denis Diderot admitted that, as its editor, his aim was to change the common way of thinking. And, to a very considerable extent, he did".[17]

Encyclopedism, in fact, became the core of what has since dominated

Ten years ago you had to visit a library to find information

Now Google can search 8 billion pages in half a second to find answers to your queries.

much Europe's school curriculum. But printed encyclopedias are now outdated almost as soon as they are printed. So new formats are needed to link in with the instant-information power of the Web.

❑ Now Google not only scans 8 billion pages in half a second to find answers on any subject; it sells adjoining space to advertise related professional services and products.

❑ Google, Yahoo, Microsoft and other search engines also compete to *personalise* information: to tailor it to the specific needs of individuals. And more and more this information is available instantly through new wireless technology: not just on the new array of mobile phones but through wireless connections in homes, offices and those tiny appliances that started out as cellphones and are now pocket multimedia PCs.

❑ On Amazon, you can not only shop for any book you want—you can download summaries, read reviews, and contribute your own.

❑ Yahoo provides dozens of ways to play games and engage in other activities with like-minded people around the world. It also provides personalised touring maps; and, through Geo-Cities, helps you design your own website.

❑ And at Altavista you can use Babelfish technology to translate this paragraph, or any other text, from English into Spanish, Dutch or eleven other languages.

So the new emphasis is on personalising the information that you want when you want it. And then you using that to actually construct knowledge: putting many forms information to practical and creative use.

Once you could only read about the adventures of such explorers as Vasco de Gama, James Cook or Charles Darwin. Now you can actually relive those journeys on the Web as you follow the cruise of the Starship Millennium Project (www.wildlands.cc).

High school students can even form a team with other countries to join Oracle's annual *ThinkQuest* competition to build a combined website on your findings. The rewards: a possible $25,000 college scholarship.

4. Your creative network

How to think for new ideas and innovate with others

Learning how to learn is now a core part of the challenge. The other is learning how to think—and learning how to create.

Here, too, new networking models are emerging strongly. Generally

Favourite new multimedia creativity tools*

Video editing (low end):

Apple iMovie	40%
Microsoft Movie Maker	18%

Video editing (high end):

Apple Final Cut series	32%
Macromedia Studio	20%
Adobe Premier Pro	20%

Painting, drawing software K-6

KidPix Deluxe	32%
Kidspiration	28%
Macromedia Studio	9%
Hyperstudio	8%

Painting, drawing software 7-12

Macromedia Studio	39%
Inspiration	25%
Adobe Illustrator	9%
The Print Shop	7%

Sound editing (low end):

Apple Garage Band	41%
Macromedia Captivate	22%
Sony SoundForge	7%

Sound editing (high end):

Macromedia Breeze	32%
Apple Logic series	23%

Desktop publishing (low end):

Microsoft Word	57%
AppleWorks	14%
The Print Shop	9%
Macromedia Freehand	7%

Desktop publishing (high end)

Microsoft Publisher	48%
Adobe Pagemaker	23%
Adobe InDesign	19%

Digital imaging (inc. photos)
Elementary grades:

Adobe Photoshop	41%
Microsoft Photo Editor	18%
ImageBlender	9%
Macromedia Studio	8&

Digital imaging (inc. photos)
Upper grades:

Adobe Photoshop range	59%
Macromedia Studio	18%
Print Shop Deluxe	9%

* Readers' Choice Awards 2005:
eSchool News, from online
survey of US educators. In some
countries Apple rates higher.

these often involve students working together in groups, using their own preferred learning, creative, thinking or working style—in partnership with others who have different talents and attributes.

New digital "templates" make it even easier to share creative ability both around your own network and around the world.

Nearly every bit of "authoring" software is already designed to include templates. Microsoft *Powerpoint* and Apple *Keynote* slides are well-known simple examples. They make it easy for even young children to insert their own videos, computer animations and self-composed music into personal presentations. Apple *iMovie* and Microsoft *Movie-Maker* video-editing templates, *Kidspiration*, *Inspiration* and *Mind-Manager* Mind Mapping software, and *Hyperstudio* and *Macromedia Director* and *Flash* animation tools are other templated products.

And once such templates are available, then anyone else with the same software can use them as a basis—and add to them. The idea is not to copy others' work but to build on its basic framework: the same way that professional authors, TV producers or journalists work individually and collectively inside professionally-designed layouts.

The New City School in St. Louis, Missouri, produced its first "multiple-intelligence" book more than ten years ago: researched, tested and written collectively by the teachers at the school. It covers the entire Missouri state curriculum, in every "subject" at every grade level, using Howard Gardner's model of multiple intelligences.[18] And it provides hundreds of easy-to-use resources for parents, teachers and students: like lists of musical tracks so that "musical learners" can learn mathematics and science to music. Many Chinese children, as an example, effectively learn to speak English by singing-along with karaoke machines.

So what happens if we involve all fiftynine million teachers in the world and their brightest students in producing not just a book but interactive, online "templates" so that all can share their knowledge?

Now imagine that done on "open source" software, and translated into every language of the world by the students of the world. That's what we mean by "mass innovation". And cooperative enterprise.

But it's also what we mean by the gap between those who shape much educational policy and today's twentyfirst-century youngsters. Look for a moment at the partial list of the new digital "authoring tools" on the opposite page: used every day by students around the world—and ask yourself why wouldn't they be bored with the old chalkboard schools.

People can now search out fellow collaborators on any subject, project or theme.

Yahoo! alone has about 300 million users and four million active groups.

THOMAS FRIEDMAN
The Earth is Flat*

* Published by Penguin: Allen Lane, London.

5. Your talent network

How to share your skills and professional knowhow

You can also use the same methods to share and expand your talents, skills and abilities: whatever your age or occupation.

Already many university disciplines link through digital networks. Type "teachers learning networks" into Google, and it will give you a choice of 898,000— within half a second. Among our favourites:

❏ **www.smartbrief.com/ascd:** the daily news summary, from newspapers and magazines around the world, on matters of interest to educators—compiled by the American Association for Supervision and Curriculum Development.

❏ **www.theage.com.au:** a daily summary of the world's best IT news, prepared by *The Age* newspaper in Melbourne, Australia.

❏ **www.building@newhorizon.org:** the website for New Horizons for Learning.

❏ **www.bbc.co.uk:** the website of the British Broadcasting Corporation, with excellent links to other sites.

In almost every academic discipline we have looked at to research this book we've found excellent websites operated by practitioners: from biology to brain research, Montessori to Comenius.

In the latest world-changing technology, the cost of international optic-fibre links has come down dramatically. For the first time ever, this enables China's 1.3 billion people, India's 1 billion and the hundreds of millions in eastern Europe and the former Soviet Union to join the global talent network.

Most of those countries have a strong core of educated talent. At its simplest, the new low-cost communications network enables competent mathematics teachers in India to coach students in Singapore. And it enables hundreds of English-speaking Indians to run American telephone call-centres from their own villages or homes.

But the ramifications are even greater. Faced with low-cost competition from China and India in particular, the brightest companies in "the West" are already gearing up for what they are calling the switch from the *Knowledge Economy* to a new *Creative Economy*.

Says *Business Week:* "What was once central to corporations—price, quality, and much of the left-brain digitised analytical work associated

By mid-2005 150,000 schools had replaced chalkboards with new interactive whiteboards.

WASHINGTON POST
The Chalkboard's Energetic New Cousin*

* September 5, 2005.

with knowledge—is fast being shipped off to lower-paid, highly-trained Chinese and Indians, as well as Hungarians, Czechs and Russians. Increasingly the new core competence is creativity—the right-brain stuff that smart companies are now harnessing to generate top-line growth The game is changing. It's not just about math and science anymore. It's about creativity, imagination and, above all, innovation." [19] And in setting up effective cross-border creative talent-sharing networks.

6. Organisation networks

New social movements linked to cooperative open partnerships

Digital networks are, of course, already transforming the corporate world—and several are now proving models for learning:

❑ Dell—the computer giant that pioneered the selling of personal computers on the Internet. Dell customers actually choose all their own PC-components on line, to their specifications. And we see similar personalised online learning programmes as a major wave of the future— where learners can choose personalised just-in-time learning options.

❑ Eighty percent of BMW's customers now design their own new car online—by selecting from 350 model variations, 500 options, ninety exterior colours and 170 interior trims. When a BMW dealer enters a customer's chosen options into BMW's Web ordering service, he receives the precise date of delivery five seconds later. The information is then relayed to thousands of suppliers who ship the components in sequence. The cars arrive eleven to twelve days later, one-third of the time it took before the online system was in place.

❑ Apple Education in New Zealand—a subsidiary of the Apple Computer distributor in that country—has done one of the finest jobs in the world in training teachers for new concepts in interactive technology. It even runs regular bus-tours to model schools.

❑ From Britain, Promethean—the European leader in electronic interactive whiteboards—also hosts an online collaborative-classroom service. This lets successful subject-teachers around the planet share interactive lesson-plans and "digital flipcharts".

By mid-2005 150,000 schools around the world had installed such interactive whiteboards, often linked up to students' own computers or "digital slates". And when the devastating hurricane Katrina and result-ing flood virtually wiped out the city of New Orleans that year, teachers and students were able to simulate hurricanes and other weather patterns:

Online study over the Web by 2007 will have spawned an industry worth $370-billion a year.

BUSINESS WEEK*

*2004 survey of potential for online learning.

from built-in software and online videos and interactive graphics.

The market has grown fastest in England, where the Government has set aside $92 million in a year to help schools buy these interactive whiteboards. And Mexico has also recently bought 30,000. So maybe the blackboard-and-chalk era is finally, slowly coming to an end.

❑ In China, Legend (now Lenova internationally) has become the biggest PC seller, largely because of the network of Legend computer-training centres, open to parents, teachers and students.

But these are not isolated minor examples. We cannot restress too strongly the way in which nearly all successful businesses today are reinventing themselves around the concept of interactive electronic webs, and as "creative learning organisations". Generally these link suppliers, manufacturers, retailers and customers. They have major lessons for education:

❑ The Apollo Group's University of Phoenix is the biggest of America's for-profit universities, with 200,000 students enrolled in its physical campuses and almost 80,000 online.

❑ *And Business Week forecasts that online study over the Web by 2007 will have spawned a $370-billion-a-year industry: mainly through distance-learning and self-directed study.*

❑ Accenture, the world's biggest business consulting company, spends $425 million a year on staff training: much of it digitised. It spends another $100 million a year on its own digital intranet to make all its best business case studies available to its global consultants. FedEx spends $500 million on internal staff training; its training and software headquarters in Memphis, Tennessee, is a model for hi-tech universities everywhere. And GE's total staff-retraining budget is now $800 million.

But probably the most important growing networks are those developed as "social movements": the open-source, collaborative networks spearheaded by Java computer applications, Linux PC operating systems, Apache Web-servers and OpenOffice-type software.

7. New global learning networks

A new society based on shared talents, cultures and "digital tools"

The inevitable end result of all this will—we suggest—be a new global learning web that will link thousands of networks where everyone can share individual talents, cultures and information.

'It cannot be said too often: all life is one. That is, and I suspect will forever prove to be, the most profound true statement there is.'

BILL BRYSON
*A Short History of Nearly Everything**

* Published by Doubleday, New York.

Already local, company, community, group, state, school and national digital networks are merging together with others around the world.

And like the Internet and the World Wide Web itself, the organisation of the new global learning web will be *chaordic:* the same dynamic combination of the unity and diversity that now underlies everything we now know about the universe, the earth and every living thing.

As Bill Bryson puts it in his brilliant book, *A Short History of Almost Everything,* in summing up the mystery of life itself:

"It cannot be said too often: all life is one. That is, and I suspect will for ever prove to be, the most profound true statement there is."

But inside that unity of all life is the uniqueness of each individual. And, in the challenge of Buckingham and Coffman: "Everyone can probably do at least one thing better than ten thousand other people. The trick is to find that something." [20]

Then to open-mindedly share and network that talent—and your culture—with the uniqueness and culture of others. Not only in your local networked teams, but with other talents around the globe.

Many, of course, will continue to share their talents commercially. Others freely through educational webs, like scientists have always done.

And yet others linked in with emerging organisations like *Wikipedia.* Says *Time* magazine, on the *Wiki* phenomena: *"Wikipedia* is a free open-source encyclopedia, which basically means that anyone can log on and add to or edit it. And they do. It has a stunning 1.5 million entries in seventysix languages—and counting." [21] (Wiki, by the way, is Hawaiian for *quick,* as in Honolulu's famous wiki-wiki buses.)

Jimmy Wales, the founder of the Internet's largest encyclopedia, says he is just getting started. He is expanding into *Wiktionary,* a dictionary and thesaurus; *Wikibooks,* textbooks and manuals; and *Wikiquote,* a book of quotations. Like *Google,* he has one simple goal: to give "every single person free access to the sum of all human knowledge." [22]

Wasn't that once the main job of schools, colleges and universities?

Now it's more and more being superseded by the combined strength of these new, interlocking networks. And by the way new breakthroughs in neuroscience are also shattering the old myths of education: to make it easier, faster and more effective to learn to learn, learn to think and learn to turn students' talents, passions and dreams into new ideas.

The talent revolution

❏ **We each have a talent to excel at something.**

❏ **The trick is to find that something.**

❏ **Focus on strengths, not on weaknesses.**

❏ **Select for talent, train for skills.**

❏ **And learn to build your own mind.**

Nature, nurture and neurons:
and how they develop talent

It's hard to believe that 400 years ago Britain's Oxford University taught that the human brain was unimportant, and that all intelligence resided in the heart.

To believe otherwise was to risk excommunication and even death.

Many similar myths have dominated learning and education right down to the present day.

Even some of world's most respected professors of education and psychology still cannot agree on a definition of "intelligence".

But hopefully new insights are emerging that will at last settle many of the debates:

❏ DNA research has produced strong confirmation that "all life is one"[1] and all living things come from the same genetic code.

❏ The multi-billion-dollar Human Genome Project has at last resolved the long-running nature-versus-nurture debate. We now know that both play a big part in our individual development.

❏ Latest *neuroscience* research, and new brain-scanning technology, has revealed new insights into how the brain, mind and body together play a much more interconnected basis for learning.

❏ The growth of electronic networks and systems may also help settle the rightful role of *standards* and *standardisation*.

❏ And the world's biggest survey of corporate employees and managers reveals individual *talent*—broadly defined— is probably much more important than any narrow definition of *intelligence.*

Everyone can probably do at least one thing better than 10,000 other people.

MARCUS BUCKINGHAM & CURT COFFMAN
First, Break All The Rules*

* Published by Simon & Shuster Business Books, London.

That latter finding comes from Gallup, the world's largest polling organisation. And it summarises two mammoth research studies over the final twentyfive years of the twentieth century.[2] In them, Gallup interviewed more than one million employees and 80,000 managers.

We know of no other survey anywhere near that large in scope.

And the results are startling in their simplicity:

❏ "Everyone has a talent to be good at something. The trick is to find that something."

❏ "Everyone can probably do at least one thing better than ten thousand other people."

❏ But *talent* is not the same as *intelligence, knowledge, skills* or specific *abilities.*

❏ Talent—as defined by Gallup—starts with each person's genetic inheritance. We are each born with, or develop early in life, a unique pattern of personality, temperament and behavioural traits that together play a big part in what and who we become.

❏ Successful managers identify specific talents and nurture them. They then make sure to create an environment in which each person develops the skills and abilities needed for those talents to flower.

❏ And so should good parents, schools and great teachers.

❏ "Don't waste time trying to put in what was left out. Try to draw out what was left in."

Which, incidentally, was the original Latin meaning of "education": *educare*—pronounced *educaray:* to draw out the unique qualities of the whole person.

Peter Drucker, with his usual common sense, says: "We've known the secret of real learning for more than 2,000 years. "The first and wisest writer on raising small children, the great Greek biographer and historian Plutarch, spelled it out in a charming little book *Paidea (Raising Children)* in the first century of the Christian era.

" All it requires is to focus on the strengths and talents of learners so that they excel in whatever it is they do well. Any teacher of young artists—musicians, actors, painters—knows that. So does every teacher of young athletes. But schools do not. They focus instead on a learner's weaknesses."[3]

Many schools already reverse this, of course. And some of the best focus on developing what several leading professors of education and

The great myths about learning and intelligence

1. That we all learn best in the same way.

2. That intelligence is fixed at birth.

3. There's only one form of intelligence.

4. It's mainly inherited.

5. It's the same as logical thinking.

6. That school is the main place to learn.

psychology call theories of "multiple intelligences" or different traits.

Gallup favours "multiple talents" as a better description—because then it is much simpler to identify potential talent, and then develop the *skills* and *abilities* to ensure that talent flourishes. And to link it in with multi-talented teams and networks.

Whichever term is used, however, the findings challenge continuing myths on which many educational policies are based:

Myth 1: that we all learn best in the same way.

What we now know: We each have a personal learning style, thinking style and working style. We each have a different way to take in information, store information, retrieve information and turn information into real knowledge.

Even geniuses learn in very different ways, think in different ways and work in different ways:

❏ **George Bernard Shaw** was at the bottom of his class at school, yet became one of the world's greatest playwrights.

❏ **Thomas Edison** was so bored with school he dropped out after only three months, but became the world's greatest inventor.

❏ **Albert Einstein** was a daydreamer. As a youth he failed his college entrance exams. Yet he became the greatest scientist of the last century. Employed as an "inspector third class" in the Swiss Patent Office, he wrote in his spare time three Papers that were to revolutionise science. The first won the Nobel Prize for physics. The second proved that atoms do indeed exist. "And the third merely changed the world." [4]

Yet even then, having just solved several of the deepest mysteries of the universe, when Einstein applied for a job as a university lecturer he was rejected. He then applied for one as a high-school teacher, and was rejected there too.

Einstein didn't keep many notes. He worked on intuition. Asked later about his method of thinking, he replied simply that "imagination is more important than knowledge". He worked out the core of his theory of relativity while he was imagining riding on a moonbeam.

And, in words that are a challenge to a new generation of creative students and thinkers: "Only daring speculation can lead us further—and not the accumulation of facts."

Myth 2: That intelligence is largely fixed at birth, and can be accurately determined by IQ or similar standardised tests.

Throw away their crutches and let children use their wings.

Help them make the most of the skills they have.

ROBERT J. STERNBERG &
ELENA L. GRIGORENKO
Our Labelled Children*

* Published by Perseus Publishing, New York.

What we now know: Says Robert J. Sternberg, Professor of Psychology and Education at Yale University: "Skills measured by IQ tests are not the only skills that, in combination, constitute intelligence." [5]

He says all children have individual strengths, and "our goal should be to help all chilDen make the most of their strengths and correct their weaknesses". He wants schools to reward excellence, but excellence broadly defined. "Throw away the crutches and let children use their wings. Help them make the most of the skills they have."

Myth 3: that there is only one form of intelligence.

What we now know: There are many forms of intelligence, and certainly many *traits* and *talents*. Howard Gardner, Professor of Psychology and Education at Harvard University, says there are at least eight separate types of intelligence, and there may be many more.

"The single most important contribution education can make to a child's development," he says, "is to help him toward a field where his talents best suit him, where he will be satisfied and competent." [6] America, he argues, has completely lost sight of this. "Instead we subject everyone to an education where, if you succeed, you will be best suited to be a college professor. And we evaluate everyone along the way according to whether they meet that narrow standard of success."

Myth 4: that all intelligence is inherited.

What we now know: For decades so-called experts argued which was most important: nature (inherited in your genes) or nurture (developed through environment, experience and culture). Now we know that nature and nurture work together. We are each born with certain traits and "propensities" for learning and specific talents. But our home, schooling, living, working and community environment is vital to develop those talents and to build new sets of skills and abilities.

Myth 5: that intelligence is the same as logical, analytical thinking.

What we now know: Professor Sternberg says intelligence takes at least three forms: analytical, creative and practical. And intelligence-quotient tests do not measure those latter two.

"A high score in an IQ test," he stresses, "is no guarantee of a high level of creative ability, practical or commonsense ability, athletic ability, musical ability or any of a number of other abilities." [7]

Again, even geniuses such as Edison, Einstein and many other analytical and creative thinkers have solved problems in different ways.

Today's schools are organised around yesterday's ideas, yesterday's needs, and yesterday's resources.

And they were not even doing well yesterday.

ROGER. C. SCHANK
Engines for Education*

* Published by Lawrence Erlbaum, Hillsdale, New Jersey.

Myth 6: That everyone has the ability to succeed at anything.

What we now know: That is simply not true.

Talent is not an all-embracing ability to be great at everything. Talent is very much based on a built-in series of aptitudes. And different aptitudes help people excel in different ways. The aptitutes that make a great accountant do not necessarily make a great drummer. And the attributes that make a fine chess-player do not guarantee success as a creative painter.

Myth 7: that school is the main or best place to learn.

What we now know: From ages five to fifteen-to-eighteen , students spend only around 20 percent of their waking hours in a school classroom. Everything else they learn is with the world as their classroom, and they generally learn more from that than from school itself.

Take almost any of the great artists, sporting achievers or movie-makers. From Mozart to Beethoven, the great composers learned well away from a school classroom. From Tiger Woods to the Williams sisters, sporting achievers learn by actually playing their sport: on the golf course, the practice range or the tennis court. And Steven Spielberg, George Lucas and Peter Jackson all learned to make movies by making movies.

Jackson, whose *Lord of the Rings: Return of the King* took eleven Academy Awards in 2004, never went to college.* When he was eight, his New Zealand parents bought an 8 mm movie camera. It didn't take their son long to get his hands on the new toy—and his life changed forever. By the time he was twelve, he and friends had dug up part of the family garden and made movies on the second world war. As a teenager, Jackson worked as an apprentice photolithographer at a local newspaper. That earned him enough to buy his first Bolex 16mm camera, and to start a career that was to see him produce, for the first time in history, three award-winning movies at the same time: the three giant episodes of J.R. Tolkien's literary classic on Middle Earth. No simple multiple-choice examination could have tested the talent of Jackson, Spielberg or Lucas.

As the Sante Fe Institute noted in 1995, in a collection of essays entitled *The Mind, The Brain and Complex Adaptive Systems:* "The method people naturally employ to acquire knowledge is largely unsup-

* *"College" is used here in the American sense, meaning post-high school. In Jackson's New Zealand, some high schools are called colleges.*

The birth of IQ and standardised tests

1900: Frederick W. Taylor introduces time-and-motion study to simplify mass production.

1905: Binet & Simon introduce first IQ test in France.

1907: Henry Ford produces first model T on Taylor-style auto mass production line.

1909: Carnegie Foundation develops 'standard unit' as basis for US high schools.

1912: Achievement tests first trialled in New York City.

1916: Stanford adopts Binet tests for America.

1917: Stanford-Binet system used to 'grade' US troops.

ported by traditional classroom practice. The human mind is better equipped to gather information about the world by operating within it than by reading about, hearing lectures about it, or studying abstract models of it."

Myth 8: That "standards" are the real test of learning, and can easily be measured by standardised written tests.

What we now know: Some standards are important, and *can* be tested. Obviously, students can be tested for their knowledge of arithmetic, chemistry symbols, spelling, geographic data and historical facts. But these are only part of a broad education. And certainly written tests cannot evaluate each students' individual talents, skills and abilities. Many tests can only measure the ability to memorise.

Some high-testing math students are brilliant at memorising the times table—but don't have the *specific creative talent* to produce a new form of calculation (1 plus or minus 1 equals anything!) that gave birth to the digital revolution and spawned Silicon Valley.

And some students are brilliant at memorising each chemical formula—but that doesn't prove they can apply the *scientific method* to analyse any challenge they may face in life.

Perhaps more importantly, the new digital and networking revolutions do depend on *agreed standards*—as anyone who has ever tried to switch from Windows to Apple Mac can testify. Now some of the world's brightest students, with a variety of talents, are working together to set new open standards that everyone can share. Fortunately, digital systems make it easy to standardise many simple concepts, from spell-checkers to calculators, allowing each person to develop and share talents.

The birth of "intelligence testing"

So how did we end up with an educational system that often seems so at variance with real life? We've already touched on some of its origins. But the history of "intelligence testing" started with a different agenda. And some of the arguments are still being fought to this day, with MRI scans and the Human Genome Project adding to the discourse.

In 1869 Francis Galton published *Hereditary Genius* and its major argument that all intelligence is inherited. This gave rise to the "eugenics" movement and its demand for "selective breeding": concepts that were later, through Hitler, to lead to the Second World War holocaust.

By 1905—while "unqualified" Einstein was presenting the first of his

Genes do not make you intelligent; they make you more likely to enjoy learning.

MATT RIDLEY
*Nature Via Nurture**

* Published by Harper Perennial, London: a summary
of the Human Genome Project.

revolutionary scientific findings—two French psychologists, Edward Binet and Theodore Simon, were publishing the world's first IQ, or *intelligence quotient,* test.

This Binet-Simon test also caused a revolution. It claimed to introduce a simple way to test who was intelligent. The duo claimed their system could determine the intelligence of a genius and the ability of those suitable only for unskilled labouring jobs.

Those IQ tests led directly to the "standardised test" model that still dominates much of the schooling in many countries.

In many ways, that model emerged from historical coincidence.

While Einstein and fellow geniuses were starting to unlock those secrets of the universe, the atom and the electron a hundred years ago, the world was just about to change. By 1900 only 10 percent of all Americans even started high school. And only 2 percent graduated. So 98 percent did not have a full high school education. But America had just started the race to perfect the ultimate Newtonian industrial model: the mass production line, with its army of bit-by-bit unskilled assemblers.

America already had several noted universities, based on separate curriculum "subjects" that had already been determined. So when a commission of university presidents was charged with recommending the new high-school curriculum, they chose the "subjects" then required for a college or university degree. This system, funded by the Carnegie Foundation, became known as the Carnegie Units for the "standard" high school curriculum. Most high schools are still based on this system, both in the United States and elsewhere.

Around the same time, American psychologists Lewis M. Terman and Maud A. Merrill, both of Stanford University, adapted the Binet-Simon model into what became known as the Stanford-Binet tests.

Their timing perfectly matched the upsurge in America's new production methods. Here was a seemingly easy way to sort out the managers from the unskilled manual workers, including migrants: each doing only one standardised, repetitive task. When America entered the First World War, the Stanford-Binet tests were used to quickly determine the "intelligence" of every recruit: with the "brightest" immediately selected for officer training and most others relegated to the ranks.

That mass-produced, factory-model of testing amazingly continues to this day. And much of the public "education debate" revolves not about how *everyone* can learn, but about the "assessment" and testing system

Your brain has 100 billion active cells, each with up to 20,000 connections

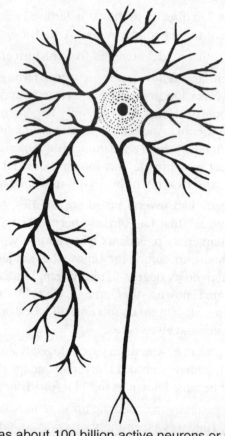

Your brain has about 100 billion active neurons or nerve cells.
Each one grows branches like a tree, to store information:
up to 20,000 branch-like *dendrites* with each cell.
Each neuron is like a powerful computer.
And each connects to other cells by sending
electrical-chemical messages along *axons*.

Illustration from *Make The Most Of Your Mind,* by Tony Buzan, published
by Pan, London, and reprinted here with permission from Tony Buzan.

designed initially to separate people on the basis of fixed intelligence.

Any new theory should instead be based on what we now know about the human brain, the varied nature of intelligence itself, and how everyone can succeed by developing individual talents.

Fortunately, we've learned more about that in the past thirty years than in the rest of recorded history. Nearly all the news is good.

First: what is the human brain?

It consists of a trillion brain cells. One tenth of these—100 billion — are neurons or active cells: one phenomenal driving force that separates human brains from every other species. A fruit fly has 100,000 active neurons. A mouse has 5 million. A monkey: 10 million. You've had 100 billion from birth.

But more important: each of those 100 billion neurons has the ability to expand from birth throughout life. The neurons themselves don't multiply after birth, but each has the ability to sprout thousands of new *dendrites*—like branches on a tree: up to 20,000 on each braincell.

The brain takes in information at a phenomenal rate: up to 3 billion "bits" of information in a second from the very first days of life.[8] It stores that information on these expanding dendritic branches. If it's new information, it grows new branches. If it relates to already-stored information, the brain files "like with like".

And the more you are open to new learning experiences, the more your brainpower soars. In a twentyeight-week-old human foetus, researchers have found 124 million connections between cells. At birth: 253 million connections, and in an eight-month old: 582 million. In the first few years of active life, these connections can explode to about 1,000 trillion.

Says Pullitzer Prize-winning writer Ronald Kotulak in *Inside The Brain*: "The amazing discovery of the brain's plasticity—its ability to physically rewire itself to become smarter—makes mental stimulation, in the long run, more essential to the body than food. That the brain thrives with good nourishment is a concept that has profound significance for individual achievement and for the way parents raise their children."

That neural "wiring" can be used both to improve your memory and to develop new connections to create even better solutions. In this way, learning becomes not only how you store and retrieve information, but how you create your own future. In many ways, this is at the heart of the new theory of learning. ***Education is not the passive accumulation of***

The interlocking brain networks

Physical networks
including brainstem, cerebellum, motor cortex, vestibular system

Sensory networks
Sight, hearing, smell, taste, touch

Emotional networks
Feelings, emotions

Chemical-electrical networks
Overall 'transition system'

Biological clock networks
Sleep and wakefulness

Cognitive networks
Linking parts of the cortex for thinking and interacting

information, passed on by a teacher or a book, but the way in which you orchestrate that information creatively and use it in practice.

How do the parts of the brain work together?

Peer through an MRI scanner and you'll see the human brain has many different interlocking components: seemingly stored from bottom to top in three main levels—with a fourth tucked in behind.

This structure of the brain gave rise, in the mid-twentieth century, to Paul MacLean's theory of a "triune" or three-tiered brain. And that seemed to fit in neatly with the other scientific trend: to "deconstruct" total systems down to their component parts. More recent research, including "functional" MRI scans, and the Human Genome Programme, shows a much more complicated system of integrated networks:

❏ A physical-movement network.

❏ The sensation and sensory-processing networks.

❏ Emotional networks.

❏ Chemical and electrical networks.

❏ Biological networks, such as those governing sleep and wakefulness.

❏ And cognitive networks—including the "association cortex": linking parts of the brain together for thinking and interacting.

And all of these are linked closely to the nerve and structural networks of the body itself.

In the anatomy, or physical structure, of the brain, several interlinked parts are easily identified on MRI scans:

At the bottom is the brainstem. Its components help process many basic instincts, such as breathing and heartbeat.

Some have called this the *instinctive* brain because of the way it seems to instinctively trigger reactions. Turn the light on in a room and any spider caught in the light will instinctively "freeze". If the spider is large, *you* may be instinctively afraid of it. A bird sitting on the highway and about to be hit by a speeding car will instinctively fly away almost the moment before impact. That was said to be the instinctive brain at work. But we now know that thus "model" is too simplistic. Instincts are triggered and processed through different parts of the brain, and not only through the brainstem.

Above the brainstem: the midbrain or limbic system—from the Latin

The two sides to your brain

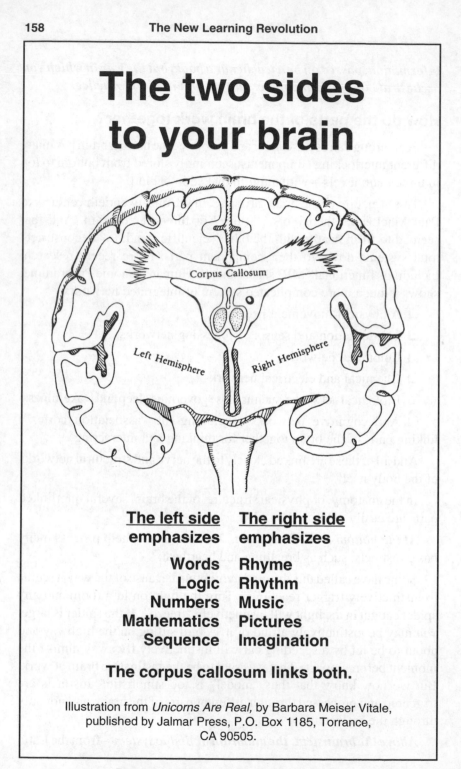

The left side emphasizes

Words
Logic
Numbers
Mathematics
Sequence

The right side emphasizes

Rhyme
Rhythm
Music
Pictures
Imagination

The corpus callosum links both.

Illustration from *Unicorns Are Real,* by Barbara Meiser Vitale, published by Jalmar Press, P.O. Box 1185, Torrance, CA 90505.

word for "collar": because of the way it seems to wrap around the brainstem.

Some earlier neuroscientists dubbed the midbrain *the emotional brain*. But again we now know that is too simplistic. The midbrain does, however, enclose some specific organs that record and telegraph emotions. And, as with the brainstem, it, too, has control-centres that instinctively trigger emotions and cause instant reactions: fear, anger, stress or joy.

At the highest level of the brain is the cortex—from the Latin word for "bark", like the bark on a tree. It sits on the top of the brain like a crumpled blanket. It's only 3 mm or an eighth of an inch thick, but it is the specific part of the brain that allows us to do many of those things that are uniquely human: to think, reason, read, write, paint, compose, speak and communicate with each other and the world. Each of those functions is processed in a different segment of the cortex, but often working in unison with other segments—and certainly with the emotions. Some scientists call this the *association cortex*.

Brain hemispheres: Scan the centre of the brain, from front to back, and you'll see that the whole brain has two distinct halves. We now know that each of these plays a different role in processing information. Some writers have called them "the left brain" and "the right brain", but that, too, is an over-simplification. They are not separate brains.

Each side plays a major role in different functions of the total brain. In right-handed people, the left side of the brain processes written words, logic, numbers, mathematics and sequential tasks. The right side deals more with more "creative" processes: rhyme, rhythm, music, pictures and imagination.

Corpus Callossum: Both sides are linked together by an electrical relay system that itself has around 300 million operating neurons. This *corpus callosum* shuttles information around instantly like an international automatic telephone exchange. And the brain works much better when using both sides together. That's why we recall the words of songs much more easily than the exact words of books: *we learn better when both sides of the brain are working in unison.*

At the lower back of the brain is the cerebellum or "little brain". It plays a big part in storing storing "muscle memory". That's the part that enables golfers to automatically store and reproduce their swing, or experienced typists to touch-type without even thinking of what their fingers are doing. The cerebellum is also closely connected to the

Six main pathways to the brain: we learn by . . .

 What we SEE

What we HEAR

What we TASTE

 What we TOUCH

What we SMELL

 What we DO

and what we imagine, intuit and feel

intricate mechanism of the inner-ear. Together they make up the *vestibular* system: very much the body's control-centre for *balance*.

If we were to compare the brain to a giant computer, that total structure would be the basic "operating system". But what a system! Today's laptops can complete millions of additions a second—but generally only one calculation at a time. Your brain, by contrast, acts as an incredibly fast "parallel processing" system. It can process billions of bits of information, on different levels, simultaneously.

Even now, we're only beginning to understand many of the brain's unique workings and abilities. For a start is its almost unlimited ability to store information on the billions of dendrites it grows on its 100 billion neurons—and to retrieve that information, merge it, synthesise it, and use it for all forms of creativity.

Information comes into the brain through all our senses: what we see, hear, touch, smell and taste—and by what we imagine, intuit, feel and actually do. The "motor control centres" of the brain send out messages to the rest of the body in a circular, automatic feedback route. Place your finger on a hotplate, and instantly your nervous system telegraphs the message to your brain to "take it off".

Your brain also stores incoming information by patterns and associations. It's almost as if each "tree" and "branch" on a neuron acts as a separate part of a multimedia library. One "tree" will store all input on fruit. And each "branch" will store information on individual types of fruit. But your brain seems to be able to almost-automatically associate and compare incoming information before "depositing" it in various memory-banks. Fruit, for example, may be round, red, yellow, green, furry, smooth, ripe or firm, yet our brain seems to be able to automatically and easily group information in all of those categories.

The main centres of the brain are connected to each other, and to the rest of the body, by millions of *axons*, or "super neural highways". Each axon in turn is covered with a "myelin" sheath. This is much like insulation around electric wires. And the better the insulation, the faster messages will speed along the "wires": up to 100 metres a second.

The brain network, in turn, is surrounded by up to 900 billion "glial" cells which "glue" the parts of the brain together, and nourish them. Until recently their role was thought to be limited. But more recent evidence indicates that glial cells may be nearly as critical to thinking and learning as neurons are.[9]

How your brain transmits its messages

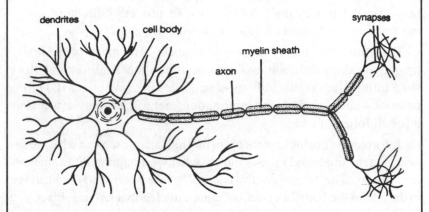

Each of your 100 billion active neurons or brain cells stores information on its thousands of *dendrites,* like branches.

It then transmits that information to other cells, and other parts of the body, by electrical impulses, along a major pathway called an *axon* (for axle or axis).

When it reaches the synapse (connecting gap) to another brain-cell, each electrical impulse triggers a chemical reaction—a neurotransmitter which jumps across the gap to transfer the message.

Each axon is insulated by a myelin sheath, which acts as an insulator. The better the insulation, the more efficient the message is transmitted. The brain has at least seventy different types of neurotransmitter, and each is affected by diet.

The entire "communication system" is surrounded by *glial* cells (for "glue"), which lay down the myelin sheathing, and generally nourish the active nerve cells. The right diet is also vital for this nourishment (see more detail in chapter 6).

Illustration is from *Accelerated Learning,* by Colin Rose, published by Accelerated Learning Systems, of Aston Clinton, Bucks, England.

And all these parts link to make up that so-called super computer—if, in fact, we can call it that; it's more like a self-renewing ecosystem.

Your brain's four wave-lengths

It even continues to work, almost autonomously, while you're asleep: subconsciously or semiconsciously. Link yourself up to an electronic scanner and you'll soon find out that parts of your brain can send and receive information on different frequencies: on four separate wavelengths. In one sense they're similar to television signals. Tune in your TV set to channel 2, or 22, and you'll be able to receive messages sent out on that wavelength.

Scan your brain when you're wide awake and it will also be transmitting or working at a certain number of cycles per second. Scan it when you're dozing and it will be transmitting on a "different frequency". Likewise when you're in the early stages of sleep and dreaming, and later when you're in deep sleep.

Many researchers are now convinced that we can absorb information much more quickly and effectively when our brains are in a state of "relaxed alertness".

That's the state we often achieve with certain types of meditation. Or by listening to relaxing music. Or doing yoga exercises.

As we'll discuss later, in the period between full waking and deep sleep, the brain automatically reviews highlights of the day just ended—and seems to "slot" the most important ones into your memory banks. Scientists using brainscans call this REM sleep—for "rapid eye movement"—because it's as if its visual system is flashing pictures of the day's events. "Digital video clips" would be a more apt metaphor.

The brain's transmission system

But, night or day, the brain's main "neural networks" work like nothing else in the mechanical world. Whether information comes in through the eye, ear, nose, mouth or touch, it is then carried through the brain and the body by both electrical and chemical impulses.

Each message starts as an electrical signal and then quickly reaches the first of a series of terminals, like switching points. Scientists call these *synapses*.

And as a message crosses each synaptic gap it is transformed by

You
are
what
you
eat.

BRIAN AND ROBERTA MORGAN
*Brain Food**

* While this quotation has been used many times before,
it forms a key theme of the Morgans' excellent book,
published by Michael Joseph Ltd., and by
Pan Books, London.

chemical catalysts. Scientists call these *neuro-transmitters (neuro* for nerve, and *transmitter* as in sending).

Some of them are triggered by our food and drink. Eat healthy food and drink lots of clear springwater, and you'll speed messages on their way, and maybe even improve their clarity. But live on a diet of fatty fast foods, washed down with tons of caffeine-rich coffee, toxic sweeteners or strong alcohol, and you'll trigger different chemical neurotransmitters.

Some of the most powerful neurotransmitters can come from drugs. such as alcohol and tobacco which can completely subvert the brain and cause addiction. Other powerful neurotransmitters are triggered by emotions and thoughts. Perhaps the best-known is adrenalin. It is often triggered by fear—fear of public speaking or fear of physical danger. Become frightened, say, by a snake or shark, and fear triggers an "alarm hormone", noradrenaline. This, in turn, "organises the brain to respond to danger, producing adrenalin and other chemicals that prepare the body to fight or flee. Noradrenaline may play a major role in both hot-blooded and cold-blooded violence."

Noradrenaline is a mood-altering chemical. And so is serotonin: known as "the brain's master impulse modulator" for all emotions and drives. It especially keeps aggression in line. In fact, dangerous impulses often arise from an imbalance between seratonin and noradrenaline.

All, of course, can affect learning. We are indeed what we eat, what we drink, what we think and what we do.

How to provide the brain's energy

Like any other complex machinery, your brain needs energy. Basically, it gets that from the food you eat. If you're an adult, your brain makes up only about 2 percent of your total weight. But it uses about 20 percent of the energy you develop.

Feed it a low-energy diet, and it won't perform well. Feed it a high-energy diet, and your personal computer will work smoothly, efficiently.

For energy, the brain needs plenty of glucose. That's why fresh fruit and vegetables are so essential. They're rich in glucose.

To send those billions of messages a minute, your brain first has to generate electricity. If you could test it now, you'd probably find it generating about 25 watts. That's the amount needed to run the smallest lightbulb in your home.

Brain functioning depends very much on what you've eaten for breakfast.

RICHARD M. RESTAK
*The Brain: The Last Frontier**

*Published by Warner Books, in arrangement with Doubleday & Co.,
245 Park Avenue, New York, NY 10017.

The source of that brain-electricity: good food combined with oxygen. Obviously you get oxygen through breathing. That's why deep breathing is recommended before and during study: to oxygenate your blood. And that's why exercise is not only good for your body, it's good for your brain. It enriches your blood with oxygen. Cut off the supply of oxygen and you destroy brain cells. Stop it completely and you die.

Your brain also needs the right type of energy to produce the best balance of those neurotransmitters. And that in turn depends on a balanced diet. Scientists have identified around seventy different types of neurotransmitters, including endorphins, the brain's natural painkillers or opiates.

And, as Brian and Roberta Morgan point out in their excellent book *Brain Food:* "Any deficiencies in nutrients can reduce the levels of certain neurotransmitters and so adversely affect the types of behaviour they are responsible for. Conversely, a physical or mental problem can be corrected by boosting the level of the relevant transmitter, and this can be done by making a simple alteration in the composition of your diet."

As an example, they point to the big increase in Alzheimer's disease among elderly people, and add: "Another characteristic of senility is the reduced ability of the brain—by as much as 70 or 80 percent—to produce acetylcholine, the neurotransmitter largely responsible for memory."

Dr. Brian Morgan, formerly a Professor at the Institute of Human Nutrition at Columbia University in New York, recommends a diet rich in lecithin to help improve everyone's memory, but especially that of older people. Foods rich in lecithin include peanuts, wheat germ and soya beans that have not been genetically modified. He also recommends lecithin and choline chloride dietary supplements to boost the neurotransmitters that are needed to improve your memory.

The Morgans also spell out other dietary deficiencies that impair mental performance, including a lack of the polyunsaturated fat called linoleic acid which the body itself cannot manufacture. "Fortunately," say the Morgans, "it is also extremely easy to find: one teaspoon of corn oil a day is enough to supply an adult with all he needs. But that teaspoon is crucial for proper brain operation. Without it, the brain cannot repair its myelin sheaths, and the result may be a loss of coordination, confusion, memory loss, paranoia, apathy, tremors and hallucinations."

Iron deficiency is a major cause of poor mental performance. It probably affects more people in Western society than any other single

Brain-friendly diet made simple

1. **A good breakfast daily**
   specially fresh fruit.

2. **A good lunch daily**
   preferably with green salad.

3. **Fish, fruit and nuts**
   plus vegetable oil.

4. **Exercise regularly**
   to oxygenate blood.

5. **Get rid of toxins**
   with plenty of water.

deficiency. It "decreases attention span, delays the development of understanding and reasoning powers, impairs learning and memory, and generally interferes with a child's performance in school". All minerals, including iron, are available when you eat a variety of raw vegetable sprouts such as mung beans, buckwheat sprouts and alfalfa sprouts.

The brain also needs a constant supply of other nutrients. Among the main ones are sodium and potassium. Each of your 100 billion neurons has up to one million sodium pumps. And they're vital for transmitting all your brain's messages. The right combination of sodium and potassium supplies those pumps with energy. Like glucose, potassium is found mainly in fruits and vegetables. Reduce your potassium intake drastically and you risk anorexia, nausea, vomiting, drowsiness and stupor. All could be symptoms of your brain's vital pumps not working.

Sodium never occurs as a separate element in nature. It combines with many other elements to form compounds. And the sodium-compounds found in a fresh vegetable diet are the best for both brain and body. Sodium chloride, or common table salt, is not recommended.

Simple tips on brain food

Fortunately, nearly all fruits are rich in potassium, especially bananas, oranges, apricots, avocados, melons, nectarines and peaches. So are potatoes, tomatoes, pumpkins and artichokes.

We'll deal with some aspects of diet in later chapters, particularly for pregnant women and children. But for now, if you want your brain to be working efficiently for all forms of learning and work:

1. Eat a good breakfast every morning, preferably with plenty of fresh fruit. Include half a banana for its potassium content—a whole one if you're pregnant—with an orange or kiwifruit for vitamin C, and any other fresh fruit in season. If you have children, make sure they do too.

2. Eat a good lunch, preferably including a fresh vegetable salad.

3. Make fish, nuts and vegetable "fats" key parts of your diet. Fish and vegetable oils have a vital role in nourishing the brain's billions of glial cells. And nuts and vegetable oils are major sources of that linoleic acid, which the brain needs to repair the myelin insulation around your brain's "message tracks".

4. Exercise regularly to oxygenate the blood.

5. Cleanse the toxins out of your body. One way to do that is to drink

We are each born with a brain. But we each construct our own mind. And we keep on doing that throughout life.

plenty of water. Coffee, tea or carbonated "soft drink" dehydrate the body, and fresh water reactivates it.

We can't stress strongly the enough the importance of a good "brain-food" and toxin-cleansing diet to truly "make the most of your mind".

But what is the human mind?

While the physical structure of the brain is now well known, how does it the brain differ from the mind?

Here we still find much less agreement.

Stephen Pinker, one of the world's leading cognitive scientists, takes more than 600 pages to explain *How The Mind Works* in the 1997 book of that name. And he starts out very simply with what he terms a note of humility: "First we don't understand how the mind works—not nearly as well as we understand how the body works, and certainly not well enough to design utopia or to cure unhappiness."

The best simple explanation he can give: "The mind is what the brain does; specifically, the brain processes information, and thinking is a kind of computation. The mind is organised into modules of mental organs, each with a specialised design that makes it an expert in one arena of interaction with the world." He goes on to underline a key message: computers have limited numbers of connections; brains have trillions.

But computers are assembled according to a blueprint; minds must assemble themselves. We each build our own throughout life: by what we eat, drink, think, do and create, plus the impact of outside influences.

Will science provide other answers?

Fortunately the converging computer, biomolecular and and quantum revolutions are producing new ways of looking at the very core of life itself—and the way in which brain, mind and body work in unison.

No part of the body lives apart from the rest. As prominent Indian-American endocrinologist and medical practitioner Deepak Chopra puts it: "There are no wires holding together the molecules of your arteries, just as there are no visible connections binding together the stars in the galaxy. Yet arteries and galaxies are both securely held together, in a seamless, perfect design."[10]

Here Dr. Candace Pert's findings are particularly important. Professor Pert first came to prominence in the early 1970s for her discovery of the

The theory of many 'intelligences'

Verbal-linguistic
Skills: listening, speaking, writing, teaching.
Careers: journalist, writer, politician, teacher, attorney.

Logical-mathematical
Skills: analytical, problem-solving, experimenting.
Careers: engineer, accountant, mathematician.

Musical
Skills: singing, musical, composing, recording.
Careers: entertainer, singer, musician, disc jockey.

Visual-spatial
Skills: designing, painting, puzzle making.
Careers: artist, sculptor, engineer, chess player.

Bodily-kinesthetic
Skills: dancing, sports, acting, hands-on, acting.
Careers: athlete, dancer, PE teacher, firefighter.

Interpersonal or social
Skills: empathy, counselling, cooperating.
Careers: sales, politician, counselor.

Intrapersonal or introspective
Skills: self-awareness, reflective.
Careers: philosophers, theorests, researchers.

Naturalist
Skills: connected to nature, apply life sciences.
Careers: naturalist, farmer, landscape gardener.

* Professor Howard Gardner's multiple intelligence model.
For fuller details, see chapter 9.

brain's *opiate receptor*. She describes receptors as "sensing molecules"— as microscopic, molecular *scanners*. Now her continuing research has revealed "the molecular basis of the emotions": the tiny *peptides* that lock into the mind's receptors. But the resulting *molecules of emotion* are not confined to the brain. They "run every system in our body". And "peptides are the sheet music containing the notes, phrases and rhythms that allow the orchestra—your body—to play as an integrated entity". [11]

Thus memories—so vital for learning—are stored in all parts of the body. And wherever new information enters the body—through sight, sound, taste, touch or smell—memory-traces are stored not only in the brain, but in the body as well. In this way, she says, the body is "the unconscious mind". And the mind and body work as one for filtering, storing, learning, and remembering: key elements of learning.

How to define intelligence?

If defining the mind is difficult, "intelligence" has at least as many conflicting definitions, as we've started to explore.

In the late nineteenth and early twentieth centuries, in the newly-developing field of psychology, practitioners lined up strongly on conflicting sides of the nature-nurture debate.

More modern research is providing much more sensible perspectives. Nature and nurture both are important. To recap:

❑ Genes DO help determine some specific traits in human beings, including temperament, personality traits and dispositions.

❑ But there is no such thing as specific overall intelligence.

❑ Nor is intelligence fixed at birth.

❑ There are many forms of intelligence—or intelligence traits.

Harvard's Howard Gardner lists eight main ones as: logical-mathematical, linguistic, musical, visual-spatial, physical or kinesthetic, interpersonal, intrapersonal and naturalistic—as we explore later.

Others say even this list is too narrow. It doesn't, for example, in include common sense. Nor does it include the ability to create entirely new concepts by combining old elements in new ways.

Gardner agrees that all his "multiple intelligences" could be described as "intelligence traits". But he says the multiple concept is much more valid than selecting analytical ability as the sole measure of intelligence.

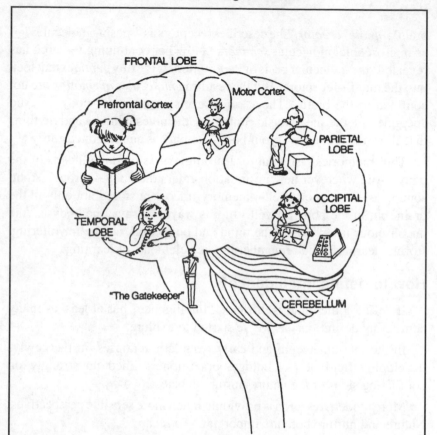

The parts of the brain that deal with different functions:

THE PREFRONTAL CORTEX, which deals with thinking.

THE MOTOR CORTEX: which controls activity.

THE TEMPORAL LOBE: the speech centre of the brain.

THE PARIETAL LOBE: which handles your spacial ability.

THE OCCIPITAL LOBE: your visual centre.

THE CEREBELLUM (or little brain), which plays a key part in adjusting posture and balance. It also acts like an "automatic pilot" when we perform learned functions like riding a bicycle or using a typewriter.

THE "GATEKEEPER": actually you have two main "gatekeepers": the amygdala and the hippocampus—all relay important messages to different parts of the brain.

Illustration from *Your Child's Growing Mind,* by Jane M. Healy, published by Doubleday, 666 Fifth Avenue, New York, NY 10103.

Yale's Sternberg says all his research[12] indicates that intelligence breaks down into three very distinct sets of abilities:

Analytical intelligence: used in analysing, judging, evaluating and comparing—very much the heart of IQ tests.

Creative intelligence: used in creating, inventing, imagining.

And practical intelligence: used in putting thoughts and ideas into practice, applying, using and implementing.

Another Harvard researcher, David Perkins, suggests three different types of intelligence:[13]

1. Neurological intelligence: the intelligence linked to IQ tests.

2. Experiential intelligence: linked to specialised knowledge and experience over time. And

3. Reflective intelligence: what some call "metacognition" or thinking about thinking and the ability to reflect.

But emotional intelligence may be more important

Other leading researchers, particularly in the last decade, have identified "emotional intelligence" as even more important than academic brilliance.

Says Daniel Goleman in *Emotional Intelligence: Why it matters more than IQ:* "At best, IQ contributes about 20 percent to the factors that determine life success, which leaves 80 percent to other forces.

"The last decade," he says "has seen an unparallelled burst of scientific studies of emotion. Most dramatic are the glimpses of the brain at work. They have made visible, for the first time in human history, what has always been a source of deep mystery: exactly how this intricate mass of cells operates while we think and feel, imagine and dream. The flood of neurobiological data lets us understand more clearly than ever before how the brain's centres for emotion move us to rage or tears, and how more ancient parts of the brain, which stir us to make war as well as love, are channelled for better or worse."

Joseph LeDoux, another American neuroscientist, was one of the first to discover the key role of the amygdala in what Goleman calls emotional intelligence. In humans the amygdala (from the Greek word for almond) is an almond-shaped cluster of interconnected structures perched above the brainstem. The brain has two amygdalas, one on each side, nestled toward the side of the head. They're very close to the hippocampus. And these are both vital gatekeepers to learning:

At best, IQ contributes about 20 percent to the factors that determine life success, which leaves 80 percent to other forces: forces grouped as *emotional intelligence.*

DANIEL GOLEMAN
*Emotional Intelligence**

* Summarised as the main theme of the book, published by
Bloomsbury, London.

The hippocampus: the gatekeeper to memory—the brain's distribution centre to sort incoming messages and send important new-information messages to specific parts of the brain for long-term storage.

The amygdala: the emotional "control centre". And, as LeDoux has proven conclusively, emotional messages—such as fright, fear, anger, tension and stress—communicate themselves direct to the amygdala and then to other major parts of the brain much quicker than those same messages go to the more "logical thinking" areas of the cortex.

Says Goleman: "In the brain's architecture, the amygdala is poised something like an alarm company where operators stand by to send out emergency calls to the fire department, police and a neighbour whenever a home security system signals trouble." [14]

LeDoux says the amygdala is an emotional sentinal able to hijack the brain. And Goleman summarises the message even more simply: "Those feelings that take the direct route through the amygdala include our most primitive and potent; this circuit does much to explain the power of emotion to overwhelm rationality."

Emotional intelligence, says Goleman, includes self-control, zeal and persistence, and the ability to motivate oneself. "And these skills can be taught to children, giving them a better chance to use whatever intellectual potential the genetic lottery may have given them."

We agree. And as we will see when we look at "the teaching revolution", emotions are the gateway to real learning. And opening that gateway is the first step towards successful teaching.

And how about temperament?

Whatever the conflicting definitions of "intelligence", it's obvious to any parent that all children, from soon after birth, show different temperaments and personalities. And that all children seem to be born with specific individual dispositions.

As early as 2,500 years ago, Hippocrates defined four separate temperaments, which he named sanguine, choleric, melancholic and phlegmatic.

In the 1920s, psychiatrist Carl Jung, in his pioneering work, identified other different ways in which people perceive information in different ways. In his ground-breaking book *Psychological Types,* he argued that we each fit somewhere on a sliding scale between four sets of extremes:

16 main types of personality

The Myers Briggs Indicator divides personalities into 16 types, generally known by four letters, graded on Carl Jung's original scale. But often these are summarised by these 16 overall descriptions:

Duty fulfiller	**Performer**
Mechanic	**Doer**
Nurturer	**Guardian**
Artist	**Caregiver**
Protector	**Inspirer**
Inspirer	**Giver**
Scientist	**Visionary**
Thinker	**Executive**

To find out your own personality, you can try:
* The official Myers Briggs test: www.DiscoverYourPersonality.com
* Or www.personalitypage.com/high-level.html—for a similar test.

1. What is the dominant way we receive stimulation: as an extravert or introvert—by relating to outsiders or delving inside ourselves?

2. How do we take in information: intuitively through our instincts or through our senses?

3. How do we make decisions: by thought and logic or by feelings?

4. What is our dominant lifestyle: organised and purposeful or flexible and diverse?

Isabel Myers and her mother, Katharine Briggs, have built on Jung's work and devised the *Myers Briggs Type Indicator.* This identifies sixteen different personality traits inside the Jung variables, and has since become one of the most widely used and popular psychological tests. You can now find your own personality-type on the Web.

But we stress, as Jung did, that many people have personalities that straddle the various types.

In more recent research, Harvard developmental psychologist Jerome Kagan renames the four most basic temperaments as: timid, bold, upbeat and melancholy. He says each is due to a different pattern of brain activity.[15]

But does our biology fix our emotional destiny, or can even an innately shy child grow into a more confident adult? Both Goleman and Kagan say a child can. Heredity is not destiny. And that is one of the most important lessons of all.

How to identify talent and let it flower

And here some of the most important research work has come from the corporate world: on how to identify specific talent and turn it into multi-talented teams.

Some of that best research has emerged from the Gallup Organisation. Marcus Buckingham and Curt Coffman summarise the results in *First, Break All The Rules,* as a guide to "great managers".

And they say that, over the last decade, "neuroscience has confirmed what great managers have always believed":

❏ *Everyone is potentially talented, but in different ways.* One of the key tasks of a teacher is to identify and draw out those unique talents.

❏ *Skills, knowledge and talents are distinct elements of a person's performance.* "The distinction between the three is that skills and knowledge can easily be taught, whereas talents cannot."[16] But they can be

Three types of inbuilt talent[1]

1. <u>Striving talent</u> includes:

Achiever: strong internal drive.
Stamina: capacity for physical endurance.
Competence: drive for expertise, mastery.
Mission: drive to put beliefs into action.
Belief: strong achievement values

2. <u>Thinking talent</u> includes:

Focus: ability to set goals and achieve them.
Discipline: a need to impose structure.
Gestalt: need to see order and accuracy.
Numerical: an affinity for numbers, accounting.
Business thinking: financial talent.

3. <u>Relating talent</u> includes:

Empathy: ability to identify with others.
Team person: ability to relate.
Interpersonal: good "mixing" skills.
Relator: need to build bonds that last.
Stimulator: ability to create enthusiasm.

MARCUS BUCKINGHAM & CURT COFFMAN
First, Break All The Rules*

*Published in paperback by Simon & Schuster, New York and London.

1. The book stresses that, as well as children showing early aptitudes in
specific future talents such as music and sporting ability,
they also show early signs of habits such as those summarised above.

developed, and differently-talented people can fit into an effective team.

❏ *"Talents are the [major] highways in your mind:* those that carve out your recurring patterns of thought, feeling or behaviour."

❏ *Talents can be separated into three categories:* striving talents, thinking talents and relating talents.

"Striving talents explain the *why* of a person. They explain why he gets out of bed every day, why he is motivated to push just that little bit harder.

"Thinking talents explain the *how* of a person. They explain how he thinks, how he weighs up alternatives, how he comes to his decisions.

"Relating talents explain the *who* of a person: who he trusts, who he builds relationships with, who he confronts, and who he ignores." [17]

❏ Great managers unlock the potential talent of each and every employee. But they also develop skills and abilities. So should schools.

❏ Nearly everyone also learns best by actually doing. We have met no one who learned to walk by attending a school lecture; no one who learned how to use a computer without actually using it; no one who has learned a sport without actually playing it; no one who has learned to draw without drawing or to paint without painting.

Nor should the concept of "talent development" restrict anyone to a predetermined future. Every parent knows that some children are later developers than others. So in early childhood, in particular, and throughout elementary and high school, students should be exposed to as many different opportunities as possible so they can in time find their "right fit".

The ideal of working in multi-talented teams at school is also ideal preparation for successful careers later. In fact, as students now work in multimedia production teams, teachers working with them are amazed at how those "natural talents" merge.

Says David Perry, the founder and chairman of Singapore's highly-successful Overseas Family School: "In our kindergarten, we've found it's great to move small children each day into different 'activity teams', so they have the simulation of different activities.

"But throughout primary and high school, we make sure to expose them to a variety of challenges in different ways. We soon find that, by working together in teams, the students themselves almost automatically sort themselves according to the strengths.

"And by working together they learn to meld their own talents with

We learn best by developing our whole body, our whole mind, our whole selves.

DAVE MEIER
*The Accelerated Learning Handbook**

* Published by McGraw-Hill, New York.

those of others; and to appreciate the strengths and talents of others." [18]

Later in life, too, as society changes so people, too, seek new challenges, and branch off in different directions.

But we cannot overstress the way in which nineteenth- and early-twentieth-century learning was based on an industrial-age society designed to produce standardised products and standardised workers.

As one of America's best corporate trainers, Dave Meier, puts it in *The Accelerated Learning Handbook:* "This approach to learning required a dulling of one's complete self. Its quest: to bring behaviour into line with routine production and thinking. The task of education and training was to prepare people for a relatively simple, static and predictable world.

"Today the task of education and training is to prepare people for a world in flux, a world in which everyone needs to exercise one's full powers of mind and heart, and act out of a sense of mindful creativity, not mindless predictability."

Meier says real learning is "based on the way people naturally learn. As children, we practised it every day of our lives. We learned all the basics not through sitting in a classroom, reading a book or staring at a computer screen, but through interacting with others and with the world, using our whole bodies, our whole minds and our whole selves." [19]

And Buckingham and Coffman spell out a similar message in almost every page of their Gallup survey-summary:

❏ Focus on developing strengths, not on weaknesses.

❏ Don't waste time trying to "put in what was left out".

❏ Try to "draw out what was left in."

❏ Select for talent, but train to develop skills and abilities.

❏ And then develop and broaden people in multi-talented teams.

Above all, as Meier puts it: learners should no longer be seen as passive consumers of someone else's information, but as developers of their own talent, and active creators of their own knowledge and skills.

When you add that incredible enriched and varied power of human creativity and potential to the explosive power of shared, intelligent, digital networks, therein lies the real emerging revolution.

20 easy steps to better learning

1   Start with the lessons from sport.

2   Dare to dream.

3   Set a specific goal—and set deadlines.

4   Get an enthusiastic mentor—fast.

5   Start with the big picture first.

6   Ask!

7   Seek out the main principle.

8   Find the three best books written by practical achievers.

9   Relearn how to read efficiently.

10   Reinforce with pictures and sound.

11   Learn by doing.

12   Draw Mind Maps instead of linear notes.

13   Easy ways to retrieve what you've learned.

14   Learn the art of relaxed awareness.

15   Practise, practise, practise.

16   Review and reflect.

17   Use linking tools such as memory pegs.

18   Have fun, play games.

19   Teach others.

20   Go digital!

How to take your talent and passion and learn other skills and ability

The Gallup organisation's survey of one million people is very clear: "Everyone has a talent to be exceptional at something." [1]

Generally that will be your passion, too. And the trick is first to define that talent—and then develop the skills and ability to achieve your maximum potential.

And while this chapter will appeal to everyone—students, teachers, parents and anyone in business—it's main emphasis is on do-it-yourself self-starters, and those who would like to be: how you can develop your skills away from a classroom or training room.

In it, you'll learn twenty simple tips to develop learning skills.

1. Start with the lessons from sport

Sport probably provide a much better learning model than many schools. There are at least eight lessons you can learn from it:

1. All sports achievers have a dream. They dream the impossible and make it happen.

The champion wants to break the 3 minute 50 second barrier for the mile. Or take the Olympic gold. Or be in a world series winning team.

All sports achievers, at every level, have dreams. It may be to break 100 at golf, then 90, then 80. Or to become the club tennis champion. Or to run the New York marathon at age 65.

2. All have specific goals. And they break those goals down into achievable steps. So while the dream is always there, they build on their

185

Eleven steps to sporting success

1️⃣ **Have a vision**
2️⃣ **Develop a plan**
3️⃣ **Set goals**
4️⃣ **Select well**
5️⃣ **Induct well**
6️⃣ **Motivate**
7️⃣ **Continuously learn**
8️⃣ **Involve players**
9️⃣ **Value mistakes**
🔟 **Encourage flair**
1️⃣1️⃣ **Use common sense**

JOHN HART
The New Zealand international rugby coach*

* Summarised from *Success in New Zealand Business 2,* by Paul Smith,
published by Hodder Moa Beckett, Auckland, New Zealand.

successes. You can't become a world champion overnight; you have to tackle hurdles regularly along the way—and celebrate each success as it is achieved.

3. All sports achievers combine mind, body and action. They know that their goals can be achieved when they link the right mental attitude, fitness, diet and physical skills.

4. They all have vision; they learn to visualise their goal. To *see* their achievements in advance. To play through their next football match like a video of the mind. Jack Nicklaus, possibly the greatest golfer of all time, says 90 percent of his success has come from his ability to visualise where every individual shot is going to land.

5. They all have passion. They have an overwhelming desire to succeed.

6. Each one has a coach, a mentor, a guide. In fact, we can probably learn more about real education from the success of the American college coaching system than we can from most school classes. If you doubt it, how many Olympic athletes, basketball and football stars have emerged from colleges—where the coaches are mentors, friends and guides?

7. All sports achievers have a fantastically positive attitude toward mistakes. They don't even call them mistakes; they call them *practice.* Even Roger Federer, John McEnroe and Martina Navratilova belted balls into the net thousands of times on their way to the top in tennis. No teacher marked those shots as failures. They were all essential parts of learning.

8. They all achieve by doing. Sport is a hands-on operation. You don't get fit by reading a book—although that may help with the theory. You don't develop the right muscles staring at a television set. You don't long-jump over 28 feet in a classroom. All sports achievements result from *action.*

Former American Olympian pentathlete Marilyn King says all astronauts, Olympic athletes and corporate executives have three things in common:

"They have something that really matters to them; something they really want to do or be. We call it *passion.*

"They can see a goal really clearly, and the 'how to' images begin to appear like magic. While the goal may seem bold, they can imagine doing all these little steps on the road to that goal. We call it *vision.*

"Finally, they are willing to do something each day, according to a

An Olympian's challenge

If you have passion plus vision but no action

You're daydreaming

If you have vision plus action but no passion

You'll be mediocre

If you have passion plus action but no vision

You'll get there but find it the wrong goal

MARILYN KING*

* American pentathlete, from her *Olympian Thinking* programme.

plan, that will bring them one step closer to their dream. We call it *action.*

"Passion + vision + action is our equation for success."[2]

Marilyn King runs courses and seminars teaching *Olympian Thinking* to corporate executives. She has also launched a *Dare To Imagine* project to pass on the same techniques to at-risk young people in her home city of Oakland, California.

So how can you apply the same principles to anything else you want to achieve and learn—and how can you do it faster, better, easier?

2. Dare to dream—and imagine your future

If, as we believe, nearly all things are now possible: what would you really like to do? What's your real *passion?* The thing you'd like to do more than anything else? Make great wine? Become the district golf champion? Get a doctorate? Start a new career?

Nearly every major achievement in the world has started with a vision: from Ford to Disneyland, Sony to Apple. So take up Marilyn King's challenge—and *dare to imagine what you'd like to achieve.*

3. Set a specific goal—and set deadlines

Ask yourself first: What specifically do I want to learn? Why do I want to learn it?

If it's a new job, a new skill, a new hobby, a trip overseas, a new sport, a musical instrument or a new challenge, what will you need to know?

It's easier to learn anything if you have a set goal. When you've done that, break it down into achievable bite-sized pieces. Then set realistic deadlines for each step, so you can see your success from the start.

4. Get an enthusiastic mentor—fast

Whatever you want to learn, many others have already learned it. When you've set your goals, find an enthusiast you can come to for specific advice. And if you can swap skills, even better.

Let's say you're a printer who wants to learn word processing. Obviously you'll be skilled in typography. So find a word processing specialist in a computer publishing field. You teach them typography while they teach you word processing. If you're new to a firm, do the same thing. Find someone who can help, regularly. Someone in the office or only a phone call away.

Remember jigsaw puzzles: they're much easier when you can see the whole picture first.

GORDON DRYDEN*

* In *Back to Real "Basics":* programme 4 in the *Where To Now?* New Zealand television series.

If you want to play golf, take professional lessons—certainly. But find a good player whose style you admire, and ask if you can play a game or two together.

The same principles apply if you're learning new technology. No one ever learned to operate a computer solely from a 700-page manual. Each student learned hands-on, with a coach.

5. Start with the big picture first

Learn from the marketers of jigsaw puzzles. If you started to assemble 10,000 pieces of a giant jigsaw puzzle one by one, it might take you years to finish. But if you can see the total picture on the package, you'll know exactly what you're building. Then it's much easier to fit each piece into place.

We're amazed at how often common sense disappears in educational systems. Subjects are taught in isolation. They're often taught in small segments, without students knowing the big picture first.

In real life, that's not the best way. It would take you years to discover New York by walking down every street. So what do you do as a tourist? You go to the top of the Empire State Building. Preferably with a New York guide. And you put yourself in the big picture. You can see Central Park, the Staten Island Ferry, the Statue of Liberty, Wall Street, the two main rivers, the key bridges, Broadway, Greenwich Village, the United Nations headquarters and the way the city is laid out in numbered avenues and streets. Then when someone tells you an address is ten blocks south of Central Park on Sixth Avenue, or four blocks east of the Lincoln Tunnel, you have a mental picture of where to go. You can build on your overall image Mind Map.

Many traditional schools still introduce subjects through textbook lectures spread over months. You're taught to read each chapter slowly and deliberately—a week at a time—without ever having the "big overview". That's crazy. It's inefficient.

Instead, try this simple experiment. Next time you're planning anything, seek out the simplest overview. If you're visiting a new city, get the colour tourist brochures in advance. They'll show you the main highlights. Or go to your public library, seek out an encyclopedia summary and duplicate it.

Then when you've got the big picture, build up the details. You'll know where they fit. Remember that jigsaw puzzle.

I keep six honest serving men, they taught me all I knew: Their names are What and Why and When and How and Where and Who.

RUDYARD KIPLING
The Elephant Child

6. Ask!

It's the best three-letter word in the learner's dictionary. Never be afraid to ask. And never be afraid to ask the best experts you can find—even if you've never met them before.

We hope it won't be long before each of us has a home computer/video/Internet terminal linked with international databanks. But even then you'll have to ask for what you want. So begin now.

Start with the Internet and the World Wide Web. It provides an incredible array of information—almost instantly. And one of the best steps you can make as a lifelong learner is to find your way around the Web. If you're a beginner, log on to *www.edutopia.org* for an introduction to some of the world's best websites for schooling. Then start navigating around the main "search engines". If you're involved in school, check out The Internet Library, set up in the tiny Nebraska town of Wayne: a well-researched guide to more than 260,000 websites vetted and graded for school and homework. It's a pay-service but you can test it free.

Then use your public library. It's not merely a book centre. It's a learning resource. Librarians are trained to help you. Call them before you visit; tell them specifically what you want to do; and ask them for the best beginner's guide. Use that for your overview; then build on it. But be specific. If you're a business executive planning a visit to Japan, ask them for simple guides to the country, its business, its culture, and the industry you're involved in.

If you learn easily by reading, that overview will probably be a book, a booklet or an article. If you learn best visually, seek out a DVD, or at least a book with plenty of coloured pictures and graphics. If you learn best by listening, get CDs or audio tapes and play them in your car.

But don't stop at the library. Find someone from college who's studying the field you're interested in. Ask the name of the best professor—the one who's the best simplifier. And phone him.

Or phone the university library, the nearest research institute, the best firm in the business. And don't be afraid to go to the top. If you want to learn about another country, call its embassy or consulate. Or its trade or tourist office. Or one of its major companies. Make asking a habit. It's probably the simplest thing you can learn from journalism. How do you think all that information gets into newspapers, on to television and radio every day?

Who?
What?
Where?
When?
How?
Why?

The journalists' creed for finding information.

7. Seek out the main principle

In nearly every field you'll find one main principle for success. Or perhaps two or three. Find them out first—before you fill in the details.

In photography, the first principle for an amateur: never take a photo more than four feet from your subject. Second principle: preferably shoot without a flash, with a semiautomatic camera. On those two principles, one of the co-authors paid for a world trip by taking photographs!

In cost accounting, the main principle: there's no such thing as an accurate cost, unless your business is running twentyfour hours a day, 365 days a year, on automatic equipment and with a guaranteed market for all you produce. Second principle: find the break-even point. Below that you're losing money. Above it you're making a profit.

In talkback radio, the main principle: no matter how big or small the city, if the host asks only for *opinions* he'll get the same 30 uninformed callers every day; if he asks for *specific interesting experiences* he'll get new interesting callers, with stimulating new information.

In education, a main principle: people learn best what they passionately want to learn, and they learn fastest by actually *doing.*

In journalistic interviewing, the first principle: ask *what* and *why.*

How do you find main principles? First you ask. Then:

8. Find the best three books by practical achievers

Don't start with academic textbooks. In the area of your interest, find the three best books written by people who've *done it.*

If you want to study advertising, call Saatchi & Saatchi or a top agency and ask their creative director what to read. She'll almost certainly recommend *Ogilvy on Advertising* as an overview. And if you want to study print-media copywriting: John Caples' *How To Make Your Advertising Make Money* and *Tested Advertising Methods.*

To practice new skills in thinking, start with the best book we know on the subject, Michael Michalko's *Cracking Creativity.* Then deal cards from Roger von Oech's *Creative Whackpack*—a brilliant ideas-starter. His first book, *A Whack On The Side Of The Head,* is also good.

To simplify business, try Robert Townsend's *Up The Organisation,,* and Buckingham and Coffman's *First, Break All The Rules.*

For three books on effective learning, try one of Tony Buzan's many books, *Accelerated Learning For the 21st Century* by Colin Rose and

The gap between what can be imagined and what can be accomplished has never been smaller.

GARY HAMEL
Leading The Revolution*

* Published by Harvard Business Press.

Malcolm J. Nicholl, and *Teaching and Learning Through Multiple Intelligences,* by Linda Campbell, Bruce Campbell and Dee Dickinson.

If you're a teacher, maybe read *The Everyday Genius* by Peter Kline, *SuperTeaching* by Eric Jensen, and *The Thinking Learning Classroom* by Glenn Capelli and Sean Brealey.

For more about your brain, try *The Amazing Brain* by Robert Ornstein and Richard F. Thompson, *Inside The Brain* by Ronald Kotulak, and *Emotional Intelligence* by Daniel Goleman.

More books are suggested at the back of this book. But in your own field ask the nearest expert to suggest a beginner's guidebook.

9. Relearn how to read—faster, better, more easily

Amazingly, few people know how to read properly. And we're not talking about super reading techniques at thousands of words a minute.

Let's start with two questions: Do you think you could regularly read four books a day and absorb the main points?* Have you read a newspaper this week?

If you answered the first question no, and the second yes— think again. If you read a daily newspaper in any major city, you've read the equivalent of at least four books. And the Sunday editions of the *New York Times*, *Los Angeles Times* or any major British paper are equal to dozens of volumes.

And how do you read a newspaper? You read only those things you are interested in. And how do you know? Because newspapers are divided into sections, so you only read the sports pages if you're interested in sports, the business pages for business. But even then you don't read every sports story or every business article. Newspaper headlines highlight the main points, and make it easy for you to select. Even the writing style of newspapers makes it easy to glean the main points. After each headline, you'll generally find them summarized in the first paragraph. So you can either read the summary or devour the whole story.

Over half of a newspaper is advertising. But you don't read every ad. Advertisers flag your attention with headlines and pictures. Classified

* *In almost eight years as a radio talkshow host, Gordon Dryden read, on average, fifteen new books a week—well over 6,000 in total—and generally skim-read two or three others a day, using the techniques covered here.*

If you can read a newspaper in an hour, you already know how to read at least four books a day.

ads are in alphabetical order. So even if you want to buy a house, you don't read all the *Houses for sale* pages. You select those in your preferred suburb, listed alphabetically.

Very simply, *you've cracked the newspaper code.* You know the formula. You know how to skim-read a newspaper every day. So you already know how to skim-read four books or anything else in print. The secret is to crack each book's code, to find each publication's formula. Court reporters, for example, know the standard format for written judgments. The judge normally reviews the case and the main arguments for many pages, then delivers his or her finding in the last paragraph. So reporters never start reading a court judgment from the front. They start on the last page—generally at the last paragraph—because they are reading the judgment to report the verdict.

And the same principle applies to all nonfiction reading. First ask yourself: *Why am I reading this? What do I want to get out of it? What new information will I want to learn? Then find the book's formula.*

Nearly every nonfiction book will state its main purpose in an introduction—as this book has done. This will tell you whether the book can provide the answers you want. Then you have to decide whether you need to read every chapter. You've almost certainly come to the subject with some basic knowledge which you're looking to extend. So you don't have to read all the material unless you want to refresh your memory.

Generally, nonfiction authors write books like speeches: in the introduction, the speaker tells you what he's going to tell you; then he tells you; then he summarises what he's told you. And often each chapter is written in a similar way: the chapter title and first paragraph or paragraphs indicate the theme, the chapter amplifies it, and it may end with a summary. If the book has subheadings, they'll help as well.

Many books have other pointers. With colour pictures, skim them and their "captions". Tom Peters' *Thriving on Chaos* summarises each chapter on a separate page at the start of each chapter. In the book you are now reading, key points are highlighted on every other page.

In brief, read every nonfiction book like a recipe book. If you want to cook pork chow mein tonight, you don't read every page in *The 1,000 Recipe Chinese Cookbook*. You read only what you need to know. This tip alone will enable you to read four books in the same time it takes to skim a newspaper.

Another tip: do NOT read "slowly and deliberately". Look out your

How to skim-read a book*

❏ **First, define what information you are seeking.**

❏ **Then hold your book about 20 inches away from your eyes: far enough to see the whole page.**

❏ **Run your index finger down the centre of the page, with your eyes looking just above your fingertip.**

❏ **Move the finger so fast that you do not have time to stop at each word and pronounce it to yourself.**

*Generally, this advice applies to nonfiction reading, where you are reading to gain information for a specific purpose. The same techniques can be used to read fiction, but even most good readers prefer to read fiction more slowly, so they can savour the atmosphere, the plot and the word-pictures.

window right now. Then reflect on your brain's fantastic ability to take in all that information instantly. You've got 130 million light receivers in each of your eyes, with a magic ability to flash that scene to your visual cortex. That's your brain's holistic ability to "photograph" a complete picture. Learn to use it.

Even those pages you think you need to read will include much information that can be skimmed. Remember your purpose, and the key answers you are seeking. For instance, school teachers, business executives and people approaching "retirement" are probably reading this book for different reasons.

So learn to skim for the points you want. Start by holding this book in one hand far enough from your eyes to see the entire page—generally about eighteen to twenty inches: about 50cm. With your other hand use your index finger or a retracted ball-point pen. Practise running either your finger or the pen quite quickly down the centre of each page, with your eyes looking just above the point of your pen or finger, following it down. You'll be amazed at what you can take in, if you know specifically what you are looking for.

This is not just speed-reading. It's sensible skim-reading and selective reading. If you're looking for main principles, then that skim-reading may be all you'll need. If you're looking for specific information and quotes to include in a report, article or book, you'll need to stop and note them. If you own the book, use it as a dynamic resource. Mark key information with a highlighter. If the book is not yours, write down page numbers. Return to them and write or type out the key points. The physical act of writing or typing will help embed them in your brain's memory-vaults—learning through the sense of touch as well as sight. Better still, highlighting will make it easy to refresh your memory when you want to retrieve the information later.

10. Reinforce with pictures and sound

Because you've read this far, you're obviously a print-oriented learner, and a linguistic learner. But you can also learn better if you reinforce the message with pictures and sound. So check out whether simple video or audio tapes are available on the subject you're studying.

And if you have family members who are not great readers, encourage them to *start* with their preferred learning style.

If one's an auditory learner, make her car into a university with a

Just do it!*

❏ **You learn to talk by talking**

❏ **You learn to walk by walking**

❏ **You learn golf by golfing**

❏ **You learn typing by typing**

❏ **You learn best by doing it!**

* The slogan for Nike footwear.

cassette-player. If one has a visual learning style, then seek out picture books, videos, digital video discs, and interactive computer programmes.

11. Learn by doing

We can't stress enough the need to engage all your senses. We give practical suggestions in other chapters.

But for do-it-yourselfers, when you check out introductory courses— or advanced ones— make sure they provide hands-on experience.

You learn to cook by cooking. You learn to play tennis by playing tennis. And even when you take golf lessons, every good professional gets you right into action.

Education is generally ineffective when it separates theory from practice. So make an effort to learn through more than one sense. If you're learning a foreign language, try to picture the scene you're learning, try to imprint the information through other senses.

To learn to count to ten in Japanese, for instance, try miming the words with actions (see routine, page 324).

Good teachers and accelerated learning courses use many other techniques, as we'll explore later. But for do-it-yourselfers, interactive technology can now help greatly. Let's take two of the most complicated non-physical games: bridge and chess. You can learn both by playing— especially with a good coach.

But bridge or chess masters don't really want to spend hours playing with a novice. So, as we have seen, some have now put their knowledge into interactive computer games. So, as well as playing with your friends, you can "play the computer."

At bridge, you can see your cards on the screen and, if you win the bidding, you can see your partner's hand to play it. The computer will play your opponents' hands. And when each hand is over you have a choice of seeing all hands—and checking how the cards should have best been played.

In most computer chess games, you can choose your level of competency, from novice to advanced; the computer will play at the same level.

12. Draw Mind Maps instead of taking linear notes

There's no use taking in important information if you can't recall it when you need it. And here traditional schooling methods are archaic.

Draw Mind Maps© instead of taking linear notes

An adaptation of the Mind Mapping principle originated by Tony Buzan, and computer-created here by Dilip Mukerjea, of The Buzan Centre, Singapore. Note:

1.   The main theme is in the centre.

2.   There is a main branch for each sub-theme.

3.   Single words are used for each concept.

4.   Where possible, each concept has a picture.

DILIP MUKERJEA
*SuperBrain**

* Originally published by Oxford University Press, Singapore.
For this book and information on other books in the series,
contact Dilip Mukerjea at: dilip@pacific.com.sg

© Mind Map is a copyrighted trademark of Tony Buzan.

Tens of thousands of students around the world right now are taking notes. They're writing down words line by line. Or in some languages, column by column. But the brain doesn't work that way. It does not store information in neat lines or columns. The brain stores information on its treelike dendrites. It stores information by *pattern and association.* So the more you can work in with the brain's own memory-method, the easier and faster you'll learn.

So don't take notes, make Mind Maps. And make them with trees, with pictures, with colours, with symbols, with patterns and associations. Mind Mapping is a method devised by Tony Buzan. Singapore-based author and Buzan facilitator Dilip Mukerjea has written and illustrated an excellent introduction to the subject, entitled *SuperBrain.*

Swedish publisher Ingemar Svantesson has produced *Mind Mapping and Memory.* And in the United States the finest book on a similar theme is Nancy Margulies' *Mapping InnerSpace.* Margulies has also written a great accelerated-learning book *Yes, You Can Draw!* and produced a first-class video to go with it.

Those books, and some of the Mind Maps in this one, demonstrate the principles in practice. The main points are simple:

1. Imagine your brain-cells are like trees, with each one storing related information on its branches.

2. Now try arranging the key points of any topic on a sheet of white paper in the same treelike format.

3. Start with the central topic—preferably with a symbol—in the centre of the page, then draw branches spreading out from it. If you're Mind Mapping New York, use the Statue of Liberty as the centrepoint. If it's Sydney, use the harbour bridge. If it's our chapter on the brain, sketch a two-sided brain.

4. Generally record only one word and/or symbol for each point you want to recall—one main theme to each branch.

5. Put related points on the same main branches, each one shooting off like a new subbranch.

6. Use different coloured pencils or markers for related topics.

7. Draw as many pictures and symbols as you can.

8. When you've completed each branch, enclose it in a different colored border.

9. Add to each map regularly. In this way it's easy to start with the

The principles of smart reading in map form

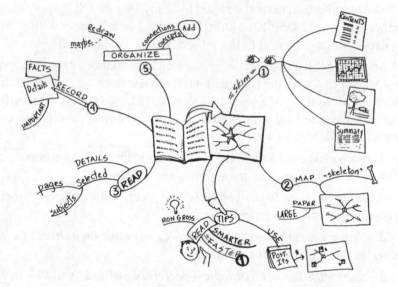

In her book, *Mapping InnerSpace,* Nancy Margulies* draws this map to illustrate the key concepts of "smart reading":

1.   Skim-check the main points first.

2.   Prepare a large map skeleton.

3.   Read not merely faster, but smarter.

4.   Record key facts and important details on your map.

5.   Organise concepts together, and when you've finished the book or other reading matter, redraw your Mind Map if you feel it needs to be simplified.

* From *Mapping InnerSpace,* by Nancy Margulies, published
by Zephyr Press, Tucson, Arizona, and reprinted
here with permission.

overview and then build up your Mind Map as you learn more key points about each subject.

13. Easy ways to retrieve what you've learned

Since the brain stores information by patterns and associations, and Mind Maps record it in the same way, then it's sensible to use the same methods for easy recall.

Here some more brain-knowledge will come in handy. Your brain has both a short-term and a long-term memory. And that's fortunate. You come to an intersection as the traffic light is turning red, and you stop. The lights turn green and you go. Your long-term memory has learned and remembered the rules about traffic lights. But your short-term memory doesn't have to remember each of the thousands of times you stop for the red light.

So how do you store and retrieve the information you need for long-term use? Partly by patterns and associations.

Mind Mapping is just one method. Another is to use all your intelligence-centres, including those involved with rhyme, rhythm, repetition and music. You don't have to spend hours on boring rote memory. As you've read this book, highlighted key phrases and subheadings and made a Mind Map of the main points, we suggest you do two things immediately you have finished:

1. Immediately reskim the key points you've highlighted.

2. Redo your Mind Map. This will also help you link your main lessons: by pattern and association. Almost certainly, if you're new to Mind Mapping, you'll have found it difficult to list each key point in only one word. But try to do so. It's very important.

Then tonight, not too long before you're thinking of sleeping, play some relaxing music. Take another look at your Mind Map. Reflect on the main lessons you have learned and visualise them.

Think of the associations—because that state of almost reverie, just before sleep, is a vital part of the learning process.

14. Learn the art of relaxed alertness

Up to now, most suggestions are for "left hemisphere" activities. But to make use of the extraordinary powers of your right hemisphere and your subconscious, *the real key to effective learning can be summed up*

Your brainwaves

1. Beta

2. Alpha

3. Theta

4. Delta

These are actual recordings of human
brainwaves—from top:
1. When wide awake—the conscious mind,
operating at 13 to 25 cycles per second,
the so-called beta state.
2. The ideal learning state of "relaxed alertness,"
8 to 12 CPS— alpha.
3. The early stages of sleep, 4 to 7 CPS—theta:
the mind is processing the day's information.
4. Deep sleep, 0.5 to 3 CPS—delta.
Note: these are approximations.

in two words: relaxed alertness—your state of mind, especially when you start any learning session.

We've already mentioned brainwaves. Now let's start to put them to use. Your brain operates, much like a television or radio station, on four main frequencies or waves. We can measure them with an EEG machine (electro-encephalograph).

If you're wide awake and alert at the moment, or if you're talking, making a speech or working out an involved problem in logic, your brain is probably "transmitting" and "receiving" at 13 to 25 cycles per second. Some call this the beta level.

But that's not the best state for stimulating your long-term memory. Most of the main information you learn will be stored in your subconscious mind. Many researchers and teachers believe that the vast bulk of information is also best learned subconsciously. And *the brainwave activity that links best with the subconscious mind is at 8 to 12 cycles per second: alpha.*

Says British accelerated learning innovator Colin Rose: "This is the brainwave that characterises relaxation and meditation, the state of mind during which you daydream, let your imagination run. It is a state of relaxed alertness that facilitates inspiration, fast assimilation of facts and heightened memory. Alpha lets you reach your subconscious, and since your self-image is primarily in your subconscious it is the only effective way to reach it."[3]

When you start getting sleepier—the twilight zone between being fully awake and fully asleep—your brainwaves change to between 4 and 7 cycles per second: theta.

When you're fully into deep sleep, your brain is operating at between .5 and 3 cycles per second: delta. Your breathing is deep, your heartbeat slows and your blood pressure and body temperature drop.

And the impact of all this on learning and memory? American accelerated learning pioneer Terry Wyler Webb says beta waves—the very fast ones—are "useful for getting us through the day, but they inhibit access to the deeper levels of the mind. Deeper levels are reached in the alpha and theta brainwave patterns, which are characterised by subjective feelings of relaxation, concentrated alertness and well-being. *It is in the alpha and theta states that the great feats of supermemory, along with heightened powers of concentration and creativity, are achieved."* [4]

And how do you achieve that state? Thousands of people do it with

Music can do in minutes what weeks of meditative practice strive towards.

COLIN ROSE
*Accelerated Learning**

*Published by Accelerated Learning Systems,
Aston Clinton, Bucks, England.

daily meditation, or relaxing exercises, especially deep breathing. But more and more teachers are convinced that some types of music can achieve the results much quicker and easier. Says Webb: "Certain types of musical rhythm help relax the body, calm the breath, quieten the beta chatter and evoke a gentle state of relaxed awareness which is highly receptive to learning new information."

Of course many types of music can help you remember messages when the music is accompanied by words—as television and radio advertising prove every day. But researchers[5] have now found that some baroque music is ideal for rapidly improving learning, partly because its main 60-to-70 beats-to-the-minute is identical to the alpha brainwaves.

Skilled teachers are now using this music as an essential ingredient of all accelerated-learning teaching. But for do-it-yourself learners, the immediate implications are simple: play the right type of music at night when you want to review your material, and you'll dramatically increase your recall.

In part that's because of how your brain works most efficiently when you're dropping off to sleep. Some call it R.E.M. sleep. The initials stand for *rapid eye movement*. And EEGs tell you why: it's almost as if your mind—even with your body asleep—is using its visual cortex to take quick frame-by-frame photographs of the day's main events.

Many researchers believe that in this state the brain is sorting out new information and storing it in the appropriate memory banks. And quiet relaxation as you review your Mind Maps, and reflect on the day's main points, opens up the pathways to those subconscious storage files.

That probably also explains why you dream: your subconscious is "dialing up" your old memories to collate the new information. And if you're thinking through a problem, your subconscious sifts through some alternative solutions, as we'll discuss in the next chapter.

The alpha state is also ideal for starting each new specific study period. Quite simply, it makes great sense to clear the mind before you start. Take your office problems on the golf course and you'll never play great golf. Your mind will be elsewhere. The same applies to study. Come straight from a high school French class to a mathematics lecture and it can be hard to "switch gears".

But take a few moments to do deep breathing exercises, and you'll start to relax. Play some relaxing music, close your eyes and think of the most peaceful scene you can imagine—and soon you'll be in the state of

Music suggestions

Use different music for different purposes.

For creating a calm atmosphere

Relaxing music, like *Mountains Are Far Away,* by the Silk Road Ensemble; most of Corelli's 12 concertos, from op. 6; and specialised, sequenced baroque music in OptimaLearning Classics, 303 and 601, from Barzak Institute.

Groovy music for getting in the mood

Especially for cooperative learning activities, *Children,* by Robert Miles; *Sweet Lullaby,* by Deep Forest; *Moments of Love,* by Art of Noise; or *At The River,* by Groove Amanda.

For "clustering" and fast writing exercises

Baya Baya, by Safri Duo; *X-Files,* by Music Sculptors; or most fast Chopin preludes.

For poetry or "reflective writing"

Most Romantic classics like Chopin and Brahms music; most George Winston or Enya music; *To a Wild Rose,* by Chris Davis; or *Novio,* by Moby.

For content put to raps or songs, such as lists, tables

Ray Ray Album Instrumentals; Safri Duo Instrumentals.

For "state changes"

Vary the music depending on the age groups, but generally any upbeat instrumental music, such as *Sand Storm,* by Darude; *Lifting Me,* by The Corrs. For teenagers, other songs by popular artists Destiny's Child, Boys to Men, Anastasia, but be sure to monitor the words of the song before using. David Bowie, Bruce Springstein or Bob Dylan music for those from an earlier era.

For getting started, as a "come in" song:

Around The World, by Planet Pop, or similar upbeat artists.

These are from selections used by Jeannette Vos. See also Chapter 8 for specific selections of music for "passive" and "active" concerts, terms covered in later text.

relaxed alertness that makes it easier to "float information" into your long-term memory.

15. Practise, practise, practise

If you're learning to speak French, speak it. If you're learning about computers, use them. If you've taken a course in Asian cooking, cook an Asian feast for your friends. If you're studying shorthand, write it. If you want to be a public speaker, join Toastmasters—and speak publicly. If you want to be a writer, write. If you want to be a bartender, mix drinks.

Remember the sporting maxim: it's not a mistake, it's practice.

16. Review and reflect

When you're learning a physical-mental skill, like typing or cooking, you can practise it with action. But in gaining other types of knowledge, make sure you review regularly. Look again at your Mind Map and review the main points immediately you've finished it. Do it again in the morning. And again a week later. Once more a month later. Then review it, and other associated data, before you have specific need for it: for an examination, an overseas trip, a speech or whatever. Before reading a new book, for instance, many people find it helps to first look at their existing Mind Maps on the subject, or skim-read the highlighted parts of three of four books that they've already read on the subject.

17. Use linking tools as memory pegs

Since the memory works best by association, develop your own "memory pegs". Associate newly acquired knowledge with something you already know.

The association can be physical or tactile: such as learning to count in Japanese by scratching your knee (see exercise, page 324).

It can be visual: like visualising scenes to remember names—forging gold in a blacksmith's shop to remember Mr. Goldsmith, a picture of a crocodile under a McDonald's arch to remember founder Ray Krok.

It can be a strong visual story: like picturing a sequence to remember, say, the planets in order from earth—the hot sun shining so strongly it breaks a thermometer, and all the Mercury spills out; this runs outside where a beautiful woman, Venus, is standing on the Earth; it keeps running over the earth into the next-door neighbour's red-earth garden—

I never worked a day in my life. It was all fun.

THOMAS EDISON

a warlike neighbour, Mars, appears and starts hurling abuse. But just then a smiling giant appears, Jupiter—the biggest planet—and on his superman-type chest he has the word SUN emblazoned, for Saturn, Uranus and Neptune, and running alongside him is a happy dog, Pluto.

It can be rhyming and visual: like memorising numbers with rhyming pictorial words, and linking them up with the items to be memorized: so that **one** becomes **sun; two, shoe; three, tree; four, door; five, hive; six, sticks; seven, heaven; eight, gate; nine, mine;** and **ten, hen.** To remember ten items, such as on a shopping list, link each one *visually* with the numbered sequence—so that if your first three items are butter, cheese and milk, you visualise butter being melted with the sun (one), cheese in a shoe (two), and milk being poured over a tree (three).

It can use the initial letter principle: as marketing people remember the key elements of advertising by AIDA: *attract Attention, arouse Interest, create Desire,* and *urge Action.*

But whichever association method you use, *try to make it outlandish, funny and preferably emotional—because the "filter" in the brain that transfers information to your long-term memory is very closely linked with the brain's emotional centre. And link your associations with as many senses as you can: sight, sound, smell, touch and taste.*

18. Have fun, play games

Ask a friend what images flash to mind when you mention education or study. Now see how they tally with Tony Buzan's experience. He says: "In my 30 years of investigating people's associations with the word 'study,' ten major words or concepts have emerged. They are: boring, exams, homework, waste of time, punishment, irrelevant, detention, 'yuck,' hate and fear."[6]

But ask a four-year-old fresh out of a good preschool centre and she'll talk about the fun she had. So nearly all progressive educators now stress the need to recapture the fun-filled joy of early learning. And humour itself is a great way to learn. So try to link humour with study. Think up games to play to reinforce the key points with someone who's studying the same subject—even *Trivial Pursuit*-type quizzes can be great aids.

19. Teach others

"Each one—teach one." That's the recommended theme for the future from California brain-researcher Marian Diamond.

It's a whole new Web, and this time it will be built by you.

BUSINESS WEEK
*It's a Whole New Web**

* September 26, 2005.

"I want to introduce the concept," she says, "that everyone can learn to be a teacher. One has to be accurate with the facts as a teacher, yet imaginative with creative ideas for new directions in the future. As we learn the facts, we can turn around and share with the next person so that the 'association cortices' can create the new ideas."[7]

Whatever your age there are few better ways to crystallise what you've learned than to teach the principles to others, to make a speech or to run a seminar.

20. Go digital!

We've already touched on the importance of *asking* for what you want to know, including asking on the Web. We cannot stress it strongly enough.

Marc C. Rosenberg, in his book *e-Learning,* says the Web is "nothing short of the world's library". But it is now much, much more than that. It's your passport to museums, art galleries and almost every newspaper in the world.

Start by learning to use Google, the world's best search engine. Contact *www.google.com* and, in the "search" line provided, type in whatever information you want. But make it specific: not simply "wine" but perhaps: *Wine United States gold medal winners 2006.*

On the same page as your search inquiry, Google tells you now many Web-site pages it can scan in half a second, before delivering its answers. *www.news.google.com* gives you instant access to the latest news summarised from 4,000 different sources, without you having to type in the name of any newspaper, TV or radio station.

But don't stop there. Check out the online courses that are available on anything you want to learn.

But do not see the Web as only the world's best library. As *Business Week* puts it in a late-2005 update special issue: "It's a whole New Web. And this time around it will be built by you."[8]

Since we all learn by actually doing, and doing with all our senses, this New Web offers almost a new sense: a way of participating, sharing, collaborating, socialising and actually creating in many different ways.

❏ In switched-on South Korea, 15 million people—almost a third of the country's population, are members of *Cyworld.* This is an Internet service which allows people to create their own Web home pages: pages

'It's not about mass media. Its about My Media.'

FARZAD NAZEM
Chief Technology Officer, Yahoo*

* Business Week, September 26, 2005.

that can accommodate an unlimitded number of photos, documents and other goodies.   You can even enter it from your mobile phone. An average of 6.2 million photos are uploaded on to *Cyworld* each day, many of them directly from cell phones.   "I use *Cyworld* as the photo archieve for my family," says Kim Joon, a 31-year-old software engineer who met his wife through a *Cyworld* club. "My one-year-old son will have a photo log of his life in *Cyworld* twenty years later."

❏ On Yahoo's *Flickr,* millions of Americans are producing their own entertainment on video, social-networking and playing games.

❏ At *MySpace.com,* some 21 million monthly visitors spend up to several hours a day sharing their thoughts, photos and music with friends on personalised home pages.

Says Yahoo Chief Technology Officer Frazad Nazem: "It's not about mass media. It's about My Media."[9]

And, to make the most of it, there's now a growing array of other services to let you tailor the Web as you like it, and to help you learn new hi-tech skills in new, much easier ways.

As we'll see later in these pages, even six-year-olds, from their first days in primary school, are learning to use digital cameras, shoot digital videos of their classsmates, and to edit these like professionals, even adding their own music, computer animations and graphics.

❏ **If you're a technology-novice,** we'd suggest you start in the same way as the six-year-olds do: with digital cameras and videos. Then seek out simple community courses in improving your skills.

❏ **If you're into your "third age",** seek out the local SeniorNet, and you'll find others delighted to share their knowledge.

❏ **If you're a teacher,** either get your students to teach you or sign up for some training. But preferably go to conferences and seminars that link new methods of learning with the new technologies. Here New Zealand has pioneered some great models: two-day, four-day and five-day seminars which alternate sessions between the new learning and teaching methods and hands-on practice to use interactive technology. In two days, teachers can easily learn to master stage-one levels for at least four different digital applications: video editing, digital-photo processing, computer animation, and compiling all these into slide presentations.[10]

Better still, the experience sets you up to provide a completely new dimension to the most exciting of all pursuits: creating your own future.

Your checklist for producing ideas

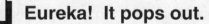 **Define your problem.***

 Define and visualise the ideal solution

 Gather the facts: specific, general.

 Break the pattern.

 Go outside your own field.

 Try new combinations.

 Use all your senses.

 Switch off — let it simmer.

9 **Use music or nature to relax.**

10 **Sleep on it.**

11 **Eureka! It pops out.**

12 **Recheck it.**

* Note: You can also reverse steps 1 and 2—start with your dream, next define where you are now, and then proceed to bridge the gap.

A creative thinking course for teachers and learners

For most of the last several hundred years, land, labour and capital have driven the economy.

For the first two thirds of the twentieth century, the mass-production methods started by Henry Ford took over as the main shapers of the industrial economy.

Now brainpower, ideas and innovation are the new drivers. And even more, the opportunity now for creative innovators in different countries to share their talents online. And, particularly for those in the "developed world", to share their creative abilities with others in emerging countries such as China and India.[1]

But, amazingly, the most important "subject" of all is not taught at most schools: how to invent your own future, how to create new ideas.

That gives us the opportunity to reinvent education and usher in a golden age of discovery and innovation: to reinvent they way we think, learn, work, live, enjoy ourselves and create. The models already exist.

Thomas Edison held 1093 patents,[2] and electrified the world. Walt Disney and Apple Computers' Steve Jobs[3] each founded giant commercial empires on the power of a new idea—and a different make-believe mouse. Ray Krok[4] was a middle-aged milk-shake machine seller when he first visited the California hamburger bar of Dick and Maurice McDonald. He was to take their basic concept, mix it with others, and turn the result into the world's biggest fast-food chain. And Sergey Brin and Larry Page took a new mathematics formula and turned it into Google.

Bill Gates is the the world's richest person firstly because he and his

An idea is a new combination of old elements.

**There are no new elements.
There are only new combinations.**

GORDON DRYDEN
Out Of The Red*

*Published by William Collins, Auckland, New Zealand.

partner, Paul Allen, had a dream to put a computer on every desk and in every home.*

Two of Europe's richest people*, the Rausing brothers,[5] owe their wealth to their father, Richard Rausing. While watching his wife prepare homemade sausages, he became intrigued by how she peeled back the skins to insert the ingredients. That idea, when reversed, turned into the system of pouring milk from cartons. And his heirs still receive royalties every day from millions of Tetrapak milk cartons.

All the great ideas in history, all the great inventions, obviously have one thing in common. All have come from the human brain. Just as the brain has fantastic ability to store information, it has an equal ability to reassemble that information in new ways: to create new ideas.

And very simply, *an idea is a new combination of old elements.* Write that down, underline it, reinforce it. It could be the most important sentence you ever write. It contains the key to creating new solutions. There are no new elements. *There are only new combinations.*[6]

Think for a moment of the thousands of different cookbooks around the world. Every recipe in every book is a different mixture of existing ingredients. Think of that example whenever you tackle a problem.

And all the breakthroughs everywhere—radio, television, the internal combustion engine—are new combinations of old bits. A push-button shower combines at least three "old" elements: hot and cold water and a mixing valve. Nylon and other "new" synthetic fibres are new combinations of molecules that have existed for hundreds of centuries. In nylon's case: recombined molecules from coal.

Since an idea is a new mixture of old elements, *the best ideas-creators are constantly preoccupied with new combinations.*

In most management courses, you learn the overriding need to define correctly the problem you want solved. *But now a new revolutionary element has emerged. We can now define the ideal solution in advance—and start creating it.*

* Swedish magazine Vecklans Affarer in 2004 puts Ingvar Kamprad, the founder of the IKEA furniture empire, ahead of Bill Gates and the heirs of Richard Rausing as the richest man in both Europe and the world, with a personal fortune of $53 billion. Kamprad denies this, stressing that he has placed IKEA control under a charitable trust. Kamprad's brilliant fortune-making idea: to sell simply-designed furniture cheaply by having the end user do his or her own assembly.

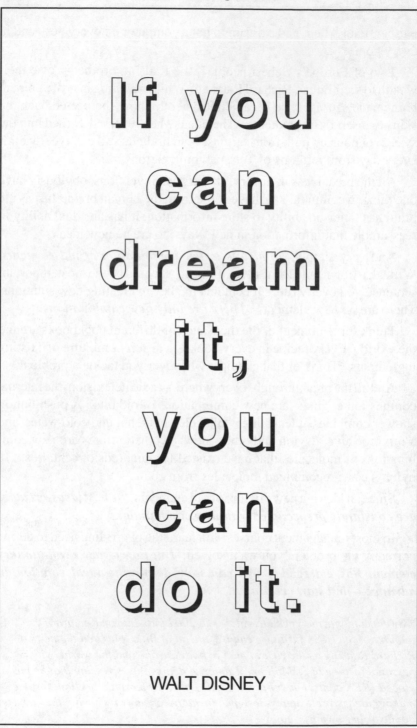

This is a revolutionary change. Whereas previously we organised our existing knowledge to solve a problem, within the limits of that knowledge, today we start by defining what we would like to achieve. And then we organise the things we don't know in order to achieve it.

Seventy years ago clothing manufacturers were stuck with such basic yarns as wool, cotton and silk. Then Wallace Corothers synthesised nylon in 1935. Today we can define the ideal garment, and then produce the fibres and mixtures to create it. Families became tired of darning socks, so science created a blend of nylon and wool to give us the benefit of both: a new mixture of old elements. Iron-weary mothers wanted shirts that would drip-dry without creases. So science created polyester fibres: a new combination of old elements. Fashion-conscious women liked the easy-care properties of nylon but pined for the fluffiness of wool. So science created acrylics—by recombining the elements of natural gas.

Peter Drucker, in *The Age of Discontinuity,* has crystallized the new innovative technique in a graphic way. He calls it "a systematic organised leap into the unknown". Unlike the science of yesterday, he says, "it is not based on organising our knowledge, it is based on organising our ignorance".

Amazingly these techniques are not taught in most schools, yet in many ways they are the key to the future.

Even worse: school tests are based on the principle that every question has one correct answer. But they don't.

California creative consultant Roger von Oech says, in *A Whack On The Side Of The Head:* "By the time the average person finishes college he or she will have taken over 2,600 tests, quizzes and exams. The 'right answer' approach becomes deeply ingrained in our thinking. This may be fine for some mathematical problems, where there is in fact only one right answer. The difficulty is that most of life isn't that way. Life is ambiguous; there are many right answers—all depending on what you are looking for. But if you think there is only one right answer, then you'll stop looking as soon as you find one." So how do you use your own brainpower to make Drucker's systematic organised leap into the unknown? These are the steps we've found most useful:

1. Define your problem

One first step is to define in advance your problem—specifically but not restrictively.

Vertical thinking is digging the same hole deeper. Lateral thinking is trying again elsewhere.

EDWARD de BONO
originator of Lateral Thinking*

*Author interview, Radio i, Auckland, New Zealand.

2. Define your ideal solution and visualise it

Step 2 is to define what you would like to achieve—ideally. And then you organise your 100 billion active brain neurons to bridge the gap between where you are and where you want to be. It also helps greatly to visualise the ideal solution, to picture "in your mind's eye" the best possible result.

Let's use a world-famous industry as a typical model: the watch industry. Up to 1970, the entire industry was dominated by Switzerland. But its business model had not changed in half a century. By 1970 it was still making sales of $10 billion a year. But "by the early 1980s, most of that value had migrated away from the traditional Swiss business model to new business designs owned by Timex, Citizen, Seiko and Casio. Employment tumbled in parallel with the drop in value. From the mid-1970s to the early 1980s, the number of workers in the Swiss watchmaking industry contracted from 90,000 to 20,000."[7]

So the industry called in consultant Nicolas Hayek. His experience in the industry: nil. But even as a boy "Hayek was always asking his family and teachers, 'Why do we do things the way we do?' He was born with an innate and incurable curiosity about the way things work and where we come from. He consumed every book he could find on physics, astronomy, the Big Bang, and Einstein's theories of mass and speed."[8]

And as an adult he applied that same curiosity to his newest challenge—and ended up reinventing an entire industry. Until he arrived on the scene, most people bought a watch to last a lifetime. And those flocking to the new Japanese brands were also doing so because of their low cost. But Hayek started with a new series of questions: What did people want from a watch? Fun? Spirit? Style? Variety? Fashion?

Those questions were to lead directly to the invention of the Swatch watch—not solely as a timekeeper but as an ever-changing fashion accessory. And with it, Hayek launched a marketing programme to persuade customers to wear a different-coloured watch with every dress or suit.

From 1983 to 1992, Swatch sold 100 million watches. By 1996 he had sold his 200 millionth.

Even the name itself emerged as typical of the innovation process. As Adrian J. Slywotzky and David J. Morrison recount in their excellent business book, *The Profit Zone:* "Hayek differentiated his watches by giving them a soul. He created a message, an emotional sense that appeals

The only dumb question is a question you don't ask.

PAUL MacCREADY
Inventor

to everyone, conveying a sense of fun, of style, and of lightheartedness. Then he wrapped it around indisputable high quality and low cost.

"All Hayek's new product lacked now was a name. 'We were working with an American advertising company,' Hayek says. 'We had the craziest names in the world and none pleased me. Finally, we went for lunch and this woman wrote on the blackboard "Swiss watch" and "second watch"' Then she wrote "Swatch". It helped that we were not very strong in English. We didn't know that "swatch" in English meant a cleaning towel. If we had known, we wouldn't have started the company with such a name!'" Problem defined. Vision set. And the two linked by new mixtures of old elements.

3. Gather all the facts

Since a great idea is a new combination of old elements, then the next step is to *gather all the facts* you can. *Unless you know a big array of facts on any situation or problem, you're unlikely to hit on the perfect new solution.*

Facts can be *specific:* those directly concerned with your job, industry or problem. And they can be *general:* the facts you gather from a thousand different sources. You will only be a great ideas-producer if you're a voracious seeker of information. A questioner. A reader. A challenger. And a storer of information, in notebooks and dendrites.

There is no substitute for personalised, purposeful homework. What comes out must have gone in. The key is to somehow link information filed in, say, "brain-cell number 369,124" on "dendrite 2,614", with another stored on "cell number 9,378,532"—or wherever.

Here your brain's patterning ability creates both problems and opportunities. Each one of us uses our brain for every waking minute to take action in a pre-patterned way —from walking to running, from driving a car to stopping at red lights. Your brain tends to store information in narrow channels, on associated "branches" for easy and quick retrieval, so we normally come up with the same answers.

4. Break the pattern

To solve problems creatively, however, you've got to *open up new pathways, find new crossover points, discover new linkages. You've got to break the pattern.*

And the easiest way to do that is to *start with questions that redirect*

Go outside your own field

❑ **The inventors of Kodachrome colour film, Leopold Mannes and Leopold Godowsky, were musicians.**

❑ **George Eastman (of Eastman Kodak) was originally a book keeper in a bank.**

❑ **Ladislo Biro, the inventor of the ballpoint pen, was in turn a sculptor, a painter and a journalist.**

❑ **King Camp Gillette (the inventor of the safety razor) was a travelling salesman in bottletops.**

❑ **John Boyd Dunlop (inventor of the air-inflated tyre) was a veterinary surgeon.**

GORDON RATTRAY TAYLOR
in *The Inventions That Changed The World**

*Published by Reader's Digest, 26 Waterloo Street, Sydney, NSW 2010, Australia.

your mind. What would happen to your problem if you doubled it, halved it, froze it, reconstituted it, reversed it, adapted it, rearranged it, combined it? What if you eliminated it—or part of it? If you substituted one of the parts? If you made it smaller, shorter, lighter? If you recoloured it, streamlined it, magnified it? If you repackaged it? Distributed it in a different way? What if you applied all your senses— and added scents or fragrances, added sounds or made it different to see or touch?

5. Go outside your own field

Put your existing preconceptions aside. The elements you use to solve problems should not only be those that are specific to the industry or process you're involved in. Use only those and you'll come up with the same old solutions.

Ask a teacher to redefine education, and generally he'll start thinking about school, and not about interactive videodiscs or life in 2010. Ask your brain to add 1 plus 1 and it will automatically answer 2. It's programmed that way.

But your brain has also stored facts about thousands of different interests: from recipes to football. The answers to problems in farming may well come from meanderings in space research. So all good inventors, innovators and creators develop an insatiable appetite for new knowledge. *Always remember to ask.*

6. Play with various combinations

Next: since an idea is a new combination of old elements, play with various combinations. Jot them down as they come to you. Try different starting points. Choose anything at random—a colour, an animal, a country—and try to link it up with your problem and solution.

Work at it. Keep your notepad full. But don't concentrate too closely on your specific field or you'll be limited by your own preconceptions.

Read as widely as you can—particularly writings away from your own speciality. Keep asking: *What if?* "What if I combined this with that? What if I started from here instead of there?" And keep asking.

7. Use all your senses

It also helps greatly to consciously try to engage all your senses. If

Who said this?

1. "The horse is here to stay, but the automobile is only a novelty—a fad."

2. "Heavier-than-air flying machines are impossible."

3. "Video won't be able to hold on to any market it captures after the first six months. People will soon get tired of staring at a plywood box every night."

4. "Everything that can be invented has been invented."

5. "Who the hell wants to hear actors talk?"

ANSWERS:

1. President of the Michigan Savings Bank, advising Henry Ford's lawyer not to invest in the Ford Motor Company.
2. Lord Kelvin, 1895.
3. Daryl F. Zanuck, head of 20th Century Fox movie studio, commenting on television in 1946.
4. Charles H. Duell, commissioner of the U.S. Office of Patents, in a 1899 report to President McKinley, arguing that the Patents Office should be abolished.
5. Harry M. Warner, president of Warner Bros., the movie company, in 1927.

your problem has been defined mathematically, try to visualise some answers. Remember how Albert Einstein's theory of relativity came to him after he'd been daydreaming, imagining that he was travelling through space on a moonbeam.

Mind Mapping, too, is an excellent creative tool—to link information together in new ways, on new branches, in new clusters, so your ideas are not merely listed in one-dimensional lines.

Work at it until your head swims. Then . . .

8. Switch off—let it simmer

Like good food after you've eaten it, let your digestive juices take over and do the work—in this case the digestive juices of your own subconscious. Note the relaxation techniques we've touched on in accelerated learning, to put your brain into its most receptive and creative mode.

9. Use music or nature to relax

Many people find it pays to play relaxing classical music, visit an art gallery or go for a walk by a river or the sea. Anything that opens up the mind to new combinations.

Different techniques work for different people. One of the present authors has always found chess a positive creative stimulant—mainly because of the way every move opens up new possibilities.

Other people find chess too focused. The other co-author finds swimming and walking more effective.

10. Sleep on it

Just before going to sleep at night, remind yourself of the problem— and the ideal solution. If you have a set deadline, feed that into your "brain-bank" too. And then *your subconscious mind will take over.* It never sleeps.

But as advertising leader David Ogilvy puts it: "You have to brief your subconscious. Then you have to switch off your thought processes and wait for something, for your subconscious to call you and say, 'Hey, I've got a good idea!' There are ways to do that. A lot of people find that to take a long hot bath produces good ideas. Other people prefer a long walk. I've always found that wine produces good ideas—the better the wine the better the idea."[9]

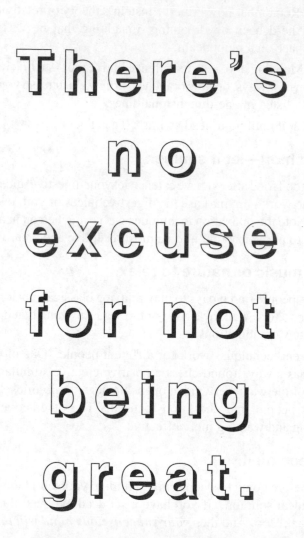

There's no excuse for not being great.

TOM PETERS
*The Circle of Innovation**

*Published by Alfred A. Knoff, New York.

11. Eureka! It pops out

The next step is the easiest of all: it pops out. You'll be shaving, or taking a shower, or sleeping—and suddenly the answer is there.

In part the process works because it's similar to the way your brain processes information in the first place. Just as you can use your subconscious to file information in patterns, so you can use your subconscious to deliberately break up those patterns and find new combinations. But only if you state your vision and your goal *specifically*. *It also pays to set a deadline, so your subconscious can feed that, too, into its data banks.*

12. Recheck it

When the new answer has popped out, *recheck it*. Does it fully solve your problem? Can you amend it or improve it?

The system we've just highlighted could be called the problem-solving way to creativity.

An alternative is a vision or mission approach. That's the same as problem-solving—except you don't start with the problem. You start with a vision of a future where virtually every dream is now possible.

Australian futurist Dr. Peter Ellyard is one of many who favour this approach. He feels that starting with a problem often limits the solution. "The dangers of a problem-centred approach can be best seen," he says, "in the inappropriately named 'health care' industry. In most first-world countries 'health care' is virtually out of control. The words 'health care' actually mean 'illness cure'. The industry consists of the activities of doctors, hospitals and pharmacies. The size of our health care budget has become an index of the nation's sickness, rather than its health. This forgets that the basic state of humans is to be healthy, not ill. We have adopted a problem-centred approach to health, largely defining health as an absence of illness, and a healthy future as an illness-free one. A *mission-directed* approach to promoting and maintaining health would be very different. It would concentrate on nutrition, exercise, good relationships, stress management and freedom from environmental contamination. This is a totally different agenda. However, the current problem is that we now pour so much money and effort into the problem-centred, technology-driven approach that there are very few resources available for a mission-directed approach."[10]

SCAMPER

is a checklist
of ideas-spurring questions.
Some of the questions were first
suggested by Alex Osborn,
a pioneer teacher of creativity.
They were later arranged
by Bob Eberle into this mnemonic:

S = Substitute?
C = Combine?
A = Adapt?
M = Modify? Magnify?
P = Put to other uses?
E = Eliminate or reduce?
R = Reverse? Rearrange?

To use SCAMPER:

1. Isolate the challenge or subject
    you want to think about.

2. Ask SCAMPER questions about
    each step of the challenge
or subject and see what new ideas emerge.

MICHAEL MICHALKO
*Thinkertoys**

*Published by Ten Speed Press, Berkeley, California.

The current authors certainly wouldn't disagree with this analysis—except to say that the "problem" was not correctly defined. And Ellyard makes a vital point: generally we all try to define a problem too narrowly. Define your problem as "unemployment", for example, and you may restrict your answers to new jobs—and not consider retraining leave or the desirability of leisure and study-time.

When consulting engineer William J. J. Gordon was given the task of finding a new way to open cans, he deliberately didn't use the word "canopener" when briefing his engineers and designers. Instead they toyed with such notions as a banana and its easy-peel abilities. Their eventual solution: the ringpulls you now see on most teartab cans. A "canopener" approach would have limited the result.[11]

Whether you use the problem-solving or mission-directed approach, you generally won't come up with a great idea unless you define a specific goal in advance.

There are, of course, many exceptions. Bacteriologist Alexander Fleming stumbled on penicillin when confronted with a strange mould growing at St. Mary's Hospital in London.

And when Massachusetts inventor Percy Spencer was working on a novel radar system in 1945, it struck him that the radiation it emitted could have a culinary use. So he hung a pork chop in front of the magnetron machine he was working on. And, as British BBC presenters Peter Evans and Geoff Deehan report, he "produced the first microwave meal in history".[12] In another of history's quirks, it was the Japanese who capitalised on the invention. "When a Japanese firm started to manufacture magnetrons, it was forbidden under the peace treaty to undertake military contracts. Therefore it concentrated on peaceful uses of microwave technology; now Japan leads the world in microwave sales." Or at least it did until the Koreans caught up.

Brainstorming checklist for ideas

But most breakthroughs come from a firm vision of the future: a specific goal. Many of those creative techniques can be adapted from other fields. Advertising, for example, has given us "brainstorming"[13]—the original idea of Alex Osborn, one of the founders of Batten, Barton, Durstine and Osborn, the giant advertising agency.

Here are some specific examples of how you can apply the brainstorming, ideas-creation process in practice:

Eureka!

Some of the innovations
that have built Nike

Phil Knight, a University of Oregon athlete, chose running-shoes as the project for a marketing essay at Stanford University: and pondered whether Japanese methods might be able to do for that industry what they'd done to Germany in watches and cameras.

He and U.S. Olympic coach **Bill Bowerman*** formed a company by contributing $500 each—on a handshake. Watching his wife make waffles, Bowerman then poured liquid urethane into the waffle iron—and, after gumming up the works, conceived the famous stipple-soled shoe.

Invited by Knight to design a shoe-stripe for the company, art student **Carolyn Davidson** came up with a curved line that looked like the swoosh of a check-mark. Said Knight: "I don't love it, but I think it will grow on me." Davidson charged only $35 for the design.

Pondering a brand name, **Jeff Johnson,** another Bowerman runner and Knight's first commission salesman, slept on it—and woke up with *Nike:* the winged Greek goddess of victory. Said Knight when he considered the alternatives: "I don't like any of them. I guess we'll go with the Nike thing for now."

Phil Knight is now one of America's richest men.

Information extracted from *Swoosh: The unauthorised story of Nike and the men who played there,* by J.B. Strasser and Laurie Beckland, published by Harper Business, New York.

* Author Dryden writes about Bowerman with a wry smile. Dryden arranged the 1960s American track team visit to New Zealand where the U.S. coach discovered jogging from Auckland coach Arthur Lydiard. Non-writer Bowerman was so impressed with Lydiard's stamina he co-authored a book on jogging—and it sold over a million copies in the U.S.

When you're looking for a new idea, can you:

Double it: like London's double-decker buses? *Halve it:* like bikinis or the miniskirt? *Expand it:* like one-stop shopping centres or the Boeing 747? *Dry it:* like packet soup? *Slice it:* like bread? *Stretch it:* like denims or stretch limousines?

What could you substitute?

Ladislo Biro substituted a ball for a nib, and the ballpoint pen was born. *The fax machine* has substituted electronic transmission for posted mail—and the Internet has superseded the fax. *Clarence Birdseye*— after finding frozen fish in Canada's Arctic Circle—substituted freezing for canning, to invent the frozen food industry. *Supermarkets* substituted self-service and trolleys for shop assistants. Xerox's Palo Alto Research Centre substituted the "point and click" method of running a computer; Apple adapted it commercially, and the world's simplest computing system was born. *Bed-and-breakfast homes* in Ireland have substituted for hotels and become the core of that country's tourist industry. CDs replaced vinyl recordings for music. And now it's the Apple iPod.

What new combinations can you make?

Sony combined earphones with a transistor radio to invent the *Walkman.* Pressure-cooked chicken and a special sauce gave us *Kentucky Fried Chicken.* Nylons combined with panties to make *pantyhose.* Walt Disney combined Mickey Mouse with tourism to invent *Disneyland.* Shops and carparks linked together to produce *shopping centres.* General Motors combined hire purchase with a choice of colours and models to build *the world's biggest car company.*

How can you adapt it?

Rollerblades are now a multimillion-dollar seller—realigning skate-wheels into one line. *Rugby football* has been adapted from soccer, *rugby league* from rugby, *softball* from baseball.

What could you magnify or increase?

McDonald's magnified hamburgers to produce the *Big Mac. Prince* has made a fortune by enlarging the tennis racquet. So has Calloway with its *Big Bertha* golf clubs. *Wal-mart* has become the world's most profitable retail chain, selling through giant discount stores. *JVC* invented *three-hour videotape* and beat off Sony to establish the world standard —because the extra length enabled buyers to record complete sports events.

Have you ever thought of this?

 All the literature that has ever been written in the modern English language consists of patterns of only twentysix letters.

 All the paintings ever made are patterns of only three primary colours.

All the music ever written consists of patterns of no more than twelve notes.

 All the arithmetical expressions we know of consist of only ten symbols.

 And for the vast computations of digital computers, everything is made up of patterns of only two components.

Thus, whenever we speak of something as being "new" we are really talking about original patterns of already existing components.

DON FABUN
*Three Roads To Awareness**

*Published By Glencoe Press, Beverly Hills, California.

What could you reduce, reverse or eliminate?

Frank Whittle reversed wind and invented the *jet engine. Bill Hamilton* adapted the principle further and gave us the *jet boat. The vacuum cleaner* is based on a similar principle. In Australia, *Kerry Packer* of the Nine TV Network reduced the time of test matches to invent *one-day cricket,* and a very profitable new summer television feature. *Computer spell-checkers* have reduced printing mistakes.

What new forms can you create?

Can you make it: *Hard,* like frozen ice blocks? *Soft,* like easy-spread butter or margarine? *Quiet,* like a Rolls Royce? *Loud,* like rock music? *Thick,* like Doc Marten bootsoles (a profitable fashion industry, based on the initial choice of unfashionable"skinheads")? *Fun,* like *Trivial Pursuit? Vertical,* like rocket takeoffs? *Horizontal,* like reclining chairs?

Can you: *Blend it,* like shampoo and conditioner? *Glue it,* like Glue Stick? *Shake it,* like a milk shake? *Cover it,* like umbrella cocktail decorations? *Uncover it,* like the miniskirt or split skirts? *Colour it,* like new lipsticks, cosmetics or blue-packed Pepsi Cola? *Compress it,* like CD-roms? *Liquefy it,* like shoecleaners? *Squeeze it,* in plastic bottles? *Spread it,* like pate? *Raise it,* with self-raising flour?

Can you repack it: *In teartab cans,* like premixed drinks? *In plastic containers,* like cask-wine? *In aerosol cans,* like hairspray? *As roll-ons,* like deodorant? *Sleek,* like Apple iMac and Acer Aspire computers?

Business innovations like these —and hundreds more —are changing the face of society. *Dell Computers* have gone from a $60,000-a-month business to $50-billion-a-year because of the revolutionary way they have customised individual computers and sold them by direct marketing and then on the Web. *Lego* has developed into a $1.5 billion business, since started by an out-of-work Danish carpenter, Olo Christiansen, as small wooden toy company. Sweden's *IKEA* has become the world's biggest home furniture retailer, with seventytnine outlets in nineteen countries, through brilliant catalogue selling and simple home assembly.

Yet where is the same innovation in the vital field of education and learning? For this book we've selected breakthroughs from around the world. But generally they've been chosen from isolated pockets.

Come up with a new idea in electronic communication—and it will be carried to a million enthusiasts immediately on the Internet and World Wide Web, and within a week or a month by scores of personal computing magazines. Inventors and early-adaptors are making fortunes by cashing

If you learn only one word of Japanese make it KAIZEN

**KAIZEN strategy is
the single most important
concept in Japanese
management—the key to
Japanese
competitive success.
KAIZEN means improvement.
KAIZEN means *ongoing*
improvement
involving *everyone:*
top management,
managers
and workers.**

MASAAKI IMAI
*Kaizen: The Key To
Japan's Competitive Success**

*Published by Random House, 201 East 50th St., New York, NY 10022.

in on the new third-wave of economic development. Why not the same verve in education?

We suspect that overwhelmingly it is because of the way schools and curricula are structured. *From the very moment of starting school, most children are taught that all the answers have already been found.* Even more: they are taught that success is learning a limited range of those answers—absorbed from a teacher—and feeding them back correctly at exam time. Yet that is not the way the real world innovates. The simple questions on the past three pages are typical of the queries posed in businesses every day as they strive to do things "better, faster, cheaper".

Don Koberg and Jim Bagnall, in their book *The Universal Traveller,* have suggested other words to encourage innovation: multiply, divide, eliminate, subdue, invert, separate, transpose, unify, distort, rotate, flatten, squeeze, complement, submerge, freeze, soften, fluff-up, bypass, add, subtract, lighten, repeat, thicken, stretch, extrude, repel, protect, segregate, integrate, symbolise, abstract and dissect.

Stanford University engineer James Adams[14] suggests thinking up your own favourite "bug list"—the things that irritate you—to start you thinking. And he lists among his own: corks that break off in wine bottles, vending machines that take your money with no return, bumper stickers that cannot be removed, crooked billiard cue sticks, paperless toilets, dripping faucets and "one sock". "If you run out of bugs before ten minutes," says Adams, "you are either suffering from a perceptual or emotional block or have life unusually under control."

Another technique is to focus on 1,000 percent breakthroughs. What can you do ten times faster, better, cheaper? What is the "killer application" in your field: the big "Aha!" that can take your company, your school or your industry to new peaks of excellence? That's what Microsoft has achieved in computer software; what Netscape has done in Internet browsers; what Canon has achieved in colour copiers.

Given the tremendous increase in technology, in almost any field 1,000 per cent improvements are possible: in some operations. Learning to typeset magazine advertisements and newspapers, for instance, once took a six-year apprenticeship. To "makeup" pages took five years of training. Today, with desktop computerised publishing, any competent typist can compress much of that eleven-year training into a week. What would it take to achieve similar breakthroughs in your field?

At the other extreme, *if you learn only one word of Japanese in your*

A hexagon
Kaizen
Think Kit

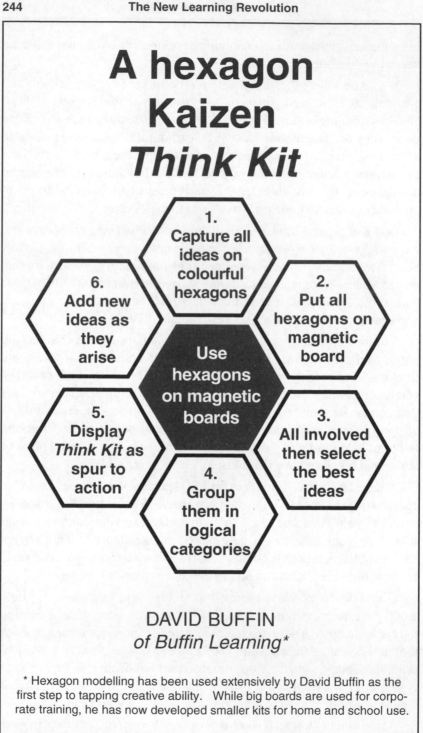

DAVID BUFFIN
*of Buffin Learning**

* Hexagon modelling has been used extensively by David Buffin as the first step to tapping creative ability. While big boards are used for corporate training, he has now developed smaller kits for home and school use.

life, make it Kaizen. It means continuous improvement. But it means much more than that. *It means a philosophy that encourages every person in an industry—every day—to come up with suggestions for improving everything:* themselves, their job, their lunchroom, their office layout, their telephone answering habits and their products.

Says Toyota Motor ex-chairman Eiji Toyoda: "One of the features of the Japanese workers is that they use their brains as well as their hands. Our workers provide 1.5 million suggestions a year, and 95 per cent of them are put to practical use."[15] And at Nissan Motors "any suggestion that saves at least 0.6 seconds—the time it takes a worker to stretch out his hand or walk half a step—is seriously considered by management."[16]

Matsushita, the giant Japanese electronics company, receives about 6.5 million ideas every year from its staff.[17] And the big majority are put into operation quickly.

It is beyond the scope of this book to cover the total secret of Japan's Total Quality Management and Kaizen movements. But to test, in part, the effectiveness of their method, try an introductory *Kaizen* on anything you're involved in. One excellent method is to use David Buffin's hexagon *Think Kit.* Staff or students are encouraged to fire in new ideas. The teacher or facilitator writes each on a coloured magnetic hexagon and attaches the hexagons to a large magnetic board. The group then arranges the hexagons around various themes or activities, and agrees on the main priorities. These are then left on display as a continual spur to agreed action (see diagram opposite).

For business we prefer to marry the two methods together: to look for the big *Aha!* idea for strategic planning (what is the really big break-through that will change the future of your company or industry?) and *Kaizen* (how can you involve all your staff in continuously striving to upgrade every aspect of that performance?). In oversimplified terms, many would describe *Aha!* as the key to American business success, and *Kaizen* as the Japanese secret weapon. Their "marriage" is *The Third Way.* And an excellent way to display them is on another David Buffin innovation, the arrowed action kit (see illustration next page): again a good permanent and colourful visible reminder of agreed goals and actions.

Many universities, of course, would say they have always taught thinking as part of logic, psychology and philosophy. But most schools don't teach what Edward de Bono[18] has termed *lateral thinking:* the

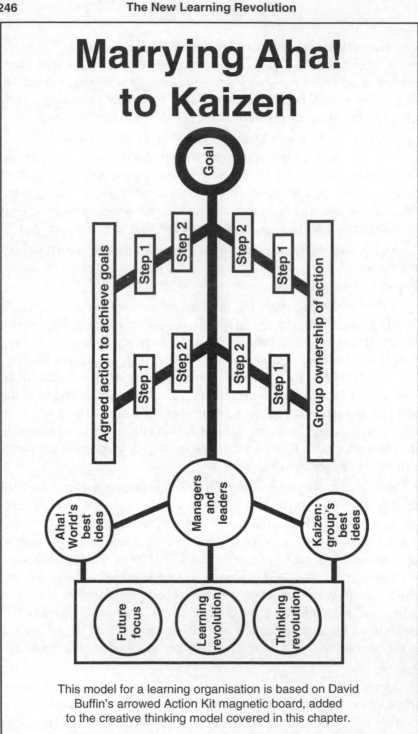

Marrying Aha! to Kaizen

Goal

Step 2 · Step 1

Step 2 · Step 1

Agreed action to achieve goals

Step 1 · Step 2

Step 2 · Step 1

Group ownership of action

Aha! World's best ideas

Managers and leaders

Kaizen: group's best ideas

Future focus

Learning revolution

Thinking revolution

This model for a learning organisation is based on David
Buffin's arrowed Action Kit magnetic board, added
to the creative thinking model covered in this chapter.

ability to open-mindedly search for new ideas, look in new directions.

Roger von Oech thinks even the terms logical and lateral thinking are too restrictive. He says we're also capable of conceptual thinking, analytical thinking, speculative thinking, right-brain thinking, critical thinking, foolish thinking, convergent thinking, weird thinking, reflective thinking, visual thinking, symbolic thinking, propositional thinking, digital thinking, metaphorical thinking, mythical thinking, poetic thinking, nonverbal thinking, elliptical thinking, analogical thinking, lyrical thinking, practical thinking, divergent thinking, ambiguous thinking, constructive thinking, thinking about thinking, surreal thinking, focused thinking, concrete thinking and fantasy thinking.[19]

But most people unwittingly limit their thinking potential. One reason is the brain's ability to file material inside existing patterns. When a new problem is tackled, we're conditioned to go down the track of previous answers. We all have preconceptions, taboos and prejudices, though few of us ever admit to them. They can be emotional, cultural, religious, educational, national, psychological, sexual or culinary.

We are also preconditioned from school to come up with "the right answer"—not the open-minded challenge for a better way. Almost every adult who has succeeded at high school or college will have firm ideas on the best educational system. And it will generally be the system that he succeeded in. Listen to anyone praise a "good school" and you will almost certainly find a school that suits that particular person's learning style.

Now that's not unusual. You could probably go through life and never find a person totally objective about everything. And fortunately no one system of education, or religion, or health, suits all. So perhaps the first step in "conceptual blockbusting"—to use James Adams' term[20]—is to accept that we all have fears, we all have biases. The best way we know to start overcoming them is to combine fun and humour. That often works for students in particular. A fun-filled atmosphere can lead to high creativity.

If you're not used to "far-out" brainstorming sessions, probably a good warm-up exercise is to start with a humorous challenge. Try inventing a new golfball—one that can't get lost. Or planning what you'd do with a holiday on the moon or underwater. Or ask some "What if?" questions. Like what would happen if pets became school teachers? Or if computers ran the government? Then use some of de Bono's tech-

Do a "PMI" on this proposition:

That all teaching should be done by computers

Write three separate columns, one headed Plus, one Minus and one Interesting.

Now list all the "plus" points
(All study could be interactive; you'd get instant feedback)

Then all the "minuses"
(No personal relationships; and how could a computer be a field-trip guide?)

Then all the "interesting" ideas
that occur to you
(How would a computer handle discipline? How would a computer be paid?
Could you make computer study a joint venture between home and school?)

PMI is one of Edward de Bono's suggestions for teaching thinking.

niques, such as PMI, CAF, C&S, APC and his "Six Thinking Hats."[21]

PMI standards for Plus, Minus and Interesting. Here the students are asked to choose a fairly outlandish statement, and in three columns write down all the points they can think of to be "plus" factors, then all the "minuses," and lastly all the reasons the proposition could be "interesting".

CAF means Consider All Factors. And again write them down, searching for new factors that don't spring immediately to mind.

C & S stands for Consequences and Sequel. Logically, both should be listed under CAF, but de Bono says that most people just do not consider all the consequences unless their attention is specifically drawn to them.

APC stands for Alternatives, Possibilities and Choices. And again the reasons are obvious: a list that encourages you to speculate.

As de Bono summarises one of his other techniques: "The theme of my book *Six Thinking Hats* is simple. There is the white hat for neutral facts, figures and information. There is the red hat to allow a person to put forward feelings, hunches and intuitions—without any need to justify them. The black hat is for the logical negative, and the yellow hat for the logical positive. For creativity there is the green hat. The blue hat is the control hat, and looks at the thinking itself rather than at the subject—like an orchestra conductor controlling the orchestra. The purpose is to provide a means for rapidly switching thinkers from one mode to another—without causing offence." [22]

All are excellent techniques. Especially the "six hats"—when you go to the trouble to obtain some bizarre models, in colours and odd shapes, and pass them around so each person can act the part.

But the simple ideas we have suggested earlier in this chapter are the ones we have found to work effectively in virtually any situation: in advertising, business, marketing, selling, exporting, market research and all aspects of learning and education. They work, we believe, because they show the logical links between sequential and creative thinking. Your critical "left-brain" logic sees the common sense in the step-by-step link-up to the "right-brain's" creative ability.

They start, of course, by tapping into the outstanding power of the brain. And the brain's potential, as we'll turn to next, is grounded in processing which goes back to the start of life itself.

Checklist for new mothers

 Most of the active brain cells a child will ever have are present by birth.

 A well-nourished foetus during pregnancy will develop an average of 250,000 new braincells every minute.

 Smoking, alcohol and drugs can severely affect that brain-growth.

 Poor diet during vital periods can cause lifelong learning disabilities.

 Eat plenty of fish, green-leaf vegetables, fruit, nuts and vegetable oil.

 Have a banana a day when pregnant, for potassium and folic acid.

 Iron- and zinc-rich foods are essential for baby's brain-growth.

 Breast-feed if possible—to add the vital "coating" to the main brain cells.

 After birth, make sure to get baby's hearing and eyesight checked regularly.

A sensible guide to producing better, brighter babies

Your body is more fascinating than any machine. Every day about two million of its cells wear out. But the body replaces them automatically. Every fifteen to thirty days your body completely replaces the outermost layer of your skin. What you see in the mirror today is not the same skin you had a month ago. But some cells your body will never replace: the 100 billion active nerve cells, or neurons, that make up your brain's cortex.[1]

Every one of them was present the day you were born. In your mother's womb you were growing them at an average of 250,000 cells every minute.

Each one continues to grow in size over the first few years of life. Each one, as we've seen, is capable of sprouting up to 20,000 dendrites. But after birth those original 100 billion neurons will remain with you throughout life, except for those that are "pruned off".*

What happens to each brain in the nine months before birth is therefore vital to later learning ability. When pregnant women are severely undernourished, their children can be born with fewer than half the brain cells of a healthy child.

As we've seen, neurons are not the only cells in the brain. We each have up to 900 billion *glial* cells to nourish the neurons. These glial cells also develop *myelin,* the sheathing that wraps around our *axons* . These are the nerve pathways that speed messages from neuron to neuron and

---

* *Until recently, most research indicated that no new cortical neurons were created after birth, although new cells are built later in other parts of the brain. New research indicates that some new cortical cells may be added later, but the 100 billion "first crop" are still the most vital ones.*

251

Within the next minute an average of 250,000 brain cells will have multiplied in each and every well-nourished growing foetus in the world.

RICHARD M. RESTAK
The Infant Mind*

*Published by Doubleday & Company, 666 Fifth Avenue, New York, NY 10103.

around our bodies—like electrical transmission wires. Both of these cell groups start growing in the womb, and continue during the first few years of life.

If the baby is poorly fed in those vital early years, it will not produce all the nourishing glial cells it needs. *And if some foods are missing from the expectant mother's diet, the nerve pathways around the brain and body will not be efficiently insulated.*

As American researchers Brian and Roberta Morgan put it in their highly-recommended book *Brain Food:* "The human brain begins growing in the womb, and the majority of this development does not slow down until the age of six. Growth in the brain of the foetus, infant and young child is time-dependent. This means that the brain grows in specific stages at specific times. If it does not have all the nutrients essential for its growth at those times, damage or malformation can result which cannot be corrected at a later date. A developing infant who is fed poorly during its period of brain growth may be left with learning disabilities which will remain for the rest of its life, no matter what is done at a later date to correct the nutritional deficiency."

Scottish Professor Michael Crawford sums up years of research into the impact of nutrition on infant and foetal brain growth: "Wherever we've found low birthweight babies, small head circumference and intellectual deficits in infants, we've found that right across the board the mothers concerned had diets before and during pregnancy that were deficient in a large number of nutrients."[2]

Even in developed societies such as Britain, the United States and New Zealand, at least 10 percent of babies continue to arrive with low birthweights. Generally that results from the mother's poor diet, smoking, taking drugs or being affected by toxic substances such as lead.

Crawford is amazed at the lack of education on diet and nutrition. And he says poor diet before birth affects more than the brain. Seven separate studies indicate that later heart problems, high blood pressure and many strokes have their roots in poor diet before birth.

One of the major deficiencies is fat. But a special kind of fat. "Unfortunately," says Crawford, "we've come to think of fat as lard and dripping. *But what the foetus really needs is a highly specialised fat— the essential fats we call them. They're the fats you need to build cells, especially braincells, and not the sort of fats that animals and humans dump on their waistlines.*

If a pregnant woman smokes one cigarette, her foetus will stop breathing for five minutes.

RICHARD M. RESTAK
*The Infant Mind**

*Published by Doubleday & Company, 666 Fifth Avenue, New York, NY10103.

"Many of those fats come from marine life. Now of course it's an old wives' tale that fish is good for the brain. It happens to be that we now have absolute scientific evidence for this. *We find that the fats found in fish and seafood of all sorts are especially relevant to the growth and development of the brain." And those same fats are vital for developing the body's immune system.*

They are also needed to build and maintain the myelin insulation.

Crawford wishes everyone would return to "the unsophisticated foods of nature": plenty of green leafy vegetables, fruit, nuts and vegetable oil.

If Crawford and his dietician, Wendy Dole, could get one message through to every potential mother in the world, it would be simply this: *the most important time for your child's brain-growth is before you become pregnant.*

Women who have used oral contraceptives should be especially careful of their diet before pregnancy. "The pill" reduces your body's stores of pyridoxine (one of the B vitamins) and folacin or folic acid, a vitamin needed for neural development. Severe folic acid deficiencies can cause serious malformations of the brain and other organs.

Crawford says pregnant women in particular should include bananas in their regular daily diet. "Not only are they a good source of potassium, they also contain good supplies of folic acid."

Zinc and iron are minerals essential for early brain growth. Where pregnant monkeys have been fed a diet low in zinc, their infants later play less with others, act withdrawn and have difficulty learning complex tasks. Iron is needed for all cell growth and multiplication. It also influences the oxygen supply to the blood.

Most dietary experts say that a simple, sensible diet is best before and during pregnancy: three meals a day, plenty of fruit, vegetables, nuts, fish and lean meat. An iron supplement during pregnancy is highly recommended. The diet should be high in foods that are rich in iron and zinc, such as beans, peas, broccoli, carrots, whole wheat bread, berries and brown rice. And don't try any special diets to keep you slim.

The other "no-no's" during pregnancy? "Smoking, alcohol and drugs,"[3] says New York researcher Ian James, Professor of Paediatrics, Obstetrics and Gynecology at Columbia University's Presbyterian Medical Centre. *He says "for every one cigarette the mother smokes, the baby smokes two". Smoking starves the foetal brain of oxygen—at a time when oxygen is vital for cell formation.*

Drugs are most dangerous to the foetus during the first three months of pregnancy, when the heart, brain, limbs and facial features are forming.

The Reader's Digest Body Book*

*Published by The Reader's Digest.

Pregnant women who smoke fifteen to twenty cigarettes a day are twice as likely to miscarry as nonsmoking mothers. In the first few weeks after birth, smokers' infants die at a rate 30 percent higher than nonsmokers' infants. Babies also absorb poisonous nicotine through breast milk. And they are later more prone to respiratory infections, and they also have a higher rate of pneumonia.

Alcohol can also damage the growing brain. Heavy drinking can cause what has become known as "foetal alcohol syndrome", which results in reduced brain size, distorted facial features, poor coordination and hyperactive behaviour.

James describes the effects of cocaine or heroin as devastating, especially for young pregnant women and their babies. Educational psychologist Jane M. Healy, of Vail, Colorado, says research estimates show that at least one of every nine babies born in the United States is drug-affected. "Many authorities warn," she adds, "that growing cocaine use by pregnant women will soon flood the schools with children who have attention, learning and social problems. And these children are not even included in our already declining test scores."[4]

Because of the caffeine content, heavy coffee and tea-drinking during pregnancy is also not recommended.

After birth, diet is still vital for all cell growth. And the importance of myelination cannot be stressed too much. Some of it is in place before birth: around the nerve pathways that enable a newborn baby to suck, cry and move its fingers. But at birth the pathways needed for walking, talking and bladder control are not yet myelinated.

"Common sense tells us that it is useless to try and get a newborn to walk alone," says Healy, "but at about one year, when those connections have myelinated, it may be difficult to prevent."

About 75 percent of myelin comes from fat—from what Crawford calls "essential fats." And the other 25 percent comes from protein. Breast feeding by a healthy mother is the best source of both. And of zinc, which is also vital to form glial cells. Breast milk also contains specific antibodies which coat the baby's intestines and respiratory tract and fight off infection. It also helps protect the baby from ear infections, eczema and other allergies. And it provides calcium and phosphorous needed for rapidly growing bones. In fact, the only thing lacking in a healthy mother's breast milk could be vitamin D. That's why many doctors recommend a vitamin D supplement. A well-balanced milk

Conception can be impaired when women consume more than 300 mg. of caffeine a day. That's 3 cups of coffee, 6 cups of tea or more than 7 sodas.

USA Today*

December 19, 1995.

"formula" can also be used in place of breast milk—but it must be one that tries to duplicate the essential elements of mothers' milk.

All this sounds like elementary common sense. But many mothers can't cope without some form of help. And around 10 percent of mothers, even in developed countries, are at "high risk".

Researchers at the Otago University School of Medicine in New Zealand, for instance, have completed a multi-year study of women having babies at the nearby Dunedin maternity hospital. Before a baby is born, hospital staff ask the mothers some simple questions, such as age, marital status, employment and home addresses over the previous year. And the figures have been consistent year by year: 78 percent of mothers can cope adequately. But 22 percent need some form of help. And nine percent of all babies are considered high risk.[5] They could be seriously abused or maltreated unless their mothers are helped.

It's not hard to identify the risk factors: young, single mothers, moving around a lot. No job. Parents who've already split up. A history of foster homes. Maybe a background of drugs. Mother suffered parental violence as a child.

Unfortunately, a similar pattern exists in many countries. The United States has 22 million children under six.[6] Five million of these are living in poverty and about two and a half million are just above the poverty line.[7] And guess who'll be the educational failures of this century unless that poverty trap is broken?

That's why we've listed parent education and early childhood health programmes as vital first priorities in any sensible education system.

Many research projects show the vital connection between nutrition and other brain-developing activities in the first five years of life.

Ideally most early brain development happens in sequence. A child learns to see before it learns to talk. It learns to crawl and creep before it walks. Walks before it runs. Learns to identify simple objects before it learns to reason. If an infant misses out on one of those steps—like walking without ever crawling or creeping—learning problems can result. To use computer terms, that's because the early activities lay down the "hard-wiring" or "hardware" of the brain—in a set sequence. When the hardware is in first-class condition, it can be used to "run" any software programme: like learning a foreign language or a new subject. But if any of the "hard-wiring" has been skipped, the brain could have difficulty running some programmes.

Alternative brain foods

❏ Nutrition research indicates that the most healing and sensible diet consists of organic fruits, vegetables and seeds.

❏ All minerals, including iron, can be obtained from kelp, organic sprouts and seeds.

❏ If you live in an area where fishing grounds are affected by mercury poisoning, organic flax seeds and walnuts are good safe sources of Omega 3.

The early-development timetable is set in part by the sequence of myelination. A thin spiral of sheathing around axons is present at birth, but the full insulation is then laid down around the body, and the brain, in sequence. Overall, in the body that starts at the top and works down. That's why you can make sounds before you learn to walk—the long axons transmitting messages to your toes and calf-muscles take longer to coat than the axons to your tongue and larynx.

In the brain, full myelination starts at the back and moves to the front. That's why you learn to see before you learn to talk and reason: your optical nerve-centre is at the back of the brain, your speech-centre is further forward, and your reasoning-centre is at the front. The process is completed in the centre of the brain—what some scientists call the "association cortex": the part you use to sort incoming information and blend it with data already in your storage files.

When axons are fully covered by their myelin sheath, they can transmit messages around the body up to twelve times faster than they could before. In fact, the speed of transmission around the body can vary from one mile an hour to 150 miles.[8]

Just as the foetus grows in spurts, so does the new infant brain. And the timing of those bursts can be vital.

Close one eye of a two-year-old for as little as a week, for instance, and you will almost certainly damage its ability to see. This is because the growing brain is laying down its main visual pathways from the eyes to the vision-centre at the rear of the brain. The two separate pathways are competing for dominance. Shut one eye for any length of time and the other one will lay down the dominant pathway. Close one eye for a week when you're twenty and it won't matter because by then your basic pathways have been laid down.

Says Stanford University human biology professor Robert Ornstein: "The critical period during which the two eyes establish their zones of dominance seems to be about the first six years in humans, six months in monkeys, and perhaps three months in cats. It is a very sensitive period. If one eye of a kitten is kept closed for only one day, it will have poor vision in that eye as an adult.

"There is a very important practical lesson from this basic work on the visual brain. Do not ever keep *one* eye of a human infant closed for an extended period of time. Keeping both eyes closed is better; after all, infants sleep a good bit of the time."[9]

In one survey of 200 inmates of Mt Eden prison in Auckland, New Zealand:

❑ **All 100 Maori (Polynesian) prisoners checked had hearing loss ten times worse than the national average.**

❑ **Eighty-two percent of non-Maori prisoners had the same degree of hearing loss.**

❑ **Most of it stemmed from lack of hearing checks and treatment in early childhood.**

Pacific Network magazine*

*Published by the Pacific Foundation, Auckland, New Zealand, February 1992 edition.

It is the same with hearing. Your inner ear is no bigger than a small nut, but it contains as many circuits as the telephone system of many cities. The ear also contains another tiny vital structure called a cochlea. It looks like a snail shell and works like a piano keyboard. But a piano has only eightyeight keys, while the cochlea has 20,000 hairlike sensory cells which pick up sound impulses and transmit them to the brain.

The whole intricate hearing mechanism is obviously vital for learning language. As with sight, the basic language pathways are also laid down in the first few years of life. English-language dialects, for example, have only beween forty and fortyfour different sounds. And all Europe's main languages about seventy. Hear all those sounds clearly in the vital first few years of life, learn to pronounce and use them, and you'll be able to pronounce other languages much better if you learn them later in life.

Most healthy children in a well-rounded environment also learn to speak fluently at least the 2,000 basic words of their language in the first four years of life. But if they can't hear, they'll find it much more difficult to speak fluently. And if they can't hear or speak, they'll have difficulty learning. Several surveys in New Zealand, for instance, found 20 percent of preschool children with hearing problems in one ear, and 10 percent with severe hearing loss in both.[10]

That's just one more reason that the most effective early childhood development programmes include regular hearing and sight checks, along with major attention to nutrition and parent education.

We are indeed what we eat—and what our mothers ate. We are also very much the result of what we do and what we think. And just as the right nutrition and exercise can provide the nourishment for a young brain's "nerve highways" and developing dendrite branches, so the right activity, involving all five senses and movement, can produce more dendritic connections. All future learning will be based on those connections—and the early nourishment that went into their development.

All the best educational programmes around the world combine elements that stimulate both a child's physical and mental development—for in truth there is no split between the two.

We are all a combination of what we eat, think and experience. And, after good care in the months before birth, the best programmes concentrate next on the most vital years of life: from birth to the early school years.

How to make the most of the vital years: from birth to 8 years

❑ Some say up to 50 per cent of a person's ability to learn emerges by age four.

❑ Another 30 percent may develop by the eighth birthday.

❑ Those vital years lay down the pathways on which all future learning is based.

❑ After age ten, the branches that haven't made connections die off.

❑ Youngsters are their own best educators, parents their best first teachers.

❑ Youngsters learn best by what they experience with all their senses, so stimulate these senses.

❑ Our homes, beaches, forests, play grounds, zoos, museums and adventure areas are the world's best schools.

❑ Simple physical routines can help infants explode into learning.

❑ Infants grow in a patterned way, so learn to build on that growth pattern.

❑ Learning anything, including reading, writing and math, can and should be fun.

How to enrich your child's learning ability from birth till age eight

Every country's educational priorities are completely back to front.

Many researchers believe that you develop more of your *ability to learn* in the first eight years of life—and especially in the first four years—than in all rest of your days.[1]

This does not mean that you absorb most of your *knowledge* or most of your *wisdom* or most of your *intelligence* by your fourth or eighth birthday. It simply means that in those first few years you form *the main learning pathways in your brain.* Everything else you learn in life will be built on that base. You also take in a fantastic amount of information in those early years, including much that is absorbed subconsciously.

Yet nearly every country spends well under 10 percent of its educational budget on the years where of your ability to learn is formed.

Marcus Buckingham and Curt Coffman, in their summary of the Gallup findings,[2] make an interesting comparison in their chapter on the latest neuroscience research: "At birth the child's brain contains 100 billion neurons, more braincells than there are stars in the Milky Way. These cells are the raw material of the mind. But they are not the mind. The mind of the child lives between these cells. In the synapses.

"From the day she is born, the child's mind begins to reach out, aggressively, exuberantly. Beginning at the centre of the brain, each neuron sends out thousands and thousands of signals. They are trying to talk to one another, to communicate, to make a connection.

"Imaging everyone alive today simultaneously trying to get in touch with 150,000 other people and you will get some idea of the wonderful

265

Male and female brain differences

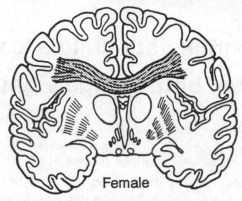

Female

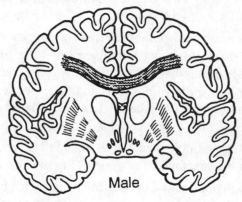

Male

Baby girls generally develop their corpus callosum
(the shaded area in the brain at top)
earlier than boys (same area in lower brain).
Girls generally develop language skills faster than boys,
but boys seem to develop distance vision
and space perception better than most girls,
giving them an advantage at some sports.

Illustrations from *The Learning Brain,*
by Eric Jensen, published by Turning Point for Teachers,
P.O. Box 2551, Del Mar, CA 92014, USA.

scale, complexity and vitality of the young mind. By the time the child reaches her third birthday, the number of successful connections made is colossal."

Many compare it to laying down an incredible mental highway system. And, in the words of neurology professor Harry Chugani: "Roads with the most traffic get widened. The ones that are rarely used fall into disrepair."[3]

Scientists have tested this infant ability in many ways. In 1964, Benjamin S. Bloom, Professor of Education at the University of Chicago, published a summary of a century of major research findings. In it, he studied five main human characteristics between birth and age seventeen and eighteen: height, general learning ability, school achievement, aggressiveness in males and dependence in females.[4]

Overwhelmingly, he found that development soared in the first few years—then tapered off. Generally it reached its halfway point before the fifth birthday. He found boys reached 54 percent of their maximum height by their third birthday, another 32 percent between three and twelve, and the last 14 percent by the eighteenth birthday.

Since Bloom's study, much other research has shown, however, that several differences between male and female brains do show up early in life.

The corpus callosum in baby girls, for instance, is generally thicker than in boys. This helps most girls to read earlier than boys. Generally girls speak earlier and learn languages more quickly. Males seem to have better distance vision and depth perception than females, making them more adept at certain sports.[5]

Two of the most thorough analyses since Bloom's have been done in the South Island of New Zealand. The first is through the Otago University School of Medicine in Dunedin, a city of around 100,000 people. In 1972, 1,661 babies were born in Dunedin. Their progress has been checked regularly ever since. And more than 1,000 of them are still being surveyed.

Research director Dr. Phil Silva says that the survey underlines the vital importance of the first few years of life.[6] "That doesn't mean that the other years are unimportant, but our research shows that children who have a slow start during the first three years are likely to experience problems right through childhood and into adolescence."

He says it's also vital to identify any special problems in the first three

If I had my child to raise over again

If I had my child to raise all over again,

I'd finger paint more, and point the finger less.

I'd do less correcting, and more connecting.

I'd take my eyes off my watch,
  and watch with my eyes.

I would care to know less,
  and know to care more.

I'd take more hikes, and fly more kites.

I'd stop playing serious, and seriously play.

I'd run through more fields, and gaze at more stars.

I'd do more hugging, and less tugging.

I would be firm less often, and affirm much more.

I'd build self-esteem first, and the house later.

I'd teach less about the love of power,

And more about the power of love.

DIANE LOOMANS
*Full Esteem Ahead**

* Published by Kramer, Tuburton, California.

years, such as hearing or eyesight defects, "because if we don't help them at the early stages then it's likely that they are going to experience long-lasting problems throughout their lives".

The other survey has checked the progress of 1,206 infants born in the city of Christchurch in 1977. One of its key findings: between 15 and 20 percent of youngsters fall behind because they don't get the necessary early-childhood health-checks and developmental experience. [7]

There are six main pathways into the brain, the five senses of sight, hearing, touch, taste and smell, and the sixth step of what we do physically. Youngsters obviously learn through all the senses. Every day is a learning experience. They love to experiment, to create, to find out how things work. Challenges are there to be accepted. Adults to be imitated.

Most important, a child learns by doing. He learns to crawl by crawling. He learns to walk by walking. To talk by talking. And each time he does so he either lays down new pathways in the brain—if his experience is new—or he builds on and expands existing pathways—if he is repeating the experience.

Youngsters are their own best educators, parents their best first teachers. And our homes, beaches, forests, playgrounds, adventure areas and the whole wide world our main educational resources—as long as children are encouraged to explore them safely through all their senses.

Research has also established beyond doubt the importance of every child growing in a positive enriched environment.

We've already quoted research by Berkeley scientists in California who have been experimenting for many years with rats—and comparing their brain growth with humans. "Very simply," says Professor Marian Diamond, "we've found with our rats that all the nerve cells in the key outer layers of the brain are present at birth. At birth the interconnecting dendrites start to grow. For the first month the growth is prolific. Then it starts to go down.

"If we put the rats in enriched environments, we can keep the dendrite growth up. But if we put them in impoverished environments, then dendrite growth goes down fast.

"In enrichment cages, rats live together and have access to toys. They have ladders, wheels and other playthings. They can climb, explore and interact with their toys. Then we compare them with rats in impoverished environments: one rat to a cage, no toys, no interaction. Again very simply: we've found that the rat brain cells increase in size in the enriched

The unstimulated and stimulated brain

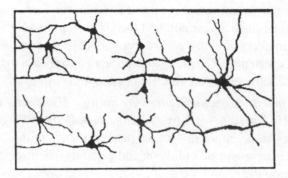

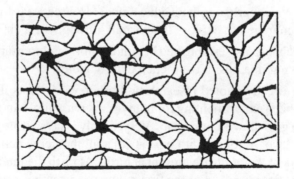

At top: a model of an unstimulated brain, with few interacting connections.
Lower: a young brain rich in connections, from stimulating activities.

These illustrations have been adapted from
Professor Marian Diamond's book
Enriching Heredity, published
by Macmillan, New York.

environment—and the number of dendrites increases dramatically. In the impoverished environment, the opposite." [8]

The rats then take an "intelligence test": they're put in a maze, and left to find food in another part of the maze. The "enriched" rats do so easily. The others don't.

Obviously, scientists can't cut up human brains to test the impact of early stimulation. But they can check with radioactive glucose. "And these checks," says Diamond, "show that the vital glucose uptake is extremely rapid for the first two years of life—provided the child has a good diet and adequate stimulation. It continues rapidly until five years. It continues very slowly from five to ten. By about ten years of age, brain-growth has reached its peak—although the good news is this: the human brain can keep on growing dendrites till the end of life, so long as it is being stimulated. Very simply, the human brain cell, like the rat's, is designed to receive stimulation—and to grow from it."

That doesn't mean turning an infant's home into a formal school classroom. The reverse, in fact: infants learn by play and exploration. It's the formal classroom that needs redesigning.

"We used to think that play and education were opposite things," say Jean Marzollo and Janice Lloyd in their excellent book *Learning Through Play*. "Now we know better. Educational experts and early childhood specialists have discovered that play *is* learning, and even more, that play is one of the most effective kinds of learning."

The key: turning play into learning experiences—and making sure that most learning is fun.

In fact, activities that good parents take for granted provide some of the best early learning. But we don't mean "academic" studies. *Scientists have proved, for instance, that regularly rocking a baby can help greatly in promoting brain growth.* It stimulates what they call *the vestibular system*. This is a nerve-system centred in the brainstem and linked very closely with the cerebellum and a baby's inner-ear mechanism, which also plays a vital part in developing balance and coordination. Scientists say this is one of the first parts of the brain to begin to function in the womb—as early as sixteen weeks after conception.

"It is this early maturity that makes the vestibular system so important to early brain development," says Richard M. Restak, M.D., author of *The Brain: The Last Frontier* and *The Infant Mind*. "The foetus floating in its amniotic fluid registers its earliest perceptions via the activity of its

All children are born geniuses, and we spend the first six years of their lives degeniusing them.

BUCKMINSTER FULLER

vestibular system. In recent years evidence has accumulated that the vestibular system is crucial for normal brain development. Infants who are given periodic vestibular stimulation, by rocking, gain weight faster, develop vision and hearing earlier, and demonstrate distinct sleep cycles at a younger age." [9]

Dr. Ruth Rice, of Texas, has shown in controlled tests that *even fifteen minutes of rocking, rubbing, rolling and stroking a premature baby four times a day will greatly help its ability to coordinate movements and therefore to learn.* [10]

And Dr. Lyelle Palmer, Professor Emeritus of Education at Winona State University in Minnesota, has completedextensive studies at kindergarten level* to demonstrate the vital importance of such simple stimulation for five-year-olds. Every day youngsters have attended a gymnasium as a key part of early schooling. There they are encouraged to carry out a simple series of routines: spinning, rope jumping, balancing, somersaulting, rolling and walking on balance beams. In the playground, they are encouraged to swing on low "jungle gyms", climb, skate, perform som-ersaults and flips. And in classrooms they play with a wide range of games, also designed to stimulate their sense of sight, hearing and touch. All activities are designed to increase in skill-level during the year, and thus help stimulate ever-increasing brain development.

At the end of each year, many of the children undergo the Metropolitan Readiness Test to measure whether they've developed enough to start first-grade schooling. Nearly all have passed the tests in the top 10 percent for the state—and most have been in the top 5 percent. Nearly all of them come from working-class backgrounds.

Palmer, a former president of the Society for Accelerative Learning and Teaching, emphasises that the children are not simply walking, running and skipping—the normal "motor" activities. "The stimulation activities we recommend," he says, "are specifically designed to activate the areas of the brain we know will promote their sense of sight, touch and hearing—as well as their ability to take in knowledge." [11]

Most parents, for instance, seem to learn instinctively that infants love to be held firmly by their hands and spun around like a helicopter blade. Palmer's Minneapolis public school research at New Vision School has shown that such activities result in important brain growth. And the

---

* In the United States, kindergarten starts at age five. In New Zealand and some other countries, it is for children aged three and four.

Helicopter spin

For ages three years and above, provided they can walk and run

Have children stand and extend their hands out from the sides of their bodies.

Invite them to spin as fast as possible,* in a standing position, for 15 seconds. Say: "We are helicopters flying to the airport." Play loud music while spinning.

Then say: "STOP and close your eyes. Keep your balance. Remain standing." (Do not say: "Don't fall down." Emphasise what to do, not what not to do.) The children stand for 25 seconds until they no longer feel dizzy. The process is then repeated.

Spin ten times. This will take about five minutes. Spin 15 seconds, rest 15 seconds, spin 15 seconds and so on. Speed is important. It keeps the ear fluid moving.

Eventually children will spin with eyes closed, opening them occasionally in order to check on safety. (Do not spin one way and then immediately spin the other way because it is important that the fluid in the semicircular canals of the ear keeps moving. When you start spinning the other way, the fluid movement stops and stimulation is reduced.)

For children having difficulty, the adult stands over the child and assists by grasping one hand and quickly pulling the child's arm around the body and to create a continuous spinning action.

This is one of the routines used by Professor Lyelle Palmer with great success to improve the learning ability of young children.

Mats and Irene Niklasson, of Vestibularis, in Sweden, have children do this exercise by spinning much slower than Professor Palmer recommends—but, they say, with similar beneficial results.

Regular updates: www.thelearningweb.net

greater the intensity of the activity the greater you see the results of the brain-growth in areas that are receptive to further learning.

The overall result is a big gain in competence and self-confidence, increased attention, faster responses and the ability to tackle learning activities of increasing complexity.

Palmer stresses that the activities are not what many schools would regard as "academic." But any classroom visit shows the youngsters "exploding" into true learning. Early reading is taught with word-card games. The youngsters get an early introduction to mathematics by playing with dominoes and big cards with dots instead of numbers. And they play games to develop pre-writing skills.

Does it help "academic development"? You bet! In another study of at-risk youngsters who were not doing well at school, Palmer's methods produced dramatic gains in reading ability. The children of the experimental group read three to ten times faster than the control group.[12]

Two Swedish vestibular-stimulation experts, Mats and Irene Niklasson, have also achieved great results using techniques similar to Palmer. At their Vistibularis organisation, they've found that slow spinning and slow movement is ideal for many children, particularly those diagnozed as having severe learning problems. Says Mats Niklasson: "Most learning problems, I found, relate to lack of balance and difficulty with the reflexes." Through spinning and other motor activities, the Nik-lassons "rewire the brain".[13]

They also agree that effective learning starts from the moment of birth. Again, the main points are simple:

1. The vital importance of step-by-step movement

Infants grow in a patterned way. They're born explorers. So encourage them to explore in a safe, but challenging, environment.

In New Zealand two Irish migrants, Jerome and Sophie Hartigan, have combined their talents to introduce a parent-involvement programme based very much on children's natural physical development. Jerome is a former Olympic pentathlete, has a masters degree from Ithaca College, New York, and is a scientist and physical training specialist. Sophie is an accomplished music teacher. Their *Jumping Beans* child-development centres, now well-established in New Zealand, involve parents in regular one-hour sessions.

How physical activity builds a child's other abilities

What a child does *physically* in the first few years of life plays a major part in how well he or she will develop other abilities. Here's a simple model of how it works:

1. The brainstem	The activity:	Leads to:
	Grasping Touching	Hand-eye coordination
	Crawling Arm-leg	Big-motor skills
	Walking movements	Prewriting ability
	Reaching Pushing	
	Turning Pulling	

2. The balancing cerebellum	The activity:	Leads to:
	Spinning Tumbling	Balance
	Balancing Dancing	Sporting ability
	Listening	Bicycle riding
	Swinging	Writing skills
	Rolling	Fine motor coordination
		Reading skills

3. The emotional brain	The activity:	Leads to:
	Stroking	Love
	Cuddling	Security
	Playing	Bonding
	together	Social skills
		Cooperation
		Confidence

4. The thinking brain or cortex	The activity:	Leads to:
	Stacking toys	Math, logic
	Assembling puzzles	Problem solving
	Recognising patterns	Fluent reading, spelling
	Making patterns	Writing, painting
	Playing word games	Good vocabulary
	Repetitive play	Memory
	Appreciating music	Musical ability

Reproduced from *FUNdamentals Guidebook,* by Gordon Dryden and Colin Rose, published by Accelerated Learning Systems, England. Chart compiled on recommendations by Jerome and Sophie Hartigan, of Jumping Beans, Auckland, New Zealand.

Regular updates: www.thelearningweb.net

Jerome Hartigan says "physical, motor learning" forms the basis for all learning, including reading, writing, arithmetic and music. "Without motor learning," he says," the brain simply will not develop."[14] He says specific movement patterns "wire up" the whole brain.

The Hartigans say it's important that physical routines should link in with the way the brain grows.

Janet Doman, director of The Institutes for the Achievement of Human Potential, in Philadelphia, agrees. And those routines should start from day one. "Give children the chance to crawl from as early an age as possible," she says. "Babies can actually crawl from birth, but generally they are restricted by so much clothing that they don't develop this ability till later."[15]

So long as children are warm, she says, parents should not limit their movements with too much clothing.

"Very simply, the more they crawl the sooner they're going to creep, and the more they creep the more they'll be able to walk. And each of these stages ensures that the next stage comes at the right moment—and that they have completed the neurological maturation that goes with it.

"If babies are bundled up for so long that they don't really crawl much at all, but go straight to creeping, then they may well pay a price for that five years later when they get to the point where they need to be able to converge their vision perfectly."

But how on earth can creeping affect a baby's *eyesight?* "Basically, a newborn baby has no ability to converge its two eyes," says Janet Doman. " But when the baby starts to crawl, the need to use two eyes together is born—because all of a sudden the baby is moving forward in space and he begins to hit the sofa or the chair. Nature's a little bit of a tough teacher, and whenever this happens the baby says: 'Wait a second; I'd better see where I'm going.' And that's when the baby begins to pull in those two roving eyes and begins to say: 'Where am I?' After that, every time the baby is moving he will turn on his vision, look to see where he's going, and bring those two eyes together. As they converge their vision, it gets better and better. But if you miss that vital stage of development you're missing out a vital stage of brain development."

Part of the reason is very simple: to creep and crawl, a baby needs to use all four limbs. And this movement strengthens the 300 million nerve-cell pathways that link both sides of the brain through the corpus callosum. Children who skip creeping or crawling—common in

Nature has built the brain in such a way that during the first six years of life it can take in information at an overwhelming rate and without the slightest effort.

GLENN DOMAN
author of *Teach Your Baby To Read**

*Author interview, Philadelphia, PA.

youngsters with severe brain damage from birth—thus find it impossible to fully coordinate both hemispheres.

2. Use your common sense

Almost everything we learn about the world comes in through our five main senses. Very early in life, infants try to touch, smell, taste, hear and look at whatever surrounds them. So encourage them from the outset.

Says Janet Doman: "A baby is born into a world in which, essentially, he is blind, can't hear very well and his sensation is far from perfect. And that's a very uncomfortable place for a baby to be. He's trying to figure out: 'Where am I? What's going on? What's gonna happen next?' Because he can't see, he can't hear and he can't feel very well. So I think the job of a parent is very clear: to give enough visual, auditory and tactile stimulation so that the baby can get out of this dilemma of not being able to see, hear or feel.

"That doesn't have to be complicated. For example, often new parents put children in a pastel environment. And this for baby is a disaster. The baby needs to see contrast, needs to see outlined shapes and images, needs to see black-and-white contrasts.

"If you put him in a room of pale pinks and pale blues, it's like putting him in a world where there's nothing to see—so he can't see it."

Or take taste. Doman says it is one of the most neglected senses. "In the normal course of events, a baby in his first few months of life would probably taste only two things: milk and vomit. Now that's not a very interesting taste variety! So we encourage our mothers to introduce some variety: a little taste of lemon or orange or nutmeg."

And sound: "Mothers intuitively speak in a slightly louder, clearer voice to babies—and that's great," says Doman. "And it's even better if you constantly tell baby what's happening: saying, 'Now I'm dressing you,' 'I'm putting your right sock on,' 'Now I'm changing your diaper.'"

Playing soothing background music is also recommended, both before and after birth. It's significant that youngsters in the Pacific islands of Polynesia, Melanesia and Micronesia almost invariably grow up with the ability to sing in harmony—an almost perfect sense of pitch. Every Polynesian also seems to be a natural dancer. Every New Zealand Maori seems to be able to sing in perfect tune. Again, experts will tell you it's because of what they did well before they went to school. They grew up in a culture where singing and dancing play a major part. And they

Why a baby needs to see sharp contrasts

In its earliest months a baby's brain lays down its main "visual pathways".

Its cortex has six layers of cells which transmit different signals from the retina in the eyes along optic nerves to the back of the brain.

One layer, for example, transmits horizontal lines, one vertical.

Other layers or columns handle circles, squares and triangles.

If a baby was to see only horizontal lines, for example, then when it crawled or walked it would continually be banging into the legs of tables and chairs because its "visual pathways" could not process vertical lines.

American scientists Torstein Wiesel and David Hubel won the Nobel prize for showing that such early sensory experience is essential for teaching brain cells their jobs.

Says Ronald Kotulak: "Even if a person's brain is perfect, if it does not process visual experiences by the age of two the person will not be able to see, and if it does not hear words by age ten, the person will never learn a language."*

That is why Glenn Doman has for more than thirty years recommended exposing babies to strong black-and-white contrasting shapes from birth, rather than using bland pastel wall coverings.

* RONALD KOTULAK
Inside The Brain
Published by Andrews and McMeel (1996),
4520 Main Street, Kansas City,
Missouri 64111, USA.

Regular updates: www.thelearningweb.net

patterned all that information in the vital early years. In a similar way thousands of three- and four-year-olds around the world can now play the violin—many in their own orchestras—thanks to programs pioneered by Japan's Shinichi Suzuki.

3. Build on all the senses

As an infant gets older, many parents feel it's even easier to encourage learning through all the senses—because you see the instant feedback.

In *Learning Through Play,* Marzollo and Lloyd stress that children learn from experiences that are concrete and active. "For a child to understand the abstract concept of 'roundness', he must first have many experiences with real round things. He needs time to feel round shapes, to roll around balls, to think about the similarities between round objects, and to look at pictures of round things. When children are at play, they like to push, pull, poke, hammer and otherwise manipulate objects, be they toy trucks, egg cartons or pebbles. It is this combination of action and concreteness that makes play so effective as an educational process."

4. Use the whole world as your classroom

Turn every outing into a learning experience.

You can search for shapes

"They're all around you," say Marzollo and Lloyd. "Point them out to your child and soon he'll point them out to you." Circles, such as wheels, balloons, the sun, the moon, eye glasses, bowls, plates, clocks, coins. Rectangles, such as doors, windows, apartment houses, cereal boxes, books, beds and delivery trucks. Squares, like paper napkins, handkerchiefs, windows and tabletops. Triangles, like rooftops, mountains, tents, Christmas trees and sails.

You can see opposites everywhere

And this is a great way to learn words—by association: if a ball goes up it must come down. So do seesaws at the park. Lights go on and off, doors get open and closed, night turns into day.

Every supermarket trip is a learning journey

Before you shop, ask your youngster to help you check through the refrigerator and pantry to see what you need: for your infant and the rest of your family.

The simple guide to learning English

 English has a total of 615,000 words

 But 2,000 make up 90% of all speech

 **400 words make up 65% of most writing**

 43 words make up 50% of daily English

 10 words make up 25% of most speech

abc **English has only 26 letters and 44 sounds**

 Most syllables can be spelled in only 70 ways

 84% of English words have simple patterns

GORDON DRYDEN*

* Summary prepared for Overseas Family School, Singapore.

Regular updates: www.thelearningweb.net

Then in the supermarket, the search is on: to find what the child needs and talk about where it comes from. But again, make it a game: "See who's first to see the cornflakes."

Learn to count with real things

Start with the things your child can touch: "This is one spoon; and these are two spoons." Then make it a natural fun game: "You've got one nose but how many eyes? You've got one mouth but how many ears? And how many fingers?" Involve him as you set the table for two, three or four people. Let him count the money at the checkout counter.

Make it fun to classify

As we've already discussed, the brain stores information by association and patterns. So start the process early. On laundry day, perhaps, he can sort socks into pairs, shirts for ironing, shirts for folding and storage.

5. The great art of communication

Language, of course, is a unique human ability. And infants learn by listening, imitation—and practice. So talk to them from the start. Tell them what you're doing. Introduce them to their relatives. Read to them regularly.

Nursery rhymes are great—simply because they do rhyme, and rhymes are easy to remember. Every child should be exposed to colorful books from the start and should be read to regularly.

Says New Zealand reading expert and author Dorothy Butler: "Keep the baby's books within reach, and make a practice of showing them to her from the day you first bring her home. The covers will be brightly illustrated, and at first you can encourage her to focus her eyes on these pictures. You can teach your baby a lot about books in the first few months."[16] Butler suggests showing even very young babies successive pages of suitable books: "Babies need people: talking, laughing, warm-hearted people, constantly drawing them into their lives, and offering them the world for a playground. Let's give them books to parallel this experience; books where language and illustration activate the senses, so that meaning slips in smoothly, in the wake of feeling."

Learning to read should be a natural and fun-filled process.

Again the principles are simple. English has about 615,000 words.[17] But 2,000 to 3,000 words make up 90 percent of most speech.[18] And only 400 to 450 words make up 65 percent of most books.[19] Introduce those words to children in a natural way, and reading develops as naturally as

First step to reading

Show your child brightly-coloured books from the day you first bring her home.
And read to her every day.

Summarised from
DOROTHY BUTLER
*Babies Need Books**

* Published by Penguin, London.

speaking. In fact the principle is so simple it's amazing there is any debate. Words, like pictures, are only symbols of reality. A picture of an apple is a symbol of a real fruit. So is the sound "apple". And so is the written word "apple". So if children can hear and see the word apple, and can taste it, smell it and touch it, they soon learn to speak and read it.

Glenn Doman has been proving this since before he first wrote *Teach Your Baby To Read* in 1964. He's also had many critics. Yet most of the critics actually recommend many of the same techniques, and often they criticize Doman for things he has never recommended.[20]

Says Doman: "It's as easy to learn to read as it is to learn to talk. In fact it's probably easier—because the ability to see is developed before the ability to talk. But don't take my word for it. Ask any producer of television commercials. They use the same simple communication techniques. Look at television any night, and you'll hear someone screaming COCA COLA, or McDONALD'S—and at the same time the brand-names appear in large colorued words, often tied in with a jingle that's easy to remember. And two-year-olds have broken the code. Now they can read because the message is large enough to be interpreted."[21]

So Doman-trained parents not only talk new words to their youngsters—loudly and clearly—they show them the words in big type, just like TV commercials or company billboards do.

In many parts of the world parents have found it simple common sense to label as many things as possible, so children can recognise written words as well as those spoken, starting with all the names of important things: from baby's own name to mommy (in America, or 'mummy' in Britain) and daddy, parts of the body and everything around the house. Printed letters, three inches high (about 7 cm.), are recommended.

When preschools were combined with parent education centres in the Pacific island of Rarotonga over thirty years ago, they labelled everything in English as well as their native Polynesian language. They found it a great way to encourage youngsters to read and speak in two languages.

In Malaysia, the Nury Institute has trained hundreds of parents to teach their three- and four-year-olds to speak and read in both Malay and English—specifically using the Doman technique.[22]

English-born teacher and author Felicity Hughes has used similar methods to teach young Tanzanian children to read in both English and Swahili.[23] Many of those children have then helped their parents read.

Felicity Hughes and the current authors agree—but Glenn Doman

Second step to reading

If an infant can see it, touch it, taste it, hear the word and see the word, she can learn both to speak and read it. So link reading with all the senses.

apple

GORDON DRYDEN

From a slide presentation on *The Learning Revolution*
to World Book International Achievers' Conference,
Barcelona, Spain, August 1996.

disagrees—that phonetics have an equal part to play with the "whole word" method of learning. Of the key words in English, about half are phonetic—written approximately as they sound: *hat, sat, mat, hit, fit, sit.* The other half are not phonetic, including such difficult spellings as *through, tough, cough, where, tight, weigh* and *bridge.*

Learn only "phonetics" and you'll be able to read and spell *set, bet, get* and *met.* You'll also quickly learn prefixes and suffixes such as *un, de, dis, re, ing* and *ed.* But you won't be able to read *Once upon a time* (phonetically: *Wunce upon uh taim).* And you won't be able to read the words from one to ten (phonetically pronounced *wun, tu, three, for, faiv, six, seven, ait, nain, ten).* You won't even be able to read *phonetically!* The long "e" in English, for instance, can be written twelve different ways: *On the quay* we could see one of these people seize the key to the green machine and give it to the chief officer who threw it in the sea.* So word-cards should include the most-used words, whether spelled phonetically or not. And fortunately 84 percent of English words do have easily-identifiable spellings, such as the "silent e" in words such as fate and kite, or syllables such as might, sight and fight.

The first cards should contain "labelling" words—the nouns of the things children first see as their parents are telling them: "That's your bottle. This is your dress. And these are your toes." Then when they can crawl, roll over and walk, they can start learning the action words, both spoken and written: "Let me see you roll over. Good boy, you can walk." Then come the adverbs: "Roll over slowly." "See how quickly you can walk." And the adjectives, too: "What a big, black dog."

But is too much early learning robbing infants of their childhood? Glenn Doman gives the simple answer:

"We have a fail-safe law. We teach all mothers this law. When teaching your child, if you aren't having the time of your life, and the child isn't having the time of his life, stop, because you're doing something wrong. That's the fail-safe law."

The early years are also the ideal time to pick up more than one language, especially if you live in an area where other languages are spoken regularly. Says Doman: "All children are linguistic geniuses— witness their ability to learn to speak a language in the first three years of life. If they live in a bilingual house, they learn two. And if they're born in a trilingual household, they learn to speak three."

* In "English English" the word "key" as in waterfront is spelled "quay".

Third step to reading: label what she can see

nose	**bath**
toes	**bed**
eyes	**plate**
coat	**shoe**

GLENN DOMAN
Teach Your Baby To Read Kit

* Published by Better Baby Institute, Philadelphia, PA, USA.
Similar word labels are contained in *FUNdamentals,* published
by Accelerated Learning Systems, Ltd., England.

Regular updates: www.thelearningweb.net

Neuroscientist Professor Diamond cautions that "love" is the most essential ingredient in early childhood education. "I think that warmth and affection is the prime consideration for healthy brain development. But from then on, expose them to a great variety of experiences. Let the child choose what interests her—and then move out from there."[24]

6. Parents as first teachers

So how can any parent become a better "first teacher"? Or better still, a first coach and mentor? Obviously you can read books on the subject, as you're doing now. But, like any other learning, hands-on experience with a mentor helps. And again the world provides many models.

In the United States, the Missouri Parents As Teachers programme has been an important trail-blazer.[25] It started in 1981 as a pilot programme—under the Parents as First Teachers title—and its early results were thoroughly researched. When all children in the pilot reached age three, a randomly-selected group was tested against a carefully-matched comparison group. In all significant areas—language, problem-solving, health, intellectual skills, relating to others and confidence—the PAT group scored much better.

PAT later became a state-funded service provided by all 543 public school districts in Missouri. On average in recent years, 60,000 Missouri families, with children from birth to three, have taken part in the programme. They've been helped by about 1500 trained part-time "parent-educators". Every month, each parent is visited by a parent-educator, who offers information about the next phase of each child's development and suggests practical ways parents can encourage sound growth. Parent-educators also offer tips on home safety, effective discipline, constructive play and other topics.

At each visit, the parent-educator takes along toys and books suitable for the next likely phase of development, discusses what parents can expect, and leaves behind a one-sheet series of tips on how to stimulate the child's interest through that next stage.

"Families receive three types of service," says parent-educator Joy Rouse.[26] "The primary part is the monthly home visit. We also provide group meetings—a chance for parents to come together with other families who have children in the same age-group. Sometimes it will be for parent-child activities, others to hear a consultant talk about child development or parenting, and sometimes it's just a fun time. The third

Fourth step to reading: label what she can do

walk	sit
run	dance
roll	talk
slowly	quietly

GORDON DRYDEN & COLIN ROSE
FUNdamentals*

* Published by Accelerated Learning Systems, England. The programme includes cards, with large blue letters, for key early verbs and adverbs.

component is screening, and this is a key component. We screen for language development, general development, hearing and vision. We also have a network where we can refer families with special needs."

Many Missouri schools link their PAT work with other programmes. The Ferguson Florissant School District, in St. Louis county, is one of the leaders.[27] It runs six separate preschool programmes: PAT; a LINK programme, with parents and infants together on courses; "Saturday School"—a half-day for four-year-olds, with group visits at home; a programme for three-year-olds; a child-care centre, with youngsters from two to five, where parents pay; and an education programme for preschoolers with special needs. The day-care centre operates at the local high school, and is used as part of a training programme for teenage high-school pupils.

Thirty percent of Missouri families with youngsters under three were on the PAT programme in the 1990s. The cost per family was approximately $250 a year, of which the state provided $180 and the school district found the rest. So to provide that service to every American family with children up to three would cost $3-billion a year for 12 million youngsters. That's only about twice what tiny Singapore (with Colorado's population) has spent equipping its schools with computers.

But Former Harvard Professor Burton L. White, who played a big part in establishing the programme, has ended his involvement with PAT because he says it is "hopelessly underfunded".[28] To do the job properly, he says, would require much higher spending—and it should be top priority. *He says not more than one American child in ten gets adequate development in the vital first three years of life.*

"This state of affairs may be a tragedy," he says, "but it is by no means a twentyfirst-century tragedy. In the history of Western education there has never been a society that recognised the educational importance of the earliest years or sponsored any systematic preparation and assistance to families or any other institution in guiding the early development of children."[29]

Professor White says the period from when a child starts walking up to two years is most important. "Every one of the four educational foundations—the development of language, curiosity, intelligence and socialness—is at risk during the period from eight months to two years."

He says bluntly that "our society does not train people to raise children".

Fifth step to reading: play phonetic games

FUNDAMENTALS

bat	got	train
cat	pot	brain
sat	hot	drain
mat		

GORDON DRYDEN & COLIN ROSE
*FUNdamentals**

* Published by Accelerated Learning Systems, England. The programme includes two sets of *Phonic Fun* cards, the first for simple "short" vowels, and the others for "combinations" such as "ai". The cards can be used for *Phonic Snap* or for the board game indicated above.

Note: Approximately half the core-words in English are phonetic; they are written approximately as they sound.

Professor Diamond, however, sounds a note of caution: "I do worry when people say things like 'Well, if you don't do something by three years of age forget it; you've closed the opportunity to stimulate that brain.' We don't want to give the impression that all of cortical input is essential that soon, though it is true for certain functions to reach optimal development, such as vision, hearing, and beginning language."[30]

Adds Professor Robert Sylwester: "The best time to master a skill associated with a system is just when a new system is coming on line in your brain. Language is a good example. It's very easy for a two- or three-year-old to learn any language. But if that person waits until eighteen or thirty, learning a new language will be more difficult because the systems governing this have been used for something else. Many skills, like learning to play a musical instrument or developing fine and gross motor skills, are best done as early as possible."[31]

Another home-based parent-education programme, which has had excellent success for children from age four to six, is called HIPPY: Home Interaction Programme for Preschool Youngsters.

It began in Israel in 1969, and has since started in over twenty other countries or states, servicing about 20,000 families a year outside Israel. It was given its biggest initial boost in America through its success in Arkansas, with the support of the former Governor and then President Clinton and Hillary Clinton. President Clinton is warm in his praise for HIPPY: "This programme, in my judgment, is the best preschool programme on earth, because it gives parents the chance to be their children's first teachers, no matter how meagre the education of the parent." [32]

HIPPY was designed by Professor Avima Lombard, initially for the nearly 200,000 refugees who came to Israel from Africa and Asia in the 1960s. They were poor and unsophisticated, and their children were sometimes neglected as their parents struggled to establish themselves in their new home. Like PAT, HIPPY takes training directly into the home, but for parents of children aged four and five. Mothers in the programme receive one visit every month, and they meet with other mothers in group meetings between home visits.[33]

Again, the results have been excellent—and in Arkansas not only have children benefitted but the programme has increased literacy among parents.[34]

In Malaysia, a parent-education programme has been taken out into

Sixth step to reading: play with key words

FUNDAMENTALS			
an	any	been	best
but	can	do	even
fun	hand	hat	must
none	now	once	slow

GORDON DRYDEN & COLIN ROSE
*FUNdamentals**

* Published by Accelerated Learning Systems, England. The programme includes all the 450 most-written English words and three sets of *Key Word Bingo* cards.
An adult or older child shows one bold word at a time, and younger children try to find a matching word on their card.
The first child to complete a line across or down wins the game.

Regular updates: www.thelearningweb.net

the villages by Dr. Noor Laily Dato' Abu Bakar and Mansor Haji
Sukaimi. They call it the Nury programme—from a word that means
"shining light". In the first ten years they trained 20,000 parents in
Malaysia and 2,000 in Singapore.[35]

7. Parents in preschool centres

New Zealand again has shown the way by piloting and researching
both the Missouri programme and HIPPY. In Missouri, PAT is very
much linked with schools, but in New Zealand the government has
associated it with that country's Plunket programme (named after a
former head of state), which has pioneered infant health-care checks,
parent education and family assistance for most of the last century. For
many years Plunket played a major part in achieving for New Zealand the
world's lowest infant death rate.

An even more thorough programme has been set up by New Zealand's
Pacific Foundation.[36] Early in the 1990s the foundation designed and
built a combined preschool and parent-training centre at Kelvin Road
School, Papakura, in the heart of an area with many deprived families.'
The centre also links in closely with most other district health and social
services. The preschool centre also provides a full HIPPY-based development programme for infants and their parents. Foundation executive
director Lesley Max describes the total project as a "one-stop shopping
center for parent and preschool services".[37] Results have been so outstanding that the government has now financed similar centres in other
parts of the country.

Again in innovative New Zealand, a parents' cooperative Playcentre
movement has been operating since 1941. It was started as a project to
provide support for mothers whose husbands were away at the war. The
women would take turns looking after a group of children to free the
others for shopping or recreation. The movement quickly spread, and one
of the early pioneers, Gwen Somerset, organised wider programmes to
train the young mothers in child development skills. Now there are 600
playcentres throughout the country, catering to 23,000 children. And
parent involvement is the key. They take turns in helping a trained, part-
time supervisor run each centre. And their own training helps make them
more competent parents.

Sweden is another country with highly advanced early childhood
development programmes—but with a tax-rate that most countries might

Children's work IS their play. Children learn from everything they do.

CAROLYN HOOPER
New Zealand Playcentre Movement*

*Interviewed by Gordon Dryden in *Where To Now?* television series,
reprinted in *Pacific Network,* February, 1992. Playcentre is a
parents' cooperative movement in New Zealand that for over
fifty years has been a world pioneer in combining parent education
with early childhood development.

find too high. For every child born in Sweden, one parent can have a year off work on almost full pay to be a fulltime parent.[38] Later, Sweden offers excellent preschool development centres.

For years it also organised one of the world's best refugee-support programmes, with migrants from 114 different countries. By law, each preschool centre employed adults fluent in both Swedish and the native language of each child. And students spoke at least two languages fluently—and many of them spoke three, including English.

But the prize for excellence in early childhood education could well go to aspects of a movement that was started over a century ago by Italy's first woman medical doctor, Maria Montessori.[39]

Most Montessori preschools are private, and often have high fees. But at French Camp near Stockton, California—an hour's drive from San Francisco—a New Zealand television crew, videotaping the world's best learning ideas in 1990, found a Montessori centre catering to America's poorest working families, Mexican fruit and vegetable pickers.[40] Both parents were working the fields from 4:30 or 5:00 each morning—for a family income of around $7,000 a year.

Yet their children were benefitting from preschool education that ranks with the top in the world. Their centre was one of eighteen set up as a research experiment by the California-based Foundation Centre for Phenomenological Research.* In the grounds of the French Camp centre the TV crew videotaped migrant youngsters dancing, singing and playing. Inside, others were engrossed in a wide variety of activities adapted from Montessori's original ideas.

They sat in child-sized chairs, at child-sized tables, used tools and implements specially designed for small hands. They also were learning advanced mathematics the Montessori way, using wooden rods of different lengths and colours to do decimals and numbers up to 2,000.

Among many other innovations, Montessori pioneered cutout sandpaper letters so infants could learn by touch as well as sight. And French Camp children were involved in a full range of similar sensory experiences. Each room had a variety of live animals and fish to help the learning process. Well-trained parents were always on hand to assist, but overall the youngsters were encouraged to be self-learners.

Like so many effective pioneering ventures, lack of finance has since forced the Foundation Centre to close many of its preschool centres, including the one visited at French Camp. Some have been taken over by other groups.

The 24 first steps to fluent writing

1. Play with big balls from crawling stage
2. Stack plastic cups from 9 to 18 months
3. Use pegboards from 12 to 18 months
4. Simple puzzles with big knobs from 18 to 24 months
5. Thread large beads at 18 to 24 months
6. More complex hand puzzles from 2 years
7. Pour rice from one jug to another, then switch to water
8. Early scribbling
9. Tons of water play
10. Hand, sponge and finger-painting
11. Switch to small balls
12. Small whiteboard
13. String macaroni between ages 2 and 3
14. Fold paper napkins from 30 months
15. Big jigsaws from third birthday
16. Draw inside big writing templates from age 3
17. Then use smaller writing templates
18. Finger-trace over stippled letters
19. Polish shoes between 3 and 5
20. Copy own name by fourth birthday
21. You write her first story, and child writes over it
22. Help her write shopping lists
23. Play writing games on home computer
24. She 'explodes' into writing before age 5

GORDON DRYDEN & COLIN ROSE
*FUNdamentals Guidebook**

* Published by Accelerated Learning Systems, England.
Note: Most activities are to develop prewriting skills.

Regular updates: www.thelearningweb.net

As one of the Foundation's then organisers, Antonia Lopez, told the TV audience: "The major job of the adult is to provide the children with as many opportunities in all of their areas, whether it's cultural, or science, art, music, mathematics or language—to provide as many opportunities that are age-appropriate and sequentially developed."[41] Something to eat was being served every two hours, with each meal a lesson in diet and nutrition: low-fat soups, whole-wheat tortillas instead of white-flour tortillas. Children set the tables as they learned to count the spoons and forks and plates. Each meal was a cultural delight.

And it didn't stop with nutrition. All family members—male, female, siblings and children—were physically examined each year.

Those who criticize Glenn Doman's early *reading* programme would probably gasp with amazement when they hear that French Camp children were *writing* fluently before they reached their fifth birthday.

As Lopez put it: "Montessori tells us that children at about four and a half literally seem to explode into writing. Now that's the official 'I can-write-a-sentence-and-a-word' version of writing. But our children are really being introduced to writing and to reading much earlier. Even as young as two and a half, they're being introduced to prewriting experiences: they're doing things left to right, top to bottom; learning relationships. And they're obviously exposed to rhymes and story-telling and all kinds of talking—so they're ready to explode into writing well before they are five."

It's perhaps significant that both Montessori's and Doman's initial research began with youngsters who were severely brain-damaged—and they then realised that these children, after multisensory stimulation, were often performing much better than "normal" children.

Montessori set out to fashion materials and experiences from which even "intellectually handicapped" youngsters could easily learn to read, write, paint and count before they went to school. She succeeded brilliantly; her brain-damaged pupils passed standard test after test.[42]

Under the Montessori method, however, a small child is not "taught" writing; she is exposed to specific concrete experiences that enable her to develop the "motor" and other skills that lead to the self-discovery of writing.

Montessori specialist Pauline Pertab, of Auckland, New Zealand, explains: "As early as two-and-a-half years of age, a child will be encouraged to pour water and do polishing, developing hand and eye

A five-year-old writes

*Vogliamo augurare
la buona Pasqua all'in-
gegnere Edoardo. Talamo
e alla principessa Maria?
Diremo che conducano
qui i loro bei bambini.
Lasciate fare a me:
Scriverò io per tutti
7 Aprile 1909.*

A sample of hand-writing, done in pen, by a five-year-old
student of Italian educator Maria Montessori in 1909.
Translation: "We would like to wish a joyous Easter
to the civil engineer Edoardo Talamo and the Princess Maria.
We will ask them to bring their pretty children here.
Leave it to me: I will write for all. April 7, 1909."*

*Reprinted from *The Montessori Method,* by Maria Montessori,
published by Schocken Books, Inc., New York.

coordination; to paint and draw, developing pencil control; and later to work with shapes and patterns, tracing the inside and outside of stencils and to work with sandpaper-covered letters about nine centimetres in depth—three to four inches—to get the feel of shapes." [43] The "explosion" occurs when a youngster discovers, by himself, that he can write.

As Maria Montessori was proving in the early 1900s, the key to early childhood deprivation lies overwhelmingly in providing a total supportive environment for all children to develop their own talents.

She demonstrated conclusively that if children can grow up in an environment structured to encourage their natural, sequential development, they will "explode" into learning: they will become self-motivated, self-learners, with the confidence to tackle any problem as it arises in life.

Yet a century later we've found only a few other early-childhood centres that combine nearly all the key principles outlined in this chapter.

Two are Montessori schools in England. The first: the London Montessori Centre, driven by its energetic head, Lesley Britton, who has also written some of the best summaries of modern Montessori early childhood education.

The second: the Montessori Farm School, run by South African-born Helen Watkins, in Bracknell, Berkshire. [44]

Elsewhere in Britain, the investment in early-childhood education has also dramatically increased in the past decade or so.

In a 2005 report, the Organisation for Economic Coopation and Development (OECD) singles out the United Kingdom for its "remarkable" improvement in preschool spending.

Britain now invests an average of $8,452 a year in early-childhood education—more than any other major nation in the "developed world", where the average is $4,294.

But the report points out that it still lags behind the more progressive smaller Scandinavian countries.

Singapore, too, has some first-rate early-childhood centres: generally one in each of the island state's high-rise housing developments. These have the added benefit of involving grandparents, many of whom live with their grownup "children".

Again, one of the best models is Singapore's international Overseas Family School. As covered in other chapters, this is one of the few schools in the world to use the International Baccalaureate "global curriculum"

Two developmental theories compared

Maria Montessori, the Italian early childhood educator, and Jean Piaget, the Swiss developmental psychologist, both proposed that children develop in sequence. But they disagreed on timing. Piaget believed children had specific periods of "cognitive" or intellectual development, with children not reaching their "concrete operational" stage until age seven. Montessori believed, however, that while children had specific "sensitive periods" for development, they should be encouraged to develop all of their senses from a very early age, and that self-learning would be based on the way the senses develop. In summary:

Montessori:

Birth to 3 years:
Absorbent mind.
Sensory experiences.
18 months to 3 years:
Coordination and muscle development.
Interest in small objects
2 to 4 years:
Refinement of movement.
Concern with truth and reality.
Awareness of order sequence in time and space.
2.5 to 6 years:
Sensory refinement.
3 to 6 years:
Susceptibility to adult influence.
3.5 to 4.5 years:
Writing.
4 to 4.4 years:
Tactile sense.
4.5 to 5.5 years:
Reading.
Overall:
The prewriting steps on page 298 are a good example of a modern-day adaptation of Montessori in action.

Piaget:

Sensorimotor period, from birth to age 2:
Obtain basic knowledge through the senses.
Preoperational period, from about age 2 to 7:
Develop language and drawing skills, but self-centred and cannot understand abstract reasoning or logic.
Concrete operational period from 7 to 11 years:
Begin to think logically, organize knowledge, classify objects and do thought problems.
Formal operations period from 11 to 15:
Children begin to reason realistically about the future and deal with abstractions.
Overall:
Piaget claimed reading, writing and mathematics should be left until the period from 7 years onwards:
Montessori: much earlier.

for all grades from age three to senior high school.

From early childhood, children from dozens of nationalities have the chance to learn in a global multicultural environment. They also benefit by the involvement of their multinational parents and grandparents in their education.

The IB's "Primary Years Programme" revolves around global and universal themes.

These start from age three in pre-kindergarten. Here three-year-olds enjoy dozens of global activities grouped around four themes:

1. Who am I? The central idea: that, as human beings, we have similarities and differences that make us unique.

2. Where do I come from? How are we part of a global family and each family is unique?

3. Once upon a time: how literature is an expression and a reflection of our cultural heritage—an introduction to classic nursery rhymes, fairy sales and poems.

4. Our best non-human friends: how we share the planet with other species which enhance our lives—and our responsibility towards them.

Youngsters are also encouraged to learn through all their senses, and through the stimulating challenge of different "learning centres".

During each week, and generally each day, the youngsters move through seven different "centres":

1. A tactile centre, where they learn from hands-on explorations.

2. A reading centre, with a great choice of books and tapes.

3. A drama centre, where they engage in pretend play.

4. An art centre, for hands-on creativity.

5. A writing centre, where they develop prewriting skills (at age three) and then writing skills (at four and five).

6. A mathematics centre, where they explore concepts with "manipulatives": concepts such as shapes and patterns.

7. A computer centre, where they learn both to use the computer as a learning tool and to try out learning software for beginners.

The global themes and learning-centre activities continue for four- and five-year-olds:

Four themes in the first-year kindergarden: Me, my family and

Brain development in the early years*

By birth: most children have 100 billion active brain cells, and these have made about 50 trillion connections with other brain cells and other parts of the body.

In first month of life: As a baby's senses react to her environment, she develops new "synaptic" connections at the phenomenal rate of up to 3 billion a second.

In the first six months: Baby will babble using all the sounds in all the languages of the world, but she will then learn to talk using only the sounds and words she picks up from her environment, particularly from her parents. Her brain will discard the ability to speak in languages she does not hear.

By eight months: A baby's brain has about 1,000 trillion connections (1,000,000,000,000,000)! After that the number of connections begins to decline—unless the child is exposed to stimulation through all her senses.

By age ten years or so: about half the connections have died off in the average child, but that still leaves about 500 trillion that last through most of life.

Up to age 12: "The brain is now seen as a super-sponge that is most absorbent from birth to about the age of 12. It is during this period, and especially the first three years, that the foundations for thinking, language, vision, attitudes, aptitudes and other characteristics are laid down. Then the windows close, and much of the fundamental architecture of the brain is completed."**

* Summarised from various sources, many of them quoted by Ronald Kotulak in *Inside The Brain,* published by Andrews and McMeel, Kansas City, Missouri.

** The exact quote is from Robert Kotulak's own summary.

friends; All around the world; Stories and rhymes; and What is in my garden?

Six themes in second-year kindergarten: *The K2 community; Your house my house; We are the world; Happily ever after (stories about different cultures); Sharing the planet with animals (including how we classify animals into five groups: mammals, fish, amphibians, birds and reptiles); and Sensational senses (how we know ourselves and our world more fully by using and appreciating our senses).*

Three-year-olds at this Singapore school find playing on computers at least as much fun as learning to swim or playing in the school's adventure playground .

Kindergarten principal Rani Suppiah says: "We encourage even very young children to treat computers just like any other learning materials: to be used with all the senses."

Wander into the kindergarten computer room and you're liable to find infants from a dozen nationalities learning to become computer literate. There is also at least one computer in each kindergarten classroom.

But obviously that is only part of a well-rounded early early-childhood education.

Overseas Family School youngsters then have the opportunity to carry on the same multisensory education, in a safe happy environment, as they move through primary school, middle school and high school.

In fact, as we'll explore in the final two chapters of this book—in looking to assemble the "best world model":

❑ When principals from New Zealand's world-class primary schools visit the infant classes at Singapore's Overseas Family School, their reaction is generally something like: "If only our students could start from the same base."

❑ And when principals from such world-leading British high schools as Cramlington, in Northumbria, and Varndean, in Brighton, visit New Zealand's best primary schools, their reaction is similar: "If only we could build on such great feeder schools."

This, in our view, is the ideal path for twentyfirst- century schooling: start from the very first early-childhood years, and then continue the same stimulating learning methods throughout the rest of schooling.

Six steps to more effective teaching

❏ **Warm environment**

Learning atmosphere

❏ **Interactive method**

Inquiry, discovery

❏ **Build thinking skills**

Specially creativity

❏ **Plenty of activations**

Play with it to reinforce

❏ **Apply it in practice**

Do it to show you know

❏ **Review and celebrate**

To retain the principles

This is model used by Jeannette Vos in all her
Learning Revolution trainings.

Regular updates: www.thelearningweb.net

New-century guideposts for teachers and trainers

This book obviously urges a total transformation in an outdated system of education and schooling.

But even without changing the entire system overnight, great teachers, principals and trainers are already showing the wave of the future.

They're doing it by combining lessons from early childhood, brain research, nature, show business, advertising, television, music, dancing, the movies, sports, art and electronic multimedia. Above all they're restoring fun to the learning process.

Some are doing this brilliantly in "subject classes": using new teaching methods to make it much easier to learn a foreign language or a science unit. And, as we'll show in later chapters, the work of these brilliant teachers can now easily be turned into multimedia "learning tools" that millions of other teachers and students can use.

Other trend-setters are doing equally innovative things inside school systems that use a "subject-based" curriculum—and where the teacher's big job is to "turn students back on to learning": to enjoy the fun and stimulation of real education.

In this chapter we touch on both, but with special emphasis on better teaching methods inside the more traditional school classroom—and also in corporate training, which often aims to develop specific new skills.

Some of the new techniques go by a variety of names. Some carry names that at first may seem strange to most. Like "suggestopedia" and "integrative, accelerated learning".

But the best all combine three things: they're fun, fast and fulfilling.

To learn anything fast and effectively, you have to see it, hear it and feel it.

TONY STOCKWELL
*Accelerated Learning
in Theory and Practice**

*Published by EFFECT (European Foundation for Education, Communication and Teaching), Liechtenstein.

And the best involve relaxation, action, stimulation, emotion and enjoyment.

Says outstanding West Australian teacher and seminar leader Glenn Capelli: "Forget all the jargon. Forget all the big names. What we're really coming to grips with can be summed up in two words: true learning."[1]

Says British-born, Liechtenstein-based educational psychologist Tony Stockwell: "We now know that to learn anything fast and effectively you have to see it, hear it and feel it."[2]

From our own research around the world, and practice in schools, colleges and business, all good training and educational programmes involve six key principles. As a lifelong learner of any age, you'll learn quicker, faster and easier in any classroom if all six are organised brilliantly by a teacher who is an *involver*—not a *lecturer*—who, acting as a *facilitator,* orchestrates these factors:

1. The best learning "state": the whole welcoming atmosphere of the classroom;

2. A stimulating format of inquiry and discovery that involves all your senses and is relaxing, fun-filled, varied, fast-paced and stimulating;

3. A process that builds thinking skills, including creative and critical thinking;

4: "Activations" to access the material, with games, skits and plays, and plenty of opportunity to practice;

5: Real-life experiences so students can put it all into practice to "show they know"; and

6: Regular review and evaluation sessions; and with them opportunities to celebrate learning.

1. The best learning "state"

Not surprisingly, each of those principles works well for an adult in almost the same way it works early in life, when learning develops quickly and easily through exploration and fun.

Orchestrating the environment

Can you imagine a two-year-old youngster learning by sitting still on a classroom seat all day? Of course not. She learns through doing, testing, touching, smelling, swinging, talking, asking and experimenting. And she learns at a phenomenal pace. She is highly suggestible, and

Learning
is
most
effective
when
it's fun.

PETER KLINE
The Everyday Genius*

* Published by Great Ocean Publishers, Inc., 1823 North Lincoln Street, Arlington, VA 22207.

absorbs information from everything that goes on around her—her total environment.

But once she gets past kindergarten, too often education starts to become boring. The fun disappears. In many classrooms youngsters are told to sit still, in straight rows, listening to the teacher and not exploring, discussing, questioning or participating.

Good teachers know that's not the best way to learn. So they plan a classroom setting that facilitates easy learning. They use fresh flowers for scent and colour. They cover the walls with colourful posters, highlighting all the main points of the course to be covered, in words and pictures—because much learning is subconscious. Students absorb the lesson-content even without consciously thinking about it.

More and more teachers have music playing to establish the mood as students enter the classroom. Many use balloons and swinging mobiles to create an almost-party atmosphere.

"The total atmosphere must be non-threatening and positively welcoming,"[3] says Mary Jane Gill, of Maryland, U.S.A., formerly in charge of staff training for Bell Atlantic. Her techniques on one accelerated learning course cut training time by 42 percent, on another 57 percent. And the very first thing they did was change the atmosphere.

Top Swedish teacher, the late Christer Gudmundsson, would agree: "The atmosphere from the time your students enter the classroom must be thoroughly welcoming."[4] And the late Charles Schmid, of San Francisco, California—a world pioneer in new teaching methods—found mood-setting music one of the major keys to achieving learning rates at least five times better than before. "And that applies everywhere, from preschool to a business seminar teaching computer technology."[5]

Liechtenstein's Stockwell—one of Europe's leading new-style trainers in both schooling and business—says the importance of well-designed colourful posters cannot be overstressed when teachers or trainers are planning a "subject" lesson: "Posters should be up around the walls before any learning session begins. They're peripheral stimuli. Their constant presence engraves their content into your memory, even when you're not consciously aware of them." He also says colour psychology is important. "Red is a warning colour; blue is cool; yellow is seen as the colour of intelligence; green and brown have a pacifying effect and are warm and friendly. Never forget that effective posters make a strong impression on the long-term memory. They create memory pictures

Accelerated learning is natural learning. As children we practised it every day of our lives:

through interacting with others and with the world, using our whole bodies, our whole minds, our whole selves.

DAVE MEIER
The Accelerated Learning Handbook*

*Published by McGraw-Hill, New York, NY.

Regular updates: www.thelearningweb.net

which can be called on when required although they were never consciously learned."[6]

It's also the kind of lesson that all educational institutions can learn from the best businesses:

❏ The Seattle-based Nordstrom chain of clothing stores is used in dozens of management seminars as a model in profitable service—and it always has freshly-cut flowers in its customer changing rooms.

❏ Every international airline welcomes passengers on board with soothing, calming music—before presenting safety demonstrations.

❏ Visit Hawaii, the tourist capital of the mid-Pacific, on a package tour and you'll soon slip into a welcoming vacation mood as you're greeted with a lei of island flowers.

❏ Visit Disneyland or Disneyworld and you're immediately struck by the cleanliness and total atmosphere.

Think of that the next time you visit a school or company seminar-room that persists with uncomfortable straight-backed wooden chairs and an atmosphere that is cold, lifeless and often colourless.

Setting the right mood and getting students' attention

Canadian teachers Anne Forester and Margaret Reinhard, in their excellent book, *The Learners' Way,* talk of "creating a climate of delight" in every school classroom. They say variety, surprise, imagination and challenge are essential in creating that climate.

"Surprise guests, mystery tours, field trips, spontaneous projects (old-fashioned days, pet displays, research initiated by the children) add richness to reading, writing and discussion. The production of plays and puppet shows is stimulated by the children's reading and is masterminded more and more fully by the children themselves.

"Your classroom will rarely be totally silent. Sharing and interaction are the vital components of a climate of delight. Discoveries, new learning, the sheer joy of accomplishment demand expression."

Creating that "climate of delight" is the first step in setting the right mood for more effective learning.

Early activity is vital

The next step is activity: precisely what students or trainees are encouraged to *do.* The colourful setting, posters and mobiles will already

Human Bingo

Typical game to break ice at seminars

Find someone who has done the following and write each name in the square

A kinesthetic learner	Owns a rowboat	Uses graphics in their workshops
Has a piece of the Great Wall	Plays an harmonica	A visual learner
Slept in an airport overnight	Has been to Bulgaria	Has taken part in a funny business luncheon
An auditory learner	Has taken a Dale Carnegie course	Is a good singer
Loves music	Is a great high school teacher	Is a fabulous cook

Not only do you meet fifteen new people, but you find fifteen specific 'teachers'

Regular updates: www.thelearningweb.net

have started to stimulate those who are mainly *visual learners.* The music will have "touched base" with the mainly *auditory learners.* And early activity makes the *kinesthetic learners* feel instantly comfortable. Interspersing these three learning styles also makes sure that all levels and networks of the brain are activated. But there are other good reasons for instant activity:

Jazzercise-type exercises to music encourage an increased flow of oxygen to the brain—and the brain runs largely on oxygen and glucose.

Other exercises to music—such as simple juggling and left-foot/ right hand, right foot/left-hand movements—can stimulate instant communication between the "right brain" and the "left-brain," as we cover in more detail in chapter 10.

Others can loosen students up—mentally and physically: to help them relax. Canadian psychologist and astronomer Tom Wujec covers many in *Pumping Ions—Games and Exercises to Flex Your Mind.*

Other activities can break the ice and help participants get to know each other—and the talents that are available to be tapped, inside and outside the specific setting.

The authors of this book frequently start international seminar sessions with a game of "Human Bingo" (see opposite). Participants have two minutes to meet as many people as possible—often to the tune of *Getting To Know You.* More importantly, in two minutes they learn all about the tremendous array of skills in the room.

At England's Cramlington Community High School, which we will meet in great detail later, all "subject" lessons start with high-participation activities for students to have fun recapping the main points of a previous lesson. All Cramlington teachers have been trained to use digital, interactive whiteboards. So if students in a previous class learned the Spanish names of body parts, at the start of this follow-up class they might play an electronic version of "pin the tail on the donkey". They'll digitally place body-part names on a projector-outline of a human body. It's fun, interactive, ice-breaking, and it quickly rehearses knowledge already learned—to quickly connect with the new lesson. The teachers have even written their own handbook of similar ideas.[7]

Other activities can put you in a positive mood. Australia's Capelli often gets his adult seminar-learners to:

❏ Sit in pairs—with someone they've never met before—and spend fortyfive seconds recounting the most interesting aspect of their back-

Since the brain cannot pay attention to everything . . . uninteresting, boring or emotionally flat lessons simply will not be remembered.

LAUNA ELLISON
*What Does The Brain Have
To Do With Learning?**

*Article in *Holistic Education Review,* Fall 1991.

ground; so that each person starts the session by focusing on projects that have been personally successful—reinforcing their ability to learn.

❏ Or massage each other's neck and shoulder muscles to encourage relaxation.

Obviously the techniques will depend on whether you are taking a regular school class, running a specific-topic seminar, or introducing an international symposium.

Eric Jensen, author of *SuperTeaching* and co-founder of SuperCamp, believes two core elements affect learning: they are *state* and *strategy*. The third is obviously *content*. "State" creates the right mood for learning. "Strategy" denotes the style or method of presentation. "Content" is the subject. In every good lesson you have all three.

But many traditional school systems ignore "state". Yet it is the most critical of the three. The "door" must be open to learning before true learning can happen. And that "door" is an emotional one—the "gatekeeper to learning", part of being in a fully resourceful state.

The right brain wavelength

One of the main steps to achieve this is to get everyone working on the "right wavelength." *And here probably the most ironic contradiction occurs: to learn faster you slow down the brain.* One of your brain's "wavelengths" is obviously most efficient for deep-sleep. Another is more efficient for inspiration. And another, the one you're most conscious of: the widewake alertness of daily living. But many studies now reveal that a fourth brainwave is the most efficient "frequency" for easy, effective learning: what some call the alpha state.[8]

Bring on the music

Dozens of research projects have found that music is a very efficient dial to tune into that alpha frequency.

"The use of music for learning is certainly not new," Californian accelerated-learning innovator Charles Schmid told us not long before his death. "Most English-speakers learn our alphabet to music, *The Alphabet song:* ABCD—EFG—HIJK—LMNOP.

"But in the last twentyfive years we've expanded our music knowledge tremendously. We've found out that in a special kind of relaxation, which music can induce, our brain is most open and receptive to incoming

Is it possible to learn 1,200 foreign words a day?

The most remarkable claims for accelerated learning in foreign-language training have come from Dr. Georgi Lozanov.

He reports* that Bulgarian students have actually found it easier to remember between 1,000 and 1,200 new foreign words *a day* than 500 words.

Here are the results he records from 896 "suggestopedic" language-training sessions:

Number of of words given in session	Number of students in session	% of words memorized per session
Up to 100	324	92.3%
100 - 200	398	96.8%
201 - 400	93	93.1%
401 - 600	53	90.4%
1000 - 1200	28	96.1%

*Dr. Lozanov's results are reported fully in his book, *Suggestology and Outlines of Suggestopedy,* published by Gordon and Breach, New York (1978).

Both the current authors were present during Dr. Lozanov's keynote presentation to the Society for Accelerative Learning and Teaching in Seattle, Washington, in 1991.

It is fair to report, however, that in all our research we have not encountered results outside Bulgaria that come anywhere near matching the ones reported above. Dr. Charles Schmid, in San Francisco, has reported students being presented with 400 foreign words in a day and being able to use them in conversation within three days (see page 335), a remarkable enough feat.

information. That type of relaxation is *not* getting ready to fall asleep. It's a state of *relaxed alertness*—what we sometimes call *relaxed awareness.*"[9]

Much of our recent knowledge in this field has been built on the pioneering research started in the 1950s by Bulgarian psychiatrist and educator Georgi Lozanov. Lozanov set out to determine why some people have super-memories.

After years of research, he concluded that we each have an "optimum learning state". This occurs, he says, "where heartbeat, breath-rate and brainwaves are smoothly synchronised and the body is relaxed but the mind concentrated and ready to receive new information."[10]

In putting that research into practice, Lozanov achieved some amazing results, particularly in foreign-language learning. By the early 1960s Berlitz, then the world's largest language-training school, promised students could learn 200 words after several days' training—a total of thirty hours.

But Lozanov's research reported Bulgarian students learning 1,200 words *a day* and remembering a remarkable 96.1 percent of them.[11]

Many others have built on his research. According to Schmid: "We now know that most people can achieve that ideal learning state fairly easily—and quickly. Deep breathing is one of the first keys. Music is the second—specific music with a certain beat that helps slow you down: anywhere from fifty to seventy beats a minute." [11]

The most common music to achieve that state comes from the baroque school of composers, in the seventh and early eighteenth centuries: the Italian Arcangelo Corelli, the Venician Antonio Vivaldi, France's Francois Coupertin and the Germans, Johann Sebastian Bach and George Frideric Handel.

Lozanov found baroque music harmonises the body and brain. In particular, it unlocks the emotional key to a super memory: the brain's limbic system. This system not only processes emotions, it is the link between the conscious and subconscious brain.

As Terry Wyler Webb and Dougles Webb put it brilliantly in *Accelerated Learning With Music: A Trainer's Manual:* "Music is the interstate highway to the memory system."[12]

Vivaldi's *Four Seasons* is one of the best-known pieces of baroque music used to start the journey along that highway. It makes it easy to shut out other thoughts and visualise the seasons.

Eight ways music aids learning

Music relaxes the mind
and lowers stress levels

Music acts directly on the body
and produces a tranquil state

Music stimulates and awakens
reviving bored learners

Music is mathematical
and stimulates specific brain circuits

Music inspires emotion
and that's the gateway to learning

Music is a state-changer
and allows you to vary the pace

Music is the universal language
and crosses all cultural barriers

Music is a powerful anchor
so it moors memory to learning

JEANNETTE VOS*

* In *How to make great presentations,* Invercargill, New Zealand, high-school teachers' five-day seminar, 2003.

In a model New Zealand school, Tahatai Coast, six-year-old children in one class not only created their own computer-animated short story of two children finding a kiwi flightless-bird trapped in a forest trap, they used *Four Seasons* as the background music. And then they computer-animated an orchestra playing it. Then, for good measure, added in a brief visual story of Vivaldi's life.

Handel's *Water Music* is also deeply soothing. And for teachers trained in new learning techniques, Johann Pachelbel's *Canon in D* is a favourite to relieve tension.

Most of those teachers also use specially-prepared tapes to start each learning session—with soothing word-pictures to match the music and encourage relaxation. Tapes can be either self-made, if you're competent in music, or bought. Their key first use in education is to put students into a relaxed, receptive state so they can focus on learning.

Break down the learning barriers

Lozanov says there are three main barriers to learning: the *critical-logical* barrier ("School isn't easy, so how can learning be fun and easy?"); the *intuitive-emotional* barrier ("I'm dumb, so I won't be able to do that"); and the *critical-moral* barrier ("Studying is hard work—so I'd better keep my head down"). Understand where a student "is coming from" and you gain better rapport. Especially in systems where students may be completely bored with old teaching methods: step into their world and you overcome any resistance quickly, smoothly.

Encourage personal goal-setting and learning outcomes

Encourage students to set their own goals—and to plan their own future. If they know where they are going, then their path is focused. In our experience, *most people will over-achieve personal targets that they set themselves*—possibly the soundest principle in management.

In classroom settings, we both encourage the "Station WIIFM" game—to focus on "What's In It For Me?" Not in a selfish sense, but to get participants, perhaps in pairs, to tell each other and teachers what they specifically hope to get from the session, the day or the year.

The way this is introduced is vital, especially in school. Many at-risk students get very angry with the traditional "You-will-learn-this today" introduction. Instead, good teachers invite students to set their own goals, right from the outset, and the outcomes they would like from the session.

How seven-year-olds explore the universe in new-model school

These are actual questions asked, and later answered, by seven-year-olds at the start of a six-week 'focused inquiry' into the planets:

❏ **What is the hottest part of the sun?**

❏ **When was space discovered?**

❏ **Why doesn't the sun have an ozone layer?**

❏ **What is inside a Black Hole?**

❏ **How hot are sun spots?**

❏ **When will the sun explore?**

❏ **What do spring, summer, autumn and winter have to do with the solar system?**

❏ **Why is there no air in space?**

❏ **What is a comet and what is a meteor?**

❏ **How were satellites put into space?**

❏ **Why is there only one sun in our solar system?**

❏ **How was the ozone layer made?**

❏ **Can there be any hotels in the universe?**

OVERSEAS FAMILY SCHOOL REPORT*

** From School of The Future tabloid, which can be downloaded at
www.ofs.edu.sg
For details of their 'focused inquiry' method, download page 3
of that publication*

In the International Baccalaureate elementary-school programme, every grade spends six weeks collectively researching one global project. It might be "endangered species", "great inventions" or "the solar system". And their research projects always start off by the students themselves listing their own questions first (see typical list, opposite). And then they set out to find the answers—and record their findings in interesting multimedia ways.

But often students in less interesting environments come with "hidden agendas"—and they don't always "buy in" to the a subject agenda. The key is to make learning a partnership, where the teacher prepares a smorgasbord of possible "curriculum pieces" and the students get a big say in what they want out of it.

Try visualising your goal

Visualising is a powerful learning tool. An ineffective teacher might well say: "Don't forget to study or you might do poorly in the upcoming test"—a negative reinforcer.

Eric Jensen suggests two better ways. One is to encourage students to visualise precisely how they would be using their new-found knowledge in the future. The other is to plant a positive thought that will encourage students to browse through their study-book looking for specific answers that might be used in the future.

We cannot stress this point too strongly: many teachers do not realise how damaging negative suggestions can be.

Trigger the emotions

Nor can we overstress that the emotional part of the brain is the gateway to long-term memory, so all good teaching encourages warm emotions. This fuses what you have been learning into deep memory.

2. The presentation: through exploration and inquiry

Positivity and linking are the first ones

All good presentations must be learner-centred and linked to students' own goals and existing knowledge. The flower is the perfect metaphor: "What does it take to make your flower grow?"

Another technique to guarantee involvement from the start is for the learners and the instructor to toss a squashy, brightly coloured Koosh ball to volunteers to tell one main point they already know about a topic, and

Prove it to yourself in two minutes

How to learn to count in Japanese by seeing, speaking and doing

English	Japanese	Say	Do
one	ichi	itchy	Scratch your
two	ni	knee[1]	knee.
three	san	Sun	Point to sky
four	shi	she	Point to girl
five	go	go	Walk
six	roku	rocku[1]	Rock 'n' roll
seven	shichi	she-she	Double sneeze
eight	hachi	hat-she	Put on hat[2]
nine	kyu	coo	Coo like dove
ten	ju	ju	Don Jewish cap[2]

1. Say 'itchy knee" and "Sun, she go rocku" as sentences as you mime the actions.
2. If you haven't a hat or cap to don, mime the actions with your hands.

to draw Mind Maps covering the same points—from a pre-prepared map that lists the main "learning branches".

The sequence is designed to encourage the learners of every subject to start by identifying what they want to know, and then proceeding from what they already know—generally an amazing amount.

The entire presentation must also be positive. The facilitator should never suggest in any way that the session is anything but fun—no "now the break's over, let's get back to the hard work" talk.

Lozanov called his fast-learning process "suggestopedia," from "suggestology"—but that is an unfortunate translation into English. Says Stockwell: "The name is rather unusual, but if you see 'to suggest' in the sense of 'to propose' or 'to recommend' then it is easier to understand the relationship." [13]

The power of suggestion is paramount in learning: we all do best when we think we can do it; we fail if we expect to fail. Every adult has seen how infants' learning abilities soar in a favourable, positive atmosphere. All good Lozanov-style facilitators try to recreate the same kind of positive fun-filled atmosphere in the classroom. And like all good advertising copywriters, they go out of their way to stress how easy the project is. Japanese-language teachers may well use the "Itchy knee; sun, she go rock!" exercise (opposite).

Business-seminars may well start with the story of Ray Krok, the fiftytwo-year-old seller of milkshake machines, who first visited a Californian hamburger restaurant in 1952 and saw the start of an idea that ended up as McDonald's—an example to show how great projects can grow from very modest beginnings.

Lozanov stresses the important links between conscious and subconscious presentation. He believes each of us has an enormous reserve of brain power waiting to be tapped. He believes that by far the most important part of all learning is subconscious; and that good teachers remove the barriers to learning by making their presentations logical, ethical, enjoyable and stress-free. Hence the importance of posters and "peripherals" as part of the total presentation: whether those posters are made in advance by a seminar presenter or, in inquiry-based school classrooms, are made by the students themselves.

Getting the big picture first

A major presentation technique is to present "the big picture" first—to provide an overview, like the total jigsaw puzzle picture, so that all the

Try this balloon test to match your abilities with others

To demonstrate to any group their individual learning and working strengths, provide each with four different coloured balloons. And get each to select, from the boxes below, his or her eight main strengths.

Creativity (red)	**Communications (blue)**
Open minded	Writing
Lateral thinking	Speaking
Brainstorming	Listening
Visionary	Visualising
Administration (yellow)	**Organisation (green)**
Financial	Leader
Structured	Simplifier
Logical	Delegator
Sequential	Self starter

Then get each person to inflate the four balloons to match his or her main strengths. Thus, if you selected all four in the red box and only one in the blue, you'd blow your blue balloon up to a quarter the size of the red one. Then split your team into groups of four so they combine strengths from each quartile.*

The balloon-match, as used above, adapted from original concept from Alistair Rylatt, Director, Excel Human Resource Development, P.O. Box 164, Newtown 2042, NSW, Australia.

later pieces can then fall into place. Again, posters or other classroom peripherals may well present the big picture—so it's always there as a focusing point.

Telling a story is also a great preview technique.

And field trips are highly recommended at the start of any study—to see the big picture in action. At the "Vivaldi trapped-kiwi story" project we've already mentoned, all classes study four schoolwide projects a year, and all other "subjects" are integrated into them. And if that schoolwide project is, for example, conservation, regular field trips will be held to explore all aspects of the subject. One of their nearby middle schools holds yearly adventure camps, videos all their confidence-building activities, and then uses the finished video to teach other teachers how to edit videos.

Drawing Mind Maps at the start of study, including all the main "limbs", allows students to draw in the smaller branches later.

Involve all the senses

All good presentations also appeal to all individual learning styles.

The most neglected learning style in nearly every school system is kinesthetic—or movement.

Every good learning experience has plenty of verbal stimulation, plenty of music, plenty of visuals—but the really great teachers make sure to have plenty of action, plenty of participation, plenty of movement. Even though students will have different combinations of learning styles, everyone *embeds* new information by *doing: by actually using it.*

Step out of the lecturing role

This is probably the major personal change required in teaching styles. All the best "teachers" are activators, facilitators, coaches, motivators, orchestrators.

Always orchestrate "non-conscious" processing

Since Lozanov practitioners say most learning is "subconscious", the room setting, posters, body language, tone of speech and positive attitude all are vital parts of the learning process.

Plenty of role playing and "identities"

Lozanov teachers also encourage students to "act the part". There are few faster ways to learn science than to act out the roles of famous scientists; or to learn history by putting yourself in the historical setting.

Because music can both calm and stimulate, it offers one of the quickest ways to influence the mood of a group.

JEANNETTE VOS*

* In her Learning Revolution seminars on
The eight ways to use music in learning, teaching and training.

Organise plenty of "state changes"

In subject-based classes, the best teachers organise plenty of "state changes" so that students switch from singing, to action, to talking, to viewing, to rhyme, to Mind Mapping, to group discussions. This has a two-fold purpose:

1. It reinforces the information in all learning styles; and

2. It breaks up the lesson into chunks for easy learning.

Both have a major bearing on how well the information is absorbed. For example, it is now well proven that, in any presentation, students can generally remember easiest the information at the start, the end and any "outstanding" examples that gripped their imagination. Regular "state changes" provide the opportunity for many more "firsts", "lasts" and graphic examples.

But in project-based study, students working in teams, and sharing their own strengths with others, generally get too caught up in the action to get bored. And the very act of learning-by-doing, while you learn the talents and skills of other team-members in the process, is stimulating enough.

Make learning-how-to-learn a key part of every course

This is probably the main overall desired result from all learning. So the techniques should be blended into all activities.

The Lozanov "concerts"

Possibly Lozanov's greatest contribution to education has again been in the sphere of music: not only to relax your mind and put it into a highly receptive state—but to use music to float new information into your amazing memory system. This is particularly useful when learning detailed information on a new subject—like a foreign language.

Lozanov recommends two *concerts*. And again, Charles Schmid has summarised the theory and practice neatly: "If, say, a class is learning a foreign language, as the first step the teacher sets out the new vocabulary in the form of a play, and with an overview of it in pictures. The student sits there taking a 'mental movie' of it. "Immediately following this comes the first concert—what Lozanov called the *active concert*. With the student looking at the text, the teacher turns on some selected music, and he reads the foreign language in time to the music. He deliberately acts out the words dramatically in time to the music.

Eight-year-olds learn French with their own fashion show

They record commentary and video the action*

* Photo: Overseas Family School, Singapore: primary school students have the choice of six international second languages. These eight-year-olds are learning French by staging a Parisian fashion show, including live commentaries. All students keep their own digital portfolio, including videoed demonstrations, on the school's digital network. *www.ofs.edu.sg*

"Now there's no magic to this; it's precisely why it is easier to learn the lyrics of a song, rather than remember all the words on a page of notes. The music is somehow a carrier and the teacher surfs along with the music—almost like catching a wave."[14]

Lozanov's second learning phase is called a *passive concert.*

Charles Schmid again: "The second concert follows immediately after the first. And here we use very specific slow baroque music—around sixty beats to the minute—very precise. And while the first reading of the language was very dramatic, the second is in a more natural intonation. Now the students are invited to close their eyes if they want—although they don't have to. They put the text aside, and imagine, say, that they are in a theatre in the country they're studying, and somebody is acting a story in the background. Generally this will be the last part of a particular language session—and the students will then go home—and probably skim through their foreign-language 'play' just before they go to sleep." Overnight the subconscious goes to work—and the seemingly automatic start of the transfer to long-term memory storage. Lozanov fans claim the use of music in this way can accomplish 60 percent of learning in 5 percent of the time.[15]

We hasten to add that even great Lozanov enthusiasts do not recommend using his full "concert" technique in every session. Even in something as clearly defined as learning a foreign language, perhaps only three "concert" sessions might be held in a week. But all the other key principles of learning would be used in other sessions.

At one of our favourite international primary schools,[16] for example, all students spend one hour a day learning a foreign language—with a choice of six: English, Mandarin, French, Spanish, German and Japanese. In three typical classes in one week eight-year-olds might be:

❑ Learning French by presenting a Parisian fashion parade, with their own French-language commentary—and then teaching French to their audience of parents;

❑ Learning the Chinese written language and spoken Mandarin by showing their parents a multimedia presentation, in Chinese, on the most healthy diet to use for better learning; and

❑ Learning German by staging a German version of Snow White.

No need for Losanov "concerts" here. The students add in their own French, Chinese and German music to their own shows. And now videos of each are on the school's website for others to share.

**The richest component of one
of our learning courses
is the activation phase.
This takes about 75 to
80 percent of the time.
We play board games,
card games, we play with
a ball, we play with
paper dolls, we play
musical chairs, we play
with construction paper.
Much like the games you
would buy in a toy shop
but adapted to
make learning fun.**

LIBYAN LABIOSA-CASSONE*

*Accelerated-learner trainer—author interview, Chicago, Illinois.

3. Thinking about it, and deep memory storage

Education is, of course, not only about absorbing new information. It involves thinking about it and storing it into deep memory as well.

Learning how to think is a major part of every educational programme, and good facilitators use "thinking games" and "mind games" to part synthesise information—and provide "state changes". In business seminars we've found it best to introduce this by fun projects: designing "a golf ball that can't get lost" or playing the "What if?" game on subjects well divorced from the activities of each group.

For deep memory storage, Lozanov's active and passive concerts are tops—specially for storing detailed new information. They are designed to access the long-term memory system in order to link new information subconsciously with data already stored.

4. Activate to draw out the learning

Storing information is also only one part of the learning process. The information also has to be accessed. So the next step is "activation".

And here games, skits, discussions and plays can all be used to "activate" the memory-banks—and reinforce the learning pathways.

Again, this needn't make more work for the teacher. The opposite, in fact. Students love to organise their own plays, presentations, debates and games. Give them the chance to present their new-found information to the rest of the class or group—any way they prefer.

Schmid explains a typical fun-based activation session, after French-language students have slept on a concert-session: "The next morning, or within fortyeight hours, the students come in; they haven't said a word of French yet—or at least not in the new vocabulary. Now comes three or four hours of what we call activation.

"Now we play games with the vocabulary. We're feeding their brains in different ways. We've already done it consciously in showing them the words and pictures of their French play. Then we've fed it into their subconscious, with the aid of music. And now they're activating their brains in different ways to make sure it's stored. And I tell you: now I wouldn't teach in any other way"

Schmid, who died not long after our interview, had degrees in music, psychology and foreign language instruction. He taught at the University of Texas and New York University for many years with traditional

Lozanov's music for the two "concerts"*

ACTIVE CONCERT

Beethoven, Concerto for Piano and Orchestra No. 5 in B-flat major.

Mozart, Symphony in D major, "Haffner," and Symphony in D Major, "Prague."

Haydn, Concerto No. 1 in C Major for Violin and Orchestra; Concerto No. 2 in G Major for Violin and Orchestra.

Haydn,Symphony in C Major No. 101, "L'Horioge;" and Symphony in G Major No. 94.

Mozart, Concerto for Violin & Orchestra in A Major No. 5; Symphony in A Major No. 29; Symphony in G Minor No. 40.

Brahms, Concerto for Violin and Orchestra in D. Major, Op. 77.

PASSIVE CONCERT

Vivaldi, Five Concertos for Flute and Chamber Orchestra.

Handel, Concerto for Organ and Orchestra in B-flat Major, Op. 7, No. 6.

J. S. Bach, Prelude in G Major, "Dogmatic Chorales."

Corelli, Concerti Grossi, Op. 6, No. 4, 10, 11, 12.

J.S. Bach, Fantasia for Organ in G. Major; Fantasia in C Minor.

Couperin, Sonatas for Harpisichord: "Le Parnasse" (Apotheosis of Corelli); "L'Estree;" J.F. Rameau, Concert Pieces for Harpisichord "Pieces de clavecin" No.1 and No. 5.

*From *The Foreign Language Teacher's Suggestopedic Manual,* by Georgi Lozanov and Evalina Gateva, published by Gordon and Breach, New York,1988.

methods before "getting hooked" on the new techniques. "I started to teach French and German and sometimes Italian with these new techniques; I wanted to see if the system worked, if it really was all it was cracked up to be. And I was amazed. I would teach students in a three and a half hour class. I'd give them 400 words of French, say, the first day. And by the end of the third day they were able to repeat them in forms of conversation. And that had never happened before.

"Previously at the university, if I gave students twentyfive words a day in the old way, they'd be lucky to remember ten the next day. I was convinced. In fact, when I first started using the techniques myself, I started dreaming in the language after about the third day. And I had never had that feedback before."

Schmid's experience left him no doubt as to the benefits of the new learning methods: "I would say the speedup in the learning process is anywhere from five to twenty times—maybe twentyfive times—over what it was in traditional methods. But it's not only the acceleration; it's the quality of learning that goes on. And the feedback. They say: 'This is fun. Why didn't I learn this way in high school?'

"Recently at a New England telephone company students were using these methods to study optic fibres and some technical telecommunications work. The trainees were sitting on the floor, playing with wooden blocks, fitting them together and understanding what goes on in an optic fiber. The trainer said: 'OK, it's time for a break.' And the trainees said: 'You take a break; we're having fun; we're learning; and we're getting this finally.' That's what I mean. It works and it's fun."

5. Apply it

In our view, the real test of learning is not a written examination through multiple-choice questions. The key is to use the learning and apply it to purposeful situations, preferably real-life.

The real test of a French course is how well you can speak French. The real test of a sales course is how well you can sell.

You learn to play a piano by playing a piano, you learn to type by typing, to ride a bike by riding a bike, to speak in public by speaking in public.

So the best teachers and business seminar organisers plan plenty of action sessions to back up the theory so students can purposefully use and apply the learning.

Knowledge is not something a learner absorbs.

Knowledge is something a learner creates.

Learners need time for integration.

DAVE MEIER
*The Accelerated Learning Handbook**

* Published by McGraw-Hill, New York, NY.

Turn your students into teachers

As in the activation phase, it makes sound sense to have students work in pairs or teams, with a free hand to prepare their own presentations of main points. Groups in a teacher-training class, for example, may each be asked to crystallise a specific aspect of educational psychology. And more and more schools are using the "buddy" system, where an older or more qualified student helps another, and both benefit.

Encourage Mind Mapping

We've already covered the principles of this and suggested you use it to preview the learning, but it is also a remarkable way to review and make notes. *It really is what it says: a map that records main points in the same way the brain stores information—like branches on a tree.* It's also a major tool in the next process.

6. Review, evaluate and celebrate

Even highly efficient learners will not always be conscious of whether they "know what they know". One way to bring the learner to that awareness is through a quick Koosh-ball throw at the end of a lesson. This will jog students' memories of all the important learnings of the day. Another way is a "passive concert" review, which also covers all the points handled.

And then comes one of the most crucial steps: the self-evaluation. This is where a student truly "digs within" to uncover those precious gems of the day. Self-evaluation is a tool for higher thinking: reflecting, analysing, synthesising, then judging.

Peer-evaluation and instructor-evaluation are also important parts in culminating a lesson, but the most important is self-evaluation.

Another way to review is to skim over your Mind Maps or "high-lighted" notes, or both:

❑ Before you go to sleep on the day you've been studying;

❑ For five minutes each morning for the next week.

❑ For five minutes once a week in the following month.

❑ For five minutes once a month for six months.

❑ And just before you need to use it—or before an exam.

If you're on a one-week course with an examination at the end, spend at least fifteen minutes a night on that day's Mind Map and highlights,

Learn a language in record time

In 1993, Bridley Moor High School in Redditch, England, tested the effectiveness of accelerated learning methods for studying a foreign language.

One group of students' German study included ten weeks of accelerated learning methods, and their examination results were compared with others studying at the same level by conventional methods.

On July 16, 1993, BBC television broadcast the examination results:

	Using new methods	Using normal methods
80% pass mark or better	65%	11%
90% pass mark or better	38%	3%

Thus, using new techniques, more than ten times as many students achieved a 90 percent pass mark.

Sources:

School examination results from Mrs Val Duffy-Cross, Assistant Head, Bridley Moor High School, Redditch, U.K. Television programme on BBC Midland TV, July 16, 1993. Course materials and methods from Accelerated Learning Systems, Aston Clinton, Bucks, England. The course is designed for do-it-yourself home study, but can be supplied with an optional kit for teachers.

and at least five minutes on each of the previous days. Or if you're writing an article or even a book, it's amazing how much you can recall by skimming your Mind Maps and underlined books.

And always remember to celebrate every victory—just as any sporting achiever would celebrate. Praise the entire class effort, and whenever possible turn that praise into a recap of the main points learned.

Putting it all together

And how does all this theory work in practice? Let's look at four examples, in two sections:

1. Teaching specific subjects—a foreign language and science.

2. A world-leading school that has taken some of the best learning theories and turned them into successsful school-wide practice.

The army learns a foreign language in record time

Learning a new foreign language has a double benefit for research:

1. Because many students don't know anything about the subject when they start, it's easy to run authoritative tests, at the end of the course, to see how much has been learned.

2. It's then equally easy to check those results against results from other teaching-methods.

In England, these methods have been tested in high school (see opposite for teaching German). And also in the American army, on the same subject, with one of the best users of the new techniques, Professor Freeman Lynn Dhority, of Boston, Massachusetts.

Dr. Dhority was already a highly successful German teacher before he studied the *suggestopedia* method with Lozanov. He then had the opportunity of testing the method and comparing it with other measured results using standard-style German teaching. All materials for the course were prepared thoroughly in advance according to Lozanov guidelines: "peripherals", including posters, music, games, songs, activities and scripts. And because of Dr. Dhority's academic training, he was able to ensure that the results could be documented.

His "control group" of eleven students studied basic German, using accelerated learning techniques, for 108 hours over three and a half weeks (eighteen days) at Fort Devens army base. The results were then compared with another group of thirtyfour army students, not taught by Dr.

How to increase the learning rate 661% with these techniques

Former Boston Professor of Education Freeman Lynn Dhority specialises in teaching second languages by many of the creative learning techniques outlined in this book.

In one well-researched study:

❏ **Three groups of American soldiers studied basic German for 12 weeks using standard educational methods (60 days, 360 hours).**

❏ **Another group studied the same subject, using "accelerated learning" techniques, for 18 days (108 hours).**

❏ **Only 29 percent of the "standard groups" reached the required level of understanding in 360 hours.**

❏ **But 64 percent of the "accelerated learning" group achieved the same ability to read German in 108 hours; and 73 percent reached the required level of understanding spoken German.**

❏ **Statistically, that is a 661 per cent better learning rate: more than twice the results in one-third the time.***

*These results are summarised from: The 661% Solution: A statistical evaluation of the extraordinary effectiveness of Freeman Lynn Dhority's U.S. Army accelerated learning German class, by Lyelle L. Palmer, Professor of Education and Special Education Chair, Winona State University, Minnesota, in a joint paper with Professor Dhority.

Dhority, learning basic German under regular "audio drill" methods over a period of 360 hours, spread over twelve weeks. And the results were dramatic: effectively, 661 percent better than other normal methods[17] (see research summary opposite).

An accelerated integrative learning teacher

For a glimpse at a new-style secondary-school teacher in action, the late Leo Wood's chemistry classes at Tempe High School in Arizona, have left a striking impression. Walk into the room and you're struck first by the paintings and photographs: a Monet, a mountain scene, portraits of Albert Einstein and Linus Pauling, and graphics on chemistry and the miracle of life. From the ceiling hang posters and models of molecules and polyatomic ions. Relaxing baroque music fills the room. The classroom is colourful, interesting and relaxing.

Wood used techniques brought to the United States by another Bulgarian, Dr. Ivan Barzakov, and perfected with his actress partner Pamela Rand. While Lozanov used his techniques mainly for foreign language-learning, Barzakov applies his principles to any subject. Effectively he combines Lozanov's "two concerts" into one. And he's developed a careful selection of music tapes which are used not just for learning and memory, but for imagination, creativity, problem solving and decision making. He carefully blends different types of music together for contrast, "because variety stimulates our minds and keeps us alert".[18] He also changes the "texture" of the music, from violin to flute through to mandolin and clavichord and piano. The result is a unique sequence that brings serenity, relaxation and anticipation. Taking part in a class with OptimaLearning music is very much like sitting through a classic movie, where the music is a powerful subconscious carrier of the total theme, and the visual art blends with it.

Visit a Leo Wood-style chemistry class, you'd soon be caught up in that same type of drama. As part of a typical demonstration, the teacher might switch the lights off, turn up a special tape for creativity and imagination, and start mixing chemicals together in a test tube. As the suspense mounts, sparks of light begin popping in the test tube, one at a time. The teacher begins talking about light and life and their interaction. The popping becomes more rapid and the sparks much brighter.

The teacher introduces the theme: "Life is a miracle, and you and I are part of that miracle."[18] The teacher walks to a demonstration table, pours

How to go from 52% achieving A, B or C grades to 92% in high school chemistry.

LEO WOOD
Science teacher, Tempe High School, Arizona

the test tube contents into a large beaker, and says: "We will learn how miraculous life really is." A big burst of fire flashes from a beaker and into the test tube as the music reaches a climax. The lights go on, the music stops, and the students are silently processing what has just happened.

As Wood put it in a note not long before his death: "The theme for the year has been introduced, properties of three compounds and density are discussed, and the relationship and interaction of light and life have been demonstrated and revealed—all in about fifteen minutes." [19]

Then he may take the students outside, to stand facing the sun with their eyes closed, before returning to class to write their impressions as Debussy music plays in the background.

Then in the teacher's finale the students learn of the fusion reaction that occurs on the surface of the sun. But not as a lecture: they actually become the hydrogen atoms as their bodies become a circle, and their fists are brought together to indicate the fusion of the nuclei.

"We have a little oral quiz at the end of the class, and everyone always gets 100 percent." And in later examinations, the results are spectacular. *Before introducing these accelerated learning techniques, 52 percent of Tempe chemistry students achieved A, B and C grades. With the new methods: 93 percent.*[20]

The tragedy, of course, is that Leo Wood died without his incredible talents being captured on video, DVDs or in other interactive ways. His work and Dr. Dhority's German classes provide graphic examples of how brilliantly innovative new methods of teaching "difficult" subjects can be improved greatly:

❏ First, by using the new, effective and interactive learning methods;

❏ Secondly, by marrying those in with new multimedia methods of making the world's best teachers and their methods available to millions, not just twenty or thirty lucky students.

5. Transforming an entire school

So is it possible to combine an integrated model of great principles and apply them to a whole school?

The answer is a resounding "yes". And one of the outstanding models is New City School in the city of St. Louis, Missouri. It serves 360 students from three years up to sixth grade.

New City is an independent school, in an area that cannot be described

Multiple Intelligence theory teaches us that all kids are smart but they are smart in different ways.

THOMAS R. HOERR
*Becoming a Multiple Intelligences School**

* Published by ASCD (Association for Supervision and Curriculum Development). Thomas Hoerr is Principal of New City School, St. Louis, Missouri. He is also facilitator of the ASCD Multiple Intelligences Network. His email address: trhoerr@newcityschool.org

as wealthy. Around 33 percent of its students are minorities, mostly African Americans. Almost 27 percent receive need-based financial aid. Other students come from all parts of the city, with parents choosing the school because of its mission and philosophy.

And that philosophy is very strong. New City is a "multiple intelligences" school. A few years after Professor Howard Gardner proposed that theory in the 1983 book, *Frames of Mind,* New City principal Thomas R. Hoerr, read it. And, in his own words: "Life has never been the same for any of us."

In that first book, as we've seen—and will see much more of in the next chapter—Harvard's Gardner identified at least seven different types of "multiple intelligence": mathematical-logical, linguistic, visual-spatial, musical, physical-kinesthetic, interpersonal and intrapersonal.

New City School has been implementing that MI theory since 1998, the second school to do so in America.*

Says Hoerr: "MI theory teaches us that all kids are smart, but they are smart in different ways." So Hoerr and his faculty started their quest to bring out that individual talent in all its students, and to expose them all the other flowering talents and learning styles in the school. To the school's principal, "MI seemed to offer another way to recognise the uniqueness of each individual".[21]

And not just in students, but in faculty, too. The early enthusiasts formed themselves into a Talent Committee, and gave themselves the task of using all their own "multiple intelligences" in studying each chapter of Gardner's book. Soon the enthusiasm spread, not just to other faculty members but to the students' parents as well.

The school started by using a yearlong, schoolwide theme. And because of the role the Mississippi River plays in their district, they chose *Life Along The River* as the first. Says Hoerr: "The theme was enjoyed by everyone. The synergy of siblings in different grades, talking at dinner or on the way to school about what they had learned about the Mississippi River in their respective classes, was great. And so was the dialogue among teachers from different grades as they were trading ideas and talking about how they were bringing the river into their classroom." [22]

But the next year they all opted to concentrate, instead, on one theme for each grade level. For three- and four-year-olds, the theme was *All*

* *Key School in Indianapolis was first, and we return to that model school at the end of the next chapter.*

Model for the future: an entire book created by the faculty of an elementary school, with complete resource guide.

Celebrating Multiple Intelligences:
Teaching for Success*

* Written and produced by the faculty at New City School,
St. Louis, Missouri.
http://www.newcityschool.org

About Me: "Who I am and how do I fit within my family and class?" For kindergarten: *Busy bodies*—"How do different systems in my body function?" Second grade concentrated on *All kinds of homes:* "Why and how to people make homes different in their communities." And fourth graders studied *Making a difference:* "What are the characteristics of someone who makes a difference?"

And all faculty, staff and parents soon discovered they *were* making a difference. As faculty delved more into the depths of "multiple intelligences", the more they realised the individual strengths in both students and teachers. And, like other great schools around the world—including those we'll meet in other chapters—that combined faculty-study led to some unusual results.

For a start, the faculty not only shared their own talents and investigations, they set out to share them with the world. In 1984 the whole school produced its first book, *Celebrating Multiple Intelligences: Teaching for Successs.* And in 1996 they followed up with *Succeeding with Multiple Intelligences: teaching through the personals.*

In the first, the faculty took the entire Misssouri state curriculum and showed how to teach that by concentrating on and sharing the great strengths and talents of each student. And by building on these strengths, all children were able to then learn from the talents of others.

That first book set the agenda to achieve that, at every grade level:

❑ How musically-talented students could learn third-grade math or social studies to music—and share that music with others.

❑ How second-graders with visual-spatial "intelligence" could use those talents to learn geography or history—and to share their resulting artwork, sculpture or demonstration-models with others.

❑ How those with great mathematical or logical strengths could use those to learn language-arts.

❑ How those with physical or kinesthetic skills could use those to learn anything—by physically doing something.

But these were not just theoretical experiments. In that first book, the faculty, students and staff pooled an enormous amount of knowledge. Every section of it includes:

❑ *A complete resource guide for teachers.* Not just a great range of books to use, but musical resources, video resources, art examples—and "tools" to develop each of the MI talents.

Not just classes. Model school also provides:

- ❏ **Before-school programme each day from 7 a.m.**
- ❏ **After-school activities till 6.30.**
- ❏ **Talent classes, run by experts with different intelligences.**
- ❏ **Ten-week summer holiday programme, including camp.**
- ❏ **Two detailed guidebooks written by faculty.**
- ❏ **Another written by principal.**
- ❏ **And school tours for visitors from around the world.**

NEW CITY SCHOOL
St. Louis, Missouri, USA*

http://www.newcityschool.org
or email Principal, Thomas R. Hoerr: trhoerr@newcityschool.org

❏ *Student resources:* a great array of things to do, in class, at home and in the community, to build and share different talents.

❏ *And resources for parents, too:* books they might read, movies they might see together with their children, galleries and museums to visit, music to play, activities to enjoy

And soon the entire school was buzzing with "multiple-intelligence" activities. Instead of pen-and-paper multiple-choice questions, all students were collaborating to actually demonstrate their multiple talents.

Even now, Tom Hoerr is amazed at how long one-dimensional "IQ" tests have dominated schooling. "Despite the fact that the misuse of tests and test-scores flies in the face of common sense, many people continue to embrace the IQ model, assuming that there is one measure that can assess an individual's intelligence. Of course, we know this is nonsense."

And not just "know": New City School students actually prove it by *showing that they know*. Regularly they demonstrate this by projects, exhibitions and presentations: what the school calls PEP.

But the innovation doesn't stop there.

❏ The faculty have together devised their own "Multiple-Intelligence Progress Report" for each child, on each curriculum subject, but related to how each student specifically demonstrates an ever-widening range of "multiple strengths".

❏ And the exercise extends well beyond school class hours. The school's day officially runs from 8.30 to 3.30. But New City offers a range of services from 7 a.m. to 6.30 p.m.

The before-school programme is free, and is staffed primarily by teacher-aids. As many as 150 of the 360 students stay after school for a fee-based Extended Day Programme. This is mainly recreational, although a study hall is offered for upper-grade students. And the school offers Talents Classes, all framed around MI, and often taken by parents, teachers and outsiders with specialist talents. The school also offers a ten-week summer holiday programme, including a live-in camp.

With 45,000 copies sold of the two faculty-produced books, New City has made its multi-talented learning model available to others. And now, of course, interactive technology and the tools of instant communications make it possible to turn that model into a world programme. Multi-talented teachers and students at one school—now multi-talented publishers co-creating with other multi-talented people around the world.

Developing your unique talent

Every human being has a learning style, and every human being has strengths.[1]

It's as individual as a signature.[2]

No learning style is better— or worse—than any other style.[3]

All groups—cultural, academic, male, female—include all types of learning styles.[4]

Within each culture, socio-economic strata or classroom, there are as many differences as there are between groups.[5]

Quotations from research by
Professors Ken and Rita Dunn*

*The sources for the quotations on this page are cited in the
chapter notes for chapter 9, to which they refer.
To obtain details of the Dunns' learning and working style checks,
contact Learning Styles Network, School of Education and
Human Services, St. Johns University, Grand Central and
Utopia Parkways, Jamaica, NY 11439.

How to find your own learning style and use your many intelligences

Winston Churchill did poorly at schoolwork. He talked with a stutter and a lisp. Yet he became one of the greatest leaders and orators of the twentieth century.

Albert Einstein, as we've seen, was a daydreamer. His teachers in Germany told him he would never amount to anything, that his questions destroyed class discipline, that he would be better off out of school. Yet he went on to become one of the greatest scientists in world history.

Thomas Alva Edison was beaten at school with a heavy leather strap because his teacher considered him "addled" for asking so many questions. He was chastised so much that his mother took him out of school after only three months' formal education. He went on to become probably the most prolific inventor of all time.

Fortunately Edison's mother—a former school teacher herself—was a pioneer in true learning. Says *The World Book Encyclopedia:* "She had the notion, unusual for those times, that learning could be fun. She made a game of teaching him—she called it exploring—the exciting world of knowledge. The boy was surprised at first, and then delighted. Soon he began to learn so fast that his mother could no longer teach him." But he continued to explore, experiment and teach himself.

Einstein, Churchill and Edison had learning styles that were not suited to their schools' teaching styles.

And that same mismatch continues today for millions of others. It is possibly the biggest single cause of school failure.

It's also obvious that everyone has different talents. Pablo Picasso

351

Multiple intelligences

Personal and professional uses

1. Linguistic intelligence.

Commonly found in: Novelists, poets, copywriters, scriptwriters, orators, political leaders, editors, publicists, journalists and speech writers.

Example of famous person: Winston Churchill, British journalist turned orator, political leader and writer.

Likely traits:	How to strengthen for learning:
* Sensitive to patterns	* Tell stories
* Orderly	* Play memory games with names, places
* Systematic	
* Ability to reason	* Read stories, jokes
* Likes to listen	* Write stories, jokes
* Likes to read	* Do vocabulary skits
* Likes to write	* Use journal writing
* Spells easily	* Interviewing
* Likes word games	* Do puzzles, spelling games
* Has good memory for trivia	* Integrate writing and reading with other subject areas
* May be good public speaker and debater, although some linguistic specialists may prefer either oral or written communication	* Produce, edit and supervise class magazine
	* Debate
	* Discussions
	* Use word processor as introduction to computers

ACKNOWLEDGEMENT:

This page and the charts on following pages have been based on and adapted from the original research of Howard Gardner, David Thornburg, Thomas Armstrong, David Lazier, Linda Campbell, Bruce Campbell, Dee Dickinson and Jeannette Vos.

was obviously a great painter, William Shakespeare a phenomenal writer, Joc Louis and Babe Ruth great sportsmen, Enrico Caruso a brilliant tenor, Anna Pavlova an outstanding ballet dancer and Katharine Hepburn a fine actress.

Every person reading this page has a different *lifestyle* and a different *workstyle*. Successful businesses depend on their ability to cater to those different lifestyles. And human-resource consultants spend their lives matching workstyle talents to jobs.

Yet many of our schools operate as if each person is identical. Even worse: most operate with an evaluation or testing system that rewards only a limited number of abilities. And those rewards early in life often separate the allegedly gifted and intelligent from those who are claimed to be less intelligent and underachievers.

Possibly the worst educational innovation of last century was the so-called intelligence test. As we've discussed, some tests may do a good job of testing *certain* abilities. But they don't test *all* abilities. Worse, they gave rise to the concept that intelligence is fixed at birth. It's not.

Better still: we each have access to many different "intelligences" or intelligence traits.

And if the current authors had to choose any one step needed to transform the world's high-school systems in particular it would be this: find out each student's combination of learning styles and talents—and cater to it; and at the same time encourage the well-rounded development of all potential abilities.

The major fault with so-called I.Q., or intelligent quotient, tests is that they *confuse logic with overall intelligence*—when logic, as we've seen, is only one form of thinking or learning skill. Some tests also confuse linguistic ability and mathematics ability with overall ability.

In recent years Harvard Professor Howard Gardner has been one of many who have made pioneer breakthroughs in shattering the "fixed I.Q." myth. For more than twenty years Gardner has used prolific research to prove that each person has at least seven different "intelligence centres", probably more. As we've touched on, he's defined:

Linguistic intelligence as the ability to speak or write well—highly developed in such people as Winston Churchill, John. F. Kennedy, William Shakespeare, Oprah Winfrey and all brilliant writers.

Logical-mathematical intelligence as the ability to reason, calculate

Multiple intelligences
Personal and professional uses

2. Logical-mathematical intelligence.

Commonly found in: Mathematicians, scientists, engineers, animal trackers, police investigators, lawyers and accountants.

Example of prominent person: Marian Diamond, Professor of Neuroanatomy at the University of California at Berkeley.

Likely traits:	How to strengthen for learning:
* Likes abstract thinking	* Stimulate problem solving
* Likes being precise	* Do mathematical computation games
* Enjoys counting	
* Likes being organised	* Analyse and interpret data
* Uses logical structure	* Use reasoning
* Enjoys computers	* Encourage own strengths
* Enjoys problem-solving	* Encourage practical experiments
* Enjoys experimenting in logical way	* Use prediction
* Prefers orderly note-taking	* Integrate organisation and maths into other curricular areas
* Enjoys strategic and analytical thinking	
* Keen on statistical reliance and verification	* Have a place for everything
* Often enjoys accounting or banking careers	* Allow things to be done step-by-step
	* Use deductive thinking
	* Use computers for spreadsheets, calculations

and handle logical thinking—highly developed in such people as Bertrand Russell, John Maynard Keynes and Ernest Rutherford.

Visual-spatial intelligence as the ability to paint, take great photographs or create sculpture or make Peter-Jackson movies.

Bodily-kinesthetic intelligence as the ability to use one's hands or body—epitomised in sports achievers and great actors.

Musical intelligence as the ability to compose songs, sing and play instruments.

Interpersonal intelligence—what we would prefer to call "social" intelligence—as the ability to relate to others.

Intrapersonal intelligence—the ability to access inner feelings.

And, more recently:

Naturalist intelligence—the natural flair that many people have to see patterns in nature, and to work as naturalists, ecologists or farmers.

The possibility of *Existential intelligence*—what some people call *spiritual intelligence.*

Others would say the first seven indicate different learning styles (as we cover in the poster pages for this chapter), while the first eight might be different talents, and the last one a *spiritual dimension* in life.

We believe Gardner's findings [6] have vital importance in planning the future of education. *Every child is a potentially gifted child—but often in many different ways.* Every person, too, has his or her own preferred learning style, working style and temperament.

Back in 1921, Swiss psychiatrist Carl Jung outlined how people perceived things differently. He classified them as feelers, thinkers, sensors or intuitors. Jung was, as far as we know, the first to classify people also as either introverts* or extraverts. It's unfortunate that many of Jung's perspectives were dropped by 1930 and relatively ignored until recently.

We all know people who embody many of the concepts he defined, and New Zealand professor of theology Lloyd Geering has summarised them in his book *In The World Today,* [2] which seeks to bridge the gap between religion and science:

The extraverted thinkers, who abound in management, military

---

* *Jung himself preferred the "intraverted" spelling of the word, while others prefer "introverted".*

Multiple intelligences
Personal and professional uses

3. Visual-spatial intelligence*.

Commonly found in: Architects, painters, sculptors, navigators, chess players, naturalists, theoretical physicists, battlefield strategists.

Example of famous person: Pablo Picasso, painter.

Likely traits:

*   Thinks in pictures
*   Creates mental images
*   Uses metaphor
*   Has sense of gestalt
*   Likes art: drawing, painting, building and sculpting
*   Easily reads maps, charts and diagrams
*   Remembers with pictures
*   Has good colour sense
*   Uses all senses for imaging
*   Likes engineering

* As mentioned elsewhere in this book, the present co-authors consider that visual and spatial traits do not always coincide. Some highly visual people may have difficulty, for instance, in following the directions from maps, even though the maps may be visually accurate.

How to strengthen for learning:

*   Use pictures to learn
*   Create doodles, symbols
*   Draw diagrams, maps
*   Integrate art with other subjects
*   Use Mind-Mapping
*   Do visualisation activities
*   Watch videos or create your own
*   Use peripheral stimuli on the walls; signs such as the posters in this book
*   Use mime
*   Change places in the room to gain a different perspective
*   Use advance organisers or goal-setting charts
*   Use clustering
*   Highlight with colour
*   Use computer-graphics

strategy and some forms of science. People such as automotive path-finder Lee Iacocca or British wartime military leader Bernard Montgomery.

The introverted thinkers, often interested in ideas for their own sake: philosophers such as Charles Darwin, Rene Descartes and Jung himself.

The extraverted feeling types, interested deeply in other people—the Mother Teresas of the world.

The introverted feeling types, including those who agonise over the world's problems but internalise them and assume them as a burden.

The extraverted sensation types: the sports-loving, thrill-seeking, pleasure-seekers.

The introverted sensation types "who find the outer world uninteresting and unsatisfying and turn inwardly to seek fulfilment"—including some of the great mystics.

The extraverted intuitive people "who enter new relationships with great gusto but do not always prove dependable. They can move quickly from one new interest to another, especially if it is not immediately fruitful. They have visions of new worlds to conquer or to build. They are promoters of new causes. We may name as examples Alexander the Great, Julius Caesar, Napoleon, Hitler, Henry Ford and builders of today's economic empires."

The introverted intuitive people, including the visionaries and dreamers who draw from their own hidden resources.

Geering says "the acknowledgment of psychological types is an essential first step if we are to appreciate Jung's concept of individuation, the process by which each of us becomes the one unique and whole human person we have the potential to become".

Many educators have now built on these concepts. Rudolph Steiner schools, for instance, place great emphasis on identifying and catering to individual temperaments.

Determining your learning style

There are currently about twenty different methods of identifying learning styles. And research by Professors Ken and Rita Dunn, from St. Johns University, New York, provides one of the most comprehensive models. But overall your learning style is a combination of three factors:

❏ *How you perceive information most easily*—whether you are mainly a visual, auditory, kinesthetic or tactile learner; whether you learn

Multiple intelligences
Personal and professional uses

4. Musical intelligence.

Commonly found in: Performers, composers, conductors, musical audiences, recording engineers, makers of musical instruments, piano-tuners, cultures without traditional written language.

Example of famous person: Mozart.

Likely traits:

*   Sensitive to pitch, rhythm, timbre
*   Sensitive to emotional power of music
*   Sensitive to complex organisation of music
*   May be deeply spiritual
*   May create own music with compute software
*   Knows a lot of music selections, artists and genre
*   Often tries to use music for learning

How to strengthen for learning:

*   Play a musical instrument
*   Learn through songs
*   Use active and passive concerts for learning
*   Study with baroque music
*   Workout with music
*   Join choir or choral group
*   Write music
*   Integrate music with other subject areas
*   Change your mood with music
*   Use music to get relaxed
*   Image/make pictures with music
*   Learn through raps such as timetables, whole language poems, choral reading
*   Compose music on computer

best by seeing, hearing, moving or touching. (The ability to taste and smell can be important in some work-styles, such as wine-tasting and perfume-blending, but these two senses are not major ones in most learning styles.)

❏ *How you organise and process information*—whether predominantly left-brain or right-brain, analytical or "global", using "global" in the sense that you are more "a broadbrush" person than a systematic thinker.

❏ *What conditions are necessary to help you take in and store information*—emotional, social, physical and environmental.

❏ *How you retrieve information*—which may be entirely different to the way you take it in and store it.

How you take in information

In the Dunns' research, they discovered that:

❏ Only 30 percent of students remember even 75 percent of what they *hear* during a normal class period.

❏ Forty percent retain threequarters of what they *read* or *see*. These visual learners are of two types: some process information in word-form, while others retain what they see in diagram or picture-form.

❏ Fifteen percent learn best *tactually*. They need to *handle* materials, to write, draw and be involved with concrete experiences.

❏ Another 15 percent are kinesthetic. They learn best by *physically doing*—by participating in real experiences that generally have direct application to their lives.

According to the Dunns, we each usually have one dominant strength and also a secondary one. And, in a classroom or seminar, if our main perceptual strength is not matched with the teaching method, we may have difficulty learning, unless we can compensate with our secondary perceptual strengths.

This has major implications for solving the high-school dropout problem. *In our experience, kinesthetic and tactile learners are the main candidates for failure in traditional school classrooms.* They need to move, to feel, to touch, to do—and if the teaching method does not allow them to do this they feel left out, uninvolved, bored.

Neuro linguistic programming specialist Michael Grinder says that of a typical class of thirty students, twentytwo will be fairly balanced in their

Multiple intelligences

Personal and professional uses

5. Bodily-kinesthetic intelligence.

Commonly found in: Dancers, actors, athletes and sporting achievers, inventors, mimists, surgeons, karate teachers, racing car drivers, outdoor workers and the mechanically gifted.

Examples: Basketball star Michael Jordan, golfer Tiger Woods.

Likely traits:

* Exceptional control of one's body
* Control of objects
* Good timing
* Trained responses
* Good reflexes
* Learns best by moving
* Likes to engage in physical sports
* Likes to touch
* Skilled at handicrafts
* Likes to act
* Likes to use manipulatives
* Learns by participating in the learning process
* Remembers what was done rather than what was said or observed
* Very responsive to physical environment
* Plays around with objects while listening
* Fidgety if there are few breaks
* Mechanically minded

How to strengthen for learning:

* Use physical exercises wherein you become the object you are learning about
* Use dancing to learn
* Use movement to learn
* Act out the learning
* Use manipulatives in science, math
* Take lots of "state changes" and breaks
* Integrate movement into all curricula areas
* Mentally review while you are swimming, jogging
* Use models, machines, Technic Lego, handicrafts
* Use karate for focusing
* Use field trips
* Use classroom games
* Use drama, role-plays
* Finger snapping, clapping, stamping, jumping, climbing

ability to take in information. They will generally be able to cope when the information is presented in either visual, auditory or kinesthetic ways.

Two to three of the youngsters will have difficulty learning because of factors outside the classroom. And the remaining youngsters—up to six in a class of thirty, or 20 percent—will be "visual only", "auditory only" or "kinesthetic only" learners. They have great difficulty in absorbing information unless it is presented in the favoured style.

Grinder dubs them VO's, AO's and KO's. And he says, "It's not just a coincidence that the initials 'KO' stand for 'knockout.' These kids are 'knocked out' of the educational system. In every study I have seen regarding 'kids at risk,' kinesthetics make up the vast majority of the 26 percent dropout rate." [8]

How you organise and process information

People with strong left-brain traits take information in logically— they can absorb it easily if it is presented in a logical, linear sequence.

People with right-brain dominance generally like to take in the big global picture first; they're much more comfortable with presentations that involve visualisation, imagination, music, art and intuition.

And if you can link together the powers of both hemispheres, and tap into those "multiple intelligence centres", you'll obviously be able to absorb and process information more effectively.

The conditions that affect your learning ability

The physical environment obviously affects learning. Sound, light, temperature, seating and body posture are all important.

People also have different *emotional needs*. And emotion plays a vital part in learning. It is in many ways the key to the brain's memory system. And the emotional content of any presentation can play a big part in how readily learners absorb information and ideas.

People also have different *social needs*. Some like to learn by themselves. Others prefer to work with a partner. Still others, in teams. Some children want an adult present or like to work with adults only. The Dunns say most underachievers are very peer-motivated.[9]

Physical and biological needs that affect learning

Eating times, time-of-day energy levels and the need for mobility can

Multiple intelligences
Personal and professional uses

6. Interpersonal or "social" intelligence.

Commonly found in: Politicians, teachers, religious leaders, counselors, sales people, managers, public relations and "people people."

Example of famous person: Oprah Winfrey, talkshow host.

Likely traits:

* Negotiates well
* Relates well, mixes well
* Able to read others' intentions
* Enjoys being with people
* Has many friends
* Communicates well, sometimes manipulates
* Enjoys group activities
* Likes to mediate disputes
* Likes to cooperate
* "Reads" social situations well
* Often likes team and group work
* Has a need to be liked
* Often likes attention

How to strengthen for learning:

* Do learning activities cooperatively
* Take lots of breaks to socialise
* Use "pair and share" learning activities
* Use relationships and communication skills
* Do "partner talks" on the phone
* Have parties and celebration of learning
* Make learning fun
* Integrate socialisation into all curricular areas
* Use "People Search" activities where you have to talk to others to get answers
* Work in teams
* Learn through service
* Tutor others
* Use cause and effect

also affect learning ability. Try learning, for instance, when you are hungry. It's hard for most of us. And some need to constantly nibble.

Some people are morning people. Others are night owls. Again, the Dunns have found that students do better when their class-times match their own "time-clocks." [10] Significantly, they've found that most high school and college students are not morning people. "Only about one-third of more than a million students we have tested prefer learning in the first part of the morning," they report. "The majority prefer late morning or afternoon. In fact, many do not begin to be capable of concentrating on difficult material until after 10 a.m." For daytime learning, the Dunns recommend 10 a.m. to 4 p.m. But who says high schools shouldn't be open evenings for the night-owls?

The Dunns confirm that "the tactile-kinesthetics" face most learning difficulties in traditional schools.[11] They often drop out because they can't focus well sitting down hour after hour. Those that stay often "get into trouble" and get suspended. Others are often unfortunately classi-fied as "learning disabled" and put into "special education" classes—where they do more of the same: lots of seatwork activity, paying little attention to their true strengths and learning styles.

Every top learning environment we have seen caters to a variety of intelligence-traits and a variety of learning styles. But many high schools in particular still seem geared to "academic" two-dimensional teach-ing—directed mainly at linguistic and logical learners. Not surprisingly, many high school teachers themselves "shine" in these attributes.

How to determine students' preferred learning styles

Again, one simple way is to ask. A simple request and discussion on learning styles and preferences is also often one of the simplest ways to break down barriers between teacher and students. You can also often tell people's preferred style by listening to them talk.

Ask a visual learner for instructions and she'll tend to draw a map. If she is starting to grasp an otherwise difficult subject, she'll say: "I see what you mean." Read her a menu in a restaurant and she'll have to look at it herself. Buy her a present and you can't go too wrong with a book—but check to see whether she's print oriented or prefers pictures. If the latter, she might even prefer a video disc. Most visual learners, but not all, tend to be organised, tidy and well dressed.

An auditory learner generally couldn't care less about reading a

Multiple intelligences
Personal and professional uses

7. Intrapersonal or intuitive* intelligence.

Commonly found in: Novelists, counsellors, wise elders, philosophers, gurus, persons with a deep sense of self, mystics.

Example of famous person: Plato, philosopher.

Likely traits:

* Self-knowledge
* Sensitivity to one's own values
* Deeply aware of one's own feelings
* Sensitivity to one's purpose in life
* Has a well-developed sense of self
* Intuitive ability
* Self motivated
* Deeply aware of own strengths and weaknesses
* Very private person
* Wants to be different from mainstream

* The core capacity of "intrapersonal" intelligence is the ability to access one's inner self. Some feel intuition is a separate intelligence trait: a seemingly innate ability to know about others or events.

How to strengthen for learning:

* Have personal "heart-to-heart" talks
* Use personal growth activities to break learning blocks
* Debrief activities
* Think about your thinking through "Pair and Shares" and "Think and Listen"
* Take time for inner reflection
* Do independent study
* Listen to your intuition
* Discuss, reflect or write what you experienced and how you felt
* Permit freedom to be different from the group
* Make "My Books" and journals of life story
* Take control of own learning
* Teach questioning

book or an instruction manual. He'll have to ask for information. He doesn't buy a car for its looks—he buys it for its stereo system. In a plane he'll immediately strike up a conversation with his new neighbour. And when he grasps new information, he says something like: "I hear what you're saying." If you buy him a present, make it a CD or a DVD player, not a book.

A kinesthetic, tactile learner always wants to be on the move. If she bumps into you accidentally, she'll want to give you a reassuring hug. When she grasps a new principle, "it feels right" to her. And for her birthday present: a laptop computer?

Now: online analysis of learning and working styles

Since the early 1990s New Zealand-based Barbara Prashnig, who heads the Creative Learning Company, first introduced the Dunn and Dunn model with great success in New Zealand primary and secondary schools, before spreading it elsewhere.

"People of all ages can learn virtually anything if allowed to do it through their unique styles, through their own personal strengths," she says in *Diversity Is Our Strength: the learning revolution in action.*

She has also built on the Dunns' research base to build a practical programme for analysing individual students' learning styles, anyone's individual working style, plus individual teaching styles and training styles. And to do this directly online through the World Wide Web.

Cramlington Community High School in Britain is one of several using Prashnig's detailed thinking-style tests for individual students as part of its programme of personalising lesson plans. This is a key part of their official "leading edge" school status, as we will see later.

Four types of thinking styles

Not only do we have preferred learning and working styles, we also have favourite thinking styles. Anthony Gregorc, professor of curriculum and instruction at the University of Connecticut, has divided these into four separate groups: [12]

❏ *Concrete sequential.*

❏ *Concrete random.*

❏ *Abstract random.*

❏ *Abstract sequential.*

Multiple intelligences
Personal and professional uses

8. Naturalist intelligence.

Commonly found in: Gardeners, farmers, explorers, biologists, ecologists, anthropologists, zoologists.

Example of famous person: Jacques Cousteau.

Likely traits:	How to strengthen for learning:
* Negotiates well	* Use nature metaphors
* Nature knowledge	* Teach via inquiry
* Sensitive to ecology	* Bring plants into class
* Sensitive to enviromental and animal abuse	* Permit sharing of pets
* Often vegetarian	* Connect nutrition to learning
* Sees pattern in nature	* Encourage project work
* Keen sense of balance with nature and the body	* Use art of nature and natural phenomenon

9. Possibly existential intelligence.

Commonly found in: Religious leaders, highly spiritual people.

Example of famous person: Jesus, Buddha, Mohammed.

Likely traits:	How to strengthen:
* Deep self knowledge	* Have time for reflection
* Sensitive to one's values	* Discuss opinions peacefully
* Sensitive to higher purpose	* Do independent study
* Often believes in transcendence	* Respect and celebrate different beliefs and perspectives
* Often sensitive to ecology	
* Often a very private person	* Use personal growth activities to break learning blocks
* Self motivated	

We're indebted to SuperCamp consultant John LeTellier for adapting the Gregorc model and providing the checklist on the next three pages.[13]

We stress, however, that no thinking style is superior; each is simply different. Each style can be effective in its own way. The important thing is that you become more aware of which learning style and thinking style works best for you. Once you know your own style, you can then analyse the others. This will help you understand other people better. It will make you more flexible. And perhaps we can all pick up tips from each other on how to be more effective.

Once you've made a graph for yourself on page 370, consider these explanations to improve your own ability to learn, think, study, work and enjoy life:

Concrete sequential thinkers are based in reality, according to SuperCamp co-founder and president Bobbi DePorter. They process information in an ordered, sequential, linear way. To them, "reality consists of what they can detect through their physical sense of sight, touch, sound, taste and smell. They notice and recall details easily and remember facts, specific information, formulas and rules with ease. 'Hands on' is a good way for these people to learn."[14] If you're concrete sequential—a CS—build on your organisational strengths. Provide yourself with details. Break your projects down into specific steps. Set up quiet work environments.

Concrete random thinkers are experimenters. Says DePorter: "Like concrete sequentials, they're based in reality, but are willing to take more of a trial-and-error approach. Because of this, they often make the intuitive leaps necessary for true creative thought. They have a strong need to find alternatives and do things in their own way."

If you're a CR, use your divergent thinking ability. Believe that it's good to see things from more than one viewpoint. Put yourself in a position to solve problems. But give yourself deadlines. Accept your need for change.

Abstract random thinkers organise information through reflection, and thrive in unstructured, people-oriented environments.

Says DePorter: "The 'real' world for abstract random learners is the world of feelings and emotions. The AR's mind absorbs ideas, information and impressions and organises them through reflection. They remember best if information is personalised. They feel constricted when they're subjected to a very structured environment." If you're an AR, use

To test your own thinking style
Read each set of words and mark
the two that best describe you

1. a. imaginative
    b. investigative
    c. realistic
    d. analytical

2. a. organised
    b. adaptable
    c. critical
    d. inquisitive

3. a. debating
    b. getting to the point
    c. creating
    d. relating

4. a. personal
    b. practical
    c. academic
    d. adventurous

5. a. precise
    b. flexible
    c. systematic
    d. inventive

6. a. sharing
    b. orderly
    c. sensible
    d. independent

7. a. competitive
    b. perfectionist
    c. cooperative
    d. logical

8. a. intellectual
    b. sensitive
    c. hardworking
    d. risk-taking

9. a. reader
    b. people person
    c. problem solver
    d. planner

10. a. memorise
    b. associate
    c. think-through
    d. originate

11. a. changer
    b. judger
    c. spontaneous
    d. wants direction

12. a. communicating
    b. discovering
    c. cautious
    d. reasoning

13. a. challenging
    b. practicing
    c. caring
    d. examining

14. a. completing work
    b. seeing possibilities
    c. gaining ideas
    d. interpreting

15. a. doing
    b. feeling
    c. thinking
    d. experimenting

After completing the test at left:

In the columns below, circle the letters of the words you chose for each number. Add your totals for columns I, II, III and IV. Multiply the total of each column by 4. The box with the highest number describes how you most often process information.

	I	II	III	IV
1.	C	D	A	B
2.	A	C	B	D
3.	B	A	D	C
4.	B	C	A	D
5.	A	C	B	D
6.	B	C	A	D
7.	B	D	C	A
8.	C	A	B	D
9.	D	A	B	C
10.	A	C	B	D
11.	D	B	C	A
12.	C	D	A	B
13.	B	D	C	A
14.	A	C	D	B
15.	A	C	B	D

TOTAL: _____

I   ___ X 4 = ☐ Concrete Sequential (CS)

II ___ X 4 = ☐ Abstract Sequential (AS)

III ___ X 4 = ☐ Abstract Random (AR)

IV ___ X 4 = ☐ Concrete Random (CR)

Now graph your results on the chart on next page.

After you have completed your personal thinking-style test on the previous page chart your results below

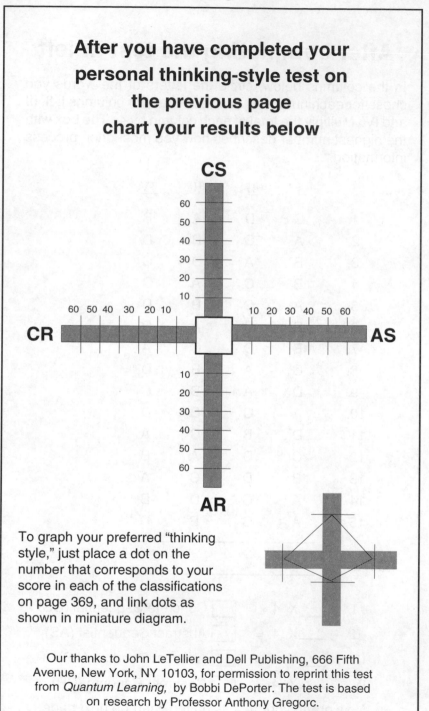

CS

60
50
40
30
20
10

60 50 40 30 20 10   10 20 30 40 50 60

CR == **AS**

10
20
30
40
50
60

AR

To graph your preferred "thinking style," just place a dot on the number that corresponds to your score in each of the classifications on page 369, and link dots as shown in miniature diagram.

Our thanks to John LeTellier and Dell Publishing, 666 Fifth Avenue, New York, NY 10103, for permission to reprint this test from *Quantum Learning,* by Bobbi DePorter. The test is based on research by Professor Anthony Gregorc.

your natural ability to work with others. Recognise how strongly emotions influence your concentration. Build on your strength of learning by association. Look at the big picture first. Be careful to allow enough time to finish the job. Remind yourself to do things through plenty of visual clues, such as coloured stickers pasted up where you'll see them.

Abstract sequential thinkers love the world of theory and abstract thought. They like to think in concepts and analyse information. They make great philosophers and research scientists. DePorter again: "It's easy for them to zoom in on what's important, such as key points and significant details. Their thinking processes are logical, rational and intellectual. A favourite activity for abstract sequentials is reading, and when a project needs to be researched they are very thorough at it. Generally they prefer to work alone rather than in groups." If you're an AS, give yourself exercises in logic. Feed your intellect. Steer yourself toward highly structured situations.

Different ways to store and retrieve information

Not only do we have different learning and thinking styles, we also each have a different way to store information and retrieve it.

And exactly the same principle applies: discuss the entire process with students and both you and they will soon work it out.

For example, co-author Dryden takes in information, like most print-trained journalists, as a print-oriented linguistic learner. But he stores information in a tactile way: by underlining, highlighting words and touch-typing—the very physical action helps embed it in his memory-banks. And he retrieves information visually: generally, as all TV producers do, by preparing visual presentations. So even if making a presentation without visual aids, he talks from mental pictures.

Co-author Vos is different. She takes information in visually and through tactile notations as she reads. She is print-oriented but enjoys a graphic format of what she reads—charts, for example. She stores information kinesthetically by exercising her body while she is reflecting and jotting her thoughts on paper. She needs time to collect information by reflection and synthesis via the subconscious. And she retrieves information through both the auditory and visual process: often listening to quiet music while preparing, for example, international seminar presentations.

How body language indicates learning styles

For intaking information

A visual learner usually sits up very straight and follows the presenter around with her eyes.

An auditory learner often softly repeats to herself words spoken by the presenter, or nods her head a lot when the facilitator is presenting spoken information. An auditory learner often "plays a cassette in her head" when she is trying to retrieve information so she may be staring off into space when she does this.

A bodily-kinesthetic learner often slumps down when she listens.

A tactual person loves to play with objects while she listens: flicking her pen or fiddling with papers, or playing with a koosh ball while she listens to someone talk.

JEANNETTE VOS*

* Six-day training on Twentyfirst Century Techniques for
Learning and Teaching: Summer Institutes.
For further details of training, email:
drjvos.mac.com

Regular updates: www.thelearningweb.net

Both are competent logical sequential presenters, but they accomplish it in different styles. One is a logical, sequential television-style presenter, and, especially when videotaping a presentation, is always conscious of the need for sequence, structure and the needs of a later, different TV-viewing audience. The other: a highly intuitive teacher, attuned to where people "are at" and the nuances of individual students' styles and patterns of learning—ever ready to "change the state" with reflection, dialogue and often a change of music. Neither style is "right". Both are completely different. In joint presentations both find that, by each presenting for alternating sessions, this provides variety and "state changes".

The implications for home study, schools and teachers

We believe every aspect of this research can greatly improve learning and schooling.

For personal home study, it makes great sense to know your own strengths, know your family's learning styles and build on them.

If it's hard for you to sit still for a long time, you're almost certainly a kinesthetic learner. So consider starting to study by previewing your material with a giant Mind Map—on a big sheet of paper. Put it on the floor and use your body while you're working. After previewing the material, play some classical music—and move with its rhythm. Then do something physical. Go for a walk, a swim, or move your body while you mentally visualise what you've just put into your brain.

Especially if you're kinesthetic, feel free to get into your favourite learning atmosphere and position.

If you are an auditory learner, record your notes on to a cassette tape over baroque music. And if you are a visual learner, be sure to draw Mind Maps, doodles, symbols or pictures to represent what you are learning. For a visual learner, a picture represents a thousand words.

For school teachers and seminar leaders, we would hope the lessons are equally obvious: analyse each student's learning style, and cater to it. You won't be able to do this for everyone all the time. But you can make sure that every style is catered for regularly throughout every learning sequence. If you do, you'll be amazed at how easily people can learn—and how much less resistance you will find.

One of the first American schools to be based almost entirely on Howard Gardner's principles is the Key Elementary School in Indianapolis.

Discover the hidden talents within you.

BILL LUCAS
Power Up Your Mind*

Regular updates: www.thelearningweb.net

Walk into the Key School and you'll find youngsters learning in all the different "intelligences". Sure, you'll find all the traditional subject areas, such as reading and math, being covered.

But you'll also find everyone involved in music, painting, drawing, physical activity and discussion. For four periods a week, children meet in multi-aged groups called pods, to explore a whole range of interests such as computers, gardening, cooking, "making money", architecture, theatre, multicultural games and other real-life skills.

"Once a week," says Gardner, "an outside specialist visits the school and demonstrates an occupation or craft. Often the specialist is a parent, and typically the topic fits into the school theme at the time." [15]

The school is also closely involved with the Centre of Exploration at the Indianapolis Museum. "Students can enter into an apprenticeship of several months, in which they can engage in such activities as animation, shipbuilding, journalism or monitoring the weather."

Key School is also alive with projects. Says Gardner: "During any given year the school features three different themes, introduced at approximately ten-week intervals. These themes can be quite broad (such as *Patterns* or *Connections*), or more focused *(The Renaissance— then and now* or *Mexican heritage).* With the curriculum focus on these themes, desired literacies and concepts are, wherever possible, introduced as natural adjuncts to an exploration of the theme."

Better yet, both New City School, in St. Louis, Missouri, and the Indianapolis school show precisely what can happen if a country finally uses its great academic research skills and blends them with well-planned schools, innovative teachers, tremendous community resources and a focus that sees all children as gifted and talented, but in different ways.

We cannot restress strongly enough our own beliefs that everyone, unless severely brain-damaged, has a unique potential to be exceptionally good at something—and we now know how to identify and build on that talent.

As Britain's Campaign for Learning found when it asked the United Kingdom public to define the aim of learning, the phrase most favoured was simply: "To discover the talents within you."

Equally important: when students learn to work together in multi-skilled teams, they not only develop their own talent but they learn to appreciate and work with the unique talents of others.

Great catch-up programmes

1. Specialised kinesiology.
2. Physical routines.
3. Ball/stick/bird teaching.
4. Catching up at spelling.
5. Back-writing for letter recognition.
6. Four-minute reading programme.
7. Finger phonics.
8. Tape-assisted reading programme.
9. Peer tutoring.
10. Reading Recovery.
11. Personal key vocabularies.
12. Beginning School Mathematics.
13. Computerised catch-ups.
14. Best programme of all: prevention.
15. 3 "health-educational" programmes.

The world's greatest catch-up programmes—and why they work

But how about youngsters who are diagnosed as *backward, slow* or *learning disabled?* What chance have they to catch-up in a world of supersonic change?

Fortunately the answers are in. And they're positive.

❏ Like Helen Keller, who was deaf, blind and mute until age ten. But by sixteen she had learned to read in Braille, and to write and speak well enough to go to college. By 1904, she graduated with honours.

❏ Or, 100 years later, the thousands of children being dosed with Ritalin for alleged "attention deficit/hyperactivity syndrome" who are then finding the real answer lies in a change in diet or exercise.

❏ Like the healthy New Zealand thirteen-year-old who tested a "normal" junk food diet on himself for two two-day periods and ended up with 35-to-50 percent slow-downs in his reading, math and typing ability—until he returned to a normal health diet.[1]

This is not to deny that some people have learning difficulties. But labelling them "learning disabled" must rank with I.Q. tests as one of the great educational tragedies of the century. *Our research convinces us that any person can learn—in his or her own way and own time.*

Dr. Mel Levine, professor of pediatrics at the University of North Carolina Medical School, confirms this in his latest book covering a lifetime of research into learning problems: *A Mind at a Time.*

All children, he says, have specific talents and abilities waiting to be tapped. Where learning problems do exist, generally these are very specific, and can be diagnosed and righted, mostly without drugs.

377

Mind-body-link research studies

1996: Study of 1,551 people:

Those who were depressed were four times as likely to have a heart attack.

Johns Hopkins School of Hygiene and Public Health

1993: Landmark Swedish study:

Men who exhibited unusual amounts of stress, over a seven-year research program, died at a rate three times greater than those who were calm.

Survey in Goteborg, Sweden

1991: US students and colds

University survey found that, when students were exposed to cold viruses, among those with stress 47% came down with colds compared with only 27% without stress.

Survey carried out by Carnegie Mellon University

MICHIO KAKU
Visions*

* Subtitled: "How science will revolutionise the 21st century".
Published by Anchor Books, New York.

Two key principles: the mind-body connection and the mind-brain connection

The first principle to restress is that learning is not only an *academic* process. Just as an infant develops his brain by sucking, grasping, crawling, creeping, walking, climbing, rocking and spinning, so too with children and adults. You can keep growing those dendrites—the brain's connecting and "storage" branches—throughout life.

Professor Diamond and her co-researchers at Berkeley have proven conclusively that the more effective the physical and mental stimulation, the bigger and better the dendritic brain growth.[2] Professor Palmer has proven in Minnesota that *physical* routines at kindergarten can dramatically improve five-year-olds' *academic* performance, because those concentrated physical activities actually grow the brain.[3]

The second principle: that the body, mind and brain act together in a continuous feedback loop: each affecting the other and causing chain reactions that trigger big changes in the body's immune system. In *Visions,* physicist Micho Kaku cites many extensive case studies to show, for example, how depressed or stressed-out adults are much more likely to die of heart attacks than those who are calm and happy. In learning, too, the continuous dialogue between brain, mind, body, diet, exercise and activity can all play major parts in overcoming learning diffiulties.

Again, Helen Keller is a classic case-study.[4] It took her three years merely to learn the alphabet. Her teacher, Anne Sullivan, was able to communicate with the girl's brain and mind through a sense of touch. She later spelled out words on her hand. Helen then learned to read and write in Braille, but in her own time. Five main factors influenced Keller's *ability* to learn: time, culture, context, support and the freedom to choose.

Time was obviously vital. Her first learnings took a long time. But once she made her initial gains she was able to build on them rapidly. Learning had nothing to do with being "disabled"; it had everything to do with having handicaps and needing *her own time-clock* to overcome them. She would never have succeeded by starting in today's regimented graded classrooms.

Culture was also important. Helen Keller's culture esteemed the ability to talk and read. By comparison, in a culture without a written language, navigation might rate much higher than reading; thus culture determines the context of learning—and learning problems. "Special education" teacher and author Thomas Armstrong puts it succinctly:

80 percent of learning difficulties are related to stress. Remove the stress and you remove the difficulties.

GORDON STOKES
President, Three in One Concepts*

*This quotation is a major theme of the book *One Brain: Dyslexic Learning Correction and Brain Integration,* published by Three In One Concepts, 2001 W. Magnolia Blvd., Suite B., Burbank, CA 91506-1704. It is highly recommended as a guide to specialised kinesiology.

"Culture defines who's 'disabled' . . . a child labelled dyslexic, hyperactive or learning-disabled in our society might excel in another culture."[5]

Keller's plight was being blind, deaf and mute. She had to learn within that limited context. Had she taken an I.Q. test, with its linguistic base, her rating would have been extremely low, if she had scored at all. Without Sullivan, she may have been placed in an institution for the retarded, instead of developing as a highly gifted person.

The support of a caring and able teacher is equally essential. Sullivan never gave up on Helen, even though the girl had wild temper tantrums.

Helen Keller also had the freedom of choice. At ten she chose to want to learn to talk. There was no rush. She did it in her own time and context. Again the message is obvious: too many people in traditional education are put in no-choice situations in both conscious and subconscious ways.

Anne Sullivan discovered the brain-body and mind-body connection because she, too, had experienced difficulties in learning. Fortunately, there is now a wealth of other research to back up those discoveries.

Specialised kinesiology

Some of the most interesting research and practical applications have come from the field of specialised kinesiology. Just as *kinesthetics,* or movement, is an important aspect of many learning styles, so is *kinesiology*, the science of motion, and *kinesthesia,* the sensation of position, movement and tension of parts of the body.

Kinesiology has become well known in some countries because of the way it has helped peak performance in sports. Brigitte Haas Allroggen, of the Munich Institute of Kinesiology, talks about the effectiveness of the science with Olympic teams: "All of a sudden things exploded. We began working with top Austrian athletes who later won Olympic medals and worldwide competitions. Then the Norwegian Olympic team came to us, and the Italians too. All had remarkable results."[6]

Similar techniques are now helping in education, and not just for people with learning difficulties. Says kinesiologist Kathleen Carroll, of Washington D.C., who links her training with accelerated integrative learning strategies: "Kinesiology improves academics for *anyone.*"[7]

This is, in part, because of the way the brain transmits messages both *electrically* and *chemically,* and the way in which stress causes blockages. In simple terms, educational kinesiologists say that when stress

How to improve your spelling, writing, reading and listening with this simple brain exercise:

1. **Stand up and, by raising your knees alternately, touch each hand to the opposite knee.**
2. **Do this about ten times whenever you are stressed.**

Variations:

1. **Do it with your eyes closed.**
2. **Do it by raising each foot, alternately behind you; touching each foot with the opposite hand.**

This is a typical exercise recommended by educational kinesiologists to integrate both sides of the brain, reduce stress and make learning easier. If you have difficulty with exercises like this, the authors recommend repatterning by a certified kinesiologist.

Exercises like this are covered in the highly-recommended books, *Brain Gym,* published by Edu-Kinesthetics Inc., P.O. Box 3396, Ventura, CA 93006-3396, and *One Brain: Dyslexic Learning Correction and Brain Integration,* published by Three In One Concepts, 2001 W. Magnolia Blvd., Suite B., Burbank CA 91506-1704.

We acknowledge the assistance of certified kinesiologist Kathleen Carroll, Three In One Concepts facilitator of Washington DC, in compiling this section of the book.

overwhelms us our brain is short-circuited—the "wiring" becomes fused. They say this is a major cause of learning problems—and labelling those problems "dyslexia" or anything else generally adds to the stress and the fusion.   Often the answer lies in simple exercises which "defuse" the blockage between the left and right sides of the brain. Get rid of the blockage and you often get rid of the problem.

Some of the most outstanding work has come from specialised kinesiology researchers and practitioners Gordon Stokes and Daniel Whiteside through their Three In One Concepts organisation based in Burbank, California. They say 80 percent of learning difficulties are related to stress. And this can be released by kinesiology.[8]

They have developed body exercises—using pressure-points, muscle testing and coordination patterns—to reorient the electrical patterns of the brain and thus *defuse* stress, clear the "blocked circuits" and turn on the ability to learn. By working through the body they've been able to change the state of both the brain and the mind.

Since the brain operates most effectively when both left and right sides are working in harmony, many of those kinesiology exercises can help you become more *centred,* more coordinated, less stressful and can make learning easier and natural—in the same way that Olympic athletes use centring exercises to prepare for competition.

Many of the best and simplest exercises have been developed by educational kinesiologists Paul and Gail Dennison and illustrated in *Brain Gym,* a highly-recommended handbook.[9]

These exercises were originally developed by Dr. Paul Dennison for people labelled "dyslexic"—people who supposedly see writing in reverse, like a mirror-image. But they help more than people with handicaps: they can be used at any age level and even for people who don't think they have learning problems. They're excellent, for instance, for classroom "state changes"—for any age group.

Unfortunately most schools are not yet using these tools, but where they are the results are outstanding. A typical example comes from the Sierra Vista Junior High School in California, where Three In One Concepts worked with eleven "special education" students who were three to seven years behind their grade level. All were considered to be handicapped by "dyslexia" . A kinesiology specialist worked with the students one afternoon a week for eight weeks. And at the end of that time 73 percent of the students showed "significant improvement" (at least

If we insist on looking at the rainbow of intelligence through a single filter, many minds will erroneously seem devoid of light.

RENEE FULLER
inventor of ball/stick/bird teaching method*

*The quotation above is the subheading of an article entitled *Beyond IQ,* by Renee Fuller, *In Context* magazine (winter 1988).

one year's growth in eight weeks) in three of six learning abilities tested, 50 percent in one and 27 percent in two others.[10]

The world abounds with other excellent catch-up programmes.

Among the best we have found:

Doman-Palmer-Niklasson-Hartigan models

Variations of the physical routine programme developed by Glenn Doman, Lyelle Palmer, Irene and Mats Niklasson, and Jerome and Sophie Hartigan are now being used effectively in many parts of the world. In the Hartigans' *Jumping Beans* programme children as young as six months go through a series of routines to music, starting with gentle rolling and balancing, then moving up to brachiating exercises: swinging from their hands on 'jungle gyms' or 'monkey bars'.

Before age three, the Hartigans recommend plenty of fun and dance to music. After three, the more structured programme can begin.[11]

In Shidchida, Japan, you'll also now find more than 100 centres where parents can do advanced developmental activities with their children.

The ball/stick/bird method

In Maryland, USA, outstanding results have been achieved by Dr. Renee Fuller while on the staff at Rosewood Hospital Centre Psychology Department. She worked with twentysix people who were institutionalised for retardation—ranging in age from eleven to fortyeight and in I.Q. tests from twentyeight to seventytwo.

Fuller taught them to read. And that achievement greatly increased both their learning ability and their self-esteem. "Not only did they learn to read advanced story material with comprehension," she reports, "they also showed some unexpected emotional and behavioural changes."[12] By learning to read they learned to think. And when they learned to think, their behaviour changed and their appearance changed.

Fuller provided them with a tool to break the reading code: the ball/stick/bird method. In this method, the ball represents all the parts of letters of the alphabet having a circle; the stick represents the parts of letters with a line; and the bird the "wings" of letters, such as an "r."

She showed her students how all the letters of the alphabet consisted of just these three simple concrete forms. With that "code" and fast-paced stories, even the most retarded students were soon learning and thriving.

Helpful hints on spelling

Try this with children having difficulty with "problem words" in English or alphabet languages.
Get them to:

a. Picture the word in their favorite colour.

b. Make any unclear letters stand out by making them look different to the others in some way, for example, bigger, brighter, closer or a different colour.

c. Break the word into groups of three letters, and build your picture three letters at a time.

d. Put the letters on a familiar background. Picture something like a familiar object or movie scene, then put the letters you want to remember on top of it.

e. If it is a long word, make the letters small enough so that you can easily see the whole word.

f. Trace the letters in the air with your finger and picture in your mind the letters that you are writing.

ROBERT DILTS and TODD A. EPSTEIN
*Dynamic Learning**

* Published by Meta Publications, P.O. Box 1910, Capitola, California 95010, USA.

Catching up at spelling

Other children are catching up at spelling using methods outlined in three excellent books, *Catchwords,* by Charles Cripps and Margaret L. Peters; *Alpha to Omega,* by Beve Hornsby and Frula Shear; and *The Writing Road to Reading,* by Romalda Bishop Spalding.

Alpha to Omega provides a particularly good introduction to the ways in which words are grouped both phonetically and in similar patterns— as pattern-recognition is particularly important to improve spelling.

Catchwords takes the core words in the Australian, New Zealand and British primary school curriculum and shows both teachers and parents how to introduce them in a natural, logical and active way.

Spelling, in fact, is one of the big casualties of the nonsensical phonics-versus-nonphonics debate. Obviously phonics can help any child learn words and syllables based on the "short" vowels: *get, set, bet; sit, hit, fit.* And simple games and whiteboard lists can help children identify the most common word and syllable patterns: *fate, mate* and *plate (the magic 'e'); light, might* and *sight; bridge, ridge, sledge* and *dredge.*

But problem words are, by their very definition, not simple ones: *spatial* and *facial; session* and *faction; cough, through* and *bough.* And even such often quoted "principles" as "i before e except after c" don't, in fact, work: as with *ancient, conscience, deficient, glacier, science, society, financier, sufficient* and many more.

Most good teachers now feel that spelling is best taught through writing. As Cripps and Peters put it: "Spelling is best remembered in the fingertips, and it is the memory of the moving pencil writing words that makes for accurate spelling." That's because "muscle memory", processed by the cerebellum, is one of the most effective forms of memory.

Nonphonetic spelling is also a visual skill, rather than a listening skill. Most children find it hard to learn nonphonetic words from spoken examples alone. So encourage them to learn by both the look and feel of words. Encourage them, too, to write words from memory, rather than copying them. By doing this, they are calling on their visual and muscle-memory ability, rather than spelling out the sounds.

Robert Dilts and Todd A. Epstein, in their excellent NLP book, *Dynamic Learning,* also make many first-rate suggestions for teaching those who find spelling difficult. In particular, they recommend using "visual imagination" in tackling tough words: visualising each word so

How back writing solves problems

Back writing, the method recommended by Peter Young and Colin Tyre in *Teach Your Child To Read*—for children who have difficulty distinguishing between some letters. Place a large sheet of paper on a smooth wall at your child's shoulder height. Give him a thick crayon or felt-tipped pen, so he can write on the paper at arm's length. Then, with your child facing the paper, write the first letter on his back, with your index finger, as if you were printing a 'lower-case' non-capital letter. Make sure he can feel it, tell him what it is, and ask him to write it on the paper.   But do only one letter at a time.   The system works because of the power of 'muscle memory': the ability to memorise through bodily actions.

The illustration is from *FUNdamentals,*
by Gordon Dryden and Colin Rose.

that the difficult letter-combinations stand out, either by making them bigger, brighter or a different colour (see hints, page 386).

Back writing for mirror writing problems

For school-age children who continue to have problems distinguishing letters such as *b* and *d,* and *p* and *q,* British educators Peter Young and Colin Tyre, in their book, *Teach Your Child To Read,* recommend "back writing". The principles are simple: place a large sheet of paper on a wall at your child's eye-level; with the child facing the poster, you use your index finger to "print" the letter *b* on his back, repeating something like, "B says buh; first down for the bat and round for the ball;" and get him to write the letter on the poster, using a thick felt pen and repeating your wording. Teach only one letter at a time.

Young and Tyre say that "over very many years we have not known this to fail".

Running fingers over the shape of Montessori sandpaper letters also helps children distinguish "similar but opposite" letters. Sets of stippled plastic letters are now available.

New Zealand breakthroughs

Other breakthroughs are often blends or developments of techniques covered in our Teaching Revolution chapter.

New Zealand's catch-up programmes, for instance, have become so successful that groups of foreign teachers now fly across the Pacific regularly to see how they work. New Zealand teachers are amazed to find that many American elementary schools still shuffle children around to several different teachers during a day: a reading teacher, for example, and a mathematics teacher.

New Zealand has "a national curriculum" but that paints only in broad strokes the educational philosophy and teaching goals. Individual teachers are regarded very much as self-acting professionals. Many are graduates of Colleges of Education , which specialise in teacher training; others from university. Blocks of all three-year teacher-training programmes are also spent in practical hands-on school experience.

Even the term *national curriculum* is probably a misnomer in that it suggests a French-style system where every year each child is learning the same set body of knowledge.

Wherever possible, students should be given choices and responsibility for their own education.

ELIZABETH SCHULZ*

* Writing in the *American Teacher* Magazine,
on her visit to New Zealand schools.

"The new national curriculum doesn't tell teachers how to run their classes," reports *American Teacher* Magazine's Elizabeth Schulz, "but it does emphasise that schools are for the students and should be organised to give them access to the skills and understanding they need to participate effectively and productively in society. School learning is meant to be relevant. Class projects should illuminate for students the interconnectedness of subjects. And, whenever possible, students should be given choices and responsibility for their own education."[13]

Perhaps more importantly, New Zealand has decentralised its school administration so that all schools, private and public, have their own "charters". These must include minimum national curriculum guidelines, but, above that, all individual schools are encouraged to innovate. And this has led to major breakthroughs. These include:

The four-minute reading programme

Like many countries, New Zealand has a large number of migrant families for whom English is a second language. Not surprisingly, many of them starting school at age five have an English reading-age equivalent of three or lower. Now many of them are catching up within a few weeks. All it takes is four minutes a day and a great link between school and home.

The entire scheme is common sense and simple. When each child starts school, teachers check his or her level of understanding. If Bobby can recognise his own name and other words starting with "B," but he can't manage those starting with "P" or "W" or "K," then the teacher works out a personalised daily list of words—beginning with those letters. Those will include the recommended first 300 most-used words in the language, and others well-known to the child, such as family and local street names.

A new list of words is provided each day, handwritten on note paper. The list is taken home for study, and a carbon copy kept at school. Each morning, the teacher spends only four minutes with each child to check progress—and provide encouragement.

But the big extra ingredient is the home involvement. Ideally, a "school neighbourhood worker" takes home the first list with each child, and explains to the parents, grandparents or brothers and sisters just what Bobby needs to learn—and how only four minutes a day is needed for him to flourish.

All it takes is four minutes a day at school, four minutes at home, and a great link between home and school.*

* The key to New Zealand's "four-minute reading programme",
as reported in the television series, *Where To Now?*
produced by Gordon Dryden for The Pacific Foundation
and broadcast on the Television One network.

Educational psychologists who developed the programme say the home-link is the real key, and "it's only half as good without that."[14] Another key is the "positive reinforcement" that comes from daily success. While the programme started over twenty years ago for five-year-old new entrants, it is now being used successfully in other schools for older children. As well as sending a new reading list home to parents each night, some have brought parent-helpers into the school. At Bruce McLaren Intermediate [middle] School in Auckland, for instance, twelve parents help out part-time.

Even senior reading teacher Beth Whitehead was a bit reluctant when asked by her principal to introduce the programme, saying "What can you do in four minutes?" But she tried it out. "I soon thought I'd show it wouldn't work. But when I started it, the children just zoomed in their reading. They were absolutely amazing."[15]

Whitehead stresses that the programme is built on positive reinforcement of everything that the child does correctly, however small.

Finger-phonics programme

At nearby Don Buck Primary School in West Auckland, teacher Mary Ashby-Green, colleague Lynne Hailey and principal Jennice Murray have achieved outstanding success with a British-based finger phonics programme. Created by Sue Lloyd of Woods Lake School, Suffolk England, the programme is known elsewhere as *Jolly Phonics*.

This takes the extremely simple approach of teaching phonetic reading by linking each sound of English with a specific action and finger movements. And it works. Kinesthetic children who have been way behind at reading early in school are now zooming ahead, proving once again the strength of "muscle memory"—and catering to different learning styles.

Before the programme was introduced at Don Buck, 40 percent of its six-year-olds were not reading. With a few months all six-year-olds were reading, and the brightest were reading twelve to eighteen months above their chronological age.

TARP—the tape-assisted reading programme

In other parts of New Zealand, primary schools have successfully linked together one of the simplest Japanese electronic innovations with the New Zealand *School Journal* [16] library—and used it to make spec-

The key ingredients of TARP: Tape-Assisted Reading Programme*

 Provide a full range of books and stories graded by age-group reading levels, with interesting photos or pictures.

 Encourage each child to choose stories on subjects that interest him.

 Have those stories recorded on audio tape, by parents, teachers or older students.

 The student reads the story as he listens, at home and at school, on a Walkman.

 When he feels confident, he reads the story without the tape.

 Then he reads parts of it to his teacher, some parts from his selection, some from her choice.

On average, children on this programme make three years' progress in eight to ten weeks.

*Details are covered fully in *TARP: The Tape Assisted Reading Programme* by John Medcalf, Training Coordinator, Special Education Service, Hastings, New Zealand. Email: medcalfj@ses.org.nz

tacular progress in overcoming reading difficulties. The innovation is the Sony Walkman cassette tape player. And in the small New Zealand suburb of Flaxmere, educational psychologist Dr. John Medcalf has taken the Walkman and used it to solve major reading problems.

The method is called TARP: tape-assisted reading programme. Each child is encouraged to read stories of his own choice—based on his own interests. But when he reads each book, at home or at school, he can hear the same story on a cassette tape, through a set of Walkman headphones.

"The readers are actually selecting stories they want to read," says Medcalf, "about subjects they're interested in: reading them when they want to read them—as many times as they like before they actually try to read them to somebody else."[17]

When the student feels confident enough, the teacher checks progress. "Some of the best results," says Medcalf, "have been four to five years' reading gain over approximately eight weeks on the programme." Overall research results show a three-year reading gain in eight to 10 weeks.[18]

In the tiny New Zealand township of Opotiki, with a low-income community and a 99 percent "minority roll", even more specular results have been achieved with TARP. Before starting it, 80 per cent of children at Opotiki Primary School were reading way below the national average. But after completing the programme, 80 per cent were away above the national average. And the entire programme was run by trained parent-volunteers. To avoid stigmatising low-achievers, all students went through the programme, taking turns each week in a separately set-up classroom. In this way, the entire school was involved in raising everyone's standards.

The programme is helped greatly in New Zealand through the graded *School Journal* material, backed by a regularly updated catalogue covering content, subjects and age-levels. Students may choose from a selection of taped stories that the school has built up, or may ask a teacher or parent to record on to a tape a story or article of special interest.

In America, results from similar programmes have also been striking. Marie Carbo, Director of the National Reading Styles Institute, refers to it as "the recorded book" method.[19]

As a strong advocate of matching reading methods and materials to learning styles, she says it can even be adapted for use with highly kinesthetic youngsters: reading a book on a music stand attached to a stationary bike while listening to the tape and pedalling.

Principles of Peer Tutoring:*

 1 Students' reading levels should be checked first.

2 Students should be matched in pairs, with the tutor only a slightly better reader.

 3 Books should be chosen for the right reading and interest levels.

4 Tutors are trained with a simple checklist, which shows them how to use "pause, prompt and praise" techniques.

5 Parents are fully informed, books taken home each night, and a list kept of books mastered.

 6 Tutoring should be done daily or at least three times a week.

 7 Each pair should record their efforts on a tape-recorder provided.

8 The teacher monitors the recordings to check progress in both reading and tutoring.

Over six months the average reading gain for tutors has been four years and for slower learners just over two years.

* Details are fully covered in *Peer Tutoring in Reading,* by John Medcalf, Training Coordinator, Special Education Service, Hastings, New Zealand.
email: medcalfj@ses.org.nz

Peer tutoring

John Medcalf has also built on earlier work by Professor Ted Glynn, of the University of Otago, in developing a successful peer tutoring programme in reading, using "pause, prompt and praise" techniques.

Here one student in an primary school simply acts as a mini-teacher for another student. Generally the mini-teacher is only a little bit more advanced—so both the tutor and her buddy benefit. The tutor very definitely is not the best reader in the class—although she may end up that way. Effectively it's one-to-one teaching without taking up the time of an adult teacher. Each "tutor" is trained in "pause, prompt and praise" techniques: to praise good work in everyday language ("Neat," or "Nice one!"); to pause for ten seconds while a reader may be having difficulty (so the tutor can think of ways to help); and to prompt with suggestions.

Flaxmere Primary School teacher Rhonda Godwin sums up the results: "We've had tutors who initially were reading about a year to a year and a half below their chronological age, and they made up to two years' gain after working on the programme for about ten weeks."[20]

Over six months the average gain for tutors has been four years—and for the slower learners just over two years.[21]

Reading Recovery programme—and its critics

All those five programmes can be operated by normal classroom teachers. But the best-known New Zealand catch-up programme is organised by teachers who need to be specially trained. It is known as *Reading Recovery,* first developed by Professor Marie Clay of the University of Auckland.

In New Zealand, while the official age for starting school is six, nearly every child starts at five. By six, many children with reading difficulties are identified in the *Reading Recovery* programme, and helped for half an hour each day by a specially trained *Reading Recovery* teacher. *Reading Recovery* has been operating as a government-funded programme throughout New Zealand since 1984. On average, youngsters catch up within sixteen weeks. About 97 percent maintain and improve their ability as they proceed through school. Despite that international praise, many New Zealand primary schools say that combinations of other programmes—as reported in this chapter—are much more effective, and certainly much more cost-effective, in teaching youngsters to read.

Learning is the greatest game in life and the most fun.

All children are born believing this and will continue to believe this until we convince them that learning is very hard work and unpleasant.

Some kids never really learn this lesson, and go through life believing that learning is fun and the only game worth playing.

We have a name for such people.

We call them geniuses.

GLENN DOMAN
Teach Your Baby Math*

*Published by the Better Baby Press, at The Institutes for the Achievement of Human Potential, 8801 Stenton Avenue, Philadelphia, Pennsylvania 19118, USA.

There has also been strong criticism in New Zealand and elsewhere that some reading programmes have downplayed the need to learn to read by blending both phonetic and non-phonetic methods. Like many other educational debates, the answer lies in combining both, and not turning either side into dogma. Around 84 percent of English words have easily-identifiable written patterns, even if not strictly spelled phonetically.

And here some of the best results of blending both methods together have been achieved by Dr. Tom Nicholson, Associate Professor of Education at the University of Auckland, summarised in his excellent book, *Reading The Writing On The Wall.* It also provides both practical guidance in teaching reading and a history of reading controversies.[22]

Personal key vocabularies

Other than Marie Clay and former Director of Education, Dr. C.E. Beeby, the New Zealand educational innovator best known in other countries is probably the late Sylvia Ashton-Warner. She first burst to prominence internationally with her book *Teacher* in 1963. It was based largely on her work teaching at primary schools in New Zealand rural areas with a mainly Maori population. And her supporters would say it provides one of the main effective answers to what some call "third wave" reading problems. In the early 1950s, New Zealand introduced into its schools the *Janet and John* series of readers, a British modification of the American *Alice and Jerry* series. But even then teachers were encouraged to make up their own books based on children's own lives.

In listening to young Maori children, Ashton-Warner "came to realise that some words—different words for each child—were more meaningful and memorable than others." When she asked a young child to write about a "train" he wrote about a "canoe".

She then started to listen to each child and selected the key words "which were so meaningful to him that he was able to remember them when he had seen them only once".

As Lynley Hood writes in *Sylvia,* her biography of Ashton-Warner: "Her pupils learned to read from their personal key vocabularies. Nearly every day, from their experiences at home or at school, Sylvia helped each child select a new key word. She wrote the word with heavy crayon on a stout piece of cardboard and gave it to the child. The word cards became as personal and precious to the children as the imagery they represented. Children who had laboured for months over 'See Spot run' in the new

Release the native imagery of your child and use it for working material.

SYLVIA ASHTON-WARNER
Author of *Teacher**

*One of the keys to Ashton-Warner's success, as covered by
Lynley Hood in *The Biography of Sylvia Ashton-Warner,*
published by Viking, Auckland, New Zealand.

Janet and John readers took one look at 'corpse', 'beer' or 'hiding' and suddenly they could read."[23]

She realised that children were more interested in their own stories than hers. So she helped her students write them. She put the stories to music. And she constructed her own graphic presentations about their dreams and experiences. She regarded each child as highly creative, and encouraged them to work with clay and paint.

Above all, she summed up her philosophy in one memorable sentence: *Release the native imagery of your child and use it for working material.*

Some of the same techniques have been used by Felicity Hughes to teach English in Tanzania[24] and by Herbert Kohl to effectively teach reading to youngsters from minority cultures in California.[25]

Beginning School Mathematics

New Zealand's success in reading recovery has been matched with some innovative approaches to teaching elementary mathematics. The *Beginning School Mathematics* programme, for example, includes very brightly-coloured puzzles and games. For their first two years at some schools, youngsters use these and other manipulative material to learn about the main relationships that underlie mathematics.

American writer Schulz summarises her impression of the programme in action: "As we enter the classroom, a glance at the six- and seven-year-olds tells us BSM is in full swing. Four students make geometric shapes by stretching rubber bands across pegs on a board. Children at a table draw pictures using cardboard circles, squares and triangles. One boy weighs household objects on a scale, guided by a sheet that asks, for example, if a cork is heavier than a paper clip. Six students stand in line by height and answer the teacher's questions about who is first, second and third in line, and who is standing between whom."[26]

Many New Zealand teachers, however, find this approach is tied far too closely with Piaget's developmental "timetable", and that much better results can be achieved by a variety of even earlier hands-on projects, including variations of the Maria Montessori's programmes.

Computerised catch-ups

Other intermediate schools have found great success by using the international *Technic Lego* programme. Others are also using some of

The best catch-up programme of all could well be a change of diet.

JEANNETTE VOS
*Who Stole the Brain?**

* Co-author Vos reached the conclusion on this page as part
of the research being completed for this new book.
If you would like to be notified when the new book is published,
please register at: www.learning-revolution.com

the excellent computer math programs that are now readily available. Among the best are those pioneered by the Computer Curriculum Corporation, based on years of research at Stanford University in California, not just for math but for a wide variety of subjects.

The best programme of all: prevention

While a minority of children do have specific learning difficulties, some of the best answers are very simple: make sure the problems do not arise. *And here the best catch-up programme of all could well be a change of diet.*

In the so-called developed world hardly a day has gone by since the start of the new century without news-media articles about the dangers of obesity, particularly among young children. But bad diet is not only a health problem. It can become a real barrier to learning.

And again a telling example of this comes again from New Zealand: this time from one of its experimental schools, Discovery 1, in Christchurh, which uses "the whole world as a classroom".

There, in 2003, thirteen-year-old student Justin Fletcher decided to test on his own body the same kind of faulty diet that ruined the health of American film director Morgan Spurlock—as covered in Supurlock's award-winning movie, *Super Size Me: A film of epic portions.*[27]

For two days Justin ate commercial sugar-rich "junk food" for breakfast, lunch and dinner. This included candies, cake, meat pies, Coco Pops and other sugar-rich foods. He repeated his junk-food again after another two days of eating his normal diet of chicken, rice, bread and lettuce.

He then put himself through as series of reading, typing and mathematics tests. The results? "His addled brain went on a go-slow when fed the sugar diet," reports *The New Zealand Herald.* "He read 43 percent slower, typed at nearly half his usual speed and solved math problems up to 35 percent slower."[28]

Justin's family also noticed behavioural changes like mood-swings, after he binged on junk food. Says his mother, Philippa, a community health promoter: "I was blown away by the impact of junk food on learning. I didn't think it would have much impact."

Their findings would come as no surprise to Dr. Mary Ann Block who outlines the key role of diet in her book, *No More ADHD: (subtitled: Ten ways to help improve your child's attention and behaviour without drugs).* Like Justin's family, she warns of the way in which too high a

13-year-old's learning scores plummet after two-day binge on sugar-rich junk food:

Reading: **43% slower**

Typing: **50% slower**

Math: **35% slower**

NEW ZEALAND HERALD
*Junk diet puts teen on go-slow**

* February 5, 2004.

sugar intake can, for many children, lead to overly aggressive behaviour.

A typical American school lunch will be high-sugar soda, chips and sweet desserts. And Dr. Block quotes a study done with 803 New York public schools and nine juvenile correction facilities to show the alternative. In the study, researchers increased fruits, vegetables and whole grains and decreased sugar and fats in diets. They then followed the children for several years. After making those simple changes "the academic performance of 1.1 million children rose 16 percent, and learning disabilities fell 40 percent. In juvenile correctional facilities, violent anti-social behavior fell 48 percent." Amazingly, the schools have not instituted these dietary changes on a permanent basis.

Three other "health-educational" programmes

This is not a book on medical problems, but no survey of effective catch-up methods would be complete without reviewing three other programmes with strong "health-educational" links.

Programme one is the method developed by Glenn Doman and his team in Philadelphia at The Institutes for the Achievement of Human Potential to assist children with severe brain damage. Following on from the pioneering work of Professor Temple Fay, Doman's team has effectively taught many blind children to see, deaf children to hear, and handicapped children to perform at "normal" levels: by physically "repatterning" other parts of the brain to take over from damaged cells and sections. His breakthrough book, *What To Do About Your Brain-Injured Child,* covers the history of the Institutes' methods, practical results and growth.

Programme two is the Tomatis Method, first developed fifty years ago by French physician, psychologist and educator Dr. Alfred Tomatis. The method uses filtered and unfiltered sound to "reeducate" the ability to listen and process sounds, both through the intricate mechanisms of the inner ear and through the body. The Tomatis method is used in more than 200 centres worldwide. Some of its results are outstanding. They improve listening ability and develop superior skills in speaking, reading, writing, sports, social interaction, motor development and music.

Programme three covers the natural alternatives, developed by Dr. Thomas Armstrong, to the medical treatment of the so-called Attention Deficit Disorder Syndrome—a malady that is claimed to inflict about two million American children.

If you're told your child has ADDS, look at his role models!

<u>Orville Wright</u>, one of the first two men to fly, was expelled from school because of bad behaviour.

<u>Ludwig van Beethoven</u> was rude and ill-mannered and was subject to wild fits of rage.

<u>Pope John XXIII</u> was sent home with a note saying he continually came to class unprepared; he did not deliver the note.

<u>Louis Armstrong</u>, the great jazz singer and saxaphone player, spent time in an institution for delinquent boys.

<u>Paul Cezanne</u>, the painter, had a bad temper and would stamp his feet in hysterical rage whenever he felt thwarted.

<u>William Wordsworth</u>, the poet, was described before his eighth birthday as a "stubborn, wayward and intractable boy".

<u>Sarah Bernhardt</u> was expelled from school three times.

<u>Will Rogers</u> was incorrigible at school and ran away from home.

<u>Arturo Toscanini</u> was an obstinate and disobedient boy; once he made up his mind not to do something, nothing could make him change his mind.

THOMAS ARMSTRONG
The Myth of the ADDS Child*

* Published by Penguin, New York.

ADDS is supposedly characterised by three main features: hyperactivity (fidgeting, excessive running and climbing, leaving one's classroom seat), impulsivity (blurting out answers in class, interrupting others, having problems waiting turns) and inattention (forgetfulness, disorganization, losing things, careless mistakes).

In recent years psychiatrists across America have prescribed, for so-called ADDS, millions of doses of Ritalin, a drug originally approved to control mild depression and senility in adults.

Now no one would deny that many children regularly display the three characteristics of being hyperactive, impulsive and inattentive. But Dr. Armstrong, who has spent years researching different learning styles, puts clearly the viewpoint the current authors have come to share: "ADDS does not exist," he writes in *The Myth of the ADDS Child*. "These children are *not* disordered. They may have a different style of thinking, attending, and behaving, but it's the broader social and educational influences that create the disorder, not the children."

Dr. Armstrong's book outlines "fifty ways to improve your child's behaviour and attention span without drugs, labels or coercion". Those ways range from changing eating habits to physical education programmes, from martial arts classes to the use of relaxing background music, from channelling energy into creative arts to computer training.

The danger of all-embracing labels

While all the programmes summarised in this chapter work well, they also underline the danger of placing all-embracing labels on *specific* learning problems.

One of the strongest warnings against such "lumping together" comes from Dr. Mel Levine, professor of pediatrics at the University of North Carolina Medical School. He is also the director of the university's Clinical Centre for the Study of Development and Learning. And he is co-founder, with Charles Schwab, and co-chair of All Kinds of Minds. This is a nonprofit institute that develops products and programmes to help parents, teachers, clinicians and children address *differences* in learning.

"Planet earth," says Dr. Levine, in his book *One Mind at a Time,* "is inhabited by all kinds of people who have all kinds of minds. The brain of each human is unique. Some minds are wired to create symphonies and sonnets, while others are fitted out to build bridges, highways and

Enable students, don't label them.

**A 'school for all kinds of minds'
will not label any of its students.
Terms such as ADD and LD lump too
many diverse children into one
deceptively simple category.**

MEL LEVINE, M.D.
A Mind at a Time*

* Published by Simon & Schuster New York.
More details on www.allkindsofminds.org.

computers; design airplanes and road systems; drive trucks and taxicabs; or seek cures for breast cancer and hypertension.

"The growth of our society and the progress of the world are dependent on our commitment to fostering in our children, and among ourselves, the cooexistence and mutual respect of these many different kinds of minds."

Dr. Levine has spent most of his life as a developmental-behavioural pediatrician. And "on countless evenings I have driven home from work feeling emotionally depleted, dejected after listening to the sad tales of children who have come to equate education with humiliation. Many have been forced to accept labels for themselves, labels that mark them as somehow permanently deviant of dysfunctional: labels like ADDS or LD (learning disability). Others have been placed willy-nilly on several drugs to somehow settle or sedate or soothe their kinds of minds."

Yet, in his view, all of those children "possess remarkable strengths waiting to be tapped". If any child is having difficulty in some aspect of learning, says Dr. Levine, it is important to determine the *specific* nature of the problem, rather than "lumping and labelling".

He likens the human mind to a complex toolbox, where not everyone may become expert in using all the implements. He prefers developing a *profile* that identifies each child's specific strengths and locates those "trouble spots where facets of a profile don't mesh" with some facets of schooling.

But Dr. Levine thinks it's much more important to identify strengths than to concentrate too much on minor weaknesses. "I believe that when your child has strengths that are suppressed, abilities he is prevented from using while growing up, he becomes a virtual timebomb primed for detonation."*

His organisation's website (www.allkindsofminds.org) is highly recommended for teachers, parents and students.

---

* *For detailed scientific back-up to Dr. Levine's judgment, we strongly recommend 'Our Labelled Children', by Robert J. Sternberg and Elena L. Grigorenko.*

Turn high schools into real-life experience and watch achievement soar.

New recipe for secondary-school reform: to learn it, do it!

Are there some guaranteed methods to overcome high-school failure?

Again the answer is "yes". But it requires a rethink of most secondary school methods.

At its simplest, the alternative can be summarised in one sentence: *If you want to learn it, do it.*

Equally simple: *Start by tapping into students' own inherent interests.* Encourage them to develop their own talents, seek out their own goals, develop their own real-life projects, so that they then find real-life solutions. In this way, most students find it much easier to develop higher-level skills in math, science and other "subjects"—because they relate directly to specific integrated tasks.

Just as simple: *Instead of relying only or mainly on standardised written memory-tests to gain a credential, make sure students "show they know" by completing real-world projects.*

This is not the complete answer, of course. But it crystallises the core of almost every successful learning experience we can think of. Yet for some strange reason most high-school systems around the world ignore that simple truth. So do most post-secondary school institutions, with the notable exception of many leading polytechnics and some of the great specialist universities.

Fortunately, an increasing number are now putting the "doing" back into learning. And by doing so they're solving the dropout dilemma at middle and high schools—again, simply because they're connecting learning to real life.

There is really only one way to learn how to do something and that is to do it.

ROGER C. SCHANK[1]
*Engines For Education**

* Published by Laurence Erlbaum Associates, 365 Hillsdale, New Jersey 07642.

❑ A survey of west coast high schools in America shows ten practices set high-achieving high schools apart from others. And nearly all of the ten involve high-quality, rigorous work, most with hands-on practical experience to "show you know".

❑ Singapore's newest institute of technology has been designed as a "teaching and learning city", and nearly all its technology students work on producing specific projects and products in partnership with some of the world's biggest hi-tech corporations, from Siemens to Microsoft.

❑ In Alaska, students from some of America's most deprived "academic" backgrounds have succeeded at high school by setting up and running four successful pilot companies. All have been run by "native Alaskan" students in a state where most of others of their background lag well behind.

❑ In California, more than 200 "school-within-a-school" Partnership Academies have been set up to provide hands-on job experience for students otherwise at risk of dropping out of high school.

❑ In Washington state several school districts are pioneering "project-based", "performance-based" or "applied learning" programmes at high school.

❑ In New Zealand schools have achieved similar results by "using the whole world as a classroom" and working out in "the real world" to put their learning into practice.

❑ And in Sweden innovations include setting up a new-style community-learning school, with even its own publishing company.

The only "surprise" is that the success of this approach should surprise anyone. Says Professor Roger C. Schank, a world authority on learning: "There is really only one way to learn how to do something and that is to do it. If you want to learn to throw a football, drive a car, build a mousetrap, design a building, cook a stir-fry, or be a management consultant, you must have a go at doing it." [1]

There's no secret in this, he says. Parents usually teach children in precisely this way. They don't give a series of lectures to their children to prepare them to walk, talk, climb, run, play a game, or learn how to behave. They just let their children do these things.

"When it comes to school, however, instead of allowing students to learn by doing, we create courses of instruction that tell students about the theory of the task without concentrating on the doing of the task." Throughout history, says Schank, youths have been apprenticed to

Ten features of successful high schools

1. **Demand more of each student and end dumbed-down tracks.**

2. **Build a schedule that gives teachers fewer than 150 student each** (switch from 45 to 90-minute class times).

3. **Get teachers talking to each other.**

4. **Design work to be showcased.**

5. **Create student advisories.**

6. **Make every minute matter.**

7. **Help students choose courses.**

8. **Turn seniors into mentors.**

9. **Give parents, students and teachers more say.**

10. **Captivate students with real-world lessons to match diverse interests.**

BETSY HAMMOND & BILL GRAVES
'Road Map To Success"

* Article in The Oregonian, Oregon, January 13, 2004.
At: www.oregonlive.com

masters to learn trades. But educators have not found it easy to apply the apprenticeship system to education. "So in its place," he says, "we lecture." And not only to lecture, but, particularly in America, to base the entire high school system around "standardised" units of study and memory-based "standardised test scores".

That system is a disastrous failure. "Fewer than 10 per cent of Californian high schools have reached optimum levels on state achievement tests," says California state Superintendent of Public Instruction Jack O'Connell.[2] "Fewer than half the students who enter the California State University system are proficient in reading and math." But when making these points at the start of 2004, O'Connell amazingly urged even more of the same type of teaching, but with more rigorous test standards.

Schools that are already achieving success are generally doing it by changing the archaic present system, not perpetuating it.

How the best schools succeed

Early in 2004 *The Oregonian,* in Portland, Oregon, completed a survey of high-schools achievement. Its conclusion: "Creating a high school that ensures success for nearly every teenager is rare. But it can be done, as shown by the results of a handful of West Coast high schools. These schools get extraordinary results, and they do it without spending more tax money than the schools around them."[3]

The newspaper found "plenty of determined principals who have turned their struggling *elementary* school into a star in a couple of years". But overwhelmingly they found high schools failing their students.

Their criteria for success? "The hallmarks of such a school would include a low dropout rate, high student achievement, a high proportion of graduates going to college and evidence that they're succeeding in college. The school would need to enrol enough minority, low-income and special education students to show it was succeeding with them too. And, on campus, students work with a sense of purpose that shows they see a connection between school and their future.

"Held to that standards, about 99 percent of high schools fall short, according to state achievement statistics and education experts."

The newspaper found ten similar key practices set the high-performing high schools apart. Two that stand out:

1. Captivate students with real-world lessons.

Two hundred high school Partnership Academies now operate in California, where at-risk students learn real-life skills, working at 500 companies.

At David Douglas High, in east Portland, Oregon, students can now find classes that match their diverse interests: electronics, Japanese and even golf-course maintenance.

"After David Douglas High paired senior Chris Czupryk with a pathologist, the teen watched him autopsy a man who had died of a massive brain infection. It involved cutting open the skull and examining the swollen brain. Now he can't wait to study microbiology and cytology, and wants to become a pathologist himself." [4]

At the Centre for Advanced Learning, a charter school in Gresham, Oregon, students build Web sites, weld furniture, and use defibrillators on mannequins to study information technology, engineering and health sciences. "Students say they shift into overdrive," says the newspaper, "to fulfil the demands of a programme that aligns with what they want to do in life."

2. Assign academic work worthy of being showcased.

"At San Diego's High Tech High, students learn by doing ambitious projects: documentaries of World War 1, a public debate on evolution, a working submarine." Every student at High Tech High is involved in producing finished "products" as he or she "learns a living". And in 2003 every graduate of High Tech High went on to college, even though fewer than half have college-educated parents.

Says *The Oregonian:* "Teachers there cover many of the same basics as other schools. But they say students understand and retain the basics better when they're tied to meaningful projects, not dictated in a lecture."

At high-achieving David Douglas High, "all juniors gather their best essays, research reports, shop projects and other work into a portfolio that showcases their advanced skills. Then they must top it up with a senior portfolio with more elaborate samples. Those get displayed at a 'portfolio' fair for students and parents."

Business-school partnership academies

Other schools are building very specific partnerships with business: some through Partnership Academies. This model originated in Philadelphia in the late 1960s. Now 200 Partnership Academies operate in California. These are linked with more than 500 California employers, in over twenty industries, including health, marketing, international trade, agriculture, electronics, construction, tourism, printing and high-tech manufacturing

96 percent pass rate at hands-on electronics academy with diplomas and hi-tech experience.

EAST SIDE ELECTRONICS ACADEMY
San Jose, Silicon Valley*

* From George Lucas Educational Foundation website:
www.edutopia.org

Each is a school-within-a-school. And each is designed to help students who are otherwise headed for failure and probable unemployment or lowly-paid jobs.

In San Jose, Silicon Valley, for instance, the East Side Electronics Academy has been successfully operating since 1985. Based on three schools in the East Side Union High School District, it sets up at-risk students with hands-on experience in the electronics, computer, semiconductor and telecommunications industries. Students work throughout the year with mentors from industry. And they take paid summer jobs for nine or ten weeks in partnership companies. *In a typical year, 96 percent of seniors graduate not only with diplomas but with strong hi-tech work experience.*[5]

Also in San Jose a Biotech Academy has been set up to link Andrew P. Hill High School with some of Silicon Valley's best-known biotechnology corporations. These companies provide guest speakers, job-shadowing opportunities and field trips. Some offer working internships. And many corporate mentors volunteer each month to work with high school students.

Erica Diaz and Miguel Villafana are typical of students who have benefitted. When Erica began high school she did not expect to graduate. "As a freshman, I just thought I was going to be a single mother and at my age—at sixteen!" she recalls.[6]

But she flowered in the academy programme, has since graduated and hopes to become a doctor. Miguel thought he would graduate from high school, but college was not in his plans. Now he's attending San Diego State University and mentoring high school students. Both say their lives were turned around by the hands-on learning methods of the academy.

In Minnesota, employers have actually helped design "an MBA for high school students": the Minnesota Business Academy, one of the state's most unusual public charter schools.

"Opened in 2000 in the renovated former Science Museum of Minnesota in downtown St. Paul, the ninth-through-twelfth-grade school known as MBA boasts a technology-oriented, project-based curriculum that incorporates a business element in everything from art to English," says a report prepared for the George Lucas Educational Foundation.[7]

"Every school should make the curriculum more practical," says Bob Kaitz, president and chief executive officer of BestPrep, the philanthropic state business group that helped MBA become a reality. "A lot

Studying robotics at Singapore's Robotic Centre, sculpturing rocket models in a math class.

Typical Middle School classes
*Overseas Family School, Singapore**

* Download four-colour tabloid on this school at: www.ofs.edu.sg
Note: Middle School details, pages 8, 9, 13, 14, 15.

of kids don't do well in school because they don't see a connection between what they're studying and what they're going to do."[8]

BestPrep conceived the idea of the 480-student MBA and mobilised 150 volunteers from the business and education community to create the school. It helped design the school building and curriculum, and raised money towards the $12 million building and operations startup costs.

Singapore shows the way

In other middle-school and high school systems around the world, students flower when producing real-world results.

Middle school students at Singapore's Overseas Family School each have to complete a specific science project every year and "show they know" in demonstrations to fellow students and parents. And to obtain an International Baccalaureate High School Diploma, as well as sitting specific subject exams, senior students have to complete a project that actually results in a finished product, showing how they are capable of integrating several "subjects" into a real-world output.

Visit any of the Singapore middle school classes, and you'll come away amazed at the output of students aged eleven to thirteen:

❑ In one art class you're likely to find students sculpturing a robot out of recycled junk.

❑ In a math class, boys and girls constructing rocket models from blueprints.

❑ In a humanities class, students tracing the history of human exploration.

❑ In drama class, students producing a fashion show featuring futuristic costumes.

❑ Or if you meet a group of students together outside the school, you're likely to find them on a field trip to the Singapore Robotic Centre, a space shuttle display or taking part in the school's many out-of-class programmes.

Says a seventh-grader after transferring from a school in another country: "It's amazing how much more I'm learning here compared to my old school. There everything was about memorisation. They wanted to stuff everything into my head, and all I had to do was memorise it and repeat it, but I don't like being a talking parrot. Although I've been here only three months, I understand complex subjects much better by doing

Singapore's Nanyang Polytechnic has been designed as a teaching and learning city, where students make robots and other hi-tech products under contract.

LIN CHENG TON
*CEO, Nanyang Polytechnic, Singapore**

* Interview with Gordon Dryden, Singapore, 2003.

the different projects. I see much better how so many things in life inter-relate: like how mathematics is needed for science." [9]

All 2,500 students at OFS assemble digital portfolios demonstrating all their major abilities; and they also have the opportunity to sit certificate and rigorous diploma examinations to qualify for college entry.

Also in Singapore, the brilliantly-equipped Nanyang Polytechnic has been designed as a "teaching and learning city". Its new 30.5-hectare campus is about the size of sixty football fields. All buildings are state-of-the-art. They include a fully-computerised library, and a "teaching factory"—where all students learn by doing, and where nearly all work is project work in partnership with, and under constract to, major international hi-tech companies. To graduate, whether in robotics engineering and design or multimedia graphics, students have to produce a finished product or programme that is actually sold to and used by these giant corporations, including Microsoft, Seimens and Oracle.

Says Principal and CEO Lin Cheng Ton: "The Teaching Factory addresses the hitherto unmet challenge commonly faced by institutions in trying to emulate a real-world environment within a typical institutional setting. An important and integral component is the industry project work where staff and students work closely as a team on real-life problems." [10] Visit the campus for a day, and you come away convinced you've been touring the tertiary learning centre of the future*.

Project-based learning takes off

But you don't have to wait till your post-high school years to benefit from project work. America's Washington state is one that has recently adopted "project-based" and "performance-based" learning as one of the cores of its high school policy.

Some schools there have built these methods into their curriculum for years. Lake Washington is one of the school districts that already has what they call "a culminating requirement" in operation. In practice, this means that, as with the IB international Diploma, all students to graduate have to produce practical project proof to show what they have learned.

"Because students choose their own projects," says researcher-reporter Diane Curtis, "the nature of their study is as varied as the teenagers themselves. Projects can range from working with real scientists on the Human Genome Project and sharing their experience through video or

Visit www.nyp.edu.sg to see the tertiary learning-centre of the future.

Mathematics makes much more sense when students move from hands-on work to abstract thinking by solving real-world problems.

SEYMOUR PAPERT
*MIT Professor**

* in *Start With the Pyramid,* article on project-based learning on
website of George Lucas Educational Foundation: www.edutopia.org

written reports to writing and producing a play, or building a 'battlebot' robot and explaining how it was built and how it works." [11]

One Lake Washington student who suffers from dyslexia conducted research on the disease and then used this information to work with younger boys troubled by dyslexia. Another student created a steam engine out of plexiglass. Another used computer-aided design (CAD) software to design a sailboat.

"Technology should be a natural component of everything students do," says Heather Sinclair, district director of secondary curriculum and staff development for Lake Washington. "It should be a natural tool they use on a day-to-day basis. It shouldn't be something that is scary or contrived. It should be authentic and realistic." [12]

But producing a "culminating project" is not done in isolation. The Washington State Legislature has laid down very rigorous educational goals for high school students: mastery of reading, writing and communications; knowing and applying the core concepts of math, the social, physical and life sciences, civics and history, geography, the arts, health and fitness; thinking analytically and creatively and integrating experience and knowledge to form reasoned judgments and to solve problems; and understanding the importance of work.

But the "culminating project" enables all students to prove how they have integrated all these learning concepts into real-world results.

Start with the hands-on experience

Too many other schools, however, start with "the academics" and wrongly concentrate first on theory and abstract principles.

Seymour Papert, distinguished professor at the Massachusetts Institute of Technology, is one who has long tried to reverse this process. He strongly believes that it's much more effective for students to move from hands-on work to abstract thinking by solving real-world problems.

"At the moment, we generally teach numbers, then algebra, then calculus, then physics. That's wrong. Start with engineering, and then from that abstract out physics, and from that abstract out ideas of calculus." [13]

That's exactly what's now being done at San Diego's High Tech High, set up in 1999 in the city's former Naval Training Centre. Since then it's built up an excellent record through courses in telecommunications,

The Mt. Edgecumbe High School model

❏ Teachers and students become co-managers.

❏ Excellence is regarded as the norm.

❏ First week each year is esteem-builder.

❏ Teachers become 90 percent facilitators.

❏ Students determine and control discipline.

❏ Everyone learns speed typing.

❏ Everyone uses computers to publish work to professional standards.

❏ School operates four pilot companies to put theory into practice.

❏ All students learn Chinese or Japanese.

❏ Russian, physics, calculus and advanced quality training have been added to the curriculum, at students' requests.

❏ Classes work without supervision.

❏ Staff training is top priority.

❏ Each teacher has own computer.

❏ Teachers, students learn to develop and use multimedia such as laser discs, hypercard and presentation software.

❏ 50 percent go on to college.

biotech, computer software, biomedical and electronics manufacturing. Again, all students study math, science, Spanish and integrated humanities while completing hi-tech projects inside and outside the school. The school also serves as a national model for educational entrepreneurship.*[14]

Setting up school-based companies

Another world pioneer in hand-on learning is Mt. Edgecumbe High School in Sitka, Alaska.

Its success is all the more remarkable because of Alaska's traditional high school record. In area it's the biggest of the 50 United States—twice the size of Texas. But it has the second lowest population: about half a million people, and only one metropolitan area, Anchorage, with a population as high as 200,000. Its native population is diverse: Caucasian, Eskimo, Eleuts and several Native American Indian tribes, many of them centred around small community towns of only 150 to 200 people, living on extremely low incomes, in a climate where the temperature in winter can reach -17 degrees Fahrenheit or -20 degrees Centigrade. Hardly a recipe for soaring educational success.

And it shows. In Alaska's 2001 high school exit examinations, 78 percent of white students passed in reading, compared with 37 percent of "native Alaskans". In writing: 56 percent of white students; 23 percent of "native Alaskans". In mathematics: 53 percent; "native Alaskans".[15]

In a damning 2002 report on Alaskan under-achievement, academics Ken Jones and Paul Ongtooguk are highly critical of the entire U.S. system that relies on testing and test results to determine educational success. Even worse, as Alaskan Natives are passing tests at half the rate of white students, "the students leave their schools for college and are assigned to remedial classes. Faced with paying college tuition to obtain what amounts to a high school education, many of these youngsters soon drop out."[16]

The notable exception, say Jones and Ontooguk,[17] is Mt. Edgecumbe High School in Sitka. For years it has been the leader in showing how great ideas can stem from other fields—in this case from Japan's quality revolution inspired originally by the American W. Edwards Deming.

TQM (Total Quality Management) and CIP (the Continuous Improvement Process or Kaizen) have been among the main processes used

Take the High Tech High video tour at www.hightechhigh.org

Deming's 14 points

as modified by students for education*

Deming's 14 points for Total Quality Management have been applied to many businesses. But here is how one class at Mt. Edgecumbe High School in Alaska has modified them for education:

1. Create constancy of purpose toward improvement of students and service. Aim to create the best quality students capable of improving all forms of processes and entering meaningful positions in society.

2. Adopt the new philosophy. Educational management must awaken to the challenge, must learn their responsibilities and take on leadership for change.

3. Work to abolish grading and the harmful effects of rating people.

4. Cease dependence on testing to achieve quality. Eliminate the need for inspections on a mass basis (standardised achievement test, minimum graduation exams, etc.) by providing learning experiences which create quality performance.

5. Work with the educational institutions from which students come. Improve the relationships with student sources and help to improve the quality of students coming into your system.

6. Improve constantly and forever the system of student involvement and service, to improve both quality and productivity.

7. Institute education and training on the job for students, teachers, classified staff and administrators.

8. Institute leadership. The aim of supervision should be to help people use machines, gadgets and materials to do a better job.

9. Drive out fear, so that everyone may work effectively for the school system. Create an environment which encourages people to speak freely.

10. Break down barriers between departments. People in teaching, special education, accounting, food service, administration, curriculum development and research, must work as a team. Develop strategies for increasing the cooperation among groups and individual people.

11. Eliminate slogans, exhortations and targets for teachers and students asking for perfect performance and new levels of productivity. Exhortations create adversarial relationships. The bulk of the causes of low quality and low productivity belong to the system and thus lie beyond the control of teachers and students.

12. Eliminate work standards (quotas) on teachers and students (e.g. raise test scores by 10% and lower dropouts by 15%). Substitute leadership.

13. Remove barriers that rob the students, teachers and management of their right to pride and joy of workmanship.

14. Institute a vigorous programme of education and self-improvement for everyone.

15. Put everybody in the school to work to accomplish the transformation. It is everybody's job.

*Published by Mt. Edgecumbe High School.

to transform Japan from a devastated, shattered and beaten society into a world economic leader.

Now Mt. Edgecumbe High School has pioneered similar methods for education.[18] Mt. Edgecumbe is a public boarding school with 210 students and 13 teachers. Eighty-five percent of its students come from small villages. Most are Native Americans, descendents of the Tlingit, Haida and Tsimpshean tribes as well as Eskimo tribes and Aleuts. Forty percent of its students had struggled at other schools. But in recent years the school has achieved one of America's highest levels of graduates moving on to higher education and interesting jobs.

In many ways it was transformed by the vision of two people: former Superintendent Larrae Rocheleau and former teacher David Langford. Mt. Edgecumbe was originally opened in 1947 as a school for Native Americans. But in 1984 it was converted into an "alternative" experimental school, with Rocheleau in charge. One of his first objectives was "to turn these students into entrepreneurs who would go back to their villages and make a difference".

Although Rocheleau is now dead and Langford has left for wider fields, their achievements live on as models for high school reform. Among the highlights of the period when they were in charge:

❏ *Teachers and students became co-managers. They set their own targets and goals, individually and collectively. And they evaluated themselves regularly against agreed standards of excellence.*

❏ The first computer course began by teaching speed typing. All students do their homework on a computer, using word processors, spreadsheets and graphic programs to produce 100 percent perfect results—just as their future businesses will demand excellence in typing, spelling, accounting, financial and sales reports.

❏ Students and staff started by drawing up their own "mission statement". Among many other points, it stressed that: "The school places high expectations upon students, administrators and staff. Programme and curriculum are based upon a conviction that students have a great and often unrealised potential. The school prepares students to make the transition to adulthood, helping them to determine what they want to do and develop the skills and the self-confidence to accomplish their goals. Students are required to pursue rigorous academic programmes that encourage them to work at their highest levels."

❏ *Students decided it was inefficient to have seven short study*

High school students' company exports packaged salmon to Asia, while learning Japanese, Chinese, Russian, and all aspects of marketing and economics.

MT. EDGECUMBE HIGH SCHOOL
Sitka, Alaska

periods a day, so the school switched to four 90-minute classes. This schedule allows time for lab work, hands-on projects, field trips, thorough discussions, varied teaching styles and in-depth study. The reorganised schedule also allows for an extra three hours of staff development and preparation time each week.

❏ Because students are viewed as customers, the school tries to provide what they want. Students repeatedly requested more technology, so the school added dozens of computers, and opens the computer lab, library and science facilities at night for all pupils.

❏ *CIP has prompted teachers to rethink their teaching styles. One science teacher says he has changed from being an 80 percent lecturer to a 95 percent facilitator.*

❏ *Because one of the school's goals is to develop "Pacific rim entrepreneurs", the students set up four pilot "companies":* Sitka Sound Seafoods, Alaska Premier Bait Company, Alaska's Smokehouse and Fish Co. and the Alaska Pulp Corporation—all under the umbrella of Edgecumbe Enterprises. The "parent company" started its first salmon-processing plant in 1985, run by students themselves. The goal was to give students the skills and experience needed to run an import-export business aimed at Asian markets. By the 1988-89 year, the company was already making four annual shipments of smoked salmon to Japan. Each subsidiary company linked hands-on experience with the academic curriculum. So mathematics students calculated the dollar-yen exchange rate. Pacific Rim geography became part of social studies. Art students designed promotional brochures and package labels for products. And business and computer students learned how to develop spreadsheets to analyse costs and project prices.[19]

❏ *All students learn either Chinese or Japanese, and their curriculum is strong in the history, culture and languages of the Pacific rim, English, social studies, mathematics, science, marine science, computers, business, and physical education.*

❏ Frequently whole classes work without supervision—as they will be required to do in the outside world—so the teachers are free to put extra time into study and further course preparation.

❏ Each curriculum is constantly being revised. As a result of student surveys and requests, Russian, physics, calculus and advanced quality training have been added.

And the success ratio? Mt. Edgecumbe's simple goal is stated

The old method of operating high schools is separated from the real world.

PAT NOLAN
Founder of Integrated Studies Programme
at Freyberg High School*

*Author interview at Freyberg High School, Palmerston North,
New Zealand. Dr. Nolan is Professor of Education
at Massey University, Palmerston North, and former Director of the
university's Educational Research and Development Centre.

boldly: to produce quality individuals. Almost 50 percent of all graduates have entered college and are still there or have graduated—much higher than the national average. There have been hardly any dropouts—in a state where dropouts are the norm among native Alaskans.

Integrated studies use the world as a classroom

If Alaska is an unlikely place to start a revolution, the lush, green, heavily-afforested national parks and soaring mountains of New Zealand seem even further removed from the traditional schoolroom. But link them with the latest computer technology, a dedicated team of university innovators and some flexible teachers from Freyberg High School in the small city of Palmerston North, and again the result is surprising.

Every innovation has its visionary driving-force. Freyberg's was Dr. Pat Nolan, now Associated Professor of Education at Massey University on the outskirts of Palmerston North. Massey was originally an "agricultural college" and it is closely linked with several nearby farm research institutes. So its hands-on tradition is a long one.

Pat Nolan marries his love of education with a passion for exploring the New Zealand outdoors: its towering volcanic snowfields, clean sparkling rivers and forests rich with native trees and birds. He's also a computer buff, who has also headed Massey's Educational Research and Development Centre, a pioneer in providing data-based services to other educational institutions.

Nolan has put all his passions together in the Freyberg "integrated studies programme". But it's no mere dream. Nolan sees it as the kind of alternative educational programne that "might go the next step in providing for all high school students the kind of results previously enjoyed by only the top 30 to 40 percent".[20]

He says "the old method" of high school studies is separated from the real world. "We've all been through the school system. What we've experienced is a compartmentalised or segmented curriculum, where subjects are locked up in their little boxes, with tight little boundaries around them. So we learn mathematics, physics and English separately. Seldom do we see the connection between subjects. Yet it's by linking subjects together and seeing the interconnections that we come to understand the real world better. And that is basically what integration is all about: developing ways of teaching—and experiencing—knowledge in a way that establishes the interconnections in the minds of the

The three key elements of integrated studies

 Interesting out-of-class project activities, combining research and exploration.

 Student use of computer as a tool for information processing and analysis.

 History, geography, science, math, economics, writing, computing and other studies are linked together, not taught separately.

Summarised from *Case Study of Curriculum Innovation in New Zealand: The Freyberg Integrated Studies Project,* by C.J. Patrick Nolan, then Associate Director of Educational Research and Development Centre, Massey University, Palmerston North, New Zealand, and David H. McKinnon, Visiting Research Fellow, Education Department, Massey University, published by Massey University.

students, and has them actually using that knowledge to create new solutions."

So Nolan's integrated studies programme has linked Massey University educational research with field-trip study projects, IBM-sponsored computer studies and the New Zealand national high school curriculum. His pilot programme started in 1986 with sixth form (grade 12) students at Freyberg. The first integrated studies course combined biology, computer studies, English and geography. The elements were drawn together around a central theme: preservation and management issues confronting New Zealand National Parks. Out-of-class field research trips were a major part of the project. In Nolan's words: "These national park field trips confronted students not only with physical adventure and challenge, but generated the experiences, data and information needed to sustain a program of integrated studies for a whole year. Computers also played a central role in supporting the theme; allowing the analysis of large and relatively complex data-sets not normally considered or done at this level."

During that pilot programme, students' examination results were checked against a similar group taking the standard high school courses. "We had hoped to demonstrate that integrated study students would do better than those experiencing normal secondary school teaching. And that's precisely what we've been able to accomplish." Because the pilot was with senior students—normally high achievers anyway—Nolan would have been happy to say that the pilot group had done no worse. *"But what we were able to show was that their academic performance was significantly better. In English and geography, students scored 20 to 30 marks higher, and in mathematics and science they on average scored 10 to 15 marks better."* [21]

"Over the next three years," reports Nolan, "we had out-of-class field trips, as short as one to two hours up to two to three days in junior school and seven to eight days in senior school." One class spent a week on the Wanganui River. But before it went, it split into study-groups. One researched the interconnection between the river and agriculture; another gathered information for an environmental impact report; another prepared to test the river's chemical composition and water-flow; another researched the Maori history of the area.

"The whole project was curriculum-driven," says Nolan, "but most activities included adventure and outdoor education components, learning bushcraft, camping and survival skills, as well as learning to work in

Students flock to new business school at secondary school.

University offers scholarships to best achievers.

groups, researching specialist subjects and then integrating them into a total report."[22]

Since 1991 all Freyberg's first- and second-year students have handled social studies and English as integrated studies. On associated field trips, science, math and related subjects have been included. "We have no separate computer studies department," says principal Russell Trethewey, "and computer work and field trips play key parts in all studies. Students revert to the subject curriculum in the third year, to sit national exams, and the results there are also well ahead of the national average."[23]

Freyberg also has shown the fastest growth in roll numbers of any school in New Zealand's North Island: almost double in four years.

High school business courses

In another highly successful New Zealand innovation, Onehunga High School in Auckland has become the country's first to set up its own business school. Students have flocked to enrol—learning real-life business skills: one of the most popular innovations in an innovative country.

Like the Freyberg project, Onehunga's business school is a three-way partnership between the school itself, the University of Auckland Business School and New Zealand entrepreneur Tony Falkenstein, a former student of the high school.

Falkenstein's Just Water company kicked in $200,000 for financial underwriting. And, when it floated publicly, it donated the equivalent of $US700,000 ($NZ1 million) in stock to the high school, and the same amont each to the university and Auckland's Unitec Institute of Technology. Since then the value of the stock has doubled.

The university has donated three scholarships a year to its business school. And it also offers students the chance to visit the university and its business incubator.

Onehunga High School has now added a hands-on building programme to its courses. In partnership with a publicly-listed construction company, Fletcher Building, students are actually building houses as hands-on projects as they learn carpentry and construction skills.

All typical, we believe, of a future in which education-business partnerships are fast becoming a gateway to the future.

The successful companies of the next decade will be the ones that use digital tools to reinvent the way they work.

BILL GATES
Business @ The Speed Of Thought*

* Published by Viking, a division of Penguin Books.

The coming marriage of learning, entertainment and business

An unusual new marriage is taking place.

The most prominent partners are Silicon Valley and Hollywood. But the most attractive potential suitors are education and business.   The challenge: to create some of the world's greatest opportunities—to merge the talents of great educators and great "business models".

Already the reasons are clear and the models exist in five related areas:

1. Electronic, interactive, multimedia software, coupled with the Internet, presents almost unlimited potential for learning and education.

2. New-method learning, teaching and training skills, in particular, provide a growing, virtually untapped, business opportunity.

3. Successful manufacturing and retailing companies can prosper even more by selling services: by providing the training necessary for customers to use their products much more effectively.

4. Every successful company has to become a continuous learning organisation—and, even more important, a leader in the drive to turn "the Knowledge Economy" into "the new Creative Economy".

5. Schools, colleges and universities can work out joint-ventures with businesses—and can learn greatly from many new business models.

Electronic multimedia opportunities

Compact discs, CD-roms, electronic games, digital video discs, and the Internet itself, provide the most striking examples of the shape of the exploding interactive learning revolution: the ability to communicate

Attend the world's greatest film seminars, led by the world's greatest producers, directors, writers.

CHRIS McGOWAN & JIM McCULLAUGH
Entertainent In The Cyber Zone

* Published by Random House, New York.

information instantly to almost anyone, and in highly-involving new ways.

The examples abound, the potential is enormous:

❏ More than ten million people have improved their health and fitness at home by exercising to actress Jane Fonda's *Workout* videos. Millions have followed up the early home experience by joining regular Jazzercise and health clubs.

❏ Now CD-rom and online courses are available to learn almost anything: from simple computer applications to advanced movie-making.

In less than two years, Atomic Learning (www.atomiclearning.com) has become the most popular software application for schools. Set up by some American school-teachers, with a deep interest in interactive technology, it now offers more than 12,500 online videoclip tutorials. These provide instant visual guides on how to use software accurately.

And, unlike complicated written handbooks, each tutorial answers only one specific question: like how to insert video clips, music or computer animations into a *Powerpoint* slide presentation.* Schools can provide continuous access to Atomic Learning for all students for around $2 per student a year.

❏ To learn something much more complicated, like advanced movie or video production, try a DVD—digital video disc—with one of the greatest movies and a built-in visual essay on how the film was made.

As a typical example, you can view the Kirk Douglas masterpiece *Spartacus,* with commentary by Douglas, novelist Howard Fast, producer Edward Lewis, production designer Saul Bass and film restorer Bob Harris, a video interview with actor Peter Ustinov, screenwriter Dalton Trumbo's scene-by-scene analysis, Saul Bass's storyboards and titles, deleted scenes analysis, additional music by Alex North, newsreel footage of the film's premiere, archival interviews and additional memorabilia. So you can learn along with the masters.

❏ Or how about music? Great interactive CD-roms are becoming teachers to a whole new generation of aspiring singers, songwriters, conductors, composers and musicians.

* The answer: from the file menu, select "Insert", scroll down to "Movies and sound", and take it from there. Incidentally, in hundreds of seminars around the world, the co-authors of this book have found no more than 5 percent of teachers know how to take this most simple step to produce interactive presentations.

Now you can even learn to be an inventor online

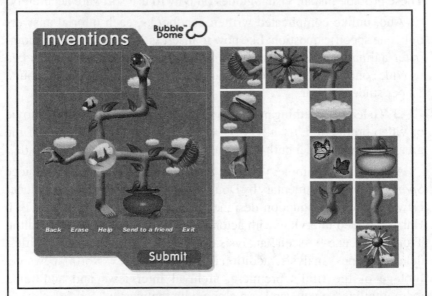

www.bubbledome.com

Even very young children learn creativity by making their own Invention Puzzle on Bubbledome's FunZone. Try it for yourself on that website. You simply click on any of the squares on the right-hand page, and drag that square to the left-hand side. In this way you construct your own completely individual design: a new combination of existing elements.

On Dorling Kindersley's *Musical Instruments* CD-rom, you can hear the tones and timbre of about 200 instruments, from the Australian *didgeridoos* to the Japanese *shakuhachi* flutes. You'll find around 1,500 sound samples, more than 500 high-quality photos and extensive text. And you can explore the instruments in four different ways.

Benjamin Britten's *The Young Person's Guide To The Orchestra* has long been a classic on both audiotape and videotape. The CD-rom version offers "musical notation of every melody, lets you know which instruments are playing at all times, and includes 50 audio examples. And you get to play conductor, too."[1]

❏ Geography? In 1985, two young Iowa trivia-game fans, Doug and Gary Carlston, turned one of their games into a computer floppy-disc hit called *Where In The World Is Carmen Sandiego?* It was a pioneer in the field to be known as "edutainment": the fusion of education and entertainment. Since 1985, the Carlstons and their Broderbund Software company have released eight titles in the series, and nearly four million Carmen Sandiego floppy disc programmes have been sold.

The deluxe CD-rom edition appeared in 1992, and today hundreds of thousands of children and their families are learning the basics of geography as they search for Carmen around the world, using 3,200 clues—including 500 in foreign languages—130 photographs, hundreds of animations, and 150 audio excerpts of traditional music.

❏ Young painters can practise with Broderbund's *Kid Pix;* young musicians can have fun with Philips's *Children's Musical Theatre;* and learn to read with The Learning Company's *Reader Rabbit.*

❏ Now infants even as young as six months can start using the family computer by touching any of the keyboard keys while using *BabyWow!* software (www.babywow.com). Former Amazon executive Tony Fernandes created *BabyWow!* and now produces it in seven languages: English, French, Spanish, Japanese, Germany, Portuguese and Chinese. The software features great photographs of bold concepts, 2,000 key words and teaches concepts such as near/far, front/back, and in/out.

❏ New Zealand teacher, software-and graphics designer Rebecca Merle has a great online series to kick-start children's creativity. It's called *Bubbledome.* Children visiting it at www.bubbledome.com can find fascinating story-starters and, in the *Fun Zone,* invent their own animated creation from Bubbledome's *Invention Puzzle.*

Older children and adults can plan an entire city of the future with

Software templates enable students to become multimedia presenters

We won $1,000 for having the most innovative raft design!

Students and teachers can now become semiprofessional movie makers with software such as Apple Computer's iMovie range.

In the model above, students from the Overseas Family School won a $1,000 prize for the most innovative entry (a Chinese dragon boat) in Singapore's annual river race—and were able to produce a video of the race highlights.

This is typical of "template" software that now allows many beginners to become skilled multimedia presenters.

Video clips from a digital camera are fed into the computer to appear in the right-hand panels, where they can be highlighted and edited on the main screen. Other controls allow you to add music and professional "fades" and "dissolves".

Microsoft's PowerPoint and Apple Keynote software comes with similar templates for multimedia slide presentations.

SimCity, learn every aspect of chess from *Chessmaster 4000,* or play a world master at bridge.

❑ And the Milnes, of Auckland, New Zealand, provide a great family example of the future, with their *SmartKids* range of products for early-childhood development: Mother Sue, the kindergarten teacher; father David, the manager; Ph.D son Duncan as the educational psychologist—and author of the book *Teaching the Brain to Read*—and other son Fraser as the producer of interactive educational CD-Roms.

Some of the biggest commercial successes have been in the form of video and computer games. Sony now makes 42 percent of its total profits from its *PlayStation* video games.

To make your own interactive, animated computer game, you can invest in *HyperStudio* beginner software. Primary schools that start their students on this as young as six or seven years find them able to master Macromedia's top-rated *Director* series by the time they leave school.

Elementary and high school students—and their teachers—can also become semi-professional movie makers by using the latest digital video cameras and simple computerised video-editing software such as Apple's *iMovie* (opposite).

Since the early 1990s the merger between Hollywood and Silicon Valley has blossomed, with Apple co-founder Steve Jobs in the innovative lead with computerised, animated movies and iPod's great instant music service.

Key aspects of the new revolution will come from the further blending of talents from the movie, computer, music and electronic games industries, linking those abilities to good educational practice. But most traditional school systems have been left far behind in the race.

Says Bill Gates: "The average primary or secondary school in the United States lags considerably behind the average American business in the availability of new information technology. Preschoolers familiar with cellular telephones, pagers and personal computers enter kindergarten where chalkboards and overhead projectors represent the state of the art."[2] Equally important, the structure of most school systems is not designed to multiply teacher talent. Great teachers are skilled in many ways: subject knowledge, empathy, communications, interactivity, music, art and perhaps some aspects of multimedia presentations. In school those talents will be confined to twenty to forty students at a time, when today they could be instantly available to the world.

Training results with accelerated learning methods

Bell Atlantic C & P Telephone Co.:[1]

4-week and 6-week customer rep.
training course and 12-day technical course.
42, 57 and 50 percent training time reduction.
Dropout rate reduced 300 percent.
$700,000-a-year saving in training costs.

Northeast Medical College:[1]

Forty percent of first-year medical students
failed their final exam in anatomy. The course
was redesigned with integrative learning
principles—and 100 percent passed.

Intel Corporation:[2]

Participants on one course achieved a
knowledge-gain of 507 percent compared with
23 percent by traditional methods.

1. Information supplied by Laurence D. Martel, President,
   National Academy of Integrative Learning,
   Hilton Head, South Carolina.

2. Information from The Centre for Accelerated Learning,
   Lake Geneva, Wisconsin. Centre Founder Dave Meier's
   Accelerated Learning Handbook (McGraw-Hill) gives other
   examples and is highly recommended.

Seldom do teachers get the opportunity to link their most outstanding talents with the diverse skills of others. To make professional TV programmes, for instance, requires a wide blend of talent: producer, director, scriptwriter, camera-sound crew, video editor, music composer, musicians, sound mixer, graphic designer and many more. What chance has "education" got to compete unless it can reorganise to blend the same kind of multifaceted talents, store the results digitally, and then "repackage" them in any interactive form required as the new multimedia platforms converge?

Now children as young as six years in leading-edge schools are learning to blend their different talents into teams to produce quite amazing primary-school versions of such professional products.

Accelerated learning business opportunities

Virtually every learning and teaching breakthrough highlighted in this book, for instance, represents an opportunity to take new methods of learning and turn them into commercial opportunities.

Every achiever in every field has the expertise that can now be multiplied a million-fold through interactive multimedia and networked communications.

One to seize the opportunities is British innovator Colin Rose. His Accelerated Learning Systems group has specialised for more than fifteen years in do it-yourself, multimedia foreign-language programmes. And now it's offering a range of similar innovations instantly online.

Other management training companies are seizing on the new combination of accelerated learning methods and multimedia communications to transform business education. These include the pioneering Centre for Accelerated Learning in America, and they're already chalking up impressive records.

Selling services and training with your products

More and more major companies are also finding that their path to the future lies in adding new services—often high quality education and training—to their traditional role as manufacturers or retailers.

Probably the most dramatic example is the world's most admired company for the past decade: America's GE, the corporation founded by inventor Thomas Edison. Its revenues have increased from $25 billion in 1980 to $162 billion in 2004. Its market worth: $360 billion.

GE has spent $80 million building a state-of-the-art training centre complete with a TV studio to develop educational programming.

'JACK WELCH'S ENCORE'
*article in Business Week**

* October 28, 1996.

For years a leader in manufacturing, GE "can no longer prosper selling manufacturing goods alone".[3]   Says its recently-retired Chief Executive Jack Welch: "Our job is to sell more than just the box."

Nearly 80 percent of GE's profits now come from services—up from 16.4 percent in 1980.   And a large slice of those profits come from GE Finance—by financing a wide range of services and products, and not only products produced by GE.

Visit the Milwaukee headquarters of GE Medical Systems and you get some idea of the scope of the changes. For years it sold CAT scanners, magnetic resonance imagers and other medical imaging equipment, to organisations like Columbia/HCA Healthcare Corp. with its 300-plus hospitals. Then in March, 1995, GE persuaded Columbia to let it service all the chain's imaging equipment, including that made by GE's rivals. By 1996 GE had added managing virtually all medical supplies to the deal—most of them product lines GE isn't even in.

Yet that is just the beginning. GE Medical has spent $80 million building a state-of-the-art training centre, complete with a TV studio, to develop educational programming.[4] For fees ranging from $3,000 to $20,000, hospitals can tune in to live broadcasts on subjects such as proper mammography techniques. And the company regularly runs management seminars for hospital executives. Topics include strategic planning, employee evaluations and time management.

But Jack Welch's successor, Jeffrey Immelt, believes concentrating only on service and learning will not be sufficient for advanced countries such as the United States and those in the European Community to compete with the low-cost manufacturing might of China and the low-cost IT skills of India..

So he's leading the American drive to turn "the Knowledge Economy" into "the Creative Economy". He's investing $5 billion in eighty initiatives under what he calls "Imagination Breakthrough".[5]

The company as a creative learning organisation

Tom Peters talks about an "organisation-as-university."[6] And more and more companies are fitting that model. In China and South Korea, in particular, company and private universities are opening regularly.

Fortune puts the challenge to business squarely: "Forget all your old tired ideas about leadership. The most successful corporation of the future will be something called a learning organisation."[7]

19th century management

Leadership based on the military pyramid

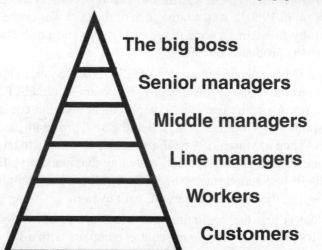

The big boss

Senior managers

Middle managers

Line managers

Workers

Customers

21st century management

All concentrated on customer service

Moments of truth

Management support

To help all staff magnify their performance

But it will be much more than that. And Bill O'Brien, former Chief Executive of America's Hanover Insurance, puts one of the real challenges: "Our grandfathers worked six days a week to earn what most of us now earn by Tuesday afternoon. The ferment in management will continue until we build organisations that are more consistent with man's higher aspirations beyond food, shelter and belonging." [8]

❏ Quad/Graphics, the Wisconsin printing company with a $500 million-a-year turnover, has been specifically set up as a learning organisation. All employees sign up as students. They work a four-day, 40-hour, flex-time week. On the fifth day they're encouraged to turn up in the company's classroom—without pay; and about half do. Everyone in the company is encouraged to be both a student and a teacher. You don't get promoted until you have trained your successor. [9]

❏ At Johnsonville Foods, also in Wisconsin, nearly every worker is taking a company-paid economics course at the local community college. Most work in small group projects. Each is encouraged to be a self-acting manager. Says one manager: "We're teachers. We help people grow. That's my main goal. Each person is his or her own manager." [10]

Business lessons for education

And probably the biggest "digital lesson" from business is the way the new technologies allow millions around the world to become "working partners" with the corporate giants:

❏ **Oracle,** with its automated teller machines, has revolutionised banking —as a leader in "relational database" systems. Now customers control their own banking.

❏ **Dell,** with its complete online ordering system, has transformed computer selling. Now the customers design their own computers, from interchangeable components.

❏ **Cisco** no longer has to answer most customer queries. Its online system puts thousands of networking customers directly in touch with other customers in the same industry who've solved the same problem.

❏ **Accenture** now employs 100,000 people in its worldwide consulting business. It spends more than $400 million a year on staff development. And it runs an enormous database of the world's best "business models"—available instantly to all its staff.

Apple, with its latest *iPod,* allows customers to download up to 15,000 music tracks, store them and play them on demand.

How to cross the chasm*

Adoption cycle for new ideas in business

The early majority

The late majority

The early adoptors

The laggards

The innovators

The chasm

| 2% | 13% | 35% | 35% | 15% |

Schools' big adoption challenge

15% brilliantly use new teaching ideas but not with ICT**

The chasm

Simplified system and professional development retraining programme needed to show all how to link the world's best teaching methods with the world's best ICT

| 2% | 13% | 85% |

15% brilliant with ICT but not with new teaching methods**

**** Information and communications technology**

* Adopted from the *Crossing The Chasm* concepts of Geoffrey A. Moore.

Just how does Silicon Valley do it? And what are its lessons for education?

Four prominent writers have pin-pointed the combined answers:

Tom Peters, in his newest book, *Imagine!*, agrees with *Future Shock* author Alvin Toffler: "Our education systsem is a second-rate, factory-style organisation pumping out obsolete information in obsolete ways." He also agrees with one of the main themes of this book: that "talent is everything, and the production of talent is significantly dependent upon schools.".

Thomas Friedman, in his newest book, *The World is Flat,* uses that metaphor to explain how all the major trends today are "flattening the world"—and changing the old top-down model of "command and control" to one of international partnerships and cooperation.

And Geoffrey A. Moore has been writing for years on the new Silicon Valley model to turn creative hi-tech inventions into widely-accepted products. He calls it "crossing the chasm".[11]

Moore argues that in most industries:

❏ 2 percent of people are innovators—the visionaries who create the new breakthroughs—from Bill Hewlett and Dave Packard, from The Body Shop's Anita Roddick to Google's Sergey Brin and Larry Page.

❏ 13 percent are "early adopters"—the first to try those products.

❏ 35 percent are "early conservatives" or "early majority" who will use the new products once they are perfected.

❏ 35 percent the "late majority" who will come on board when forced by their customers; and

❏ 15% are "laggards" or "sceptics" who'll resist almost any idea.

And the major task of all business today, says Moore, is to "cross the chasm" from the first 15 percent to the big majority.

The easiest way to do that is to design "templates" that make the ideas easy to use by almost anyone. And the same, from our experience, applies to spreading new educational ideas.

❏ The best-known digital-template in the world is probably Microsoft's *Powerpoint* software. Instead of hiring a computer-design specialist, *Powerpoint* users can themselves produce high-quality colour-sides, and chose from a toolbox of background designs, typefaces and sixteen separate layouts for every slide. Unfortunately, most teachers and students don't get past the simple "colour slide" part of the programme.

Now it's easy to learn 3D computer graphics

and personalise each students' lessons

Students can easily learn three-dimensional computer graphics, and how to turn themselves into fantasy or historical characters. Illustrations from Southland Innovator seminars in New Zealand, organised by The Learning Web and taught by the crew at www.bubbledome.com, with support from the staff of Tahatai Coast Primary School.

Regular updates: www.thelearningweb.net

So instead of using it as a base for inserting their own creative videos, computer animations and music-compositions, the result is "death by *Powerpoint*"—well-known to anyone attending conferences.

❏ Apple *iMovie* and Microsoft *MovieMaker,* as we've seen, provide simple templates for anyone to edit video like a professional.

❏ Adobe's *inDesign* publishing software—upgraded from the original *Pagemaker* software—provides a wide variety of templates for magazines, newspapers, books, advertisements and desktop publishing.

❏ And now Atomic Learning provides those 15,000 videoclips on demand so any student at a subscribing school, anywhere in the world, can get instant online instructions on how to use these and other software applications.

From our experiences around the world, education works on a similar bell curve to industry: again with around 2 percent of teachers very strong innovators and another 13 percent eager to be first to adopt those new ideas in practice.

But education generally lacks a system to make those great break-throughs instantly available to teachers everywhere.

Even worse: quite often the 15 percent "innovators and early adopters" of new teaching and learning methods know little about information and communications technology.

And the 15 percent ICT "innovators and early adopters" generally know little about new teaching and learning methods.

But put those two groups of innovators together, and you've found the a great new way to transform education, schooling and learning.

Not by putting all students and teachers into "death by *Powerpoint*" straight-jackets, but creating templates which allow individual talent to flower.

Bring that talent, creativity and technology together, and you just might change the world.

You'll certainly change schooling—as innovators and early adaptors have already proven.

Only a fool worships his tools but they can be the catalyst to start the revolution.

How to use interactive technology as the catalyst to reinvent schooling

If Geoffrey Moore's *crossing the chasm* model is fairly accurate—and we think it is—then only about 15 percent of adults readily welcome change.

Another 70 percent come on board only when the new hi-tech break-throughs become so easy to use that their benefits are self-evident. And in another twenty years the final 15 percent may consider them.

It happened with the telephone. If we still used old manual phone exchanges, under the old gender barriers, half the world's female population would now be manning telephone exchanges and switchboards. But simple touch-dialling has put the world instantly at out fingertips.

It even happened with the printed book: Produced in Europe by Gutenberg in 1451-53; but it took Comenius's reinvention of the text-book, with pictures, 200 years later, before the idea was transferred into mass education.

It certainly happened with the Internet: It started more than thirty years ago. But not till Tim Berners-Lee created the World Wide Web in 1991, and Mark Andreessen and his team produced the Netscape *Navigator* browser, did it really take off.

It has not yet happened in education. As Reed Hundt, Chairman of the U.S. Federal Communications Commission, put it in the early 1990s: "There are thousands of buildings in this country with millions of people in them who have no telephones, no cable television and no reasonable prospect of broadband services. They're called schools."

But now the tipping point is about to come in education, too: as the

New Zealand's change-model

❏ **Abolish Education Department.**

❏ **Abolish Education Boards.**

❏ **Make all schools charter schools.**

❏ **Schools run by parent-boards.**

❏ **ICT as change-catalyst.**

❏ **Innovation flowers in some.**

❏ **But chasm needs to be crossed.**

❏ **So link schools in clusters.**

❏ **Innovative schools as leaders.**

❏ **Bus tours to model schools.**

❏ **Regular teacher retraining.**

❏ **Online back-up by State.**

❏ **Share best practice online.**

science of learning finally links with the art of great teaching and the innovative strength of the digital age.

Again, as we've seen throughout this book, the *innovators* and early *adopters* have already shown the way. And fortunately the models are already in place for the planet's 59 million school teachers and 1.5 billion students to cross the chasm into a different, more exciting world.

Again, the best examples come from separate parts of the world. And again in small pockets: either small countries, small states, small provinces or counties:

From New Zealand: both a new system to release the brilliant creativity of trend-setting principals and teachers, specially in primary or elementary schools—and a chasm-crossing model to spread that change to all schools.

From the American state of Maine: laptops for all seventh and eighth-graders in the state.

From the north England county of Northumbria: the model to transform secondary schooling, inside a standard national curriculum.

From Singapore: how to add interactive school networks to a global curriculum.

From the combined world of computer science and business: the simple digital templates to make the transfer much easier

And from the open-source movement: the new system to share the benefits of networking the digital learning revolution to the rest of the developing world.

1. From New Zealand—the innovation begins

Imagine a country the same size as the United Kingdom or the American state of Colorado, and around the same population as Singapore: four million people, 500,000 primary and secondary students at 2,700 schools, and a Government that has:

❏ Abolished its entire national Department of Education, and replaced it with a scaled-down policy-advising Ministry.

❏ Abolished all its district School Boards.

❏ Turned all its schools—public and private—into charter schools, run by community-elected boards.

❏ Then challenged those boards to reinvent "tomorrow's schools".

What if we set aside all discussion of things as <u>they were</u>, as <u>they are</u> and as <u>they might become</u>, and concentrated on <u>what they ought to be?</u>

DEE HOCK*

* In *Birth Of The Chaordic Age,*
published by Berrett-Koehler Publishers, San Francisco.
"Chaordic" comes from the "seamless" combining of chaos and order,
what Hock sees as the self-governing organising system of nature.

❏ Not just to reinvent them: but to say how they'll achieve excellence in any field they chose, over and above minimum national standards.

And to do all this in 1989-90, at a time when, unknown to the New Zealand Government:

❏ The free World Wide Web, free Internet browsers and free Web search engines were about to be invented.

❏ Microsoft was just about to give away a completely free digital encyclopedia, *Encarta,* to help sell its Windows system And . . .

❏ Before long a couple of American college students would invent a completely new-type search engine that can scan 8 billion pages in half a second to provide alternative answers to almost any question.

Now it would be great to report that 2,700 New Zealand community boards, elected by parents and teachers, immediately reinvented schooling. They didn't. But the 2 percent of innovators did.

And a chance appointment hastened the process. Because any new schools about to be built had no students and thus no parents to elect the boards, the Minister of Education had to appoint interim ones.

The first new school of all was near the country's biggest exporting port: the departure point for New Zealand's giant export industry of timber, logs, pulp and paper.*

So the new Minister appointed a senior executive from the port company to be the interim board chair.

We suspect the new chair must have studied the writings of Visa inventor Dee Hock, with his theories of organisation and education. Or maybe he'd also read "the ancient bit of philosophy" that Hock has since quoted in his book, *Birth of The Chaordic Age:* "Understanding requires mastery of four ways of looking at things: as they *were,* as they *are,* as they *might become,* and as *they ought to be."* For that is what the new chair recommended at the first meeting of the Interim Board: to set up a new primary school where the students would become fully confident

---

* *In the 1930s, when a quarter of the country's workers could not find work, two other New Zealand innovators decided to employ thousands to turn the pumice-lands of the volcanic North Island into the world's biggest man-made forest. And the pinetrees they planted grew to maturity in half the time anywhere else on the planet. Many ended up as into pulp and paper and have been exported ever since through the Bay of Plenty port of Tauranga.*

How to produce global citizens

Competent and confident to analyse any problem on a four-step basis:

❑ **The present:**
Where are we now?

❑ **The past:**
How and why did we get here?

❑ **The alternatives:**
Who else has a better way?

❑ **The future:**
How do we invent a better one?

TAHATAI COAST SCHOOL MODEL*

* Tahatai Coast Primary School, Papamoa, New Zealand.
www.tahatai.school.nz

and competent globally-minded citizens, able to tackle any challenges in life on the basis of:

❑ **THE PRESENT:** *Where are we now?*

❑ **THE PAST:** *How and why do we do it this way?*

❑ **THE OBVIOUS ALTERNATIVES:** *Who else is doing better, anywhere in the world? (in business terms: bench-marking)*

❑ **AND THE FUTURE:** *How can we create even better answers— not just to invent "tomorrow's school", but invent tomorrow's world?*

The new Interim Board of Tahatai Coast Primary School agreed. And that is what they set out to do, in the Papamoa suburb of Tauranga in the well-named Bay of Plenty.

That simple aim became the "job specifications" for the school's first principal, Mark Beach, in the mid-1990s.

❑ It was to become not only a model school, but a model for marrying new interactive technology with new methods of learning and teaching.

❑ It was also to become one of the models for the new national challenge to build tomorrow's schools.

❑ And a model for providing rich learning experiences for what emerged as a low-income population with a 35 percent "minority" school roll: from New Zealand's indigenous Maori culture—generally failed by traditional learning methods.*

But New Zealand, as we've seen, has a tradition of innovation in schooling, specially primary schooling. From the late 1930s it was one of the first countries to follow John Dewey's theories of education: to learn by doing, with all the senses, learn by practical discovery, and to involve all children as creators of their own knowledge and future.

New principal Beach was a fan of Dewey, of Gardner's concept of Multiple Intelligences, of Edward de Bono's *lateral thinking* methods, and many of the other innovations already covered in this book.

But Beach also sensed the rising tide of interactive technology and the new era of instant information. So he recommended the new school board should spend all of its $NZ400,000 "establishment grant" on big-ticket items. These included a satellite receiving dish, a full set of orchestral equipment and the first of the school's new Apple Macintosh computers.

* For funding purposes, the New Zealand Ministry of Education ranks communities on a decile scale, from 1 to 10—with 1 the lowest incomes and 10 the highest. When it opened, Tahatai was a decile 2 school.

Welcome to the primary school of tomorrow: already here

- ❏ **All five-year-olds do computer animation.**
- ❏ **Six-year-olds compose stories on laptops.**
- ❏ **Seven-year-olds design their own websites.**
- ❏ **Eight-year-olds win online short story competition with Internet links to museums.**
- ❏ **Nine-year-olds design 3-D animation to invent their ideal school of the future.**
- ❏ **Ten-year-olds write, shoot, edit and record music for award-winning video.**
- ❏ **Eleven-year-olds produce own musicals.**
- ❏ **Twelve-year-olds make video on how to make a professional TV show.**
- ❏ **No graffiti or truancy.**
- ❏ **Students line up at 7 a.m. to start school.***
- ❏ **They press their own school reports on CD-Roms or duplicate them on DVDs.**

Tahatai Coast Primary School

Public primary school at Papamoa, Bay of Plenty, New Zealand.
See samples of students' work at: www.tahatai.school.nz
* Regular school classes do not start until 9 a.m.

He also agreed with Hock: that "only a fool worships his tools". And not one teacher was employed at the new school on the basis of any hi-tech knowledge. Instead, all were judged on their enthusiasm to introduce change, and to make a real difference to the lives of their students.

The result, as they say, is history. And by the start of 2005, the school had been visited by more than 7,500 teachers, including 2,500 from all parts of the world.

All visitors are struck by the differences between what they see and most other typical school practice:

❑ Students themselves show visitors around.

❑ There's a complete sense of democracy in action: open dialogue between students, teachers and principal.

❑ The school actually has fewer classsroom computers than many schools elsewhere in the world. But at Tahatai they are used much more effectively. The school even bars *Powerpoint* in favour of creativity.

❑ A sense of happy creativity pervades the place, from the entrance displays right around the corridors and classroom walls.

The New Zealand school-year is divided into four "terms", not two semesters. And in each of those terms, all Tahatai students study an overall "global theme". It could be "learning how to learn", "learning how to think", "communications" or "conservation". But in all cases, the students use it to investigate that topic on the four-basic questions we've already outlined.

But walk into any class and you'll finally get the "big Aha!" at what this all means. Instead of "reading for an hour", "math for an hour" and other subject-divided study, students will be using all their varied talents and skills to research and report their findings on the same project. But not just in the classroom. Their world has become the classroom.

They could be studying a New Zealand novel or short story on that same theme. And, inside that, they might be using all their different "learning styles" or "intelligences" to both research and report their group findings.

So instead of multiple-choice questions about the story, the students would almost certainly be recreating it in a "Stephen Spielberg" or "Peter Jackson" way: producing a multimedia, almost movie-like version of their version of the story.

❑ And in producing their multimedia findings: The *mainly visual*

Continual professional development for teachers is at the heart of our school's success.

VIKI LAWRENCE
Ex-Principal, Tahatai Coast School*

* *"How to create a twentyfirst-century school"* presentation
to "Southland Innovator" seminar series,
Invercargill, New Zealand, 2003.
See www.thelearningweb.net/southland

learners might be making television storyboards of the finished product, or designing the titles and graphics. *The mainly kinesthetic, tactile* learners might be making *Claymation* models of the characters. The video experts might be shooting background scenes. And the animation experts might be producing professional computer animations.

And innovation abounds with the staff. The school's year even starts a week later than others, and makes it up with an extra fifteen minutes a day. But in that advance week, the entire staff, at an live-in "retreat", plan the year's "learning how to learn, learning how to think" programme .

Of course Tahatai was not the only change-making school under the new Government policy. But as the first one built from scratch, it was soon seen as a model for the rest. It doesn't even look like a school: more like the kind of buildings you'd find as a Californian gated golf resort. And all this for low-income families.

But Tahatai wasn't the only coincidence. By 1995, when the school was being set up, Apple Computer in America had just completed the first decade of its ACOT programme (Apple Classrooms of Tomorrow). And the American company's New Zealand distributor had set up an Apple Education subsidiary to pioneer similar trends.

Tahatai was to be its model. And, working in partnership, the two brought to New Zealand, to work with the new school, Canadian Lane Clark. She had been one of the pioneer teachers at the River Oaks ACOT school near Toronto, Ontario. She spent twelve weeks fulltime at Tahatai, and trained the new staff in how to link the new tools of interactive technology with the Dewey principles of *inquiry, discovery* and *students creating their own future.*

It was the start of a three-way partnership that exists to this day. Some of its follow-on highlights:

❏ An annual series of two-day weekend teacher retraining conferences, where teachers from other schools would learn to marry great new teaching and learning ideas with the ICT tools.

❏ Apple bus tours, where teachers from around the country would spend a week visiting other trend-setting schools: again all linking the best learning and teaching methods with the new technology.

❏ The sharing of teacher training methods: what schools like to call "professional development"—but, under the Tahatai model, an almost daily programme of this. Not a static series of lectures, but collaborative sharing of information. Once a week, for example, the teachers hold a

How New Zealand schools crossed the ICT chasm: 23 began to train others. Now half the rest have joined the fun.

"techie breckie": a breakfast where each one passes on any new technical tips they've picked up.

❏ A coordinated staff reading programme, in which all teachers share copies of articles recommended by other teachers—and then discuss how to put the best research into practice.

By the end of 1997, when a third edition of *The Learning Revolution* appeared, the Tahatai success story started to spread nationally and internationally. The school took pride of place in that new edition, and the trickle of foreign visitors started to become a flood.

By then, too, it was obvious that not all New Zealand's schools were *crossing the chasm* at the same pace—even if they'd ever heard of the term. Of the country's 2,700 schools, many in farming districts were small, often one-teacher or two-teacher schools. And of the total, only between fifty and sixty appeared to be using the new technology well. Amazingly: that validates Geoffrey Moore's 2 percent.

So to spread the message of how information and communications technology could be the catalyst for change, the Government appointed an ICT coordinator. And that task went to another creative country school principal, Carol Moffatt, then head of the Oxford Area School in the South Island province of Canterbury. Then ICT Manager Murray Brown, who had coordinated the Freyberg High School integrated studies project, with its school, university and IBM partnership.

In a small, closely-knit community like New Zealand, innovator Moffatt knew the other pacesetters and invited them to a two-day conference to brainstorm how best to make excellence the norm.

Not surprisingly, they recommended the concept of "ICT clusters", with one "leading school" acting as the coordinator to share the new methods with up to eight other schools. All 2,700 schools were invited to apply for cluster leadership, and twentythree were chosen for the first two-year contracts. Their only payment: the salary of an extra teacher, with Tahatai being paid the equivalent of two teachers, to act in a broader advisory role.

That system has worked wonderfully well. By early 2005 1,100 of the country's 2,700 schools had been involved in the ICT clusters.

And the innovation had spread even further:

❏ Apple has expanded its bus tours to cover both New Zealand's two main islands.

'Where the art of teaching meets the science of learning.'*

CRAMLINGTON COMMUNITY HIGH SCHOOL

* Its website slogan at:
www.cchsonline.co.uk

❏ Two public primary schools, Sherwood and Gulf Harbour, have set up "digital classrooms"—with parents wishing to take advantage of this paying $NZ500 per student a year in extra fees (about $US350).

❏ Discovery 1, in Christchurch, has become the country's first public primary school to use "the city as a classroom", where students study out in "the real world" but return to their central-city base to collate their findings on computers and in other "show you know" projects.

❏ And New Zealand's southern-most region has extended the concept to its region with the Southland Innovator Project.* This included two five-day seminars to retrain many of the district's principals and teachers. And a follow-up project to help all Southland schools coordinate enterprise and ICT programmes with local businesses.

Other similar "ICT cluster models" have been tried elsewhere, noticeably the *Navigator* schools in the Victorian state of Victoria and the United Kingdom's *Beacon* schools. But most visitors award top marks to the New Zealand effort. So do we. Our only reservation: why has the programme not yet been introduced in all schools?

The Government has also chipped in with grants to provide every New Zealand school principal with a laptop, and to subsidise laptops for teachers.

The Government's Education Ministry also runs two main websites to provide online information and share it: www.minedu.govt.nz and www.tki.org.nz (the initials for the Maori words for "three baskets of knowledge: *Te Kete Ipurangi).*

2. The United Kingdom high school model

If New Zealand is a model for decentralised schooling, the United Kingdom is providing an equal one for introducing interactive technology to a national curriculum, specially at secondary level.

And just as New Zealand's innovation started off with a business-school partnership, England's was to benefit from the same pattern.

But its business partner is a home-grown one, the Lancashire based

* *The programme for the Southland Innovator seminars, coordinated by The Learning Web Ltd., can be downloaded from that publisher's website (www.thelearningweb.net). It shows how to alternate hands-on training sessions for interactive technology with equally-interactive sessions to "walk the talk" can demonstrate new learning and teaching methods.*

Cramlington's digital network and its role:

❏ **To research**

❏ **Experiment**

❏ **Explore**

❏ **Create**

❏ **Communicate**

❏ **Transform**

OFSTED REPORT*
on Cramlington Community High School
Northumbria, United Kingdom

* Ofsted is the United Kingdom Government organisation
charged with checking school standards in education.

firm Promethean, designers and manufacturers of ActivBoard digital, interactive whiteboards. Promethean now has many school partners. But one of the frontrunners has been Cramlington Community High School, on the outskirts of the Northrumbrian city of Newcastle-Upon-Tyne. Like Tahatai and the other great New Zealand schools, it's almost impossible to do justice to it solely in writing. Even its informative website (www.cchsonline.co.uk) can convey only a little of the story:

❑ The first to provide an accelerated-learning cycle in each class schedule—even fifty-minute ones—and link it with both interactive technology and the Internet.

❑ Among the first to make full use of Promethean's ActivBoards and that company's online "collaborative classroom" project, which shares lesson-plans and "learning and teaching tools" through the Internet.

❑ Its own digitised accelerated-lesson plans stored on the Internet—and, in the words of *The Guardian* newspaper: "accessible at lightning speed from all 700 networked computer stations around the school".[1]

❑ Interactive whiteboards in every classsroom, and used by fully-trained teachers to provide almost George Lucas-type dramatic movie effects to stimulate class discussion.

❑ Two-hour weekly planning and training sessions for all staff on ICT and on individualising learning.

❑ Three fulltime graduate web-designers plus a video technician.

❑ Personalised learning for all students, including free time to study at home and out in the community.

❑ A special grant from the U.K. Ministry for Education and Skills to set up a separate interactive-whiteboard training centre, to share the message with other schools.

❑ An exchange programme with schools around the world.

❑ Rave reviews from England's Ofsted school-review authority, as the model for training teachers to integrate interactive technology into the national curriculum.

❑ One of only 100 U.K. schools accorded "leading edge" status.

❑ And, like Tahatai and other excellent schools: continuing professional development for all teachers as the key to the school's performance—apart from its excellent leadership.

Innovative head Derek Wise and Deputy Head Mark Lovatt have even written two books on how to create a technology-linked accelerated

How's this for a high school exam report?

- ❏ **Highly effective school.**

- ❏ **Exciting place to learn.**

- ❏ **Very high standards.**

- ❏ **Leadership outstanding.**

- ❏ **Students challenged.**

- ❏ **Bold emphasis on learning**

- ❏ **Creative, enterprising.**

CRAMLINGTON COMMUNITY HIGH SCHOOL*
Northumbria, United Kingdom

* Report by Ofsted, the United Kingdom Government organisation
charged with inspecting the nation's schools.

learning school.[2] And the school's teachers and students have produced a detailed guide filled with bright ideas as part of upgrading their learning programme to the next level. Wise sees that as "a completely personalised curriculum", where every student is helped to identify his or her talents and then develop the skills and abilities to improve them.

Cramlington, too, benefits from the U.K. Ministry's excellent online backup for interactive technology, and the British Broadcasting Corporation's world leadership in online services.

Only one problem: Wise and Lovatt wish all England's primary schools could produce student-graduates at the same level as the best they have visited in New Zealand.

He also sees the Tahatai and Cramlington examples as a great marriage of talent-development, personalised learning and the Promethean "collaborative classroom" concept of sharing "the best with the best" online.

3. Singapore's networked global curriculum

Like New Zealand, Singapore also has only four million people. But all crammed into an area the size of New Zealand's biggest lake.

And while it's public investment in school ICT dwarfs its fellow-Commonwealth country, one of Singapore's best educational initiatives also stems from New Zealand leadership.

New Zealand businessman David Perry—a former successful Apple dealer—first visited Singapore in the early 1990s, on a consulting assignment . That involved visits to an international school. And soon afterwards he received a phonecall from one of its key executives, Irene Chee. The Singapore Teachers College had moved, and all its giant central-city campus was empty. Why not set up a model school there?

So together they did: the Overseas Family School, one of several international schools in Singapore licensed to service the island city-state's successful policy of attracting more than 3,000 foreign companies and their state.

Like Cramlington and Tahatai, it's impossible to convey its model in mere typescript. (You can download its sixteen-page *School of The Future* full-colour tabloid from its website—www.ofs.edu.sg—and see a much fuller story with photos).

But its *chasm-crossing* can be briefly summarised:

❏ The first school in Singapore, and one of the first in the world, to

When children can turn out computerised art like this (and in full colour)

why should they settle for less?

adopt the International Baccalaureate global curriculum for all age groups from early-childhood to senior high school.

❏ Now almost 2,500 students from sixtyfive nations.

❏ Extensive use of interactive technology as part of that programme, and effective staff training in the IB philosophy and methods.

❏ An open-source digital network that links all administrators, teachers, students and their families—so the entire school programme becomes a family affair.

❏ And many of its staff now digitising lesson plans and or "curriculum maps", using a wide variety of interactive software, including Macromedia *Flash* and professional animation applications.

But the Overseas Family School model has ramifications way beyond its international-school concept.

The IB curriculum it has embraced is a truly international one—and ideal for every student, not just those who are "academically gifted".

It is based around a multi-cultural, global model: trying to develop students as globally-minded citizens, with an open-minded understanding of what it means to be a participating global and local citizen.

It has both widely-accepted international *academic* assessment standards and, in Singapore, offers all students the facilities to carry through life, on the school's electronic network, a digital portfolio of all their individual achievements, talents and strengths.

Like Tahatai and Cramlington, it sees a "curriculum" not as a narrow set of subjects, but as an interlinked way of becoming both a global-thinking citizen and a personal creator of a talented future.

And through its open-sourced digital network it has the built-in possibility of sharing some of its methods with schools around the world.

4. Learning templates for the new digital age

Sharing that knowledge internationally will, we believe, involve the use of "digital templates". Elsewhere in business, those lessons already abound:

❏ Every newspaper, magazine, television station and all successful publishing programmes use such templates as a framework.

❏ For some reason, even many great teachers don't. That probably stems from the "death by *Powerpoint*" syndrome. Many university

Templates

for you to share online

www.cyworld.com (Korea)

15 million with 3D personal Web sites

www.wikipedia.org

Biggest online encyclopedia

www.google.com

8 billion pages, 1.1 billion images

ww.Fotolog.net

57 million photos to share

www.ebay.com

147 million trading partners

www.yahoo.com

300 million users

www.altavista.com (Babelfish)

For instant translations

www.MySpace.com

21 million share ideas every month

* See much fuller list, page 510.

lecturers have finally moved up from black-and-white overhead-projector transparencies to *Powerpoint,* in the mistaken belief that this represents the full scope of "interactive technology". It doesn't.

❏ But fortunately, as we've seen, some of the brightest schools in the world have their children displaying their full creative talents inside real digital frameworks or templates.

❏ That's why most Apple schools regard *iMovie* video-editing software as among the most versatile creative tools. Once even young students have been taught to use a digital video camera, they can now edit their final movies to professional standards.

❏ That's why middle and high-schools are using *Mind Manager, Inspiration* and other mind-mapping software applications for creative thinking, brainstorming, TV storyboarding and writing.

❏ That's why even small children are using *KidPix* and *Kidspiration* software to create great artwork and junior mind maps.

❏ And some New Zealand teachers are learning the basics of eight interactive-technology applications in four days of training—actually two days because in the other half of their training time covers many other new learning and teaching methods.

Let's illustrate with three examples, one from a primary school, one from a business, and one from Asia:

❏ **The school example:** When eight Beijing-based professors of education visited Sherwood Primary School in New Zealand, they were greeted by an eight-year-old Korean lad. A year earlier, he couldn't speak a word of English. But this morning he welcomed them in English, which they spoke. And then took them into the school Espresso coffee bar and showed them his multimedia presentation on the history of New Zealand—in both English and Maori. It included a video he'd shot himself, and edited using the Apple *iMovie* editing software template. And with animations he'd also created himself inside another digital template.

Then he took the guests—from the Beijing Academy of Educational Sciences—into one of the school's digital classrooms. And there another eight-year-old showed them the computer-animated interactive game he had created on Tolkien's *Lord of The Rings.* And finally the guests were interviewed by ten-year-olds on the school's radio station. It broadcasts twentyfour hours a day, seven days a week, to all homes in their area—all operating, of course, to the same kind of templated and automated format as successful commercial music stations.

Use the entire world as a talent pool.

ERIC RAYMOND
The Cathedral and The Bazaar*

* First used as the title of address to the
Linux Kongress, May 1997, on the concept
of the open-source movement.

As the professors drove off to the airport, the leader was the first to exclaim: "If eight-year-olds can do that here, then China had better catch up, or we'll be left behind the rest of the world."

Not long after this, when two former Silicon Valley executives from India were interviewed on the same school's radio station, they were fascinated at the first question from a ten-year-old: "What do you personally intend to do this year to change the world?" Indeed.

❏ **The business example: again from Auckland:** the Trends international publishing company. In 1985, it became New Zealand's first company to install a new Apple Mac network, and designed a *Pagemaker* digital template so that any journalist could, within a day, be producing fully professional layouts for the company's four-colour *Kitchen Trends* annuals.* But that year it exhausted all the supplies of kitchen colour photos it could find. So the next year it launched the annual *Trends Kitchen Designer of the Year Award.* To enter: talented kitchen designers had to send in a portfolio of colour photos, professional sketch plans, and a write-up of the design problem and how it was solved. The company now has the world's best library of kitchen colour-photos, and of *New Home Trends, Renovation Trends, Bathroom Trends,* and enough others to produce seventy international home-improvement annuals every year.

Change "kitchen designers" to "international students and teachers" and hopefully the connection becomes clear: the world's "teachers and students of the year" sharing their talents online.

❏ **And from Asia:** South Korea, China, Japan and India are among those leading the open-source revolution: the groups combining to build free software in competition with the international commercial giants.

Singapore's Overseas Family School is linking in with the same concept. It's a fee-paying private international school. But its leadership is committed to the cooperative, collaborative open-source principle in sharing international learning ideas, methods and interactive "tools".

Says founder and chairman David Perry: "We regard that as the way science is supposed to operate. To freely share scientific knowledge, to test it, and, where it doesn't measure up, to amend it, and pass on the results to others."

Add Wikipedia and Google to the mix and the stage is set to reinvent schooling: and use the world's 59 million teachers and 1.5 billion students as the talent-pool.

* Co-author Dryden founded Trends in 1984 with partner David Johnson.

What do you personally intend to do this year to change the world?

* First question asked by ten-year-old interviewer on school radio station to two Indian computer software experts from Silicon Valley. See previous page.

How any country can lead the learning revolution: and so can you

Now it's your turn. The New Learning Revolution is yours to shape.

And whoever you are, wherever you live, the solutions you choose will be different—but, we suspect, with much in common.

Some countries, like England, have strong regional structures for schooling. And, in the case of Britain, the incredibly powerful central mass-communications network and "international brand" of the BBC.

United States leadership seems much more likely to come from corporations like Google, eBay and Apple—with their ability to change entire industries— and some of the giant philanthropic foundations.

Australia and America have self-governing states. Other small nations, such as Singapore, Qatar, Ireland, Finland and Sweden, have strong central Governments with the power on institute change.

Yet other giants, like China, India and Brazil, have enormous potential.

But within those parameters, the main pathways to the future are clear.

1. The big-picture challenge

Almost everything is now possible. We now know how to create the world's first full *learning society*—for all its people.

That requires no less than a revolution. But a gentle one. No modern, advanced nation can continue to run an education system locked into a model designed at least a century ago or even longer.

And billions currently ensnared in poverty cannot not cross the digital-divide by trusting a system that has consistently failed them.

We are living in an education system designed for a different era.

JOHN ABBOTT & TERRY RYAN
The Unfinished Revolution*

*Published by Network Educational Press, Stafford, United Kingdom.

China alone needs to retrain its 10 million teachers—and find probably twice that many new ones. It cannot do this with the old, failed system.

In India, up to 40 percent of children never get to school. And of those who do, 40 percent drop out by age ten.

So even if the developed world has money to waste on inefficient systems, poor countries have neither the cash nor time to spare.

2. Bring on the real public debate

Almost everywhere the public education debate is nearly always about wrong alternatives.

In most Western countries the debate is nearly always about "test scores" and senior high-school assessment systems.

But it matters very little whether senior academic exams are for British "A levels", the International Baccalaureate Diploma or other similar qualifications. The top *academic* scholars who achieve these are not the problem. They'll fly through any standardised memory test.

The problem lies with the under-achievers in a system not designed for them. And there are now many ways to correct that.

More importantly, true democracy is based on an *informed* choice of alternatives. And that challenges educational authorities and the mass media to find the best alternatives that work, and then present them as key points for the needed national debates. Here the national television networks, particularly in countries with strong State broadcasting systems, have major parts to play, as certainly Britain's BBC recognises.

But again, in the new digital age, it seems much more likely that the real leadership will come through the online "social entrepreneurs".

3. Raise the sights

Again, for the first time in history, it is now possible to "dream the future and then create it". In the new digital, electronic age of instant communications, every successful major corporation is regularly reinventing itself—and completely changing entire industries.

Google, Yahoo, Amazon, Dell and eBay are classic examples of new-era corporations that could not have existed even a few years ago. They have reinvented completely new *business designs*. So have Ireland's Ryanair and Richard Branson's Virgin, which have left the conservative giant airline networks floundering in their profitable jetstreams.

Relearn the best from the past, too

As Confucius said 2,500 years ago:

❑ **Blend the best of the new with best from the old.**

❑ **Learn by doing.**

❑ **Use the world as classroom.**

❑ **Use music and poetry to learn and teach.**

❑ **Blend academic and physical.**

❑ **Learn how to learn, not just facts.**

❑ **Cater to different learning styles.**

❑ **Build good values and behaviour.**

❑ **Provide an equal chance for all.**

CHEN JINGPAN
*Confucius as a Teacher**

* Published by Foreign Language Press, Beijing, China.

One has only to visit corporations like FedEx, Accenture or giants like GE to see what can be done when leaders unleash creative talent and share it through new communications technology. Or marvel at what will happen as Skype joins eBay to offer free global Internet phonecalls to their combined membership of 200 million.

Or visit Wellington, New Zealand, to see how an entire city can be transformed by the creative genius of Peter Jackson. He has almost single-handedly turned it into one of the world's major movie capitals. Little wonder that the kids of New Zealand have a new hero—and are lining up from their first day at school to become digital movie-producers.

Or the next time you join the other 147 million registered traders on eBay—and Skype's 50 million—think also of these lessons for world education. If it's possible to link that many people on a trading site, what is the problem in linking 59 million school teachers?

Or will the leadership come from such sleeping giants as China: not only racing to take over what remains of the Industrial Age, but also finding guidance in its quite incredible past? Only arrogance could suggest that all breakthroughs will come from the Western world.

4. To learn it, do it

If there is any lesson that shines strongly from our researches and experience, it is simply this: *if you want to learn it, do it.*

The traditional lecture model is now hopelessly flawed—and probably always has been. Both Carnegie Mellon University and Singapore's Nanyang Polytechnic have already shown the way:

❏ CMU by redesigning its university to get rid of boring lectures.

❏ Nanyang by ensuring that students genuinely qualify for diplomas by producing finished products under contract to major companies.

Sure, standardised written tests can check such one-correct-answer subjects as mathematics and spelling, but the real test is: *show you know.*

This presents major challenges for teacher training. That's simply because, in most countries, teacher training is controlled by people who have spent their careers operating an old system.

5. Lifelong personalised learning

Learning is not the same as schooling. And lifelong learning is everyone's individual responsibility.

If knowledge is the new capital then innovation is the new currency.

KEVIN KELLY
*New Rules for the New Economy**

* Published by Viking Penguin, New York.

Note: Kevin Kelly uses this quote in his annotated Bibliography
to crystallise the message of *Innovation Explosion,* by
James Brian Quinn, Jordan J. Baruch and Karen Anne Zien,
published by The Free Press.

Kelly, former Executive Editor of *Wired* magazine, recommends
www.sims.berkeley.edu/resoources/infoecon/
as the most complete web site for the new economy.

No one can rely on existing skills for even a few years. And most new skills now do not depend on one's age. Demographics are changing everything. Now if you want to learn desktop publishing at age eight or eighty, you can use the same just-in-time, personalised learning methods.

Cramlington High School head Derek Wise puts *personalised learning* as top of his agenda in planning the future direction of his school: just-in-time programmes when any learners want them, where they want them.

This means everyone now needs to *learn how to learn.* Amazingly, that most important subject of all is not taught at most schools.

Neither is its partner: *learning how to think, how to create.*

But those will be the two most important skills to add to your own specific talents for a satisfying future in the emerging society.

For those who live in the "developed world", those creative skills, along with the ability to learn new ones, will actually decide whether living standards can be maintained.

Even becoming *learning organisations* will not be sufficient in a narrow sense. Creativity is moving to the top of the corporate agenda.

There is no way, short of complete trade boycotts, for countries such as Britain, Germany, France and the United States to compete, on price, with the new-found manufacturing might of China or the low-cost IT skills of India.

6. Leading the new Creative Society

Here General Electric's new CEO Jeff Immelt is correct. Certainly in the Western world each country is moving from *The Knowledge Economy* to the *Creative Economy.*

And each country's future will rest on its ability to create new products, new services, new experiences, and new designs:

❏ Like Apple *iPod*, with its great fit-in-the-pocket design and its ability to store up to 15,000 *personally-selected* music tracks, now linking with computer-in-the-pocket cellphone technology. Stand by for the music, phone, videophone and classroom-in-your-pocket revolution.

❏ Or Sony's *PlayStation*—the core of that giant corporation's profitability, but yet to really tackle the problem of interactive learning.

❏ Or the ability of the world's Peter Jacksons, Stephen Spielbergs, George Lucases, J.K. Rowlings and Cirque du Soleil circuses to produce completely new experiences.

How to turn your teaching talent and passion into a successful world industry.

GORDON DRYDEN
The Aha! Talent Game*

Yet most schools, and most teacher-training establishments, do not teach creativity —except in the sense of a few arts subjects.

Surprisingly, the "evidence-based" practices that underly most public education policies are generally based on the old, outdated classroom model, and don't include the evidence from great business change.

Here again Britain has taken a partial lead. Chancellor Gordon Brown has created a special fund for teaching *enterprise education* and *entrepreneurship* in schools.

The co-authors of this book have a special interest here, as we've combined to run seminars on similar subjects, in places as far apart as the cold north of Sweden and the far south of New Zealand.

And in a 2004 series of nine one-day seminars in England, on enterprise education, it was a delight to see how school principals and teachers were at first a little nervous, and then amazed, to sit alongside Government-appointed "enterprise advisers" from business, and find what fun the "enterprise-creation" process can be.

The "accelerated-learning" game we played: *AHA! How to turn your own teaching talent into a successful world industry. Your market: The world's 59 million school teachers.*[1]

The specially-designed board game included 121 great ideas: from Barbie to Nike, Disney to Nintendo, McDonalds to Tesco, Starbucks to Doc Marten boots, Harry Potter to Richard Branson and Anita Roddick.

Within ten minutes, nearly all the teachers were enthusiastically working out how to develop their own talents to match those leaders.

Within two hours, the original trickle of ideas had turned into a flood. It was the first time that most had ever even thought that their great specialist teaching talents had potential outside a class of thirty students.

But, perhaps more importantly:

❏ They learned how anyone can turn talent into a world-changing business: even bigger than the New City School's great effort in writing and publishing two books. Now it can be done digitally, interactively.

❏ They learned a little of how to turn a very complex subject—the entire "mix of international business"—into an accelerated-learning lesson: methods and a process that can be used to teach anything.

❏ They learned stage-one of how to get their own students to design "games for learning"—just like Lego, Sony, Nintendo; only better.

❏ And they started to grasp what Nelson Thornes, Europe's biggest

The challenge lies in creating a workplace in which people can be the best they can be.

FREDERICK W. SMITH
in *The Book of Leadership Wisdom**

* Edited by Peter Krass, published by John Wiley & Sons, New York.

textbook publisher, is now doing: switching old-type books into "blended interactive lesson plans". Students can now combine illustrated books with interactive, do-it-yourself, just-in-time digital "learning tools". And self-assessment is built-in—online. Each student is then instantly provided with suggestions to improve his or her performance.

Still think interactive and online technology won't change the future of education?

7. Creating a Creative School

So what questions does that raise for tomorrow's schools?

In many ways: the same challenges faced by progressive business. And as FexEx founder Frederick W. Smith says in *The Book of Leadership Wisdom:* "The challenge lies in creating a workplace in which people can be the best they can be."

Significantly, when Nelson Thornes' international development manager last visited New Zealand she was amazed to see six-to-ten-year-old students also creating their own interactive learning games. Just like the former teachers who've inspired the blended-learning programme in her own company.

We would also be the last to suggest that a few schools provide the only model for the world. What New Zealand's *Tomorrow's Schools* experiment does prove, however, is the enormous creative talent that exists, among principals, teachers, students and parents, when the *structure* of schooling is changed to unleash it.

And that new technologies allow John Dewey's "construct your own future" concept to be reinvented for a completely new-type economy.

So the real challenge is how to turn school, from the very first years, into a new form of *creative workshop,* with the latest do-it-yourself tools.

Top-selling American management writer Tom Peters, in his latest book, *Imagine!,* says he "despairs of the [American] education system more than any other part of society that I can imagine".[2]

❏ *"Classrooms are abnormal places, unless you dream of a career as a prison guard. They have nothing whatsoever to do with the real world."*

❏ *"Our school system is getting it all wrong, for an age in which creativity and intellectual capital drive the economy. The school 'system' abhors creativity."*

Turn the future over to the students.

JOHN TAYLOR GATTO
A Different Kind of School*

* Summarised by Tom Peters in *Imagine!*, published by
Dorling Kindersley. London.

❏ *"Talent is everything"* . . . *but "schools teach to the test. Standardisation? Ye gads. Not in my Silicon Valley!"*

And then Peters—who worked for years as a senior consultant with the giant McKinsey group in Silicon Valley—presents alternatives very similar to those canvassed in this book:

❏ *"Turn the future over to students,"* in the words of John Taylor Gatto, author of *A Different Kind of School,* three times New York City School Teacher of the Year and once State Teacher of the Year.

❏ *"Learning is more about good questions than good answers,"* as Christopher Phillips puts it in *Socrates' Cafe.*

❏ *"School is an insult to the intelligence,"* as Frank Smith writes in his book of the same name. Adds Peters: "The timebomb in every classroom is that students learn exactly what is taught. And schools spend most of their time contriving contexts in which kids learn *not* to like particular subjects. Research shows that such brilliant anti-learning sticks! Standardised testing mostly teaches kids that they are not competent. And so they drop out of science . . . they drop out of math. The school system really does accomplish something after all: it *discourages* large numbers of competent human beings from exploring things they might actually care about."

That's a devastating critique, and certainly doesn't describe the great school experiences we've highlighted throughout these pages. But Peters also presents Frank Smith's positive alternative version of *The Learners' Manifesto:*

❏ The brain is always working.

❏ Learning does not require coercion.

❏ Learning must be meaningful.

❏ Learning is incidental.

❏ Learning is collaborative.

❏ The consequences of worthwhile learning are obvious.

❏ Learning always involves feelings.

❏ Learning must be free of risk [actually fear of failure].

And Peters, like us, sees alternatives: "There are hundreds of fabulous schools. Some are our public schools, in wealthy communities. Some are public schools, in poverty-strikken communities. Some are charter schools. Some are Waldorf schools. Some are Montessori schools."

Create the right environment and even small children will 'explode' into learning.

MARIA MONTESSORI

So to get the public and political debate really on track, find those brilliant role model schools and present them for that debate: in glowing technicolour, not in the bland, unread ritual of yet more academic reports.

8. Keep it simple

Our next conclusion: *keep it simple.* As Geoffrey Moore's model shows: the chasm won't be crossed unless the solution is easy to grasp.

Some of the really great "accelerated learning" models come from teachers who are brilliantly gifted. If we're lucky, each of us has probably been taught by someone like that at least once in our life.

But not every one of the world's 59 million teachers can be as inspiring as many of the gifted ones featured in these pages. And most teachers would shudder at the thought of having to turn every classroom lesson into the kind of multimedia interactive experience of a Leo Wood-style bells-and-whistles chemistry class (from page 341).

We favour a simpler route. Paraphrasing the words of Montessori: "If you create the right environment, then all students will 'explode' into lifelong learners, and creators of their own future."

Create the right environment and turn it over to the kids. Get them to create, and co-create, their own future. Amazingly it works.

But how to do that in a sensible, easy-to-use crossing-the-chasm curriculum?

9. The new curriculum: the early years

A curriculum is not a mere body of information to be passed on and later tested. Some aspects of that subject-based approach may be sensible in high school and university, but even there we challenge it. Overall a modern curriculum involves four inter-related parts:

THE CONTENT: *What information is studied and learned.*

THE PROCESS: *How it is studied, so that lifelong habits are formed to inquire, investigate, probe, analyse, present, reflect and create.*

THE METHOD: *The format, so that every project also involves learning how to learn and learning how to think.*

PERSONAL GROWTH: *What attitudes are "caught"—the life-skills that help create a well-rounded, fully-participating citizen.*

All the great primary-elementary school models covered in these

One model for a new global curriculum

1. Global Culture

6. Global Qualifications

2. Global Explorers

A new six-part school system

5. Global Citizens

3. Global Knowledge

4. Global Network

---

1. Pre-kindergarten

First fun-filled multisensory programme from aged 3.

2. Kindergarten

Hands-on learning for 4 and 5-year-olds.

3. Elementary

Inquiry-based global projects: includes foreign language.

4. Middle school

Focused-inquiry curriculum with integrated themes.

5. High School

Global qualifications and portfolios of strengths.

6. College level

Two years general, then rigorous specialised study

OVERSEAS FAMILY SCHOOL*

* This is the International Baccalaureate model, as applied by Singapore's Overseas Family School, on a combined site. www.ofs.edu.sg—to download *The School of The Future*.

pages incorporate all four: Tahatai Coast, the Key School in Indianapolis, the New City School in St. Louis, Missouri. And so do dozens we have visited in places as far apart as Sweden, Singapore, Shenyang and San Diego, as we've covered in earlier editions of *The Learning Revolution*. And many more that have worked wonders under a gifted principal, but no longer shine "under new management".

But we come back strongly to the best curriculum for *crossing the chasm* and thus making it easy for any school to put it into practice—even when a brilliant principal retires or moves on.

And, at elementary-level, the vote almost certainly goes to the International Baccalaureate Primary Years Programme (PYP) for children from three to eleven years. The reasons:

It is a "think global, act locally" curriculum. The IB mission statement sees students becoming " critical and compassionate thinkers, lifelong learners and informed participants in local and world affairs, conscious of the shared humanity that binds all people together while respecting the variety of cultures and attitudes that makes for the richness of life." Inside that, it allows maximum local participation.

THE CONTENT: *Its school year is based around global themes, like many of the other schools we have covered. But it has the great benefit of being international, so that, by using the new networking technologies, it can be shared with schools and students everywhere.*

Time is too short for the world's under-privileged to stay under-educated while a great "scalable" system already exists.

Those six-weekly topic-themes enable students to absorb the building-blocks of their world: the planets of the universe, continents, minerals, oceans, rivers, inventions, ancient civilisations and technologies of the world, including one's own country and current global issues.

All other building-block "subjects"—reading, writing, spelling, basic mathematics, science, art and music—are integrated into those topics, so they link to the real world. And, with the Overseas Family School's additional content curriculum, all students learn a second international language, also integrated with the topic theme.

THE PROCESS: The whole approach is built on identifying and developing one's own talents inside multi-talented teams, so that concepts such as "multiple intelligences" are constantly, and almost automatically, blended and absorbed into the learning process. Create the right environment, and children automatically start with their strengths—then

Focused inquiry

Eight key questions to discover the world

FORM:

What is it like?

FUNCTION:

How does it work?

CAUSE:

Why is it like it is?

CHANGE:

How is it changing?

CONNECTION:

How is it connected to other things?

PERSPECTIVE:

What are other points of view?

RESPONSIBILITY:

What is our responsibility?

REFLECTION?

How do we know?

INTERNATIONAL BACCALAUREATE*

* From its Primary Years Programme:
www.ibo.org

share these with each others. This process also develops a wide range of multimedia skills: to discover information, turn it into creative knowledge, test it, reflect on it, create with it and apply it.

THE METHOD: What the Overseas Family School* calls *focused inquiry:* starting with the IB's eight-question method of tackling every possibility. To any non-teacher visiting the school for the first time, all students seem to be developing the combined skills of multimedia investigative journalists. All teachers are trained NOT to volunteer ready-made answers but to act as inquiry-stimulators. By contrast, we've visited many schools in the world where teachers say they feel guilty if they are not themselves talking for at least 90 percent of the time.

THE QUESTIONS: The students quickly learn to use eight main questions to start their *focused inquiry* into whatever they are studying, so the inquiry process becomes second nature:

Form: *What is it like?* Everything has a form with recognisable features, which can be observed, identified, described and categorised.

Function: *How does it work?* Everything has a purpose, a role or a way of behaving which can be investigated and categorised.

Cause: *Why is it like it is?* Things do not just happen. Everything has a cause, and actions have consequences, which need to be considered.

Change: *How is it changing?* Everything is in a state of change. Change is universal, and one of the best tests of an educational system is how it develops students' ability to manage change.

Connection: *How is it connected to other things?* We live in a world of interacting systems, in which the actions of individuals, communities, nations and elements affect others.

Perspective: *What are other points of view?* We all view issues and concepts through different perspectives, and often preconceptions.

Responsibility: *What is our responsibility?* We are not passive observers of events. We can and must make choices. By doing so we can make a difference, on a personal, community and global scale.

* Disclosure of interest: when the first edition of The Learning Revolution appeared in late 1993, the first big international order came from the Overseas Family School: one copy for every staff member and others to send to every international candidate applying for a teaching job in the new school. Co-author Dryden regularly consults for the school, and is the author of "School of The Future", its online newspaper.
www.ofs.edu.sg

Isn't this what you'd like your children to be?

Inquirers: using their natural curiosity to acquire the skills needed to conduct purposeful research.

Lifelong learners: with an active love of learning.

Thinkers: skilled in using thinking skills critically and creatively to make decisions and solve complex problems.

Communicators: confident in receiving and expressing ideas and information—in more than one language.

Risk-takers: confident to explore new roles, ideas and strategies.

Knowledgeable: with a critical mass of significant knowledge of themes and topics of global importance.

Principled: with integrity, honesty and a sense of fairness and justice.

Caring: with a personal commitment to action and service—and sensitive towards others' needs and feelings.

Open-minded: committed to exploring a range of views, and understanding the values and traditions of other cultures.

Well-balanced: with an understanding of the importance of physical and mental balance and personal well-being.

Reflective: with the ability to reflect wisely, and constructively analyse their personal strengths and weaknesses.

INTERNATIONAL BACCALAUREATE AIMS*

* From the aims of the International Baccalaureate Primary Years Programme. See full aims: www.ibo.org

Reflection: *How do we know?* And how do we know when we are correct? Reflection also encourages us to focus on our way of reasoning, and the quality and reliability of the evidence we have considered.

Now many of the other schools highlighted in these pages also have similar inquiry models. But the benefit of the IB PYP is the way these tie into universal themes, to unlock the building blocks of knowledge.

And those of us who are journalists would say they resemble the famous *Who? What? When? Where? How? and Why?* questions of investigative reporters: even nonfiction book writers.

PERSONAL GROWTH: PYP teachers also have to build, into their daily lesson plans, projects to cultivate eleven distinct attitudes, all designed to develop balanced, real-life skills.

And, when added to the eleven-step attitudes checklist, the unified power of the programme becomes obvious. Isn't this what you would like your children to be:

Inquirers: using their natural curiosity to acquire the skills needed to conduct purposeful research?

Lifelong learners: with an active love of learning, way after they have left school?

Thinkers: skilled in using thinking skills critically and creatively to make decisions and solve complex problems?

Communicators: confident in receiving and expressing ideas and information—and competent in more than one language?

Risk-takers: confident to explore new roles, ideas and strategies?

Knowledgeable: with a critical mass of significant knowledge of themes and topics of global importance?

Principled: with integrity, honestry, a sense of fairness and justice?

Caring: with a personal commitment to action and service—and sensitive towards others' needs and feelings?

Open-minded: committed to exploring a range of views, and understanding the values and traditions of other cultures?

Well-balanced: with an understanding of the importance of physical and mental balance and personal well-being?

Reflective: with the ability to reflect wisely, and constructively analyse their personal strengths and weaknesses?

And all that as the basis for *elementary-primary* schooling. But with

Are you sure what you are testing?

1. Basic knowledge

6. Specialist knowledge

2. Surface knowledge

The many facets of knowledge

5. Personal knowledge

3. General knowledge

4. Global knowledge

Basic knowledge: Reading, writing, arithmetic.

Surface knowledge: Often in standardised tests.

General knowledge: On a wide variety of topics.

Global knowledge: Worldwide 'cultural literacy'.

Personal knowledge: Best shown by portfolios.

Specialist knowledge: Deep 'subject' knowledge.

GORDON DRYDEN*

* United Kingdom enterprise-education, seminar tour, 2004

the added benefit that the total curriculum is transferable. And can easily be shared with others. It already involves 1,595 schools in 128 countries.

International Baccalaureate schools employ curriculum coordinators, to work in with teachers. And while teachers are workng with students on the current six-week project, the coordinators are helping plan the next six weeks: checking on satellite television programmes, confirming the latest research. And, when linked to international networks, sharing some of the great new ways that interactive-technology tools can be used.

10. The new curriculum: middle and high school

Middle schools and high schools will continue to be different to the building blocks of the primary years. And if those early building blocks of *content, process, method* and *personal growth* are firmly in place, then students are stimulated to involve themselves, in increasing depth, over a wide range of both specialist and integrated-studies projects.

Again, the IB curriculum is an excellent start: because, at middle and high-school level (at public or private schools) it encourages such depth and integration as part of the concept of developing open-minded, globally-minded, responsible citizens. And at all high school levels, the International Baccalaureate places major emphasis on a *Theory of Knoledge** and students producing multi-discipline, case-study projects to blend their "subject knowledge": again to *show you know*.

The programme therefore acknowledges the distinction between many different forms of knowledge, and thus different methods to "show you know"—and those that can be proven by "standardised tests".

11. Sharing with the rest of the world

Anyone who has visited Nelson Thornes' new "blended learning" headquarters, Singapore's Overseas Family School's "digital curriculum" group, or studied Cramlington's "personalised learning plans", is struck by the similarity.

Here are three organisations—an international European company, an international, multicultural, Asian-based preK-12 school, and a state high school in the industrial north of England—all working on almost identical projects. And with similar aims.

* We believe the IB Theory of Knowledge component is one of the few aspects of the curriculum that can be substantially improved, by adding in the latest research to change many theories on learning and thinking.

The world
is
hurtling
towards
the
on-demand
pan-media
universe.

MARK THOMPSON
Director-General, Britain's BBC*

* Paraphrased from speech to Edinburgh International Television
Festival, August 27, 2005.

All are working on personalised lesson plans for use by anyone, anytime, at school and at home. Self-learning, self-correcting, self-assessing. And even with online help to spot and help overcome any weaknesses:

Nelson Thornes: digitising subject-based textbooks, CD-roms and online support for international multimedia and personalised study.

The Overseas Family School: digitising methods of taking the full K-12 International Baccalaureate curriculum and making a range of interactive "learning tools" available free online to share it.

And Cramlington: digitising the U.K. secondary-school curriculum—but with special emphasis on personalising it, including relating it to individual learning styles for when-you-need-it study.

Now consider nine other projects, and the possibilities become clear:

❏ **Britain's BBC,** with its *Creative Future, Beyond Broadcast* and *Digital Curriculum* projects: digitising the incredible resources of the world's biggest public-service television and radio broadcaster. Then planning to make them available to what Director-General Mark Thompson calls "the on-demand, pan-media universe we're hurtling towards". [3] The BBC's "producers, commissioners and content creators have started with a blank sheet of paper and begun to re-imagine drama, news, music, children's and other key genres from scratch": in the march to plan interactive content and experiences. Now add that to the enormous value of the BBC's high-prestige "international brand".

❏ **MIT's MediaLab in America:** and Director Nicholas Negroponte's $100 laptop project, with China as the first big user. (The price can be kept to that level only with minimum bulk orders of one million units, with China first in line.)

❏ **Novatium's similar project in India:** with their $100 network computer, ready to link with India's villages—and plans to develop village-based community learning centres. And, we forecast, that group's ability to tap into the brilliance, drive and wealth of the big Indian contingent of venture capitalists and start-up experts in Silicon Valley.

❏ **Promethean's** *ActivBoard collaborative classrooms* **project:** to link together subject-specialising teachers who are experts in preparing electronic, interactive flipcharts for sharing lesson-models online.

❏ **Jeffrey Sachs' United Nation's Millennium Project**: to halve world poverty within ten years. And, within the same timespan, provide

How students tap into global knowledge

A selection of global websites

Google
www.google.com

National Geographic
www.nationalgeographic.com

Smithsonian Institute
www.si.edu/intro/html

Atomic Learning
www.atomiclearning.com

Science Learning Network
www.sln.fi.edu/org/behind.html

Adventure On-Line
www.adventureonline.com

GlobaLearn
www.globalearn.org

Kidlink
www.kidlink.org

Kidspace
www.plaza.interport.net/kids_space

Multimedia in Education
www.unit-sb.de/sonstige

Edviews
www.edviews.com

Exploratorium
www.exploratorium.edu

BBC Education
www.bbc.co.uk/education

OneLook Dictionaries
www.onelook.com

Learn 2
www.learn2.com

MapBlast
www.mapblast.com

MapQuest
www.mapquest.com

Topmarks
www.topmarks.co.uk

Homework Solver
www.homeworksolver.com

Atlapedia (world's maps)
www.atlapedia.com

Telephone directories
www.teldir.com

World Time Zone
www.isbister.com/worldtime

Schoolzone (UK)
www.schoolzone.co.uk

Learnfree
www.learnfree.co.uk

Other lists: www.edutopia.org*

* This is the home page of the George Lucas Educational Foundation. On it, type *Learn & Live* on the "search" space, and then, when the Learn & Live book chapters are on screen, select, at the end of the book, *Glossary, Electronic Resources and Index*—download from the Internet, and print out the entire list.

primary education for all the world's poor countries. (Imagine the lesson in cooperation, culture and learning if each school in the developed world adopted a partner-school in a poorer country—to share education and health programmes by learning together).

❏ **China's Li Ka-Shing Foundation:** and its project to train new teachers by satellite—specially if China adds some of the newer learning methods to some of its own great traditions.

❏ **Google:** and its well-advanced project to digitise a world library of books and research documents. Google represents the very essence of America's entrepreneurial brilliance: the combination of innovators and great management. The innovators: students, Russian-born Sergey Brin and American-born Larry Page. The outstanding manager: CEO Eric Schmidt, with his pioneering background as the CEO of software maker Novel and chief technology officer at Sun Microsystems. And with a history in charge of Java, Sun's ground-breaking project to develop multi-platform software to make sharing easy.

❏ **eBay:** combining the creative talent of founder Pierre Omidyar and the management competence of CEO Meg Whitman. And Omidyar's foundation already showing how peasants in Guatemala and other countries can develop their great handcraft skills and sell them on the Internet.

❏ **The open source software movement:** the new method of openly and freely sharing the learning and creative talents of computer scientists, Internet hobbyists, and participating students and teachers around the world. A movement epitomised by Tim Berners-Lee and the World Wide Web, Linus Torvalds' Linux, Wikipedia and its inspirers.

❏ And this summary from Michael Clark, leader of the Overseas Family School's digital team, and their own efforts to provide a stable, low-cost digital network for sharing interactive learning methods: "Effectively we're creating one of the world's most efficient multi-platform IT systems for schools. One of our big aims is to take what is available free on the Internet and, in the spirit of the free software movement, to make our adaptations and improvements available to the world."[4]

Now imagine those sharing facilities coming together with some of the great interactive learning models highlighted in this new book, and in the previous four editions of *The Learning Revolution*.

But now the opportunities are soaring with the rise of *glogal templating*.

Now join your own creative revolution

The world's best online sites where you join millions of others to co-create

Research
www.wikipedia.org
www.del.icio.us.com
www.answers.org

Share photo albums
www.fotolog.net
www.webshots.com
www.flickr.com

Getting together
www.cyworld.com (Korea)
www.MySpace.com
www.match.com

Customised music
www.pandora.com
www.itunes.com
www.yahoo.com (music)

Tech news
www.dig.com

Collaboration
www.basecamp.com

Free phone calls
www.skype.com
www.vonage.com

Podcasting
www.odeo.com
www.itunes.com

News
www.topix.net
www.news.google.com
www.news.yahoo.com

Donations
www.donorschoose.org
www.freecycle.org
www.freesharing.org

Blogs
www.postsecret.com
www.Feedster.com

Services
www.craiglist.org
www.freecycle.org
www.backpackit.com

Open source
www.jibjab.com

Auctions, trading
www.ebay.com

It's almost as if a new Web is being born:

❏ **Cyworld:** the soaring South Korean website with 15 million members—almost a third of the population, and including 90 percent of those in their early twenties. Using online templates, every member has a personalised, three-dimensional website. An average of 6.2 million digital photos, from members, are shared on the site every day—and stored for reuse.

❏ **MySpace:** the American-based sites where some 21 million visitors a month share thoughts, photos and music with friends on per-sonalised home pages.

❏ **PostSecret:** where hundreds of people every day send in their often-hilarious postcards, and an art-and pop-culture lover, Frank Warren, picks out the best and posts them on the site. The result has rocketed PostSecret to the tenth most-popular position of the 13 million blogs montored by Feedster.com, a blog search engine.

❏ **Flickr.com:** with its 39 million digital photos and 1.2 million users all over the world adding theirs and downloading others'.

❏ **Fotolog.net:** with its 57 million photos—and rising. Only here members are restricted to sending in only one family photo a day. Result? Visitors can click through photo journals of hundreds of thousands of lives all over the world.

As Business Week puts it in a major 2005 report: "A whole new Web is emerging from the wilds of cyberspace. It's no longer all about idly surfing and passively reading, listening or watching. It's about doing, sharing, socialising, collaborating, and, most of all, creating." [5]

For years politicans have talked about "a Third Way" in national and international leadership: how to blend the best features of cooperative enterprise, entrepreneurial business and social conscience. And this new collaborative movement provides a strong alternative basis.

12. The Foundation model

Some charitable foundations are also showing the way—often set up with grants from business following the patterns originally set by the Ford and Carnegie Foundations in the United States.

❏ The International Baccalaureate's global curriculum programme, for example, was initially supported by grants from the Twentieth Century Fund and the Ford Foundation.

The 'best of British'

Leading-edge websites to share with all

National Grid for Learning
http://www.ngfl.uk/

Curriculum Online
http://www.curriculumonline.gov.uk/

Culture Online
http://www.cultureonline.gov.uk/

Parents Online
http://www.parentsonline.gov.uk/

Connexions
http://www.connexions./gov.uk/

National Curriculum
http://www.nc.uk.net/home.html

National Curriculum in Action
http://www.ncaction.gov.uk

ICT in schools
www.dfes.gov.uk/ictinschools

UK Online
http://www.ukonline.gov.uk

Teachers' portal
http://www.teachernet.gov.uk/

Parents' portal
http://www.dfes.gov.uk/parents/

❑ The Bill and Melinda Gates Foundation has become the world's biggest charitable trust. As well as big donations to help fight AIDS, it has put hundreds of millions into American schools—if, unfortunately, still seemingly mesmerised by the American mantra of standardised testing.

❑ The George Lucas Educational Foundation continues to provide excellent guides to school breakthroughs, with books, videotapes and on-line services.

❑ Pierre Omidyar continues to look for ways to expand the philosophy that inspired him to found eBay: "What would happen within a marketplace if everyone had equal access to information and tools?"

❑ And in Britain, the Royal Society for the encouragement of Arts, Manufactures and Commerce has launched its nationwide Campaign for Learning, also backed by some of Britain's leading philanthropic found-ations. Its aim: "To change the culture and gradually transform the United Kingdom into a 'learning society'."

To that founding Chairman Sir Christopher Ball adds a personal vision: "For every individual to have a Personal Learning Action Plan, every organisation to become a learning organisation, and for everybody to be in reach of an accessible provider of learning opportunities— whether in a school, college, university or in employment or in the home."

13. Britain's own leadership role

It would be presumptuous for two non-citizens to prescribe the exact nature of Great Britain's march into *The New Learning Revolution.*

But both co-authors are regular visitors and seminar-presenters in the United Kingdom. Co-author Dryden has lived there for three years in the past decade. Two of those years were with Accelerated Learning Systems in Aston Clinton, near Aylesbury, preparing the *FUNdamentals* multimedia programme for early-childhood development. And one year in London with Speakers International as a consultant in corporate training. From our combined experiences, these models stand out to place Britain at forefront of change:

Early-childhood programmes: some of the best in the world. And an incredible Government effort over the past decade to take Britain's spending on preschool education to the top of the major nations.

Primary schooling: some excellent work on literacy and numeracy. But from accompanying British school principals and deputy-principals around New Zealand primary schools, we can confirm: it's here where

Some people see things as they are and ask why. I dream of things that never were and ask: Why not?

GEORGE BERNARD SHAW
Back to Methuselah, Act 1.

Britain can perhaps benefit most from other models.

High schools: Cramlington sets the pace, but is only one of several great trend-setters.

Leading-edge schools: Again, at least 100 exemplars. And schools like Varndean in Brighton are also models for the world, with Headteacher Andy Schofield an inspiring example.

National leadership: The BBC and Britain's Open University are the best of their type on the planet. Under its new leadership, expect exciting innovation from your national broadcaster.

But it's in interactive technology, with strong Ministry leadership and cutting-edge commercial partners, where the U.K. is really set to shine. Promethean and Nelson Thornes are obvious corporate models. And the National Grid for Learning, Curriculum on Line and other similar initiatives are outstanding (see websites, page 512).

Then if Britain could, like New Zealand, unleash the creative flair in its primary schools, and marry that with the strength of the ICT division inside the Ministry for Education and Skills, the crossing-the-chasm results would be unbeatable. It would also provide the missing link between Britain's great early childhood achievements and outstanding high-school breakthroughs.

Add in the power of the BBC's incredible "brand", with its upcoming interactive online innovations, and Britain could play by far the biggest role in the United Nations Millennium Project. Not only to cut world poverty in half by 2015, but to provide good preschool and primary education for every child on earth.

14. Invent your own model

But why wait for anyone else when you can create your own model?

Behind every one of the positive examples we've highlighted lies a person or people who decided to make a difference.

So the catalyst to change the way the world learns can be anyone, anywhere: in business, at school, in a community or a family. It needs to be, for the evidence is overwhelming. A new learning revolution is overdue to match the revolution in communications and technology.

The tools are here. The time is now. The script is yours to write — or dance, or sing, or play, or act, or draw, or orchestrate.

Anyone can lead the world into this new century. Why not you?

Chapter reference notes

Where the same reference source is used more than once, subsequent references are abbreviated in this way:

6: 1.2 — meaning: chapter 6, see chapter 1, note number 2.

GD is Gordon Dryden, and JV is Jeannette Vos.

Other page references refer to pages in this book.

Introduction

1. Mark Thompson, Director-General, British Broadcasting Corporation, speech to Edinburgh International Television Festival (August 27, 2005).

2. John Medcalf, *TARP: The Tape Assisted Reading Programme,* summarised on pages 392-393 of this book.

3. Steve Ham, *The Wired Campus,* article in *Business Week* e-biz supplement (December 11, 2000).

4. Matt Ridley, *Nature Via Nurture,* Harper Perennial (2004).

5. Full details from page 427.

6. Robert J. Sternberg, *Beyond IQ,* Cambridge University Press (1985) and, with Elena L. Grigorenko, *Our Labelled Children,* Perseus (1999).

7. Intro.3.

1. The converging revolutions

1 Peter Drucker, *The New Realities,* Harper & Row (1989).

2 www.etforecasts.com

3 Dee Hock, *Birth of the Chaordic Age,* Berrett-Koehler (1999).

4. Margaret Wheatley, *Leadership and The New Science,* Berrett-Koehler (2001).

5. George Gilder, *Telecosm,* Free Press (2000).

6. Kevin Kelly, *New Rules For The New Economy,* article in *Wired* magazine (September, 1997).

7. Peter Drucker, in *Managing in the Next Society,* Butterworth Heinemann (2002).

8. Thomas Goetz, *Open Source Everywhere,* article in *Wired* magazine (November, 2003).

9. John Naisbitt, interview with GD, Boston, Mass (1990).

10. 1.7.

11. 1.9.

12. Anita Roddick, *Body and Soul,* Greenleaf (2003).

13. Jeffrey D. Sachs, *The End of Poverty,* Penguin (2005).

14. 1.7.

15. 1.7.

2. The network revolution

1. Seymour Papert: various articles, all available at www.papert.org

2. Graham Nuthall, *The Cultural Myths and Realities of Classroom Teaching and Learning: a Personal Journey,* article in *Teachers College Record,* New Zealand (May 2005).

3. William D. Plaum, *The Technology Fix,* ASCD (2004).

4. Marc Prensky, *Digital Natives,*

Digital Immigrants, article on his website, www.marcprensky.com (2001).

5. Marc Prensky, *Do They Really Think Differently?,* article on his website, www.marcprensky.com (2001).

6. Marc Prensky, *Proposal for Educational Software Development Sites,* article on his website, www.marcprensky.com (2003).

7. www.wisdomquotes.com

8. Quoted by Matt Ridley, *Nature Via Nurture,* Harper Perennial (2004).

9. 2.1.

10. John Holt, *How Children Fail,* Delta (1982).

11. *The Promise and Limitations of Smart Drugs,* cover story in *Business Week* (September 26, 2005).

12. Michio Kaku, *Visions,* Anchor (1997).

13. Mark Thompson, speech to Edinburgh International Television Festival (August 27, 2005).

14. 2.1.

15. Karl Popper, *The Open Society and its Enemies,* Philosophy Books (1945).

16. Matt Ridley, *Nature Via Nurture,* Harper Perennial (2004).

17. Denis Diderot, quoted by Bryan Magee in *The Story of Philosophy,* Dorling Kindersley (2001).

18. *Celebrating Multiple Intelligences: Teaching for Success,* New City School, St. Louis, Missouri (1994).

19. Bruce Nussbaum, in *Get Creative,* Business Week cover story (August 8/15, 2005).

20. Marcus Buckingham & Curt Coffman, *First, Break All The Rules,* Simon & Shuster (2000).

21. *It's a Wikipedia World,* article in *Time* magazine (June 6, 2005).

22. 2.21.

3. The talent revolution

1. Bill Bryson, *A Short History of Nearly Everything,* Doubleday (2003), but also Matt Ridley, *Genome,* Fourth

Estate (1999), and *Nature Via Nurture,* Harper Perennial (2004).

2. 2.20.

3. Peter Drucker, *The New Realities,* Harper & Row (1989).

4. 3.1.

5. Intro.6.

6. Howard Gardner, *Frames of Mind,* Basic Books (1983).

7. Intro.6.

8. Ronald Kotulak, *Inside The Brain,* Andrews and McMeel (1996).

9. Douglas R. Fields, *The Other Half of the Brain,* article in *Scientific American* (April 2004).

10. Deepak Chopra, *Quantum Healing,* Bantam (1989; also in *Perfect Health,* Harmony (1990).

11. Candace B. Pert, *Molecules of Emotion: Why You Feel The Way You Feel,* Simon & Schuster (1997).

12. Intro.5.

13. David Perkins, *Outsmarting IQ,* Simon & Schuster (1995).

14 Daniel Goleman, *Emotional Intelligence,* Bloomsbury (1996).

15. Jerome Kagan, *Galen's Prophecy,* Basic Books (1994), but also chapter 14, 3.14.

16. 2.20.

17. 2.20.

18. Dave Meier, *The Accelerated Learning Handbook,* McGraw-Hill (2000).

4. The teach-yourself revolution

1. 2.20.

2. Marilyn King, from *Dare To Imagine,* an article in *On The Beam,* published by New Horizons for Learning (Fall, 1991).

3. Colin Rose, *Accelerated Learning,* Dell (1985).

4. Terry Wyler Webb, with Douglas Webb, *Accelerated Learning With Music—a Trainer's Manual,* Accelerated Learning Systems, Georgia (1990).

4. Georgi Lozanov, *Suggestology and Outlines of Suggestopedy,* Gordon and Breach (1978); Donald Schuster and Charles Gritton, *Suggestive Accelerative Learning and Teaching,* Gordon and Breach (1985); Lynn Dhority, *The ACT Approach: The Artful Use of Suggestion for Integrative Learning,* Gordon and Breach (1991); Richard Bandler and John Grindler, *Using Your Brain For a Change,* Real People Press (1986); Georgi Lozanov and Evalina Gateva, *The Foreign Language Teachers Suggestopedic Manual,* Gordon and Breach (1988); Tony Stockwell, *Accelerated Learning: in Theory and Practice,* EFFECT (1992).

6. Tony Buzan, *Make The Most Of Your Mind,* Linden (1984).

7. Marian Diamond, interview with GD in Berkeley, CA (1990). For more scientific data, see Marian Cleeves Diamond, *Enriching Heredity,* Macmillan (1988).

8. *It's a Whole New Web,* cover story, *Business Week* (September 26, 2005).

9. 4.8.

10. Taught at four-day teacher training seminars organised by The Learning Web Ltd. See *Southland Innovator* programme at www.thelearningweb.net

5. The creative revolution

1. Thomas Friedman, *The World is Flat,* Penguin/Allen Lane, London (2005), provides graphic examples of the creative links between the developed world, on one hand, and India, China and Eastern Europe on the other.

2. *The World Book Encyclopedia.*

3 Frank Rose, *East of Eden: The End of Innocence at Apple Computer,* Arrow Books (1989).

4. John F. Love, *McDonald's: Behind The Arches,* Bantam (1986).

5. *The Sunday Times Rich List* (1996).

6. Part of this chapter originally appeared in Gordon Dryden's *Out Of The Red,* William Collins (1978).

7. Slywotzky, Adrian J.; and Morrison, David J., *The Profit Zone,* Times Books, (1998).,

8. 5.7.

9. Ogilvy, David, *Ogilvy on Advertising,* Crown Publishers (1983).

10. Peter Ellyard, speech to New Zealand school principals (1992).

11. William J.J. Gordon is the founder of Synetics Educational Systems Inc.

12: Peter Evans and Geoff Deehan, *The Keys to Creativity,* Grafton (1988).

13. Alex Osborn, *Applied Imagination,* Charles Schribner's Sons (1953).

14. James L. Adams, *Conceptual Blockbusting,* Penguin (1987).

15. Masaaki Imai, *Kaizen: The Key To Japan's Competitive Success,* Random House (1986).

16. 5.15.

17. Toshihiko Yamashita, *The Panasonic Way,* Kohansha International (1987).

18. Edward de Bono, *De Bono's Thinking Course,* BBC Books (1982).

19. Roger von Oech, *A Whack On The Side Of The Head,* Warner Books (1983).

20. 5.14.

21. 5.18.

22. Edward de Bono, *Teaching Thinking,* Penguin (1977).

Chapter 6: Right from the start

1. Professor Marian Diamond points out (letter to authors, June, 1993) that, while no one develops another cortical brain cell from the time of birth, brain cells do continue to multiply after birth: in the dentate gyrus of the hippocampal complex; granule cells in the cerebellum; and nerve cells in the olfactory epithelium.

2. Interview in London with GD (1990).

3. Dr. Ian James, interview in New York, with GD (1990).

4. Jane M. Healy, *Your Child's Growing Mind,* Doubleday (1987).

5. Ten-year research project carried out by the Psychology Department, University of Otago Medical School, Dunedin, New Zealand.

6. *Children in Crisis,* article in *Fortune* (August 10, 1992); figures will have varied since that but the same trend remains.

7. 6.6.

8. The Diagram Group, *The Brain: A User's Manual,* Berkley Books (1983); Richard M. Restak, *The Brain: The Last Frontier,* Warner Books (1979).

9. Robert Ornstein and Richard F. Thompson, *The Amazing Brain,* Houghton Mifflin Company (1984).

10. GD, *Where To Now?* television series, produced by Pacific Foundation, New Zealand (1991), scripts reproduced in *Pacific Network* (February, 1992).

Chapter 7: The vital years

1. Benjamin S. Bloom, *Stability and Change in Human Characteristics,* John Wiley (1964).

2. 2.20.

3. 2.20.

4. 7.1.

5. Research on male-female brain differences summarised in *The Learning Brain,* by Eric Jensen, published by Turning Point for Teachers (1994).

6. Dr. Phil Silva, Director of the Dunedin Multidisciplinary Health and Development Research Unit, University of Otago Medical School, interview in Dunedin New Zealand, with GD (1991).

7. The Christchurch study is financed by the New Zealand Medical Research Council. Percentages are from Dr. David Fergusson, Programme Director, in interview with GD (1991).

8. Professor Marian Diamond, interview with GD in Berkeley (1990).

9. Richard M. Restak, *The Infant Mind,* Doubleday (1986).

10. Ruth Rice, *The Effects of Tactile-Kinesthetic Stimulation on the Subsequent Development of Premature Infants,* University of Texas (1975).

11. Prof. Lyelle L. Palmer, *Kindergarten Maxi-Stimulation: Results over Four Years,* at Westwood School, Irving, Texas (1971-75); *A Chance to Learn: Intensive Neuro-Stimulation in Transition Kindergarten,* at Shingle Creek Elementary School, Minneapolis (1989-90); and *Smooth Eye Pursuit Stimulation Readiness in Kindergarten,* at Shingle Creek Elementary School, Minneapolis (1990-91).

12. Palmer interview and correspondence with JV (1993).

13. Interview with JV (1996).

14. Notes provided by Jerome Hartigan to GD (1995).

15. Janet Doman interview in Philadelphia with GD (1990)

16. Dorothy Butler, *Babies Need Books,* Penguin (1984).

17. Oxford English Dictionary.

18. J.A. van Elk, *The Threshold Level for Modern Language Learning,* Longman Paul)1976) for Council of Europe. The most-used 1700 words in the English language, from Extended Ayres List, are listed by Romalda Bishop Spalding in *The Writing Road to Reading,* Quill/Williaml Morrow (1990).

19. Peggy Kaye, *Games for Learning,* Noonday Press (1991).

20. GD first interviewed Glenn Doman, in Melbourne, Australia, for New Zealand radio and television in 1974; he has studied the Doman method in action in Australia, New Zealand and especially at The Institutes for the Achievement of Human Potential in Philadelphia, in 1988 (for one week), 1989 (for one week), in 1990 (during a three-day television recording session) and during the preparation of this book. Dryden has yet to meet one published critic of Doman who has actually visited The Institutes or studied his work at first hand. In fact, one highly qualified professor, and the leader of a model school, interviewed

for this book, publicly criticized Doman's methods while admitting to using them extensively.

21. Glenn Doman interview in Philadelphia, PA, with GD (1990).

22. Dr. Noor Laily Dato' Abu Bakar and Mansor Haji Sukaimi, *The Child of Excellence,* The Nury Institute, Malaysia (1991).

23. Felicity Hughes, *Reading and Writing Before School,* Jonathan Cape (1971).

24. 7.8.

25. All details of the Missouri Parents As Teachers programme obtained by GD during videotaping visit to St. Louis, Missouri (1990).

26. 7.25.

27. Ferguson Florissant School District data from visit to the district by GD (1990).

28. Phone interview with GD (1994).

29. Burton L. White, *The First Three Years Of Life,* Prentice Hall (1986). Note that, while this is an excellent book overall, many other child-development specialists disagree with Dr. White on the use of "baby bouncers" and "walkers". Dr. White correctly recommends that these should not be used for more than 15 minutes at a time; others say that any use of them encourages some parents to use them as "baby sitters", and prolonged use can cause developmental problems, particularly if they are used as a substitute for the important neurological stage of crawling.

30. Interview entitled *The Brains Behind The Brain,* in *Educational Leadership* (November, 1998).

31. 7.30.

32. Article, *Forward* (October 9, 1992).

33. The HIPPY programme has been introduced into New Zealand by the Pacific Foundation. Details have come from Foundation Executive Director Lesley Max.

34. Amy J. L. Baker and Cyaya S. Piotrikowski, in *The Effects of Participation in HIPPY on Children's Classroom Adaptation: Teacher Ratings,* published by the National Council of Jewish Women, Centre for the Child, New York.

35. 7.22.

36. Co-author Dryden was the original Chief Executive of the Pacific Foundation.

37. Interview with GD (1997).

38. GD visit to Sweden (1990).

39. Paula Polk Lillard, *Montessori: A Modern Approach,* Schocken Books, provides an excellent guide to Montessori's work.

40. Details of the Foundation Centre for Phenomenological Research gained on a visit by GD to the Artesia II Montessori centre, at French Camp, CA. (1990). Information updated from Foundation Centre email to authors.

41. 7.40.

42. Maria Montessori, *The Montessori Method,* Schocken Books (1964): first published in English in 1912.

43. Pauline Pertab interview with GD in Auckland, New Zealand (1993).

44. GD videotaped the Montessori Farm School programme in 1995 for *FUNdamentals.*

8: The teaching revolution

1. Tony Stockwell, *Accelerated Learning in Theory and Practice,* EFFECT, Liechtenstein (1992).

2. From Glenn Capelli's seminar at SALT Convention in Minneapolis, MN. (1992).

3. Interview with GD, Washington, D.C. (1990).

4. Interview at Sodertalji High School, Sweden, with GD (1990).

5. Interview in San Francisco, California, with GD (1990).

6. 8.1.

7. *500 Tips for Teachers,* produced by the staff of Cramlington Community

High School, and available their website: www.cchsonline.co.uk (Accelerated Learning books).

8. 4.4.

9. GD interview with Charles Schmid, San Francisco (1990).

10. 4.4.

11. Sheila Ostrander and Lynn Schroeder, *Superlearning,* Dell (1969), reported claims that some students had learned up to 3,000 foreign words in a day. Lozanov in 8.6 records 1,000 to 1,200 words being learned per day, with a recall rate of 96.1% (see table, page 318). The present co-authors have seen no authenticated research evidence to justify higher claims than this, and have seen no evidence outside Bulgaria of figures as high as 1,000 to 1,200.

12. 4.4.

13. 8.1.

14. 8.9.

15. 8.9.

16. Overseas Family School, Singapore. GD actually saw each of these demonstrations to parents in Singapore (2005).

17. Written analysis of Dr. Dhority's results, provided by Dr. Palmer, but summarised here, with details, on page 340.

18. Conversation with JV (1993).

19. Personal letter to JV (1993).

20 School results summary provided by Leo Wood (1996).

21. Thomas R. Hoerr, *Becoming a Multiple Intelligence School,* ACSD (2000).

22 8.21.

9:   Learning-styles revolution

1. From *Learning and Teaching Styles and Brain Behaviour,* newsletter of the Association for Supervision and Curriculum Development and the Oklahoma State Department of Education, Oklahoma (1988).

2. *Survey of Research on Learning Styles,* in *Educational Leadership* (Vol.

46, No. 6, March 1989).

3, 4 and 5. 9.1.

6. Howard Gardner, *Frames Of Mind,* Basic Books (1983).

7. Lloyd Geering, *In The World Today,* Allen & Unwin and Port Nicholson Press, Wellington (1988).

8. Michael Grinder, *Righting The Educational Conveyor Belt,* Metamorphous Press (1989).

9. Rita Dunn, Jeffrey S. Beadry and Angela Klavas, *Survey of Research on Learning Styles,* in *Educational Leadership* (Vol. 46, No. 6, pages 53-58).

10. 10.9.

11. From a summary of the Dunns' research, *Learning and Teaching Styles and Brain Behaviour,* published by the Association for Supervision and Curriculum Development and the Oklahoma Department of Education Newsletter (1988) .

12. Anthony Gregorc, *An Adult's Guide to Style,* Gabriel Systems, Maynard, Mass. (1982).

13. This test, while adapted from Anthony Gregorc's, first appeared in this form in: Bobbi DePorter, with Mike Hernacki, *Quantum Learning,* Dell Publishing (1992).

14. Adapted from book in 9.13.

15. Howard Gardner, *The Unschooled Mind,* Basic Books (1991).

10: The catch-up revolution

1. *Junk diet puts teen on go-slow,* New Zealand Herald article (February 5, 2004).

2. 4.7.

3. 7.11

4. Helen Keller, *The Story Of My Life,* Doubleday (1954); Helen E. Waite, *Valiant Companions: Helen Keller and Anne Sullivan Macy,* Macrae (1959); Norman Richards, *Helen Keller,* Children's Press (1968).

5. Thomas Armstrong, *In Their Own Way,* J.P. Tarcher (1987).

6. Brigette Allroggen, *Munich Institute of Technology,* in *Three In One Concepts Newsletter,* Three In One Concepts, Burbank, CA. (1993).

7. Kathy Carroll, interview with JV (1993).

8. Gordon Stokes and Daniel Whiteside, *One Brain: Dyslexic Learning Correction and Brain Integration,* Three In One Concepts, Burbank, CA. (1984).

9. Paul and Gail Dennison, *Brain Gym,* Edu-Kinesthetics, Ventura, CA. (1988).

10. Sierra Vista Junior School results reported in *Diffusing Dyslexia,* by Lee Wasserwald, special education teacher, in *1985 Grant Results Report,* available through Three In One Concepts, Burbank, CA.

11. GD videotape interviews with Hartigans (1996).

12 Renee Fuller, *In Search of the I.Q. Correlation* and *Ball-Stick-Bird Series,* Ball-Stick-Bird Publications, Stony Brook, New York; and *Beyond I.Q.,* an article by Fuller summarising her work, *In Context* magazine (winter 1988).

13. Elizabeth Schulz, *A Long Way To Go,* article in *American Teacher* magazine (February 1993).

14. Four-minute reading programme. developed originally by educational psychologist Donna Awatere.

15. Interview with GD (1991).

16. *The New Zealand School Journal* is published by Learning Media Ltd., Wellington, New Zealand.

17. John Medcalf, quotes from interview with GD (1991), and some material summarised from his book, *TARP: The Tape Assisted Reading Programme,* Special Education Service, Flaxmere, Hastings, New Zealand.

18. 10.17.

19. See: Marie Garbo, *Igniting The Literacy Revolution Through Reading Styles,* article in *Educational Leadership,* Association for Supervision and Curriculum Development, Alexandria, VA. (October, 1990).

20. Rhonda Godwin, interview with GD (1991).

21. Research data gathered by John Medcalf and related to GD in interview (1991).

22. Tom Nicholson, *Reading The Writing On The Wall,* Dunmore Press (2000) is an excellent guide to the phonics-versus-whole language debate, and a synthesis of what actually works.

23. Lynley Hood, *Sylvia: The Biography of Sylvia Ashton-Warner,* Viking, Auckland, N. Z. (1988). Sylvia Ashton-Warner, *Teacher,* Penguin (1966).

24. Felicity Hughes, *Reading and Writing Before School,* Jonathan Cape (1971).

25. Herbert Kohl, *Reading, How To,* Penguin (1973).

26. 10.13.

27. New Zealand Herald article, *Junk Diet Putts Teen on Goslow* (February 5, 2004).

28. 10.27.

11: The High School Revolution

1. Roger C. Schank, *Engines for Learning,* Laurence Erlbaum (1995).

2. Jack O'Connell, quoted by George Lucas Educational Foundation, www.edutopia.org

3. Betsy Hammond and Bill Graves, *Road Map to Success,* Oregonian (January 13, 2004).

4. 11.3.

5. 11.3.

6. 11.3.

7. 11.3.

8. 11.3.

9. Overseas Family School's online newspaper, *School of The Future:* www.ofs.edu.sg

10. Lin Cheng Ton, CEO, Nanyang Polytechnic, interview with GD, Singapore (2003).

11. 11.3.

12. 11.3.

13. www.papert.org for an excellent collection of Dr. Seymouth Papert's writings.

14. 11.2.

15. Our thanks to The Management Edge Ltd., P.O. Box 12461, Wellington, New Zealand, and especially to Ross Peddler, Director, for assembling various reports on Mt. Edgecumbe High School.

16. Ken Jones and Paul Ongtooguk, *High Stakes Testing in Alaska,* article filed at www.edst.edu.abc

17. 11.16.

18. Myron Tribus, *The Application of Quality Management Principles in Education at Mt. Edgecumbe High School, Sitka, Alaska, (1990),* reprinted in *An Introduction to Total Quality for Schools,* American Association of School Administrators (1991).

19. 11.18.

20. Dr. Nolan: interview in Palmerston North with GD (1991).

21. C.J. Patrick Nolan and David H. McKinnon, *Case Study of Curriculum Innovation in New Zealand: The Freyberg Integrated Studies Project,* Massey University (April 23, 1991).

22. 11.20.

23. Interview with GD (1997).

12: The Corporate Revolution

1. Chis McGowan and Jim McCullough, *Entertainment in the Cyber Zone,* Random House (1995).

2. Bill Gates, *The Road Ahead,* Viking Penguin (1995).

3. *Jack Welch's Encore,* cover story in *Business Week,* international edition (October 28, 1996).

4. 12.3

5. *Get Creative,* cover stories, Business Week magazine (August 8/15, 2005).

6. Tom Peters, *Liberation Management,* Knopf (1992).

7. Peter M. Senge, *The Fifth Discipline,* Random House (1992).

8. 12.7.

9. 12.7.

10. 12.7.

11. Geoffrey A. Moore published his first *Crossing The Chasm Book* in 1991, and has revised it under various titles since. See www.amazon.com for details and reviews of all editions and books.

13: The digital revolution

1. *In a class of their own, The Guardian* online newspaper (September 23, 2003).

14: How to reinvent the world

1. *The Aha! Game: How to turn your talent into a successful world industry,* devised by Gordon Dryden for corporate and school seminars. The board game includes 121 examples of great ideas: 11 from each of 11 aspects of business. Coordinated by The Learning Web Ltd., Auckland, New Zealand.

2. Tom Peters, *Imagine!,* Dorling Kindersley (2003).

3. Mark Thompson, speech to Edinburgh International Television Festival (August 27, 2005).

4. Michael Clark interview with GD, Singapore (2005).

5. *Best Of The Web,* special Business Week report (September 26, 2005).

Acknowledgments and thanks ■■■■■■■■■■■■■■■■■■■■

Both authors thank:

* The pioneers in many fields on whose shoulders this work stands. These include: Maria Montessori, Dee Dickinson, Georgi Lozanov, Jean Piaget, Roger Sperry, Robert Ornstein, Marian Diamond, Tony Buzan, Colin Rose, Howard Gardner, Robert Sternberg, Joseph DeLoux, Antonio Domasio, David Perkins, Mary Ann Block, Richard Restak, Karl Pribram, Joseph King, Dale Purves, George Augustine, David Fitzpatrick, Lawrence Katz, Antony-Samuel LaMantia, James O. McNamara, S. Mark Williams, Michio Kaku, Matt Ridley, Barbara Given, Burton L. White, W. Edwards Deming, Don Schuster, John Grassi, Lyelle Palmer, Peter Kline, Laurence Martel, Rita and Ken Dunn, Paul and Gail Dennison, C.E. Beeby, Daniel Whiteside, Gordon Stokes, Bobbi DePorter, Eric Jensen, Don Campbell, Charles Schmid, Richard Bandler, John Grinder, Michael Grinder, Freeman Lynn Dhority, Anthony Gregorc, John Le Tellier, Peter M. Senge, Charles Handy, Christopher Ball, Tony Stockwell, Glenn Capelli, Barbara Prashnig, Bettie B. Youngs, Ivan Barzakov, Pamela Rand, Betty Shoemaker, Thomas Armstrong, Donald Treffinger, Tim Berners-Lee, Alan C. Kay, Steve Jobs, Glenn Doman and those whose names appear at the bottom of each left-hand "poster page" of this book.

* To all the other people around the world who have helped with interviews and assistance in many ways, notably:

* The Americas: *United States:* Bradley and Cathy Winch, Tom Hoerr, John Naisbitt, Leo Wood, Mary Ellen Maunz, Janet Doman, Mary Jane Gill, Michael Alexander, Libyan Labiosa-Cassone, Philip Cassone, Joy Rowse, Sue Treffeison, Nancy Margulies, Marilyn King, Judith Bluestone, Lily Wong-Filmore, Susan Schmidt, Antonia Lopez, Lynn O'Brien, Valerie Barlous, Diane Loomans, Kim Zoller, Greg Cortepassi, Kathleen Carroll, Steven Garner, Mary Regnier, Von and Donna Stocking, Nancy Ellis, Peter and Anne Kenyon, and Mahesh Sharma. *Canada:* Paul Ruta, Tom Rudmik, Lane Clark, Jim Muckle, Doreen Agostino and Ed Gimpelj. *Brazil:* Eliana Rocha and E. Silva.

* The United Kingdom: Jim Houghton, Chris Dickinson and the crew at Network Educational Press, Derek Wise, Mark Lovatt, David Lewis, Michael Crawford, Vanda North, Peter, Paul, Katie and Claire Templeton, John Abbott, John Hoerner, Lesley Britton and the staff at Lansdowne College.

* Rest of Europe and Africa: *Sweden:* Ingemar Svantesson, Christopher Gudmundsson, Bam Bjorling, Stein Lindeberg, Stefan and Lola Holm, Pontus Pedersen, Ulla Eriksson. Agnetta Nilsson, Bengt-Eric Andersson, Bengt Lindquist, Barbara Martin, Bo Naesland, Agneta Borg, Barbro Martensson, Anders Larsson, Helena Wallenberg, Michael Bogolea, Bitte Johannesson, Gunilla Garde, Annike Airijoki, Tim Sefton, Ulf Lundberg, Mickey Thornblad, Mats Oljons, Thomas Dahlqvist, Ingrid Bjorkegren-Frode and Kim Frode, Ann-Marie Odebas, Monica Lundberg, Kerstin Palmn, Onni Varg, and Mats and Irene Niklasson. *Germany:* Sven Stroczynski, Petra Witt, Peter Susat. *Norway:* Anne and Neil Carefoot. *Finland:* Camilla Newlander and Martin Grippenberg. *Liechtenstein:* Tony Stockwell. *Germany:* Rudolf Schulte and Claudie Monnet. *The Netherlands:* Peter Schade and Nick van den IJssel. *South Africa:* Antony Lovell and Pita Ward.

* Asia-Pacific: *Singapore:* David Perry, Irene Chee, Pat Keenan, Michael and Jamie Clark, Bhim Mozoomdar, Dilip Mukerjea, Carmee Lim, Teo Chee Hean, principals and staff of Overseas Family School. *China:* Ji Mingming and the leaders of the Beijing Academy of Educational Sciences. *Australia:* Lindy Capelli, Keith McDonald, Alistair Rylatt, Eric Frangenheim.

* New Zealand: Kate Whitley, Noel Ferguson, Jonathan Gunson, Mark Beach, Viki Lawrence, Jenny Griggs and the staff of Tahatai Coast School, Warren Patterson and the staff of Sherwood School, John Petrie and the staff of Gulf Harbour School, Tony Falkenstein, Vicki Buck, Jerome and Sophie Hartigan, Lesley Max, Pacific Foundation, ASB Charitable Trust, John Medcalf, Lloyd Geering, Murray Brown, Carol Moffatt and all the crew at Video and Television Resources.

Our thanks to those involved in the publishing team in nineteen countries.

Jeannette Vos thanks:

* John Green for his incredible support while taking on this project yet another time. And my immediate family members, Leisha and Summer Groenendal, and Elly Van Barneveld. Also, a special thanks to the many personal friends who have supported my work. And to Gordon Dryden, for all the areas of content that he contributed, plus his journalistic ability to make the book so readable, and his cooperation and joint effort in making The Learning Revolution concept such a best-seller internationally.

Gordon Dryden thanks:

* Margaret Dryden, for 49 years of love, wisdom, tolerance, patience, support, great parenting and good fun. And Jeannette Vos, for suggesting this book, for the outstanding teaching experience distilled into these pages, and for tolerance at seeing volumes of other material slashed and simplified in an editor's drive to make academic research understandable to general readers.

The New Learning Revolution library

To start learning any subject (if you're a print-oriented learner) the co-authors recommend you first read three or four simple books on that subject by practical achiever. Then try "more depth".

GETTING STARTED: OVERVIEW

Buckingham, Marcus, and Coffman, Curt, *First, Break All The Rules,* Simon & Schuster, New York (1999).

Meier, Dave, *The Accelerated Learning Handbook,* McGraw Hill, New York (2000).

Rose, Colin, *Master It Faster,* Accelerated Learning Systems, UK (1999).

GETTING STARTED: TEACHERS

Loomans, Diane; and Kohlberg, Karen, *The Laughing Classroom,* Kramer, Tiburon, CA (1993).

DePorter, Bobbi; Reardon, Mark; and Singer-Nourie, Sarah, *Quantum Teaching,* Allyn & Bacon, Boston (1999).

Grinder, Michael, *A Healthy Classroom,* Michael Grinder & Associates WA, (2000).

TO START SCHOOL REFORM

Smith, Alistair, *Accelerated Learning In Practice,* Network Educational Press, UK (1998); see their catalogue for other Alistair Smith books in series.

Lovatt, Mark; and Wise, Derek, *Creating an Accelerated Learning School,* Network Educational Press, UK (2001): the Cramlington experience.

Smith, Alistair; Lovatt, Mark; and Wise, Derek, *Accelerated Learning: a user's guide,* Network Educational Press, UK (2004): the Cramlington Accelerated Learning Cycle.

George Lucas Educational Foundation, *Learn & Live,* kit includes book and one-hour videotape hosted by Robin Williams, covering U.S. breakthrough school models, direct from: *www.edutopia.org*

Hoerr, Thomas R., *Becoming a Multiple Intelligence School,* ASCD, Alexandra, VA (2000).

Faculty of New City School, *Celebrating Multiple Intelligences in the Classroom,* New City School, St. Louis (1994).

GETTING STARTED: MUSIC

Campbell, Don, *The Mozart Effect,* Avon Books, New York (1997).

Barzakov, Ivan and Associates, *Essence & Impact* (includes *How to Use Music*), Barzac Institute, Novata, CA (1995).

Andersen, Ole; Marsh, Marcy; and Harvey, Arthur, *Learn with the Classics,* LIND Institute, San Francisco (1999).

GETTING STARTED: THE BRAIN

Restak, Richard, *The New Brain: How The Modern Age Is Rewiring Your Mind,* Rodale Ltd., UK (2001).

Bragdon, Allen D; Gamon, David, *Use it or Lose it,* Bragdon Publishers, San Francisco (2000).

Le Doux, Joseph, *The Emotional Brain: The Mysterious Underpinnings of Emotional Life,* Simon and Schuster, New York (1996).

Ornstein, Robert; *The Amazing Brain,* Houghton Mifflin, Boston (1984).

Robert Kotulak, *Inside The Brain,* Andrews and McMeel, Kansas City, Mo. (1997).

Sylwester, Robert, *A Celebration of Neurons,* ASCD, Alexandria, VA (1995).

Diamond, Marian; and Hopson, Janet, *Magic Trees of the Mind: How to Nurture Your Child's Intelligence, Creativity, and Healthy Emotions from Birth Through Adolescence,* Plume, New York (1998).

GETTING STARTED: DNA

Ridley, Matt, *Genome: the autobiography of a species,* Fourth Estate, London (1999).

Ridley, Matt, *Nature Via Nurture: Genes, Experience and What Makes Us Human,* Harper Perennial, London (2003).

John Sulston & Georgina Ferry, *The Common Thread,* Bantam, UK (2002).

MIND MAPPING

Mukerjea, Dilip, *Superbrain: Train Your Brain To Unleash the Genius Within By Using Memory Building, Mind Mapping, Speed Reading,* Oxford University Press, Singapore (1996).

Buzan, Tony, *The Mind Map Book—Radiant Thinking,* BBC, London (1993).

Margulies, Nancy, *Mapping Inner Space,* Zephyr Press, Tucson, AZ. (1991).

ACCELERATED LEARNING

Rose, Colin; and Goll, Louise, *Accelerate Your Learning,* Accelerated Learning Systems, UK (1993): a kit.

DePorter, Bobbi, *Quantum Learning,* Dell, New York (1992).

Rose, Colin; and Nicholl, Malcolm. J., *Accelerated Learning For the 21st Century,* Accelerated Learning Systems, UK (1997).

CREATING NEW IDEAS

Michalko, Michael, *Cracking Creativity,* Ten Speed Press, Berkeley, CA (1998).

von Oech, Roger, *A Whack On The Side Of The Head,* Warner, New York (1990).

Adams, James L., *Conceptual Blockbusting,* Penguin, New York (1987).

von Oech, Roger, *Creative Whack Pack* (playing cards), U.S. Games Systems, Stamford, CT.

Michalko, Michael, *Thinkertoys,* Ten Speed Press, Berkeley, CA (1991).

MEMORY

Squire, Larry; and Kandel, Eric, *Memory: From Mind to Molecules,* Scientific American Library, New York (1999).

Higbee, Kenneth L., *Your Memory: How it Works and How to Improve it,* Piatkus, London (1989).

Buzan, Tony, *Use Your Perfect Memory,* Plume-Penguin, New York (1991).

INTELLIGENCE

Goleman, Daniel, *Emotional Intelligence,* Bloomsbury, London (1996).

Siler, Todd, *Think Like a Genius,* Bantam, New York (1997).

Gardner, Howard, *Frames Of Mind,* Basic Books, New York (1983).

Gardner, Howard, *The Unschooled Mind,* Basic Books, New York (1991).

PERSONAL DEVELOPMENT

Rosenberg, Marshall B., *Nonviolent Communciation: A Language of Compassion,* Puddle Dancer Press, CA (1999).

Demartini, John F., *The Breakthrough Experience: A Revolutionary New Approach to Personal Transformation,* Hay House, UK (2002).

FOR STUDENTS

Rose, Colin; and Civardi, Anne, *Champs,* Accelerated Learning Systems, UK (2001).

Martel, Laurence, *School Success,* Learning Matters, Arlington, VA (1992).

Ellis, David B., *Becoming a Master Student,* College Survival, Rapid City, SD (1985).

FOR PARENTS

Kline, Peter, *The Everyday Genius,* Great Ocean Publishers, Arlington, VA (1988).

Armstrong, Thomas, *In Their Own Way,* Jeremy Tarcher, LA (1987).

Clark, Faith and Cecil, *Hassle-Free Homework,* Doubleday, NY (1989).

FOR TEACHERS

Nicholson, Tom, *Reading The Writing On The Wall,* Dunmore, New Zealand (2000). Excellent to teach reading.

Capelli, Glenn: and Brealey, Sean, *The Thinking Learning Classroom,* The True Learning Centre, Perth, Western Australia (2000).

Campbell, Linda and Bruce; Dickinson, Dee, *Teaching and Learning Through Multiple Intelligences,* Allyn and Bacon, Boston (1999).

Jensen, Eric, *SuperTeaching,* Kendall/Hunt, Dubuque, Iowa (1988).

Caine, Renate Nummela and Geoffrey, *Unleashing the Power of Perpetual Change,* ASCD, Alexandria, VA (1997).

PARENTING FOR INFANTS

Eliot, Lise, *What's Going On In There? How the Brain and Mind Develop in the First Five Years of Life,* Bantam Books, New York, (1999).

Dryden, Gordon; and Rose, Colin, *FUNdamentals,* Accelerated Learning Systems, UK (1996): complete kit; and as book, HarperCollins, UK (2000).

Beck, Joan, *How To Raise a Brighter Child,* Fontana, London (1985).

Marzolla, Jean; and Lloyd, Janice, *Learning Through Play,* Harper & Row (1972).

White, Burton L., *The First Three Years of Life,* Prentice, Hall, New York (1986).

EARLY READING

Milne, Duncan, *Teaching The Brain To Reid,* SK (SmartKids) Publishing, Auckland (2005).

Hughes, Felicity, *Reading And Writing Before School,* Jonathan Cape (1971).

Young, Peter; and Tyre, Colin, *Teach Your Child To Read,* Fontana (1985).

Doman, Glenn, *Teach Your Baby to Read,* Better Baby Press, Philadelphia (1979).

EARLY WRITING

Martin, John Henry; and Friedberg, Andy, *Writing To Read,* Warner (1986).

Spalding, Romalda Bishop and Walter T., *The Writing Road To Reading,* Quill/William Morrow, New York (1990).

CREATIVE WRITING

Rico, Gabriel, *Writing The Natural Way,* J.P. Tarcher, Los Angeles, CA.

SPELLING

Cripps, Charles; and Peters, Margaret L., *Catchwords,* Collins, London (1993).

Hornsby, Beve; and Shear, Frula, *Alpha to Omega,* Heinemann, UK (1993).

MATHEMATICS

Help Your Child With Maths (the book

of the BBC TV series), BBC Books, London.

Johnson, Virginia, *Hands-On Math,* Creative Teaching Press (1994).

Doman, Glenn, *Teach Your Baby Math,* Better Baby Press, Philadelphia (1979).

GAMES FOR LEARNING

Kaye, Peggy, *Games for Reading,* Pantheon Books (1994).

Kaye, Peggy, *Games for Learning,* The Noonday Press (1991).

Perry, Susan K, *Playing Smart (four to 14 years),* Free Spirit (1990).

GAMES FOR TEACHERS AND TRAINERS

Thiagarajan, Sivasailam (Thiagi), *Diversity Stimulation Games* (1994); *Teamwork Games* (1994); *Cash Games* (1994); *More Cash Games* (1995); *Matrix Games* (1995); *Lecture Games* (1994); *Instructional Puzzles* (1995); *Creativity Games* (1996), all published by HRD Press.

LEARNING DIFFICULTIES

Levine, Mel, *A Mind At A Time,* Simon & Schuster, New York (2003).

Bluestone, Judith, *The Fabric of Austism: Weaving the Threads Into A Cogent Theory,* Handle Institute, Washington, USA (2004).

Reichenberg-Ullman, Judyth; Ullman, Robert, *Ritalin Free Kids,* New York, (2000).

Sternberg, Robert J.; and Grigorenko, Elena L., *Our Labelled Children,* Perseus, New York (1999).

Block, Mary Ann, *No More ADHD: 10 Steps to Help Improve Your Child's Attention and Behaviour Without Drugs,* Block Books, Texas, USA (2001).

Doman, Glenn, *What To Do About Your Brain-Injured Child,* Better Baby Press, Philadelphia (1974).

Armstrong, Thomas, *The Myth of the ADDS. Child,* Dutton, NY (1995).

Vitale, Barbara Meister, *Unicorns Are Real: A Right-Brained Approach to Learning,* Jalmar Press, Torrance, CA (1982).

MUSIC FOR LEARNING

Brewer, Chris Boyd; and Campbell, Don, *Rhythms of Learning,* Zephyr Press, Tucson, AZ (1990).

Campbell, Don, *100 Ways to Improve Teaching with Your Voice and Music,* Zephyr Press, Tucson (1992).

Merritt, Stephanie, *Mind, Music and Imagery,* Asian Publishing, Santa Rosa, CA (1996).

Barzakov, Ivan, *How to Read with Music,* Barzak Educational Institute, Novato, CA (1995).

MONTESSORI

Elizabeth G. Hainstock, *The Essential Montessori,* Plume, New York (1997).

Britton, Lesley, *Montessori: Play And Learn,* Vermilion (1992).

Lillard, Paula Polk, *Montessori: A Modern Approach,* Schoken Books, New York.

LOZANOV METHOD

Lozanov, Georgi; and Gateva, Evalina, *The Foreign Language Teacher's Suggestopedia Manual,* Gordon and Breach, New York (1988).

Lozanov, Georgi, *Suggestology and Outlines of Suggestopedy,* Gordon and Breach, New York, (1978).

Stockwell, Tony, *Accelerated learning in Theory and Practice,* EFFECT, Liechtenstein (1992).

DIET, ECOLOGY & LEARNING

Hills, Sandra; Wyman, Pat, *What's Food got to do with it?* Windsor, California (1998).

Pfeeifer, Carol C., *Nutrition and Mental Illness: An Orthomolecular Approach to Balancing Body Chemistry,* Healing Arts Press, Vermont, USA (1987).

Rapp, Doris J., *Our Toxic World: A Wake Up Call,* Environmental Medical Research Foundation, Buffalo, New York (2003).

Robbins, John, *May All Be Fed: Diet For A New World,* Avon Books, New York, (1992).

Morgan, Brian and Roberta, *Brain Food,* Pan, London (1987).

Roberts, Gwilym, *Boost Your Child's Brain Power: How To Use Good Nutrition,* Thorsons, England (1988).

Ausubel, Kenny, Harpignies, J.P., *Nature's Operating Instructions: The True Biotechnologies,* Sierra Club Books, San Francisco, (2004).

FOREIGN LANGUAGE TEACHING

Dhority, Freeman Lynn; and Jensen, Eric, *Joyful Fluency: Brain-Compatible Second Language Acquisition,* The Brain Store, San Diego, CA (1998).

Dhority, Lynn, *The ACT approach: The Artful Use of Suggestion for Integrative Learning,* Gordon & Breach, New York (1991, expanded edition).

FOREIGN LANGUAGE LEARNING

Colin Rose, *Accelerated French, Accelerated Spanish, Accelerated Italian, Accelerated German,* Accelerated Learning Systems, Aston Clinton, Bucks, U.K. (full programmes).

LEARNING & WORKING STYLES

Prashnig, Barbara, *The Power Of Diversity,* Network Educational Press, UK (2002).

Markova, Dawna, *How Your Child Is Smart,* Concari (1992).

Carbo, Marie; Dunn, Rita and Ken, *Teaching Students to Learn Through Their Individual Learning Styles,* Allyn and Bacon, Boston (1991).

Keirsey, David; Bates, Marilyn, *Please Understand Me,* Prometheus, Del Mar, CA. (1984).

TEACHING THINKING

De Bono, Edward, *Teaching Thinking,* Penguin, London (1977).

De Bono, Edward, *Edward de Bono's Thinking Course,* BBC Books, London (1982).

SELF ESTEEM

Loomas, Diane with Julia, *Full Esteem Ahead,* Kramer, Tiburon, CA (1994).

Youngs, Bettie, *The Vital 6 Ingredients of Self Esteem: How to Develop Them In Your Students,* Jalmar Press, Torrance, CA (1992). For teachers.

Borba, Michele, *Esteem-Builders,* Jalmar Press, Torrance, CA (1989). For elementary teachers.

EDUCATIONAL KINESIOLOGY

Dennison, Paul E. and Gail E., *Edu-K for Kids! The Basic Manual on Educational Kinesiology for Parents and Teachers of Kids of All Ages,* Edu-Kinesthetics, Ventura, CA (1987)..

Dennison, Gail E. and Paul E; and Teplitz, Jerry V., *Brain Gym for Business,* Edu-Kinesthetics, Ventura CA (1994).

MIND-BODY CONNECTION

Pert, Candace, *Molecules of Emotion: Why You Feel the Way You Feel,* Simon & Schuster, New York (1997).

Hannaford, Carla, *The Dominance Factor: How Knowing Your Dominant Eye, Ear, Brain, Hand & Foot Can Improve Your Learning,* Great Ocean Publishers, Arlington, VA (1997).

Promislow, Sharon, *Making The Brain Body Conection,* Kinetic Publishing, West Vancouver, BC, Canada (1998).

Hannaford, Carla, *Smart Moves: Why Learning is Not All in Your Head,* Great Ocean Publishers, Arlington, VA (1995).

Hartley, Linda, *Wisdom of the Body Moving: an introduction to body-mind centering,* North Atlantic Books, Berkeley, CA (1995).

TOMATIS METHOD

Tomatis, Alfred, *The Ear of Language,* Stoddard, New York (1997).

Gilmor, Timothy M.; Madaule, Paul; and Thompson, Billie (Editors); with Wilson, Tim, *About The Tomatis Method,* Listening Center Press, Toronto, Ont., Canada (1989).

TEACHING VALUES

Eyre, Linda and Richard, *Teaching Your Children Values,* Simon & Schuster, New York (1993)..

Glenn, H. Stephen; and Nelson, Jane, *Raising Self-Reliant Children in a Self-Indulgent World,* Prime Publishing (1989).

BUSINESS TRAINING

Rylatt, Alistair; and Lohan, Kevin, *Creating Training Miracles,* Jolley-Bass, San Francisco, CA (1997).

Gutherie, Richard L., *Working With Spirit: to replace control with trust,* Integrated Systems Thinking Press, Walled Lake (2000).

LEARNING ORGANISATIONS

Senge, Peter M., *The Fifth Discipline,* Random House, Sydney (1992).

Senge, Peter M.; Roberts, Charlotte; Ross, Richard B.; Smith, Bryan J.; and Kleiner, Art, *The Fifth Discipline Fieldbook,* Nicholas Brealey, London (1994).

THE FUTURE

Friedman, Thomas, *The Earth is Flat,* Penguin/Allen Lane (2005).

Hock, Dee, *Birth of the Chaordic Age,* Berrett-Koehler, San Francisco (1999).

Kaku, Michio, *Visions: how science will revolutionise the 21st century,* Anchor, New York (1997).

Friedman, Thomas, *The Lexus and The Olive Tree,* HarperCollins, UK (2000).

Handy, Charles, *Beyond Certainty,* Hutchinson, London (1995).

THE DIGITAL ECONOMY

Kelly, Kevin, *New Rules For The New Economy,* Viking, New York (1998).

Tapscott, Don; Ticholl, David; and Lowy, Alex, *Digital Capital,* Harvard Business School, Boston (2000).

Tapscott, Don (Editor), *Blueprint to the Digital Economy,* McGraw-Hill, New York (1998).

Martin, Chuck, *The Digital Estate,* McGraw-Hill, New York (1996).

Tapscott, Don, *Growing Up Digital,* McGraw-Hill, New York (1998).

Negroponte, Nicholas, *Being Digital,* Vintage, New York (1996).

Downes, Larry; and Mui, Chunka, *Unleashing The Killer App.,* Harvard Business School Press, Boston, Mass (1998).

LEADERSHIP

Covey, Stephen, *The 7 Habits Of Highly Effective People,* Simon & Schuster, New York (1989).

Goleman, Daniel, The New Leaders: *Transforming the Art of Leadership Into The Science of Results,* Little Brown Book, UK (2002).

Drucker, Peter, *Managing in the Next Society,* Butterworth Heinemann, Oxford (2002).

TOTAL QUALITY MANAGEMENT

Imai, Masaaki, *Kaizen: The Key to Japan's Competitive Success,* Random House, New York (1986).

Other recommended reading and resources ■■■■■■

Adams, James L., *The Care and Feeding of Ideas*, Penguin, London (1986).

Andreas, Connie and Steve; *Heart Of The Mind: Engaging Your Inner Power to Change*, Real People Press, Moab, Utah (1989).

Bandler, Richard; and Grinder, John; *Transformations*, Real People Press, Moab, Utah (1981).

Beadle, Muriel, *A Child's Mind*, MacGibbon & Kee, London (1971).

Beeby, C.E., *The Biography of an Idea: Beeby on Education*, New Zealand Council for Educational Research, Wellington, New Zealand (1992).

Blakemore, Colin, *The Mind Machine*, BBC Books, London (1990), accompanies television series.

Bloom, Benjamin (Editor), *Developing Talent In Young People*, McGraw Hill, New York (1981).

Bloom, Benjamin, *Stability and Characteristics in Human Change*, John Wiley, New York (1964).

Brewer, Chris Boyd, *Music and Learning: Seven Ways to Use Music in the Classroom*, LifeSounds, Kalispell, MT (1993).

Butler, Dorothy, *Babies Need Books*, Penguin, London (1984).

Caine, Renate Nummela and Geoffrey, *Making Connections: Teaching and the Human Brain*, Association for Supervision and Curriculum Development, Alexandria, Virginia (1991).

Campbell, Don, *Music, Physician for Times to Come*, Quest Books, Wheaton (1991).

Campbell, Linda; Campbell, Bruce; and Dickinson, Dee, *Teaching and Learning Through Multiple Intelligences*, Allyn & Bacon, Boston, Mass (1996).

Carroll, Kathleen, *Science Songs and Stories For the Big Question*, Brain-Friendly Teaching and Learning, Washington DC (1999).

Carroll, Kathleen, *Sing a Song of Science*, Brain-Friendly Teaching and Learning, Washington DC (1995).

Cherry, Clare; Godwin, Douglas; and Staples, Jesse, *Is The Left Brain Always Right?* Fearon Teacher Aids, Belmont, California (1989).

Christopher, Robert C., *The Japanese Mind*, Pan, London (1984).

Clay, Marie, *The Patterning Of Complex Behaviour*, Heinemann, Auckland (1979).

Costa, Arthur, *Supervision for Teaching Thinking*, Pacific Grove, California (1989).

Crum, Robert; Cran, William; and MacNeil, Robert, *The Story of English*, Faber & Faber/BBC Books, London (1986), with TV series of same name.

Csikszentmihalyi, Mihaly and Isabella, *Flow: The Psychology of Optimal Experience*, Harper & Row, New York (1991).

Davenport, G.C., *An Introduction to Child Development*, Collins, UK (1994).

De Bono, Edward, *Lateral Thinking*, Harper & Row, New York (1979).

Diagram Group, The, *The Brain: A User's Manual*, Berkley Books, New York (1983).

Diamond, Marian, *Enriching Heredity,* Macmillan, New York (1988).

Dickinson, Dee, *Positive Trends in Learning;* IBM Educational Systems, Atlanta, Georgia (1991).

Dilts, Robert; and McDonald, Robert, *Tools of the Spirit,* Meta Publications, Capitola, CA.

Dreikurs, Rudolph, *Happy Children,* Fontana, London (1972).

Drucker, Peter L, *The New Realities,* Harper & Row, New York (1989).

Dryden, Gordon, *Out Of The Red,* Collins, Auckland (1978).

Dunn, Rita and Ken; Treffinger Donald, *Bringing Out The Giftedness in Your Child,* John Wiley, New York (1992).

Dunn, Rita; and Griggs, Shirley A., *Learning Styles: Quiet Revolution in American Secondary Schools,* National Association of Secondary School Principals, Reston, Virginia (1988).

Dychtwald, Ken, *Age Wave,* Bantam, New York (1990).

Evans, Peter, and Deehan, Geoff, *The Keys To Creativity,* Grafton, London (1988), with BBC radio series.

Fahun, Don, *Three Roads to Awareness,* Glencoe Press, Beverly Hills, CA (1970).

Forester, Anne D.; and Reinhard, Margaret, *The Learners' Way,* Peguis, Manitoba, Canada (1990).

Fuller, Renee; Shuman, Joyce; Schmell, Judith; Lutkus, Anthony; and Noyes, Elizabeth, *Reading as Therapy in Patients with Severe IQ Deficits,* Journal of Clinical Child Psychology (1975, Spring, Volume IV, No. 1).

Gallwey, W. Timothy, *The Inner Game of Golf,* Pan, London (1979).

Gallwey, W. Timothy, *The Inner Game of Tennis,* Random House, New York (1974).

Goleman, Daniel; Kaufman, Paul; and Ray, Michael, *The Creative Spirit,* Dutton, New York (1992).

Goodlad, John, *A Place Called School,* McGraw-Hill, New York (1984).

Gorney, Roderic, *The Human Agenda,* Guild of Tutors Press, Los Angeles (1979).

Grassi, John, *Introduction to Geometry: A Curriculum Guide For Elementary Teachers,* ALPS Products, Framingham, Mass (1985).

Grassi, John, *The Accelerated Learning Process in Science,* ALPS Products, Framington, Mass (1985).

Gregorc, Anthony, *An Adult's Guide To Style,* Gabriel Systems, Maynard (1982).

Handy, Charles, *The Age Of Unreason,* Hutchinson, London (1989).

Harvey, Neil, *Kids Who Start Ahead, Stay Ahead,* Avery, Garden City Park, NY (1994).

Herbert, Nick, *Quantum Reality,* Doubleday, New York (1987).

Hirsch, E.D. Jr, *Cultural Literacy,* Bantam/Schwartz, Moorebank, NSW, Australia (1988).

Holt, John, *How Children Fail,* Pitman, New York (1968).

Hood, David, *Our Secondary Schools Don't Work Any More,* Profile, Auckland NZ (1998).

Hood, Lynley, *Sylvia: The Biography of Sylvia Ashton-Warner,* Viking, Auckland, New Zealand (1988).

Hutchinson, Michael, *Mega Brain,* Ballantine, New York (1986).

Israel, Lana, *Brain Power For Kids,* Buzan Center, England.

Jung, Carl, *Man And His Symbols,* Doubleday, New York (1964).

Kao, John, *Jamming,* Harper Business, New York (1997).

Kantrowitz, Barbara; and Takayama, Hideko, *In Japan, First Grade Isn't Boot Camp,* Newsweek (April 17, 1989).

Kantrowitz, Barbara; and Wingert, Pat, *An "F" in World Competition,* Newsweek (February 17, 1992).

Keller, Helen, *The Story of My Life,* Doubleday, New York (1954).

Khalsa, S., *Edu-K for Everybody,* Edu-Kinesthetics Publications, Glendale, CA.

Kohl, Herbert, *Reading, How To,* Penguin, London (1973).

Kovalik, Susan, *ITI: The Model, Integrated Thematic Instruction,* Covington, Kent, Washington (1994).

Kriegel, *If It Ain't Broke . . . Break It!,* Warner Books, New York (1992).

Lewis, David, *You Can Teach Your Child Intelligence,* Souvenir Press, London (1981).

Lewis, Katherine, *Cooperation and Control In Japanese Nursery Schools,* Comparative Education Review, (Vol 28, No. 1, 1984).

Lindgreen, Henry, *Educational Psychology In The Classroom,* John Wiley, New York (1962).

Macrae, Norman, *The 2024 Report,* Sidgwick & Jackson, London (1986).

Maguire, Jack, *Care and Feeding of The Brain,* Doubleday, New York (1990).

Maltz, Maxwell, *Psycho-Cybernetics,* Pocket Books, New York (1966).

Merritt, Stephanie, *Mind, Music and Imagery,* Aslan, Santa Rosa CA (1996).

Martel, Laurence, *A Working Solution For The Nation's Schools* (validation report on integrative learning at Simon Guggenheim School), Interlearn, Hilton Head Island, South Carolina (1989).

Martel, Laurence, *Testimonials and Comments from Corporate Customers,* Interlearn, South Carolina (1991).

Madaule, Paul, *When Listening Comes Alive: A Guide to Effective Learning and Communications,* Moulin, Buffalo, NY (1994).

Max, Lesley, *Children: Endangered Species?* Penguin, Auckland (1990).

Medcalf, John, *Peer Tutoring in Reading,* Flaxmere Special Education Service, Hastings, New Zealand.

Medcalf, John, T.A.R.P.: *The Tape Assisted Reading Progamme,* Flaxmere Special Education Service, Hastings, New Zealand.

Morita, Akio, *Made In Japan,* Signet-Dutton, New York (1986).

Nash, Madeleine, *Fertile Minds,* Time magazine Special Report, February 3, 1997.

Naisbitt, John, *Megatrends,* Warner Books, New York (1982).

Naisbitt, John, *Megatrends Asia,* Simon & Schuster, New York (1996).

Noor, Laily Dato' Abu Bakar; and Sukaimi, Mansor Haji, *The Child of Excellence,* Nury Institute, Malaysia (1991).

Ohmae, Kenichi, *The Borderless World,* Fontana, London (1990).

Ornstein, Robert, *Multimind,* Houghton Mifflin, Boston (1986).

Ornstein, Robert, *The Nature of Human Consciousness,* Freeman, NY (1973).

Ornstein, Robert, *The Psychology of Consciousness,* Penguin, NY (1977).

Ornstein, Robert; and Sobel, David, *The Healing Brain,* Simon & Schuster, New York (1987).

Osborn, Alex, *Applied Imagination,* Charles Scribner's Sons (1953).

Packard, David, *The HP Way,* Harper-Business, New York (1996).

Parnes, Sidney, *Creativity: Unlocking Human Potential,* Dok Publications, New York (1972).

Penfield, Wilder; and Jasper, Herbert, *Epilepsy and the Functional Anatomy of the Human Brain,* Little Brown, Boston (1954).

Peters, Thomas J.; and Waterman, Robert H. Jr, *In Search of Excellence,* Harper & Row, New York (1982).

Peters, Tom; and Austin, Nancy, *A Passion for Excellence,* Collins, UK (1985).

Postman, Neil; and Weingartner, Charles, *Teaching as a Subversive Activity,* Dell, New York (1987).

Pribram, Karl, *The Neurophysiology of Remembering,* Scientific American (January 1969).

Pribram, Karl; and Goleman, Daniel, *Holographic Memory,* Psychology Today (February 1979).

Rapp, Stan; and Collins, Tom, *Maxi-Marketing,* McGraw-Hill, New York (1987).

Restak, Richard M., *The Brain: The Last Frontier,* Warner, New York (1979).

Restak, Richard M., *The Infant Mind,* Doubleday, New York (1986).

Roddick, Anita, *Body and Soul,* Ebury Press, London (1991).

Rogers, Carl, *Freedom to Learn,* Charles E. Merrill, Columbus, Ohio (1969).

Rohwer, Jim, *Asia Rising,* Butterworth-Heinemann, Singapore (1995).

Russell, Peter, *The Brain Book,* E.P. Dutton, New York (1979).

Schuster, Donald H.; and Gritton, Charles E., *Suggestive Accelerated Learning Techniques,* Gordon and Breach, New York (1986).

Sheff, David, *Game Over: Nintendo's Battle To Dominate an Industry,* Hodder & Stoughton, UK (1993).

Sheridan, Mary, *Spontaneous Play In Early Childhood,* Routledge, UK (1993).

Shih, Stan, *Me-Too Is Not My Style,* Acer, Taiwan (1996).

Sperry, Roger, *The Great Commissure,* Scientific American (January 1964).

Smith, Paul, *Success In New Zealand Business,* Hodder Moa Beckett, Auckland, N.Z. (1996).

Sternberg, Robert, *Beyond I.Q.,* Cambridge University Press, New York (1985).

Suzuki, Shinichi, *Nurtured By Love,* Exposition Press, New York (1975).

Svantesson, Ingemar, *Mind Mapping and Memory,* Swan, Auckland (1989).

Thornburg, David, *Multiple Intelligence Inventory,* Thornburg Centre for Creative Development.

Toffler, Alvin, *PowerShift,* Bantam, New York (1990).

Townsend, Robert, *Further Up The Organisation,* Michael Joseph, UK (1984).

Treacy, Michael; and Wiersema, Fred, *Discipline of Market Leaders,* Addison-Wesley, Reading, MA (1995).

Vance, Mike; and Deacon, Diane, *Think Out Of The Box,* Advantage Quest, Kuala Lumpur, Malaysia (1995).

Vos-Groenendal, Jeannette, *An Accelerated/Integrative Learning Model Programme Evaluation: Based on Participant Perceptions of Student Attitudinal and Achievement Changes,* unpublished dissertation, ERIC and Northern Arizona University, Flagstaff, Arizona (1991). [UMI Dissertation Services Number: 9223732; DAI: 5304A; at www.uni.com]

Waite, Helen E., *Valiant Companions: Helen Keller and Anne Sullivan Macy,* Macrae (1959).

Wallace, Rosella R., *Active Learning: Rappin' and Rhymin',* Upbeat Publishing, Anchor Point, Alaska (1990).

Ward, Christine, and Daley, Jan, *Learning to Learn,* published by the authors, Christchrch 2, New Zealand (1993).

Watson, Lyall, *Supernature,* Coronet, London (1973).

Wenger, Win; and Poe, Richard, *The Einstein Factor: A Proven New Method for Increasing Your Intelligence,* Prima Publishing, Rocklin, CA (1996).

Wenger, Win, *Beyond Teaching and Learning,* Project Renaissance, Singapore (1992).

Wujec, Tom, *Pumping Ions: Games and Exercises To Flex Your Mind,* Doubleday, Toronto (1990).

Index

Author biographies

Jeannette Vos *is a Netherlands-born, Canadian-raised American doctor of education. She received her doctorate from Northern Arizona University after seven years' research in accelerative and integrative learning and teaching.*

She is the founding President of The Learning Revolution International, and one of the founding members of the National Institute for Teaching Excellence at Cambridge College in Boston, Massachusetts. She is also a senior faculty member at their Ontario, California, campus, to which her Academy is accredited.

From a thirty-year background in teaching and corporate training, she is a well-known international seminar and conference presenter, with particular specialties in the use of music and the arts, digital technology, metaphor, movement, nutrition and overall brain-body fitness, creativity, neuro-linguistic programming and general accelerated-learning methods.

Dr. Vos is currently researching and writing two further books, on breakthroughs in brain-mind-body research and on natural nutrition.

Website: www.learning-revolution.com
Email: vos@learning-revolution.com

Gordon Dryden *is a New Zealand-based award-winning broadcaster, author, journalist, publisher, television host and businessman, with a multimedia career that also spans public relations, international marketing and advertising creative directing.*

In 1990, he obtained a $2 million grant to set up the Pacific Foundation in his home country, New Zealand, to mount a public debate on education in the twentyfirst century. That project involved touring the planet with a TV crew and shooting 150 hours of videotape for six one-hour documentaries.

Given his multimedia background, it's not surprising that he brings a deep interest in creative thinking and interactive-technology to education. He also heads his own multimedia publishing company, The Learning Web. Its activities include organising teacher retraining programmes to link new learning methods with new technologies. He has an abiding interest in bridging the digital divide between rich and poor nations.

Website: www.thelearningweb.net
Email: gordon@learningweb.co.nz